Memories from The Marshes of Glynn

World War II

Sonja Olsen Kinard

Memories from The Marshes of Glynn

World War II

Compiled and edited by

Thora Olsen Kimsey
and
Sonja Olsen Kinard

Illustrations by Michael B. Gardner

Published by Looking Glass Books
730 Sycamore Street
Decatur, Georgia   30030

Copyright © 1999 Sonja Olsen Kinard
- Second Printing 2004

All rights reserved. No part of this book may be reproduced in any form or by any means without prior written permission of the publisher, excepting brief quotations used in connection with reviews, written specifically for inclusion in a magazine or newspaper.

ISBN 978-1-54395-300-8

Manufactured in the United States of America

Thora Olsen Kimsey
1929-1999

Six years ago my sister Thora and I set out on a journey together. We had no idea where the road would lead, but we looked forward to getting there together.

Over the years, as our "walking-talking" history of the World War II era in Glynn County evolved, we spent many hours together laughing and crying over our neighbors' stories of love and loss, of life and death, of humor and tragedy. When Thora and I weren't together, we burned up the telephone lines between our houses sharing with each other the letters we had received from new correspondents.

Our six-year partnership brought Thora and me closer together than ever. The process of creating a book became more important to us than the book itself. Over the years I came to depend on Thora's creativity and her eye for detail. Her tenacity and intensity ensured that the project, which on many days seemed overwhelming to both of us, would be completed.

We had gathered almost all of the material when Thora was diagnosed with cancer. Her dedication to the project at that point seemed only to intensify, although she never insisted that we rush the process. Even though she knew she might not see the book, she would not risk mistakes by working too hastily.

In the midst of the final stages of preparation for printing, Thora sat in her chair in the living room with our publisher and our book designer, uncomfortable but attentive to details such as font selection and column widths.

Thora did not see her idea become a reality, but she experienced the joy of pursuing every step in the process. For that we are grateful.

Sonja Olsen Kinard

Dedicated to the memory
of our
father and mother
Olaf Helmer Olsen and Lillie Mae Quick Olsen

MEMORIES FROM THE MARSHES OF GLYNN

WORLD WAR II

TABLE OF CONTENTS

Acknowledgments
FOREWORD
PRE-WAR ERA 1
Chapter 1 - Scenes of Glynn County 2
RUMBLINGS OF WAR 7
Chapter 2 - Activities in Glynn County 8
EARLY WAR YEARS 15
Chapter 3 - Torpedoed Tankers 16
PROTECTING THE COAST 27
Chapter 4 - Civilian Volunteers 28
Chapter 5 - Georgia State Guard 31
Chapter 6 - Civil Air Patrol 37
Chapter 7 - Coast Guard Auxiliary, Reserve and Sea Scouts 43
Chapter 8 - U. S. Coast Guard 51
MILITARY INSTALLATIONS 61
Chapter 9 - St. Simons Naval Air Station 62
Chapter 10 - Glynco Navy Blimp Base 72
LAUNCHING LIBERTY 87
Chapter 11 - Shipyards 88
GLIMMERINGS FROM THE PAST 125
Chapter 12 - Stories From the Home Front 126
STARS IN THE WINDOWS 261
Chapter 13 - Our Men and Women in Service 262
Casualty List for Glynn County 280
EPILOGUE 282
APPENDIX A A-1
APPENDIX B B-1
BIBLIOGRAPHY

ACKNOWLEDGEMENTS

We are indebted to all the contributors who made this book possible. They unselfishly shared their stories, wonderful photographs, and time.

The book is their story and we express our sincere gratitude for support and inspiration to: our brother, Olaf Olsen, Jr. host and storehouse of knowledge of the area and its people; his wife, Gloria, gracious and accommodating hostess; our sister, Virginia O. Horton for her down-to-earth advice; Sonja's daughter, Karol for her candid appraisal and her son, Olaf for his marketing expertise. Especially are we grateful to Thora's husband, Dexter Kimsey, whose patience, caring, chauffeuring and critiquing were invaluable.

Jack Lang opened doors to numerous people, willingly arranged and accompanied us on interviews, and traveled to Bremen, Germany to interview the captain of U-boat 123, Reinhard Hardegen; Winn Baker flew into the Winder airport to share his father's stories, scrapbooks and pictures.

Susan Richard Boswell, whose friendship began when she was a child in Thora's children's choir, graciously and beautifully used her talents in designing the book's interior.

As the book drew closer to press time, Martin (Skip) Owens offered his services for the printing of our marketing flyers; Rick Lubrant enthusiastically designed the jacket; and Brian Davis, cartographer, donated his time and services.

Special thanks for courtesies of the librarians at the Brunswick and St. Simons Libraries, Gail DeLoach at the Georgia State Archives, and Joyce Seward through her oral history of Cumberland Island.

Sam Goldman, Executive Director of the Callanwolde Fine Arts Center, whose offer for Callanwolde to co-sponsor the publishing of this project opened the final door for the completion of our memories of World War II.

Last, but not least, Dick Parker, our publisher, who took on this project of working with sisters showed much patience, offered invaluable advice, and displayed encouragement and confidence in our work and in us.

We are truly blessed.

Special Thanks to Callanwolde Fine Arts Center for assistance with the publishing of
Memories from the Marshes of Glynn: World War II.

FOREWORD

The scene is the dining table after a meal when old friends and family are visiting. Someone begins, "Do you remember when . . . when I was a child, my parents . . . during the war we had to . . ."

The seed for this book was planted each time we heard the stories of Olaf Olsen, our father. He was the firstborn in America of Norwegian parents. He ran away to sea at age thirteen and by age sixteen had survived the shipwreck of one vessel and jumped ship from another that was never heard from again. Except for his seafaring, he lived his entire life in Glynn County, Georgia, witnessing two world wars, major industrial and transportation changes, and the everyday rhythms of coastal life. Our favorite stories were about the World War II years and Dad's part in the rescue of the crews of two torpedoed tankers.

The idea for this book was germinated when my sister Thora visited the St. Simons Library during the years our aging mother was in a local nursing home. The library's location in the Old Casino's bowling alley was full of youthful memories. Listening to old friends reminisce at the library, Thora began to appreciate how our father and others in the area contributed to the war effort and realized that the old timers were a walking, talking history of that era in Glynn County.

The concept of recording this history grew as Thora talked with former classmates at reunions. Then one day she told me the plan for a book. Thora knew what she wanted -- a book about Glynn County during World War II as seen through the daily lives of the local people . . . what they experienced, how they lived, how the war changed their lives, how they laughed and loved . . . what they lost and how they worked for a common goal: to protect their homeland and win the war. I said, "Let's do it!"

We soon realized that we had engaged ourselves in a major undertaking just to contact those who might share their stories. We mailed more than 1,000 letters, focusing on the 1939-1951 graduating classes of Glynn Academy High School. We also contacted people we knew who lived in Glynn County during World War II.

Several widely-read publications carried our requests for information, including *The Atlanta Journal/Constitution*, *The Islander*, *The Brunswick News*, and *The Market Guide to Georgia*. Responses poured in from people delighted to share their memories with us. Thora and I were at times overwhelmed with the photographs, newspaper articles, written and tape-recorded recollections. Thora and I interviewed several subjects, and we received help from others who conducted, taped, and transcribed interviews.

When we learned that the captain of the German U-boat that sank two American ships within sight of the Georgia Coast was still living, we knew we had to interview him. Jack Lang, a native of Brunswick who was traveling to Germany, offered to interview Kapitan Reinhard Hardegan.

We received help from others whom we have not met, but who were committed to preserving the memories of their friends and family. Some traveled quite far to conduct interviews. Mary Lee Childs, for example, drove from Thomasville, Georgia, to a nursing home in Florida to interview Ruby Shane Johnson.

We are proud to share the memories of those who took time to contribute their stories, and we hope that you too will cherish them and the people who helped defend our homefront during World War II. This is their story.

Sonja Olsen Kinard

Pre-War Era

CHAPTER ONE

Scenes of Glynn County

Knollis Holmes

In the days before the war, when the shipyard was small, Brunswick was a great place to live. Most people left their doors unlocked and you could walk safely down Albany Street in the city. Brunswick was a "Saturday town." The people liked to come to town to see and be seen while shopping. Newcastle Street was the destination. The best spot for sitting and watching was in front of Kress ten-cent store or close to the Gloucester Street intersection. Of course, the younger folks would "drag the main," doing U-turns at the Mansfield and G Street intersections with Newcastle Street. You could get a big bag of mixed candy from Kress for about 10 cents.

Brunswick was a naval stores shipping port. The Downing Company, located on the river at approximately the foot of Monk Street, had hundreds of 50-gallon barrels filled with rosin and stacked four or five high. A good job in the pre-war years, maybe at Hercules*, usually paid less than $20 weekly.

The Oglethorpe Hotel, located in front of the train station, was built, as I understand, to service the train traffic and primarily the Jekyll Island owners. Had it been at a later time when it was demolished, it would have been fought for and preserved as an architectural treasure.

Most people don't know that the only way to go to Darien and north was by the GC&P [Georgia Coast and Piedmont] Railroad! Some dubbed it the "Get Out, Cuss, and Push Railroad!" U.S. 17 was built right on top of the railroad bed, including the crossties, which gave it the corduroy, roller coaster-type ride. In flood time, the Altamaha River would cover the road for a few days.

* The Hercules Powder Company of Wilmington, Delaware, bought the Yar-Yan Rosin and Turpentine Company, a company that distilled pine tar from pine tree stumps. One of its plants was in Brunswick.

Curtis Burch

At one time there were four railroads running in and out of Brunswick: the AB&C (Atlanta, Birmingham and Coast); the ACL (Atlantic Coastline); the GC&P (Georgia Coast and Piedmont); and the Southern.

I remember seeing the stevedores up and down the waterfront all during the '30s, loading crossties and barrels of rosin on big ships going to all corners of the earth. I also remember in the '30s when the USS *Constitution* (Old Ironsides) came into the Brunswick Harbor and was docked at the foot of Mansfield Street. I went on board. [Live oak timbers were shipped from St. Simons Island, Georgia, and were used in the construction of the USS *Constitution*.]

About 1934 or 1935, many foreign ships came into Brunswick to the sugar docks. They were called the Hershey Sugar Docks. A musician friend of mine, Troy Davis, would carry his guitar and harmonica down to the docks. The sailors would come off the ships with their accordions and harmonicas to have music right there on the dock.

Before World War II when I was about 12 years old, I had a *Brunswick News* paper route for a couple of years. A U.S. government dredge, *The Calibre*, docked at the foot of F Street, diagonally behind the Oglethorpe Hotel. When the other boys and I got through with our paper routes, we would go down there and either sell or give the sailors a paper. Many times they would invite us on board and give us pie and coffee. They were a great bunch of guys and for a kid to get to go on a big ship like that was something! *The Calibre* was what they called a hopper dredge, as opposed to a pipeline dredge. A hopper dredge stored the silt on the vessel until it held all it could accommodate. Then it went out into the deep ocean and dumped the dredged silt.

Some of the black people would go in the Front River in Brunswick, row across, cast a net, and catch fresh mullet. Sometimes they would use a hook and line to catch speckled trout. They would string the fish up on marsh grass or a palmetto frond, put them in a wheelbarrow, ice them down, and from the Bay Street riverfront push the wheelbarrows up and down the streets of Brunswick selling fresh fish. These were very good fish. Times were hard in the '30s and many, many able-bodied men could not get a job. People would do just about anything to feed their families.

My grandmother owned 88 acres that backed up on the slave-dug Altamaha Canal, which the government took when it built Glynco Blimp Base.

I knew some old gill-net fishermen and trappers that trapped raccoon and mink from the marshes—a rough lot of people.

Malcolm Seckinger

Just before the war, down by the sugar docks, someone started building a boat that looked like an airplane fuselage. It was all aluminum. It had seats in it like an airplane and was named the Nassau Clipper. It was to be a light, fast boat that was supposed to revolutionize sea travel, carrying passengers back and forth to Nassau. The boat was from 120 - 130 feet long and was on the ways ready to be launched. Every Sunday it was a ritual for the residents in Brunswick to view the progress of this boat. The war came along and all that area was taken into the shipyard. I don't know what happened to the Nassau Clipper.

George Parmelee

We had a café business down at the pier on St. Simons, and prior to World War II it was rough making a living. Most of the business was during the summertime. If you didn't make it during the summer, you didn't fare too well in the winter because there just weren't that many people on St. Simons. One guy came in the café one night after Labor Day and I remember his comment. He says to my mother, "Lady, you know, this is the first graveyard I've ever seen with neon signs."

Curtis Burch

Things started picking up in Brunswick when the Scott and Mead Paper Companies formed a joint venture and opened the Brunswick Pulp and Paper Company. A great many jobs, good jobs, became available, and this, in turn, created other jobs in the community.

Rumblings of War

CHAPTER TWO

Activities in Glynn County

England had been at war with Germany since September 1939. By June of 1940 the Scandinavian countries and France had surrendered to Hitler's forces. The United States was taking steps to prepare the home front, but at the same time most of the American people were not alarmed. The draft was enacted, and military facilities—including Camp Stewart at Hinesville, Hunter Air Force Base at Savannah, and Moody Air Force Base in Valdosta—were being built and equipped. "Even before the war started, as early as 1940, families were displaced from their homes in Flemmington, Georgia, for the construction of Camp Stewart (now Fort Stewart)," recalls Karl Meschke, a Brunswick resident. "Many of these people were very resentful of losing their homes to a cause which at that time was not supported by everyone. We knew one family named Ran who had lived there almost since the Civil War who lost their farm and home."

Between September 1939 and October 1941, just two months before Japan bombed Pearl Harbor, reports in *The Brunswick News* traced the effect of the war on Glynn County from initial subtle influences to actual preparation for war by the residents. The month after England declared war on Germany, the National Guard in Brunswick was ordered to begin drilling twice a week and to prepare for seven days of field training by the end of January. The Oglethorpe Guard, a part of the Brunswick National Guard, immediately began formulating plans for an intense course of study to prepare for the increased work and the responsibility that were anticipated. By November the newly organized Naval Aviation Club on St. Simons Island at McKinnon Air Field purchased a government-approved plane, and lessons in flying and ground work were taught.

Two industries in Brunswick were affected by the war in Europe early in 1940. An increase in markets for naval stores boosted sales for the Hercules Powder Company. The Brunswick Pulp Mill, which had been purchasing pulp from the Scandinavian countries, sought new sources in the United States as these countries were occupied by Germany.

As early as May 1940, General George Marshall made a plea to businessmen of the nation to allow their employees who were members of the National Guard to serve in the now three-week training camps to be held in the summer. All Georgia counties instigated home defense measures in June 1940. The aim was to defend the highways, manufacturing and hydroelectric plants, railroads, gasoline, and telephone lines and similar public services, as well as to prevent an invasion along the coast. As Mussolini declared war against Germany's enemies and the Nazis were within twelve miles of Paris, the Georgia Militia was preparing for maneuvers.

The nation's five-year $5,000,000 Rearmament Fund, approved in July 1940, meant that Brunswick consumers began paying more taxes but also that they would receive a new armory. By now the public was barred from power plants, and a month later the telephone offices were closed to all visitors. Brunswick wasn't without aliens: by mid-1940 more than 150 had registered.

This also was the month that Ryburn S. Clay, State Defense Corps Manager, notified key men in every county in the state to call local meetings. Glynn County's key men—James D. Gould, J. M. Exley, and Paul Killian—helped in the organization of the local group. The plan was to organize the volunteer service of local citizens who were over 35 years of age, of excellent character, in good health, and commonly recognized as loyal and patriotic, so that should the necessity arise, they would be prepared to assist in the preservation of peace and order, protect vital installations and public works, and keep the activities of aliens in the state under close observation.

A month later Glynn County was notified to supply 68 men on the first army call, and a site for a proposed army camp on the land near the Hercules Powder Plant was revealed. In September 1940 local troops of the National Guard left for Camp Jackson in Columbia, South Carolina, for a year's training. Ruth Croft Kent, whose father, Carl E. Croft, was among this group, recalls that "on September 16, 1940, the Brunswick Riflemen, Company E, Second Battalion, 121st Infantry and the Oglethorpe Guards, Headquarters Company, Second Battalion, 121st Infantry of the National Guard were summoned into active duty due to the war in Europe."

By fall 1941, emphasis was placed on the aviation school at McKinnon Field. Having been awarded a contract by the Army Air Corps, the school now provided the primary training for the regular cadets. Due to a delay in constructing new facilities, a bottleneck had been created and the Army Air Corps was seeking adequate facilities. McKinnon Field was one secured to solve the problem.

High officials of the Navy were continually on the speaking circuit at civic clubs to promote the advantages of Navy service. Generals inspected the recreational facilities in Glynn County for the soldiers who would be stationed at Camp Stewart.

During these years of war in Europe, the St. Simons and Sea Island volunteers were organized to aid the Brunswick Red Cross in making supplies for war victims. Even the Boy Scouts had been asked to be ready to contribute to the national welfare.*

*See Appendix, Chapter 2 - "Rumblings of War"

Calvin Allen

I was born February 4, 1925, in Brunswick, Georgia. My earliest memories were of talk about the Depression. My family knew the distress of the situation, although my father was one of the lucky ones who had a job as a civil servant, hired by the city of Brunswick. This branch of the government often didn't have enough money to pay employees. Instead, they were paid in script, pieces of paper insuring that the holder would be paid at some time in the future. Brunswick was like a modern-day Eden. Its semitropical climate produced lush and beautiful vegetation, and the style of living was typically southern, relaxed, and comfortable. The area was attractive not only to its inhabitants, but also to wealthy northern tourists—and to bugs. The former served as a source of income to many of the area's inhabitants, the latter as a source of aggravation.

I remember my parents and their friends talking about the election and their hopes that Mr. Roosevelt would save us from the nightmare that had been created by the despised Republican administration. The election came, and with the installation of Mr. Franklin Delano Roosevelt as president, there was a decided improvement in the economic conditions, as had been predicted. New schools, government buildings, roads, and many other improvements were occurring through employment of the masses who had survived the recent situation. Numerous new programs, with such initials as WPA and NRA, appeared. No one thought of these changes as socialistic, and indeed the word itself brought terror to the minds of most of the people we knew.

The Political Climate of Germany

There were also conversations about a similar situation that existed in Germany and the civil unrest created by that environment. I remember my uncle, who was an engineer in the merchant fleet, talking about the riots in the streets of Germany, which he personally had witnessed, when people protested the lack of food and vital necessities. No one heeded their plight because we were just emerging from similar conditions in the United States. The name Hitler began to appear in the newspapers, and many thought that he might be the deliverer of his country as Roosevelt had been of ours. His ideas were somewhat scorned as he proclaimed the German people a superior race who should rule others not so fortunate. Many people dismissed him as a raving madman.

The news from Germany became more threatening, and the concern of England and France became apparent as Germany invaded Czechoslovakia. All efforts to settle the conflict peaceably failed, and both of the large European countries hesitated to do anything that might promote another global conflict. Our country developed a policy of neutrality, which later became known as isolationism. After Germany usurped Czechoslovakia, it invaded Poland, and, France and England finally realized that Hitler planned to conquer the entire western hemisphere and probably the entire world. Eventually, the United States also realized that the madman in Germany posed a threat to our country and developed a program of shipping ammunition and war materials to oppose the evil force. We still staunchly refused to send troops to our Allies, although in 1939 a draft system was imposed and suddenly a huge army of soldiers, sailors, marines, and merchant marines appeared on the streets. Also, a host of plants and factories appeared in the country. Glynn County, because of its location on the Atlantic Coast, had several small shipbuilding and repair companies that received sizable war contracts.

Japan, A Small Island Empire

I recall Mrs. Wood, our eighth-grade literature teacher, talking about the people of Japan. I had never thought much about Japan aside from memorizing the name for geography lessons. Mrs. Wood stated that Japan was a small island empire, only recently visited by western civilizations. The inhabitants were of small stature, generally attractive in appearance, and of inscrutable nature. When I visited the World's Fair in New York in 1939, I went to the Japanese pavilion and was astounded by the large silver and pearl-encrusted replica of the Liberty Bell, the beautiful gardens, the rich silks, and the differences in dress and customs. I was most intrigued by the women, who were extraordinarily beautiful.

I remember a huge fire that occurred at the Atlantic Refining Plant in the ARCO district of Glynn County and almost destroyed everything at the plant. The company decided that it would be cheaper and better to refine the oil in Texas, close to the oil fields, and ship it out from there, so the Glynn County operation was terminated. Many jobs and a huge loss of income to Glynn County occurred at that time.

The refining plant's huge storage tanks were dismantled, and a Japanese ship landed at the harbor in Brunswick and carried them back to Japan. The boys would often ride to the piers to watch the ships load cargo, and I remember wondering what the Japanese would do with all that junk. I later had the misfortune of learning first hand of their intentions for those tons of steel. The Japanese crews, in contrast to the seamen from other foreign ships, didn't leave their ships.

December 7, 1941

On December 7, 1941, I had the great luck of getting a first date with the girl whom I had almost worshiped for years. We went to the Ritz Theater to see *Gunga Din*, starring Errol Flynn. During the middle of the movie the lights came on and a voice announced that the Japanese had bombed Pearl Harbor in Hawaii and had inflicted grave damage to our Pacific Fleet. My first thought was "I don't believe that those beautiful Japanese women could be involved in such a nefarious plot." The movie continued, but everyone left and gathered at the soda fountain at Andrew's Pharmacy, which for some reason was open on that Sunday afternoon, to discuss the situation. I recall that everyone was stunned to think that a place as small and unknown as Japan would have the audacity to challenge the mighty power of the United States. The consensus was that the United States would declare war and Japan would be entirely destroyed in two or three weeks at the most. Little did we realize the Japanese people's ardor and devotion to their purpose.

The following day, Monday, classes were disrupted by talk of the "Japs"'dastardly act, and even the teachers were distracted by our suddenly being thrust into a state of war. An assembly was called, and the radio message from President Roosevelt was heard announcing that the United States had declared war on the Japanese. Shortly thereafter Germany and Italy declared war on the United States.

OUR LIFESTYLE SUDDENLY CHANGED

A huge shipyard appeared in the south end of Brunswick, and the population of the town suddenly seemed to double. Classrooms bulged with new students, children of the families who had moved to Brunswick to find employment in the war industries. People went from door to door searching for a place to live until they could find a permanent place to locate their families. The Brunswick Pulp and Paper Company and the Hercules Powder Company, as well as some of the smaller industries, were suddenly the recipients of large war contracts, and the size of their work forces increased dramatically. Many of the men who had shown up in the defense plants almost immediately went into the armed services to make quick work of our despised enemies, and women appeared in jobs that were usually considered the bailiwick of men. New words began to appear in our vocabulary—*selective service* (the draft), *rationing* (limiting the civilian use of materials strategic to the war effort), *4F*, and *1A*, to name a few. Certain foods, gasoline, some medicines, and tires fell into the category of rationed items, and the country suffered these shortages with absolutely no complaints. The war was on and it promoted a surge of patriotism such as no one had seen since the First World War. President Roosevelt proposed a series of rights for veterans, known as the G. I. Bill of Rights, one of which was college tuition at government expense. These proposals were gladly accepted by everyone as an obligation to those who were risking their lives to preserve our freedom.

Rumors abounded that there were U-boats lurking off the Atlantic coast and that they were using the southern coast to deposit spies in the United States. The loss of two ships, tankers, off the coast of St. Simons brought us to the realization that the rumors weren't altogether false. Blackouts were imposed; sirens would alert citizens that an air raid was eminent and that all lights should be extinguished. Of course that was an exercise in futility, but we realized that we were indeed involved in a war that could come into our homes.

Those of us who were in high school were anxious to finish so we could join the armed forces to fight the fiends who were perpetrating the horrors we read about in the newspapers. Those who didn't want to fight were deemed cowards and faced almost universal contempt. The exceptions were those who were physically or mentally unfit to engage in conflict, and even they were often looked upon with scorn. The conscientious objectors, people excused from military duty because of their religious or moral convictions, probably drew the greatest contempt of all.

NEW AGE

The war brought the country into a new age of prosperity; defense plants were paying prodigious salaries, and people were spending money without regard to what might occur in the future. The horrors of the Depression were quickly forgotten. This was the era of the big bands, and people would buy out tickets to see performances by these national heroes. Our philosophy had suddenly changed from an existence of laid-back complacency to one of "we may die tomorrow, so let's get all we can out of today."

Tipperary (Tune)
Takes a long time to save a million!
Takes a long time I know.
Takes a long time to raise a billion,
But Uncle Sammy needs the dough!
Goodby, Sunday joyrides!
Farewell, silk-shirt flare!
When the school buys Bond, on next Monday
Yes, my Bond'll be there!

Most people contributed in whatever way they could to the war effort. I remember my mother and other women from our church gathering to roll bandages for the Red Cross. I, along with most of my friends, worked at various jobs and participated in the voluntary withholding programs to purchase war bonds. There was a sense of patriotism existing then that I never expect to see again. I remember an auction that was held for the purchase of war bonds. The big prize was a date with a celebrity—a movie star, I believe. Two young ladies, children of wealthy parents, waged their own war that morning to see who would get the honor. As the price rose, one would leave the auditorium to call her father for approval to bid higher. The final price reached the astounding figure of several hundred dollars . . . a staggering amount for that time.

G. I. Joe

All of my friends had chosen which branch of the service they would join and were just waiting to be called. Most of us didn't have to wait too long. I, along with some friends, had signed up for the U. S. Army Air Corps, and while I waited, I worked at the Hercules Powder Company for a few months.

World War II forced a lot of boys to become men, many of whom were not ready to relinquish their youth. I went into the Air Force and served three years as a radar mechanic and operator. After the war, I returned to college on the G. I. Bill and completed medical school at the Medical College of Georgia.

Karl Meschke

Just before the United States entered the war, there were a number of rumors about Fifth Column activities. One school teacher actually told her class that one Karl G. Meschke was caught making a short wave radio broadcast in German. Ralph Hood, School Superintendent, called my dad to apologize. The German name, plus some personal animosity, probably prompted the story.

Hoyt Brown, Jr.

I spent very little time in Glynn County during the war. My father, Hoyt Sr., was very active in the American Legion before the war, and I know he and the Legion worked on "coastal planning" with the FBI, whose agents were frequently in our home during 1941. He, therefore, had some insights into the political situation and encouraged me to take the competitive exams for the U. S. Merchant Marine Academy (USMMA; Kings Point, New York) in July 1941. This I did and was notified that I was in the 1942 class. I also applied for pilot training in the Royal Canadian Air Force (RCAF). I was also accepted there and told to await further orders.

In the meantime, I was working at Brunswick Pulp and Paper in the power plant. On Saturday, December 6, 1941, I received orders from the RCAF to report to Windsor, Ontario, on January 1, 1942. On the same day I also received USMMA orders to report to New Orleans on December 30th for Midshipman School. I chose USMMA and left home on Christmas Day to report to New Orleans

In the weeks between December 6th and December 25th, I continued at Brunswick Pulp and Paper and worked the night shift (11 p.m. - 7 a.m.) on Saturday, December 6th and Sunday, December 7th. Since I slept during the day, when the news about Pearl Harbor was announced my mother woke me up to listen to the radio .

During that three-week period before I reported to duty, I could not walk down Newcastle Street without being stopped and asked, "When are you leaving?"...not "Are you leaving?" Everyone my age was assumed to be going.

Patriotism

Brunswick and Glynn County were most patriotic. Parades on Confederate Memorial Day, July 4th, and, of course, November 11th were a way of life. On these occasions there were two or three U. S. Navy ships in port and the National Guard was a big deal year round. Open house parties were sometimes held for the ships' crews. I recall two of my older cousins and others married men from these Navy visits. We still had Civil War and Spanish-American War, as well as World War I veterans around at that time. Glynn County was an excellent recruiting source even in peace times.

At USMMA, part of the training was sea duty. I went on sea-going merchant ships from March 1942 to November 1942. I came home on survivor's leave in July 1942. I had 10 days to get from New York to Houston for my new ship. I rode the train from New York to Brunswick with my new uniforms and put them in Cranford Cleaners for pressing. The shop caught fire and all my uniforms were destroyed.

Later in November I came home on five days' leave and I remember riding in the lead convertible during the Armistice (not Veterans) Day parade. I also went to a football game and the dance after the game. Life was normal.

After graduation from Kings Point, I went on active duty in the Navy and did not return to Brunswick until March 1946 upon my release from active duty. My dad went back in the Navy in 1944. He and Mom were among the original sponsors of the USO in Brunswick. My sister, Betsy Ross, met her husband, William Feeney, there. I ran into many Glynn County people during the war....at Times Square...Pearl Harbor...New Guinea...and Japan. It was always a wonderful experience, and I could never get over seeing so many from so small a town. My class of 1941 did not have a single person killed in action. Hard to believe.

Early War Years

CHAPTER THREE

Torpedoed Tankers

War had been declared. But to us its reality was distant. That is, until the early morning hours of April 8, 1942, when two oil tankers off the coast of Glynn County were torpedoed by a German U-boat. The explosions jolted many out of their beds. The sound of artillery from the surfaced U-boat firing at the waterlines of the tankers echoed across the water, and the dark sky glowed as oil seeped onto the calm ocean and burst into flame.

Burning Torpedoed Tanker
Picture taken from lifeboat.
From the files of Mrs. Olaf H. Olsen, Sr.

Glynn County was on the front line, and the home front rose to the occasion. Men bravely rescued survivors; homes and hearts opened to the oil-smeared, sunburned, water-soaked crews; and teenage boys eagerly assumed manly tasks. Olaf Olsen was the first to reach the survivors. His story of the rescue is recalled by his son, Olaf Jr., who, sixteen years old at the time, was already knowledgeable of boats and the waters around Glynn County and ingeniously got himself onto the guarded docks where they brought in the survivors.

Olaf H. Olsen, Jr.

CAP'N OLSEN'S RESCUE

Dad was on the north end of Cumberland Island at the Candlers' estate, High Point, when a plane piloted by Lt. Col. Robert Ferguson circled the house and dropped a note attached to a wrench. Dad picked up the note and read that the tankers had been torpedoed. He noted their locations and instantly got into the car and headed for High Point dock on the Cumberland River where the Candlers' yacht, *Lourine II*, a 42-foot Fairform Flyer built by the Huckins Yacht Corporation, Jacksonville, Florida was moored. He was in the middle of St. Andrew's Sound before he took out the note and finished reading it. It said, "If you can go, sit down in the field."

Lourine II
Owner, Charles Howard Candler
Courtesy of Sam and Betsy Candler

This is the one time that Dad ran the *Lourine II* wide open at 17 knots. He went to the Sea Island Yacht Yard located on the west bank of the Frederica River beside the drawbridge. Taking on fuel and a crewman, he headed toward St. Simons Sound. Knowing the shallow draft of his boat and familiar with the tides and the waters around St. Simons, he didn't follow the channel but sped in front of the King and Prince Hotel through the Portuguese slough.

The Coast Guard, with slower boats, followed the channels, and Dad reached the survivors first and took three lifeboats in tow with 54 men in them. He met the Coast Guard, took on board Dr. Avera to attend to the wounded, then transferred the wounded to the Coast Guard boat. He then proceeded towing the survivors in the lifeboats back to the Coast Guard Station on the Frederica River, where he docked at the Weescot Dock next to the station.

Lt. Olaf H. Olsen, Sr.
From the files of Mrs. Olaf H. Olsen, Sr.

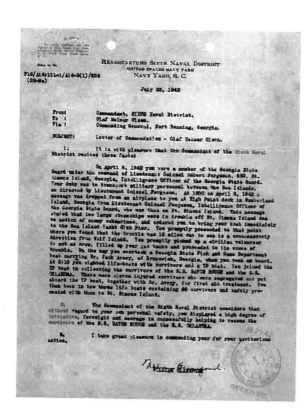
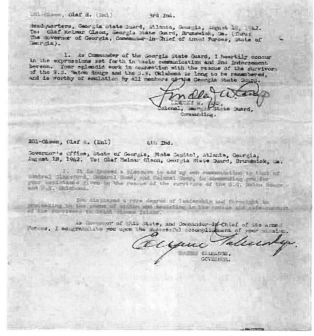

Letters of commendation received by Olaf H. Olsen, Sr. for his rescue of survivors of the torpedoed tankers

Antonio Barboza
Survivor of the SS Baton Rouge
Courtesy of Mary T. Martin

Antonio Barboza
Merchant seaman and a survivor of the torpedoed ship Baton Rouge

BARBOZA'S STORY

Most of the men were asleep in their bunks at that time, except the few men on watch. I was on watch in the engine room just before the torpedoing. I had gone up to the second officer in the fireroom and asked him regarding blowing the tubes. He said it would be right to do it at 3 o'clock.

I returned to the engine room intending to fill the water tanks. Just at that moment, I heard a funny noise and felt the ship tremble. I had no idea what had happened and thought that possibly one of the boilers had blown.

The second officer was with me. The lights went out and it was pitch dark. I stood still. I didn't know what to do. I noticed water coming into the engine room with great force, with oil mixed in it. I sought to locate the fireman and find out what the trouble was, but the engineer was in the way so I crawled around the boilers. I found machinery and debris floating everywhere with the water rushing in fast. Then I realized that the boat had been torpedoed. I tried to reach the ladder to get out of the room, but I was unable to. The water, which was rising all the time, was forcing me up between the boilers and the grating overhead.

I followed the grating to the opening and was finally able to crawl out and get up onto the deck and to a lifeboat. The crew were all there with the exception of one of the firemen and the engineer, who I found out later were believed to have drowned following the torpedoing.

ONE JUMPS OVERBOARD

One of the oilers was also drowned when he became excited and jumped overboard. The torpedo had apparently hit between the engine room and the bunkers, and the ship had stopped immediately. The men remained cool and calm in the face of death.

I got into one of the lifeboats and assisted in lowering it. We pulled away from the ship within about five minutes after the torpedoing. The commander of the submarine in a guttural German tone told us to pull alongside of this undersea craft and he would save us.

We all lay down in the two lifeboats as we were afraid we might be victims of machine gunning, and we drifted slowly away from the submarine in the darkness. None of us saw the face of the commander who gave the order to us. Apparently the attack on our tanker was without any warning.

FALL RIVER MAN ON SHIP SUNK BY SUBMARINE OFF GEORGIA

"Even though it was my first disaster at sea and I lost all of my clothing and other belongings, I am anxious to ship again and I will know what to do the next time," Antonio Barboza, 28, of 237 Field Street, son of the late Mr. and Mrs. Manuel Barboza, stated this afternoon in discussing his experiences of being on a torpedoed ship off the Georgia coastline on April 8 [1942].

Mr. Barboza, who has followed the sea for the past 12 years, was an oiler on a tanker which was torpedoed on the early morning of April 8. During the past year or two, he has seen the remains of numerous torpedoed ships, but this was the first time he was an active participant in such a drama. In telling his story of what took place, Mr. Barboza, whose brother is Manuel Barboza of 616 Orswell Street, related how he left Texas for a New York port and the tanker was on the way up the coast, off Georgia, when the torpedoing took place at 2:45 a.m., April 8.

Fall River Herald Times

Merchant Marine

Several of the men were injured in escaping from the ship. My back was bruised and scratched and I was cut under the left arm. The submarine commander started to play his search light on the two lifeboats containing approximately 38 men, but no attempt was made to fire on us or to force us to come aboard the submarine.

Apparently the submarine had sunk another ship shortly before it attacked us. We slowly drifted away and when at a safe distance we began to use our oars. When daybreak came, we set our course to the west and continued rowing.

CREW PICKED UP

About twelve hours later, a Coast Guard vessel picked us up when we were still some distance from land, which we had not yet sighted, and brought us into Brunswick, Georgia. I spent two days in the hospital and then came north, arriving in Fall River Thursday night.

Our tanker may yet be salvaged as it was sunk in about 30 feet of water, with the front of the vessel protruding from the waves. Captain James Poucher (Poche) was in command.

Fall River Herald Times

Gladys Cothran Long

After graduating in 1939 from Glynn Academy, I went to work for the Southern Bell Telephone Company. I was on duty the night the two tankers were torpedoed off St. Simons. Our manager, Mr. Ross, heard the explosion from where he lived and called the switchboard and asked it we had heard any report of gunfire. We said no, and he asked us to ring the Coast Guard on St. Simons. You know the rest. Many of the crew of each ship were lost, and of course, we handled calls from the survivors to their families.

Sara Corbett

When the oil tankers were torpedoed, I was working at Nolan's Photography Studio. Mr. Nolan was commissioned to make pictures of the tankers and the graves of the men who lost their lives. I went with Mr. Nolan to make these. It was some sight! You could have driven a big car through the hole in the tanker. I couldn't believe it did not sink. Later, one of the tankers was towed to the pier on St. Simons. I could have gotten pictures, but as a youth, I never dreamed that some day I would want to show them to my children. Who was thinking of children? I wasn't even married!

"The German sub sank two tankers off the coast and we had the bodies of 26 men out in our garage in body bags. Some had drowned. Because their bodies were so filled with water, it was impossible to embalm them. The bodies that were not claimed are buried in Palmetto Cemetery."

James (Sonny) Miller
(son of Edo Miller who owned the Edo Miller Funeral Home.)

Hollis Cate

During the war, I worked at Miller's Funeral Home while I was in high school. My most poignant recollection of that time was our having to handle the bodies of the seamen lost when a German U-boat torpedoed two tankers only a few miles off the coast. We had no room for them but had to "make" room. Previously, while I was there, we never had more than two bodies at one time.

Lillian Marie Lang Meyers

When the tankers were sunk off the coast, boys I knew who were good divers helped bring the bodies to Miller's Funeral Home and I went to look at them. It was horrible and the war began to be more real to me.

Lt. Commander Albert Fendig
U. S. Naval Intelligence
Recollections by Albert Fendig, Jr.

My memories of World War II, oddly enough, do not focus on St. Simons since Dad left his law practice in about 1939 and entered the Naval Intelligence Service. We were in Savannah and Charleston until late 1944, when Dad went to the Pacific.

From our home on the marsh's edge, east of Savannah, I can recall times when my father's tradition of telling us bedtime stories, which he made up about animals in the Okefenokee Swamp who personified my sister, my brother, and myself, was interrupted by booms and flashes on the horizon. We later learned that American tankers were being torpedoed and shelled just offshore. It was Dad's job as intelligence officer to go aboard the tankers and get the flag and code book before the ships went down. I later saw tankers in St. Simons Sound at anchor with holes in the hull large enough to drive a Greyhound bus through.

My memories of St. Simons focus on visits when I stayed with Edwin and Neal Fendig, my cousins. I recall vividly the PT boats as they raced past the pier. We would stand on the beach and use our semaphore to find out if any German subs had been spotted. It was fun to attempt to evade the guards who patrolled the beach at night, and, of course, our memories have to include the strange sensation of an island blacked out on all seaward windows.

Lt. Commander Albert Fendig
Courtesy of the Coastal Georgia Historical Society

"It was Dad's job as intelligence officer to board the tankers and get the flag and code book."
                  Albert Fendig, Jr.

Graves of the Merchant Mariners who lost their lives when their ship was torpedoed off the coast of Georgia
Palmetto Cemetery, Brunswick, GA
Courtesy of Jack Lang

DECLASSIFIED
Information on the Sinking of the Tankers off St. Simons
Declassified - Navy Department
Office of the Chief of Naval Operations
Washington, D. C.
April 21, 1942

Subject: Summary of Statements by Survivors, SS *Oklahoma*, American Tanker, Texas Company

1. The 9264-gross-ton SS *Oklahoma* was torpedoed without warning at 0100 CWT. (0200 EWT) on April 8, 1942, 8 miles, 25 degrees, from the second gas buoy off Brunswick, Georgia, in a water depth of 40 feet. The vessel remained afloat approximately 45 minutes and drifted approximately one mile to the northeast, sinking stern first on even keel until the stern touched bottom when it listed about 3 degrees to starboard, the bow remaining above water.

2. The ship was en route from Port Arthur, Texas, to Providence, Rhode Island, on the inshore route, 2 miles off buoys, with a full cargo of 66,000 bbl. of kerosene, 30,000 bbl. of gasoline, and 4,000 bbl. of diesel oil. She was on course 25, speed 16 knots, not zigzagging, completely blacked out, radio not used. Three lookouts were on watch, two on the bridge and one atop the bridge. The weather was clear, sea small, wind SE force 2, visibility good, no moon.

3. According to most survivors the torpedo struck the engine room, probably ten feet below the water line, causing an immediate flooding of the engine room and crew quarters, and a billow of smoke arose. A bluish vapor was also observed by some. The vessel did not catch fire from the torpedo explosion. It was at first believed the *Oklahoma* had collided with another ship and an SOS was sent to this effect on the emergency transmitter, the main set having been damaged.

4. Three lifeboats containing 18 survivors immediately abandoned ship. Hearing screams aboard, the Master and 3 others reboarded the ship. They found one of the officers critically wounded while 18 of the crew were apparently trapped below. The wounded officer subsequently died. While aboard the second time, the radio operator sent an SOS. Ship was again abandoned. Soon after, at about 0200 CWT, the submarine surfaced about 3 points off the port bow northwest by north of the ship about ½ mile to 200 yards distant. About twelve rounds were fired by the submarine, five being hits. Subsequent examination indicates the shells were from a 5-inch gun and apparently tumbled and glanced, possibly indicating poor rifling in the gun. A smoldering fire in the forepeak was evidently started by shellfire, which was incendiary. When firing ceased, the submarine was about 50 yards from the *Oklahoma*. The submarine circled the vessel and disappeared leisurely eastward, surfaced at 0210 CWT.

5. The submarine was approximately 250 feet long and answered the description of the German 750-ton SS boats. It had a long, low conning tower, cruiser bow, spoon stern, no net cutter, painted black, one 5-inch gun forward of the conning tower.

6. Comments are:
    1. That life rafts were held by goose necks so tightly that a hammer was required to get them loose.
    2. That there should be more entrances to crew quarters and an engine room sky-light to prevent the crew from being trapped below.

A. J. Powers, Ensign USNR

Photos are in sequence, clockwise from upper left.

Raising the SS Oklahoma
Courtesy of the Coastal Georgia Historical Society

22

Sonja O. Kinard

THE SINKING OF TANKERS OFF THE GEORGIA COAST BY U-BOAT 123

The Battle of the Atlantic started on September 3, 1939, the day war was declared in Europe, and didn't end until VE Day, May 8, 1945. By January 1942, when Germany declared war against the United States, U-boats were sinking merchant ships along the northeastern Atlantic coast, and by April 1942 they had entered the waters along the Georgia coast.*

Around the time of the fiftieth anniversary of D-Day, we learned through a *National Geographic* documentary that the captain of the U-boat that sank the *Oklahoma* and the *Baton Rouge* was still living. Michael Gannon's book *Operation Drumbeat* relates the German plan to wreck the merchant shipping along the Atlantic coast and prominently features Kapitan Reinhard Hardegen, commander of U-boat 123 that torpedoed the tankers on April 8, 1942, and in the early morning hours of April 9 sank the *Esparta*, a United Fruit Company ship, off the coast of Cumberland Island. We wrote to him. He replied, sending a picture of himself at the age of 28, when he was the captain of the U-boat, and including the phrase "Yesterday's enemies are today's friends."

We had heard rumors of submarines being captured with bread wrappers and theater ticket stubs from Brunswick onboard, of fuel oil being sold to the U-boats, and of U-boats being sunk. Jack Lang, who was planning a trip to Germany, offered to interview Captain Hardegen, who lives in Bremen, Germany. In March 1996, he met the captain and his wife at their home and asked about these rumors.

*Additional information on U-boats can be found in the appendix.

Kapitan Reinhard Hardegen
Interviewed by Jack Lang. Jack's account of his interview with Hardegen was published in the December 7, 1996, issue of The Brunswick News.

Today, older Americans are remembering the Japanese air attack on our naval fleet moored at Pearl Harbor 55 years ago. This triggered America's entry into World War II as then-President Roosevelt had Congress declare war on Japan the next day. Although our country had been helping beleaguered England with "lend-lease" war materials in its war with Germany, we were not prepared to fight a "two front" conflict at the time of Pearl Harbor. President Roosevelt did not include Germany when he asked Congress for a declaration of war against Japan. However, Japan's aggression pact with Germany and Italy forced Hitler to declare war on the United States five days after the December 7 blow.

Utilizing his powerful submarine fleet, generally referred to as U-boats, Hitler immediately devised a plan to disrupt shipping off our Atlantic seaboard, bringing the war to our doorstep here in Glynn County.

In 1990, Florida State professor Michael Gannon published a book titled *Operation Drumbeat* in which he chronicled the U-boat successes. He described the sinkings as the "Atlantic Pearl Harbor." Professor Gannon had researched both the American and German naval

Kapitan Reinhard Hardegen
Age 28
Courtesy of Reinhard Hardegen

files and interviewed many still-living naval veterans. He talked at length with Reinhard Hardegen, captain of U-boat 123, at his home in Bremen, Germany. Hardegen started his sinkings outside New York Harbor in January of 1942. As he worked his way down the Atlantic coast, he sank two tankers off the coast of St. Simons Island, the SS *Oklahoma* and the SS *Baton Rouge* on April 8, 1942.

Many local residents remember being awakened in the early hours of that spring day as explosions reverberated into Brunswick and the islands as the two ships sank to the bottom of the shipping channel. (Later the ships were raised from the relatively shallow water and anchored in the St. Simons Sound for a period of time.) A total of 21 seamen were killed on the two tankers and all but five were identified and shipped to their hometowns for burial. The five unidentified (badly burned) were buried in separate graves in the Palmetto Cemetery in Brunswick with metal markers reading "Unknown Seaman - 1942." One of the unknown dead was identified years later and bears a marble headstone with his name and dates. These graves can be seen today in the cemetery on 23rd Street. The reality of being in World War II was vividly brought home to the Glynn County residents by these sinkings and deaths.

Brunswick native Jack Lang interviewed Captain Reinhard Hardegen at his home in Bremen, Germany, in the spring of 1996. This meeting with the 83-year-old robust former U-boat captain proved to be very interesting. His recall of the war was vivid, including his sinkings of the two ships off St. Simons Island. In the interview, Captain Hardegen emphasized that he was a German Navy U-boat captain, not a Nazi.

Hardegen had the distinction of being honored by both Germany and the United States. First, after his initial successful sinkings (measured in tonnage), Hitler gave him the Iron Cross with oak leaf clusters at a private banquet. In a documented account of this event, Hitler asked Hardegen how he thought the war was going for Germany. The brash 28-year-old captain answered to the effect, "I think you should build more U-boats and less tanks and not look towards the East (Russia)." A red-faced Hitler shot back, "Young man, you don't know what you are talking about."

Second, in 1990, Hardegen and his wife were brought to Jacksonville, Florida, and honored for his gesture of saving lives when a tanker ablaze from a torpedo hit from Hardegen's sub had to be shelled by deck guns to effect sinking. Noticing the people on Jacksonville Beach, Hardegen maneuvered his U-boat, at the risk to his crew, between the shore and the ship to fire. This avoided his shells over-shooting the tanker and hitting into the large crowd gathered on shore to watch the spectacle. Amusingly, Hardegen told Lang about an incident during a book tour of the United States with Michael Gannon. He said that a lady had refused to shake his hand and termed him "still the enemy." In the next breath, she added, "I don't shake hands with Yankees either." This puzzled Hardegen, as he considered all Americans "Yankees," until his host explained the sectional differences in America.

Reinhard Hardegen and Jack Lang
Bremen, Germany 1996
Courtesy of Jack Lang

Hardegen recalled the austere life aboard the 50-man U-boat. Leather coveralls were worn most of the time and there were beds for half the crew. They took turns between being on duty and sleeping.

Many narrow escapes were cited by the captain and included depth charge attacks by American destroyers and a bomb dropped on the U-boat's deck by a British plane which proved to be a dud.

Despite an unbelieving German naval command, the Allies had broken the German communicating codes (by way of the Enigma machine). This enabled the British and the Americans to ultimately track and sink most of the U-boats. Of approximately 39,000 men in the German U-boat service, 35,000 never returned home.

Lang asked Hardegen a series of questions which had gnawed in his and other locals thoughts for over 50 years including: 1. Did your sub or others ever refuel in America or Georgia waters? Answer: "Definitely not. Our range of operation was 12,000 miles and we operated from the French port of Lorient, which is closer than German ports." Hardegen said that refueling was done in the Canary Islands (owned by neutral Spain), but this was stopped by British diplomacy. 2. Did you or any English-speaking crewmen ever come ashore in Brunswick and attend movies or buy bread at the Vienna Bakery? Answer: "No. Hitler didn't send me to America to go to movies, but to sink ships!" He did confirm that his sister U-boats had put ashore German spies near Jacksonville, Florida, and on Long Island, New York, but they were captured and most executed in New York after trial. 3. When did you realize Germany had lost the war. Answer: "By mid-1944."

Following the war, Hardegen was mistakenly imprisoned by the British as a war criminal for one and a half years before his wife could assemble necessary records to release him. Destitute, he worked for an American oil company in Germany and eventually started a marine oil business. He and his wife have traveled throughout the world and he has been aboard most of the latest American and Russian submarines. As an avid golfer, he expressed a desire to attend The Masters in Augusta one day.

His departing words to Lang were: "Enemies yesterday, friends today."

Protecting The Coast

CHAPTER FOUR
Civilian Volunteers

Thomas Gignilliat

Civilians unselfishly volunteered to serve as air-raid wardens and airplane spotters as part of the Civil Defense Program. They also assumed a military role in patrolling until the military could be equipped and trained to protect the coast.

On the day following Pearl Harbor, my dad, Harry Gignilliat, came home in the evening with a khaki uniform and a World War I rifle that he had been issued as a member of the Home Guard. The Home Guard was a quasi-military militia of some type formed to defend the shores until help arrived. He later transferred to the Coast Guard Auxiliary, where his talents could be better utilized. During these first days of the war there were many plans formulated that fortunately were not implemented until much later when they had been refined.

The Army and later the Coast Guard had armed personnel, some with dogs, patrolling the beach during hours of darkness. It certainly curtailed any long walks on the beach after dark unless you were prepared to be challenged frequently.

One of the Coast Guard operations was the conversion of private yachts to patrol craft. Most of this was accomplished by the addition of two-way radios and mounting machine guns fore and aft and, if the yachts were large enough, depth charges on the stern, in racks. You could see these boats coming and going at all hours of the day and night. Whether they could have dropped those depth charges without blowing themselves out of the water was a questionable matter. I remember my dad coming home from work, changing into uniform, and going on patrol with the Coast Guard Auxiliary for all or most of the night.

The Civil Air Patrol flew its light planes off the old St. Simons Airport (Redfern Field), a dirt strip where one of the shopping centers is presently located. Members of the patrol wore Army uniforms with red lapels and flew small civilian aircraft equipped with two-way radios and later bomb racks under the wings that carried a 50-pound bomb. These people flew offshore anti-submarine patrols.

Virginia Kent Jackson

St. Simons Lookout

Civilian volunteers manned an airplane-spotting outpost. It was located on top of a flat-top building near the King and Prince Hotel close to the beach. My father and I were on duty from 8 p.m. to 12 midnight two nights a week.

World War II Arm Bands worn by Mrs. Bob H. McGinnis
Top: U.S. Army Air Force, Women's Air Warning Service
Bottom: Civil Defense Driver
Courtesy of Gloria S. Ramsour

Gloria Smith Ramsaur

My maternal grandmother, Mrs. Bob McGinnis, lived on St. Simons and patrolled the beach at night. She drove a 1938 black four-door Ford up and down the beach.

Woodie Angela Estes

My daddy was an air-raid warden during World War II. The tower from where he patrolled was on the south end of the King and Prince Hotel in what was then the pool area.

Catherine Wynne Gleason

CODE THEO-33

High school students worked as aircraft spotters atop one of the flat-topped buildings at the King and Prince Hotel. Whenever planes flew over, we called Jacksonville (code: Theo 33) and gave information about the number of engines and the direction of the aircraft.

Stella Morton Harned

SEA ISLAND LOOKOUT

As volunteers at the beginning of the war, our job was to man the tower on top of the administration building on Sea Island at night to look for enemy planes. We all took turns.

Patricia Sikes Jobe

My dad was a neighborhood air-raid warden (in Brunswick). When we had a blackout, my mother and I would huddle in the hallway with all of the doors closed so the light wouldn't project from the radio until the all-clear siren sounded.

Airplane Spotters and Air Raid Wardens
Front row, second from left: Marion McKendree
Courtesy of Georgia McKendree

Mrs. Hubert W. Lang, Sr.

BRUNSWICK COUNTRY CLUB LOOKOUT

Before I went to work at the shipyard, I was a volunteer plane spotter. A high tower was erected at the Brunswick Country Club. If we saw a strange plane, we had to report it to the authorities. My daughter, Lillian Marie, was also a plane spotter.

FLASH MESSAGE FORM A

Call your telephone central and say, "ARMY FLASH" 7/4 M
Give your phone number

Central will connect you with an Army Information Center.

When you hear, "ARMY, GO AHEAD, PLEASE", you say, "FLASH" and continue message you have checked on form below, in the order indicated.

When reading message to Army operator, do not repeat titles of columns. Read clearly and distinctly.

Do not hang up until operator says, "Thank you."

1	2	3	4	5	6	7	8	IMPORTANT	
Number of Planes	Type of Plane	Altitude of Plane	Seen or Heard	YOUR OBSERVATION POST CODE NAME	Location of Planes from OP	Distance of Planes from OP	Planes headed toward	DO NOT TELL ARMY OPERATOR THIS INFORMATION.	
NUMBER FEW MANY	Single motor Bi-motor Multi-motor BLIMP	Very Low Low High Very High	Seen Heard		N nw ne W E sw se S Planes radius OVER	Report distance in MILES only in ½ report HEAD	N nw ne W E sw se S	Time placing Call	Seconds To Local Operator	Total Seconds to Army Operator
1	BM		Heard	29	East			10:29	5	55
1	BM	high	Seen	29	Overhead		N	10:45	3	35
1	BM	high	Seen	29	East	3	S	11:05	10	30
1	BM	high	Seen	29	East	5	S	11:16	3	58
1	BM	high	Seen	29	E	5	S	11:20	2	45
3	BM	high	Seen	29	E	5	Circling	11:23	5	43
6	BM	high	Seen	29	E	5		11:27	2	260

Sample of Observer's log. Courtesy of Clara Marie Gould. Information on form from Mrs. Gould's log.

Sample of Airplane Observer's Log
Information on this form is from Mrs. James Gould's log
Courtesy of Clara Marie Gould

Mrs. James D. Gould, Airplane Observer Identification Card
Courtesy of Clara Marie Gould

John B. Morris

CODE DOG-101

I remember being a plane spotter at the observation tower erected near Highway 17 on the grounds of the Brunswick Golf Course. The code name for this post was 'Dog-101.' When a plane flew over, we picked up the direct phone and called Savannah with our code name and some identifying description of the plane.

Lynn Gillican Sikes

WHAT KIND OF PLANE WAS THAT?

Mother was a member of the Air Observation Team. She would go up in the observation tower with binoculars and report any air traffic. Much to our embarrassment, she was forever reporting buzzards or some kind of bird!

Mary Curry Ward

We moved from Brunswick to St. Simons in 1937 when I was three years old to establish Ward's Drug Store at the pier. During the war my dad, Carl Ward, was an air-raid warden and turned on the huge siren in our backyard to warn the residents of East Beach to turn lights out to blacken the coastline when enemy ships approached or the Coast Guard warned.

CHAPTER FIVE

Georgia State Guard

**Georgia State Guard
(1942 - 1947)**

When it appeared that the Georgia National Guard units would be brought under federal control in 1940, Governor Eugene Talmadge organized the Georgia State Defense Corps.* By September 19, 2,955 officers and 3,000 men were assembled. On December 10, 1941, just three days after the Japanese bombed Pearl Harbor, the Defense Corps was ordered into active duty. The units were under the leadership of the commanding general of Fort Benning, Georgia, who was (then) Brigadier General Omar Bradley.

In early 1942 the Georgia State Defense Corps was renamed the Georgia State Guard with no change in headquarters in Atlanta. James D. Gould, who had been appointed unit commander of Glynn County in August 1940, became commander of the 23rd District in April 1943.** J. M. Exley had been commander before then.

Our state was divided into two defense zones with the Georgia State Guard guarding the vital areas.*** The enemy in Europe could try raiding by land and sea in order to penetrate the interior of our state to sabotage our military installations and industrial plants and to cripple our major traffic arteries. The islands off the coast were vulnerable to enemy infiltration and needed patrols and observation posts established. Thus in June 1942 a boat detail of the Georgia State Guard was formed with men knowledgeable of the coastal waters. Civilian boats were pressed into service to transport men and supplies to the various islands.

* See appendix, "The Georgia State Defense Corps, the Georgia State Guard."
**Georgia Department of Defense - Georgia State Guard - Brunswick District 23: Lamar Q. Ball Collection, Georgia State Archives.
*** See appendix, "The Georgia State Guard Is Ready" by Lindley W. Camp.

Boat Detail of the Georgia State Guard
Docked at Boat Yard on Terry's Creek
Courtesy of Olaf H. Olsen, Jr.

BOAT DETAIL OF THE GEORGIA STATE GUARD

Excerpts from the following letter explain the situation along the coast, express the need to form the Georgia State Guard Boat Detail for Coastal Patrol, and document the dates of formation and dissolution of the organization.

```
HEADQUARTERS INTERNAL SECURITY DISTRICT NO. 4
          Office of the Commanding General

                                    Fort Benning, Georgia
                                    June 16, 1943

TO:    Olaf H. Olsen, c/o Brunswick Combat Team,
       U.S. Army, Brunswick, GA.

       ...A year ago the Georgia coastal area,
topographically vulnerable to raiding and spying and to
submarine operations by the German enemy, was without
any net of outposts and patrols. . . .Army troops of the
Eastern Defense Command, and Fourth Service Command
troops attached to them, had become available to establish
such a net. But since many of the more important of
these patrols and posts had to be established and
maintained on the offshore islands and along the coastal
waterway, boats were necessary. None were at that time
available for these purposes either in the Army or from
the Navy Coast Guard. Nor was personnel available
knowledgeable of the tricky local problems of weather,
tides, and navigation.
       This problem was solved by the organization as of
June 15th, 1942, of a Boat Detail, having a civilian
status, of which Detail you were a member. You volunteered
for this work. . . .These services were invaluable. You
became the Technical Officer of the Detail, based upon
your lifelong, intimate knowledge of the waters and upon
your professional standing as a seaman, which included
your having held a license as a Master for ships up to
10,000 tons burden. The Detail . . . was attached to the
Brunswick Combat Team, of the Carolina Sub-Sector, of
the Southern Sector of the Eastern Defense Command. ...
       This commendable activity is now about to be
terminated, as of June 20th, 1943, due in part to the
fact that the Coast Guard with its newly established
beach patrols and outposts and the Navy's newly completed
Brunswick Heavier-than-Air Base with its blimps have
now partially filled the gap which originally existed.

Signed:   Eric Fisher Wood, Brigadier General,
U. S. Army, Commanding
```

Members of the Georgia State Guard Boat Detail
Back row (l to r): Lts. Frank Horne, Holland, Reginald Taylor, and Hanson
Front row (l to r): Capt. C.H. Candler, Jr., Capt. Charles King, Lt. Robert Ferst, and Lt. Olaf H. Olsen
Courtesy of Olaf H. Olsen, Jr.

Richard Waters
Richard Waters' father, C. O. Waters, was chief of staff of the Georgia State Guard in Atlanta until elevated to commander in 1942.

The headquarters of the Georgia State Guard (GSG) were in Atlanta. The Georgia State Guard Boat Detail for Coastal Patrol was a division. Sometimes it was called the Georgia Guard Navy.

I came down to the coast a couple of times with my father, Col. C. O. Waters, and remember some of the boats, especially the *Cherokee*, a 52-foot Elko that Mr. Charles Howard Candler, Jr., had bought for use by the Guard. I remember that boat well because we traveled on it to Cumberland Island and stayed aboard it when we were down at the coast. I don't recall who operated the *Cherokee*, but the deckhand was a fellow named So. He was a funny little Oriental guy and the captain had a habit of always saying the word *so* as an exclamation to most anything. This guy would jump up and say, "Yes, So."

The other crew member I remember was John, the cook and stand-in deckhand when needed. He was a poor choice for that vessel because he must have been six and a half feet tall and the galley was down forward. He had to work down there with his head bent over to keep from hitting the overhead all the time. He had long hands. He sure could cook up a good meal!

On Cumberland Island, the headquarters of the GSG Coastal Patrol was at High Point on the North End. I remember just before you crossed the dunes to the beach from the land side was a little encampment with a pyramid tent over wooden floors where they kept the horses used for patrolling the beach. We stayed in an old cottage at High Point. There were no screens in the windows and they put mosquito netting over our beds. They also used some of the buildings at the Carnegies' on the South End. There were only two military vehicles on Cumberland Island, one Jeep and one truck. The rest belonged to civilians. My father, being a colonel, got to ride in the Jeep.

Headquarters for the boats was at the old Sea Island Yacht Yard, now the Sea Island Marina. There were officers' quarters at Captain Olaf Olsen's Boat Yard on Terry's Creek in Brunswick near the old radio station, WMOG.

The Georgia State Guard patrolled the barrier islands along the coast. There were some regular Army personnel and they were augmented by the GSG. On Sapelo Island was a Georgia State Guard training area.* The men were housed in the old cow barn that had a statue of a turkey in front of it. They put the cots in where the old cow stalls were. Over the head of the cots were signs such as Daisy and Gertie, the names of the cows.

A lot was going on prior to our actual involvement in the war. There may have been evidence that Nazi U-boats were off the coast prior to the time we became involved. Obviously the United States felt it was going to be involved in the war and formed the Georgia Civil Defense Corps. My father was employed by the Atlanta Gas Light

Company in 1929 as general superintendent and in 1943 became the assistant to the president and chief engineer. At the gas company, he was involved in putting together emergency response teams. In the event of sabotage to the gas lines, these units could go to the damaged area, correct the problem, and get the gas customers back on line.

At the beginning of the Georgia Civil Defense Corps (GCDC), Colonel George Sweeney was the commanding officer. My dad started in the unit in Avondale Estates, Georgia (DeKalb County), and accepted his first commission in the corps as a lieutenant. Then he went on up through the ranks. He went from lieutenant to captain and became the G-3 in headquarters, which was the training officer. In early 1943, the command was passed to Colonel William Whelchel. Also at that time my father had been promoted to lieutenant colonel as chief of staff.

Colonel Whelchel at some point late in 1944 or early 1945 resigned, and my father was made commander of the Georgia State Guard. Having become assistant to the president of the gas company in January 1942 and acquiring more administrative responsibilities as the Guard was being federalized, my father realized that he couldn't hold two full-time jobs. Sometime in 1945, my father resigned his position. The war was also winding down.

* See appendix for article by Dr. Louie D. Newton.

Georgia State Guard in Training
Sapelo Island, Georgia
Courtesy of Richard Waters

L to R: Lt. O. Claire Waters, Col. William B. Whelchel

Maneuvers in the Sand Dunes

Barracks in Cow Barn
Note the names of cows on each stall

Georgia State Guard Drilling

Wallace Sullivan

Wallace Sullivan is a highly decorated World War II serviceman, having received two Purple Hearts, two Bronze Stars with a V for Valor, and a Combat Infantryman Badge for the 26th Division of General Patton's 3rd Army. He returned to Brunswick in July 1945.

In May of 1942 I came to Brunswick from Massachusetts with the U.S. Army G Company of the 104th Regiment of the 26th Division. Our assignment was coastal patrol. There were outposts on all islands off the coast, and they were reached by boats. We organized the Coastal Patrol Unit and ran 25 patrols from Savannah to St. Marys. We were stationed outside of Hercules in tents that, at the time, were a recreation center for the men from Fort Stewart who came to enjoy the beaches of St. Simons. We took over that encampment and built showers and a kitchen to feed our troops. We had a large group assigned to our company—border patrol men, MPs, etc., about 700 men all together. Our company was under the command of Captain Stevens.

We stayed in Brunswick 11 months to complete our assignment. The shipyard was under construction at that time. Brunswick's population of 15,000 grew to 75,000 before we left for ETO (Europe). I saw everything develop, including Glynco Blimp Base. No Navy at that time, only Army. Before going overseas I married a Brunswick girl, Victoria Holland, on May 10, 1944.

Mary Stevenson Melnyk

Nick and Mary Melnyk
Courtesy of Mary and Nick Melnyk

Mother met Nick before I did. I was away at school, but Mother informed me that she had someone she wanted me to meet. His name was Nick Melnyk, and he was a soldier stationed in Brunswick, headquartered in the tents on the grounds in front of the Hercules Powder Company. He was in the 104th Infantry Regiment, 26th Yankee Division. Its assignment was to patrol the area halfway to Savannah and halfway to Jacksonville. The sole mission of the patrol was to apprehend or report the landing of German troops with the purpose of sabotage on the East Coast. Nick was in the clerical section.

I was scheduled to meet him but called to cancel. The person taking messages was an Oriental, and every time I gave him the message, he said, "So." His name was Eddie So.[He was the deckhand on the *Cherokee,* which was in the Boat Detail of the Georgia State Guard.] I was never able to communicate and kept my date with Nick. Six months later, in 1942, we were married. After Nick and I married, I went to see him at Camp McCain in Grenada, Mississippi. I couldn't buy a ticket to Grenada because no one knew where it was. So the ticket master at the train station, located behind the Oglethorpe Hotel in Brunswick, sold me a ticket to Memphis. I told him that I did not want to go to Tennessee, but to Mississippi. He said, "Well, you have to go to Memphis and when you get there, ask 'em."

It was a hot summer Saturday when I finally got off the train in Grenada. I was dead tired and dirty. I said to Nick, "Get me a motel or something." He replied, "There is nothing here . . . no motels in this town."

That evening we went to a USO dance and kept asking local people if anyone in town had a room. When we asked one of the chaperones, she said, "Oh, no, but I do have what used to be slave quarters which we have made into a barn." The first night in Grenada, Mississippi, we slept in a barn!

Camp McCain was huge and hot! Residents of Grenada used every room in their houses for the wives of the soldiers. Where we eventually stayed the dining room and the living room were divided by a sheet down the middle and used for sleeping quarters. We finally got the bedroom as the guests rotated. There was no air conditioning . . . they didn't even have a fan! Because of the heat, the Army changed the whole routine in Grenada. The soldiers went to work at 5 a.m., got back to base at 9 a.m., and then went back at 5 p.m. for a few hours. These guys would be going on five-mile hikes for training, plus an occasional 25-mile hike.

In December 1943, I went to New York to meet Nick. The trains were crowded, and I rode the train sitting on duffel bags all the way. Nick met me, and we got a room in a hotel. Within 15 minutes, he was called to report. He said, "If you don't hear from me in three days, go back to Brunswick." I spent Christmas alone in the hotel. He was shipped out to England, where he was being readied for the D-Day invasion. On June 6, 1944, Nick landed late in the day at Omaha Beach. He, being a personnel officer, had to report all happenings, casualties, and progress of his engineer combat battalion to higher headquarters. I came back to Brunswick, went to work at the shipyard, and worked the third shift in the payroll department.

CHAPTER SIX

The Civil Air Patrol

Civil Air Patrol

Aviators in the United States sensed a national emergency might be eminent because of the situation in Europe, and as early as 1939 began proposing a plan to relieve the military of patrolling our coast. The proposed plan resulted in the formation of the Civil Air Patrol on December 1, 1941, just six days prior to the bombing of Pearl Harbor. The CAP was a group of civilian pilots from all walks of life who, because of age or physical condition, were prevented from serving in the military or had already been sworn into service and were waiting to be called.*

A fleet of German submarines was roaming the Atlantic and in January 1942 methodically started down the Eastern Seaboard, torpedoing our supply ships and other vessels vital to wartime shipping. The Civil Air Patrol's Coastal Patrol operation started in January 1942 out of an Army base at Fort Screvens, Savannah, Georgia. From February 28, 1942, until August 31, 1943, civilian pilots flew all kinds of single-engine civilian planes as far as 40 miles out to sea searching for German U-boats.**

The sixth base to open along the Atlantic seaboard was the CAP Base Headquarters at St. Simons Island, Georgia, which opened May 22, 1942, in offices attached to the hanger at McKinnon Airport.

*"When Antiques Went to War: The 50th Anniversary of the Civil Air Patrol," by Roger Theil, 1319 Naylor Court, N.W., Washington, D.C. 20001.
**Civil Air Patrol - Historical Monograph - History of Coastal Base # 6 - St. Simons Island, Ga.

Francis A. (Sam) Baker
Courtesy of Winn Baker

Samuel Winn Baker

My dad was Francis A. Baker, but everyone knew him as Sam. His father was Samuel Winn Baker, and so my dad was "Little Sam." I am named after my grandfather. Before World War II, Dad was a pilot and flight instructor, but his main job was sales manager for the Georgia Power Company.

When the Civil Air Patrol was organized on St. Simons Island, he was second in command at CAP #6, as they called it. This unit was located at McKinnon Air Field in the old original hanger, which is still there by the tower. When the Navy came in, the CAP moved across the road. About halfway down the runway where it parallels the road, there was a little path that went clear out in the woods over there. That area is all the Island Club now. I have an aerial picture, and you can see where they taxied across the road to use the runways at McKinnon Field from their headquarters in the woods.

I really don't know where the men in the CAP came from. From all over, I guess. Some of the men I remember were Ned Egbert, Walt

Nicoli, Andy Cochran, David Black (later he was one of my professors at GMC), George Dixon, Duckworth, Ernie Helms, Bosarge, Ernie Jenkins, and Joe Mangum. Joe Mangum later became an executive with Delta Air Lines and hired me there when I became a pilot. Mr. Charlie Gowen was the oldest member. I believe he was in his 70s.

Ernie Jenkins got hurt in a crash off the end of the runway. Ned Egbert was one of the first to go down offshore. His propeller came off. He had put the propeller on and had been flying the plane for a week or so before it came off and the plane went down. He was rescued.

The CAP flew mostly Stinsons, Fairchilds, and Ryans. There also was a bigger Stinson called the "Gull-wing" Stinson. The Stinson 10-A was smaller, and the Fairchild 24 was sort of in between the two. They did not fly Taylorcrafts and Cubs on submarine patrol.

Did Dad Spot a Sailboat?

I remember Dad talking about some of his experiences. Sometimes he would come home at night and talk about an airplane that had gone down. There was one documented case of my dad spotting a sub. They didn't carry bombs on the planes at that time. Dad saw what he thought was a sailboat while he was flying south of St. Simons off Cumberland Island. This was in the spring of 1942. When he approached the sailboat, it suddenly submerged, leaving the sails floating on top of the water. He realized it was a sub and notified the base. Since he had no bombs, there was nothing he could do.

We lived at the end of Ocean Avenue on the boulevard in Brunswick. One night Mom and Daddy took me out in the yard and we watched these flashes. In my mind, I thought they were in the marsh. I didn't realize they were offshore.

When the torpedoed ships were raised, I sat in my mother's lap while Daddy flew us in a Taylorcraft over one of the torpedoed ships in St. Simons Sound. I was five years old at the time. As we flew over, I remember seeing a bateau near the ship go up in the hole in the side of the ship. That scene has stuck with me all these years. After they closed the CAP base on St. Simons, my dad transferred to Texas and flew the border patrol for about three months.

My mother, Fenton Burroughs Baker, repaired airplanes. She was good at fabric work and woodwork. She was Dad's best mechanic. She actually had learned how to fly but never soloed. Mother also played the piano in an orchestra . . . Chester Anderson's among others. She played with different people at different times, played at clubs if they had a dance, and played the piano off and on at the little bars on St. Simons.

The Navy still had McKinnon Field in 1944, but people were able to again start flying civilian airplanes. Dad, Ned Egbert, and the other guys took their planes back over to Redfern Field. Redfern Field was located about where the Kentucky Fried Chicken is now on St. Simons. Right after the war, when the Navy still had McKinnon Airport, Daddy and Ned Egbert were at the Brunswick Air Park. When the Navy released McKinnon, Ned went to McKinnon and Dad stayed at the Brunswick Air Park.

Civil Air Patrol Pilots and Observers
Courtesy of Winn Baker

Dad was still district sales manager with the Georgia Power Company after the war. He also had a little flight school to teach the returning G.I.s who wanted to learn to fly on the G.I. Bill. After that fizzled out, he continued at the Brunswick Air Park. It was where Brunswick College is now. As a matter of fact, the new stadium is sitting right in the middle of where the old runways were . . . right off Fourth Street.

Charles Daniel, Jr.

Early in the war the Civil Air Patrol, which was made up of civilian pilots who volunteered their planes and their services, came to St. Simons. There were probably 12 to 15 planes and about 30 volunteers. They flew submarine patrol with 250-pound depth charges affixed to these civilian planes. Several different planes were used—the Ryan SC, a Stinson, and others. My uncle, Walter Nicolai, was one of the pilots for the CAP and flew the Ryan SC. After about 18 months, the CAP began to phase out. [The base closed in February 1943.] All CAP people were moved out of St. Simons to Texas to fly border patrol on the Mexican border.

*See appendix for names of original staff of officers and additional information.

Ann Wynne McMichael

Our family moved to St. Simons Island in the 1930s. Our parents, Morgan and Irene Wynne, were in the hotel business. We lived at Wynne Gables. Our father built the first King and Prince Hotel, which later burned.

Catherine, my sister, and I went to school in Brunswick via the causeway on the school bus. The whole screaming load of us interrupted our singing of "Red Sails in the Sunset" to yell out the windows to the toll gate keeper: "Heeeeeyyyee Mr. Chitty!" St. Simons was a little bit of heaven, and the hours were filled with time on the beaches, swimming, and dancing. We must have danced away most of those years. I graduated from Glynn Academy in 1940 and went to Brenau College that fall. As the war clouds gathered, I decided to come home to our island.

St. Simons turned out the lights. Everyone seemed to have a job to serve our country. Friends and neighbors joined the Red Cross, worked with the USO, served as spotters, and filled their shoes with sand walking endless patrols on the beach. I went to work at McKinnon Airport at the crossroads on the island. It was closed to public air traffic and taken over by the Civil Air Patrol.

The Air Force took control of the CAP units up and down the East Coast and designated them Coastal Patrol. The staff who worked at these bases joined the CAP. They were carefully scrutinized and sworn in, as were pilots, copilots, mechanics, maintenance crews, and radio operators. No one else was allowed past the gate guards without authorization. I believe the nucleus of this CAP unit originated at the University of Georgia School of Aviation. It packed up and moved to St. Simons and was soon joined by other CAP members from Atlanta and nearby cities. Many of the pilots brought their own planes.

After rigging their Wacos, Pipers, and Stinsons to carry demolition bombs, our fleet was a bit slow, but perfect for the assignment of hours of patrolling our coastal area searching for oil slicks, debris, and shadows of subs. Where our parameters ended, other CAP units took over. They stayed in touch with all coastal bases. One of my jobs was to operate teletype machines—the Model T of communications with its clanging bell to indicate incoming messages. At the base we worked long hours, seven days a week. We lost planes, a pilot, and saw several severe injuries from crashes. There was one forced landing on Hilton Head . . . a totally undeveloped Mecca for mosquitoes. Who knew!

In December 1942, I married Billy Burchhalter, a pilot at our base who was from Aiken, South Carolina. Ours was the first formal wedding at the new Methodist Church on St. Simons. That next summer he answered a call for pilots needed as flight instructors in Army Air Force schools. We moved to Douglas, Georgia. As with most groups who live with danger, we had to have a touch of humor. Ours was a ghost pilot . . . a non-existent Lt. Hagreen who left us frantic, crazy messages in the most unlikely places. As we visited our CAP base for the last time, I looked back over my shoulder to read the message on the bulletin board: LT. HAGREEN CALL YOUR MOTHER!

Charles Gowen

At age 73, my father was a member of the CAP and flew a plane. All were privately owned airplanes. Pilots flew whatever kind of planes they had. Single engine—don't think they had any two- engine planes. Some single-engine planes were better than others. They would send the planes out with bombs on the wings. Don't know if they ever saw a submarine. They used to laugh about it and say they were more worried about my father landing when he came back with that bomb on the wings.

Clarence B. Gowen
Courtesy of Winn Baker

Ray Cameron

The Civil Air Patrol at the St. Simons Airport was transferred to Eagle Mountain Lake, Texas, for the border patrol along the Rio Grande River. The Navy commander at the naval air station on St. Simons wanted it off the base, so he wrote Washington, saying the planes were too slow to follow the traffic pattern and they also didn't have any radio communication. At the beginning of the war, they were vital for patrolling the coast when the Navy was unprepared, but when the blimp base was built, the blimps took their place.

Airplane Hangar at McKinnon Air Field St. Simons Island, GA

Aerial View of McKinnon Field St. Simons Island, Georgia
Note: West of the field across the road is where the Civil Air Patrol was located. Planes had to be taken across the road to the runways.
Courtesy of Winn Baker

Airplanes Used to Patrol the Coast at the Beginning of the War
Courtesy of Winn Baker

Ralph Dorris

CIVIL AIR PATROL CADET CORPS

After I became a Life Scout, one step away from Eagle, I left scouting and joined the Civil Air Patrol as I wanted to take flying lessons. My dad said if I earned money for lessons, I could go with others up to the old Darien golf course grass runway on Sunday afternoons. My grandmother in Tennessee thought it was amusing that I had learned how to fly planes before I learned to drive a car. I became the Civil Air Patrol Cadet commander in 1944 after Harold Friedman graduated and went off to college. We had drills and classes in navigation and weather and continued with flying lessons. Also we got to fly with senior pilots on patrol for German U-boats off the coast. I was never aware that we cadets participated in actual finds, but we did feel like we were contributing to the war effort.

Civil Air Patrol Cadets
Far left: Sam Baker
Third from left: Julian Flexer
Center: Ralph Dorris
Third from right: Royce Tarret
Second from right: Benny Pye
Courtesy of Ralph Dorris

CHAPTER SEVEN

Auxiliary-U.S. Coast Guard Reserve-Sea Scouts

United States Coast Guard Auxiliary

VOLUNTEER GROUP IS DOING FINE SERVICE
SOME FACTS ABOUT DUTIES OF THE COAST GUARD AUXILIARY
THE BRUNSWICK NEWS, JULY 23, 1942

Most of the anti-sabotage patrol of the Sixth Naval District, a volunteer group of some 400 former yachtsmen and fishermen who sail the inlets from Jacksonville, Florida, to Wilmington, North Carolina, are keeping a constant dusk-to-dawn vigil for fifth columnists.

These civilian boat-owners, old salts who know their home waters like the palms of their hands, are members of the Coast Guard Auxiliary. They serve, without pay, aboard their own vessels and the vessels of their friends, doing a man-sized part in the man-sized job of patrolling the coast.

It's their specific job to investigate and report all suspicious craft and activities. Is their work important? The answer lies in the now established fact that Axis submarines have landed saboteurs, armed with devastating explosives, on our Atlantic coast.*

The 400 members of the Sixth District Auxiliary own a total of about 350 boats. The reason there are more members than boats is that in some cases two or more members own a boat in partnership. The craft range in size from 25 feet to 100 feet; some are swanky cruisers, some battered shrimpers; some cost $1,000, some upwards of $10,000.

From this array of boats, mostly pleasure craft, the Coast Guard has selected 75 vessels for actual patrol duty in the Sixth District. These boats have been painted battleship gray and marked with the identifying letters CGA.

The owners of the 75 selected craft usually go out with their vessels and the other 325 auxiliary members serve as the crews.

When the boats are used for duty, a Coast Guardsman is assigned to each vessel. Uncle Sam pays for the gasoline, maintains the crafts, and supplies meals for all hands on the job.

The amount of time which members of the auxiliary spend on patrol duty is left up to the individuals and depends largely on their outside business obligations.

GEORGIA'S VOLUNTEER NAVY

The organization of the U.S. Coast Guard Auxiliary followed the passage by Congress of the Auxiliary and Reserve Act. The submarines lurking off the Georgia coast brought an urgent appeal from the government. It was directed to all yachtsmen and motorboat men.

In Brunswick, one flotilla for daily patrol was organized in June 1942 and continued until October 1943. All coastal areas of the United States had been divided into naval districts. A Coast Guard officer, either in regular service or reserve, was named director of the auxiliary for each district. Men from all walks of life joined.

The usefulness of the auxiliary did not lessen, however, when the subs disappeared. Lt. Ralph McCrary was captain of Division No. 2, which Savannah and Brunswick flotillas compose. Ensign Nelson Niall was commander of Flotilla No. 4 in Brunswick.

Jack McQuade
Atlanta Journal, December 10, 1944

"Early in the war the old Bernice, *which had been painted gray, as were other civilian craft that had been commandeered by the Coast Guard Auxiliary, was tied up at the pier."*

Charles B. Daniel

"I was on temporary Coast Guard duty one night a week. It was bad losing sleep, but we got to eat beef, which tastes real good when you can't have it often."

William H. Backus

Some of the members go out every night, some two or three times a week, and some only once a week.

But all of the members are former yachtsmen or fishermen, and they love the sea. Consequently, almost all of them go out just as often as they possibly can.

Members of the auxiliary should not be confused with other former yachtsmen who are actually members of the Coast Guard Reserve. Under the program, the Coast Guard has granted various ratings to yacht owners who have volunteered for active duty. These yacht owners are assigned as the skippers of their own boats.

Those in this area who are members of the auxiliary and the name of their boats follow (only a portion of the boats listed, however, have been designated at this time for actual patrol duty):

St. Simons: Percy S. Bacon, *Lucky*; George H. Stevens, *Bobsuelaine*; Bruce W. Winpenny, *Penny II*; Olaf Olsen, *Skeeter*; A. G. Johnson, *Amelia W*.

Brunswick: Jas. E. Royall, *Bernice*; R. G. McCrary, *Irene*; R. L. Bennet, *Bernecliff*; Chas. E. Gray, *Ora C*; Edward R. Gray, *Charles E. Gray*; L. A. Miller, *Two Friends*; Wesley Greenfield, *W. H. Greenfield*; L.S. Miller, *Ranger*.

Officers of the flotilla are Percy S. Bacon, commander; J. E. Royall, vice-commander; R. G. McCrary, junior commander.

Madeline Thomas Rouse

In April 1940, I married the man I loved. My husband, Jimmy Rouse, was a crewman on the yacht *Elizabeth McCaw*, which was owned by R. J. Reynolds, Jr. This yacht was particularly important to me since I spent the first six months of my marriage aboard this beautiful sailboat. Not too many of us can look back to having spent their honeymoon in such a way.

Mr. Reynolds owned Sapelo Island, one of the islands that form the Golden Isles of Georgia. Jim and I lived on this island for many years of our married life. Our firstborn came into our lives on July 25, 1941, and needless to say, she was the joy of our lives. We lived in a little green cottage down by the sea, and at night, we could hear the waves as they broke along the beach. It was a quieting sound, and one that I treasure to this day.

During one of the interludes of not being at sea, Jim had brought his car, a Graham-Page, to Sapelo to work on the engine. Afterward, we drove down to the Marsh Landing Dock. Marsh Landing was where all the barges bringing supplies and produce docked to unload their merchandise. Jim had the radio turned on when the announcement came with the disturbing news that Japan had attacked Pearl Harbor and had destroyed a great part of the American fleet. At that moment, it seemed that all my new world had suddenly fallen apart. I knew that this man whom I had married would enlist to serve his country. When he registered and was classified as 1-A, he enlisted in the Coast Guard Reserve.

America had been caught off guard. Although it was common knowledge, even to the populace, that there were German U-boats just 30 to 40 miles off the coastal United States, this great land was caught unprepared. Once this country had officially gotten into the war, Germany saw America as its enemy. The East Coast was in jeopardy, as was the West Coast. Patrol boats of some sort were needed until the proper kinds of boats could be built. All yachts were confiscated by the government in order to fill the need. The *Elizabeth McCaw* was among the many. She was stripped of her sails and fitted with a machine gun and one depth charge. Sounding devices and radar were installed.

We were still on Sapelo as Jim was awaiting his order to go to Charleston, South Carolina, for training. We were awakened in the early hours of the morning by the sound of a great explosion. Every dish and window in our little cottage shook. The cottage had a garret that was accessible by stairs. From the upstairs window, we saw a fire that lit up the whole sky and billowing black smoke that rose upward with the flames. The Coast Guard was alerted and the next day the survivors were brought to St. Simons Island. Most of them were charred from the heat and sun, the result of exposure while waiting to be rescued. Those who were present said that they would carry memories of those men to their graves.

Jim went on to Charleston for assignment, then on to Maryland for basic training. When he finished his basic training, he scored high enough to be classified as a chief petty officer. With this rating, it meant that he could be in command of many of the vessels that were destined to do the patrolling. He was re-assigned to go back to Charleston for further orders. Much to his surprise, the *Elizabeth McCaw* was also there. The greater surprise was that he had been assigned to be the navigator in charge.

Here is how these patrols were to operate. The entire East Coast had been sectioned off into "X" number of nautical miles, and each area within the range was to have its home port. Where one's particular range ended, another began within its vicinity. In this way, the whole coastline was protected. As more men and boats became available, boats and crews were dispersed to patrol other areas. When disbursement was enacted, Jim, in charge of the *Elizabeth McCaw*, was stationed at the Coast Guard Station on St. Simons Island. The pieces of my shattered world once again fell into place.

These yachts and sailboats stayed within the limits of what we consider our nation's waters. This means that they were never more than 15 to 20 miles offshore. When you are out at sea, the skyline of the city lights is highly visible. Any object that is offshore at this given distance becomes fairly visible. These boats and men were targets for U-boats, which they heard on their sounding devices as well as their radar. Most of them had one machine gun and one depth charge. Larger yachts may have had more, but the vast majority were highly unequipped for the tasks they faced on daily maneuvers. When the PT boats were built and put into practice their operation was ended.

In Brunswick, the residents were facing an influx of people who came here to work in the newly built shipyard. In looking back, it was absolutely unbelievable. Because of the closeness of our harbor to the ocean, Brunswick had been chosen to build Liberty ships. People were

Left:
James Rouse, U.S.C.G.R.
Courtesy of Madeline Rouse

Elizabeth McCaw
Courtesy of Madeline Rouse

coming into Brunswick from all over the United States. Housing was inadequate. Where were all these people and their families going to live? Every vacant lot within the city was condemned and allocated to build temporary housing for those coming here. The understanding was that at the end of the war, the property owner could opt to purchase the housing at a low price, or they could have the buildings torn down. In a matter of a few months, the population had about tripled.

Many of those who had come to build ships were also master musicians. Seeking relaxation from their daily work, they formed a symphony orchestra. They needed a conductor and a pianist. My sister, Helen Thomas, who was playing the organ at her church, St. James Lutheran, applied for the job as pianist and was hired. Some of the musicians who were down here had played in a symphony orchestra in Babylon, New York. They got together and asked their conductor, Christos Vironides, to come to Brunswick and be their conductor. He came. Two years later my sister and Christos were married.

Charles B. Daniel

St. Simons Sea Scouts

One of the things we got involved in was the Sea Scout ship *Asao*, which was sponsored by the Coast Guard Station and the Coast Guard Auxiliary. Nelson Niall was the Sea Scout captain. We, being juniors and seniors in high school, functioned as an auxiliary to the Coast Guard. If they didn't have enough people, they would call on us to go out on the boat with them. Naturally, we had a lot of fun and really appreciated all the work.

The St. Simons Sea Scout ship crew, which was composed of 12 of us, was invited to go on a shakedown cruise of one of the Liberty ships. We boarded the boat in Brunswick and went out about 20 or 30 miles, which took a whole day. Various tests were made on the ship to get it ready for duty. Our skipper, Nelson Niall, had arranged for this. Various members who are still around here are Edwin Fendig, who is now a harbor pilot, his brother, Neal Fendig, Ray Cameron, Noel McCay, Allen Frye, Buddy Edwards, Skippy Edwards, and me. We had a lot of fun and learned a lot from Skipper Niall.

During the hurricane of October 1944, a tug and a barge were grounded. Assistant Sea Scout Skipper Hollis, who was a Coast Guardsman, decided it would be a very good idea for the Sea Scouts to try to salvage the tug, which had washed up into the marsh across from the Cumberland Wharf on the west side Cumberland River. So off we went! There were six or eight of us in the Coast Guard self-righting lifeboat. We got there in jig time. As we tried to get close to shore to anchor we ran hard aground and the tide was going out. In four hours we could get off the boat and walk in the mud. Luckily we weren't in any danger. We spent the night there. The next day Skipper Nelson Niall came in one of the other Coast Guard boats and rescued us. We finally got the Coast Guard lifeboat off the mud. It was a fun thing for a group of boys to be involved in but wasn't too smart a move. We had about as much a chance of salvaging that tug up in the marsh as we had of flying to the moon. Somebody much later salvaged the tug.

Sea Scout Ship Asao
L to R: Neal Fendig, Noel McKay,
Allen Frye, Red Brady,
Ray Cameron, Skipper Nelson Niall,
John Hollis, Edwin Fendig,
Chip Daniel, and Johnny Clark
Courtesy of Charles B. Daniel

For July 4th, in 1944 or 1945, the Jaycees prevailed upon the blimp base to put on a mock rescue mission and use one of the blimps to hoist someone out of the water within sight of the pier to show everyone how it was done. The Sea Scout ship was asked to supply one person to be the victim. I was chosen and was hoisted up almost into the blimp. Then they let me back down to be picked up by a boat. This was very exciting for me. I don't know how exciting it was for those standing on the shore.

William H. Brown

SEA SCOUT ADVENTURES

During my employment at the Brunswick Marine, I also served as skipper of the Sea Scout ship with my friend Louis Keiffer, a supervisor at Hercules, serving as mate. We had about 15 Sea Scouts in the unit. We also had the use of a 32-foot catboat donated by a man in Stanford, Connecticut. We used to go out nearly every Sunday afternoon for a sail in the St. Simons Sound. We tied up at the St. Simons pier one afternoon right behind a PT boat with depth charges on its stern. The boom on our catboat extended about 10 feet beyond the stern of our boat. After mooring our boat, we noticed the boom was swinging right over the depth charges. However, both boats were rising and falling in the same sequence, so we didn't dislodge any depth charges.

One afternoon as we came into Back River our auxiliary engine conked out and we had to sail through the Back River drawbridge. At our slow pace, we had Sunday traffic backed up all the way to Brunswick and the island.

Late one afternoon we bought fuel at the Gulf dock on East River and started back to our dock on Terry Creek. I decided to ride on the board we were pulling. Dark caught us as we approached the north end of Jekyll. It was an eerie feeling to be riding behind the boat unable to see it, only hearing the exhaust. I finally called for them to pick me up. Fortunately they did.

Man Overboard

Another afternoon, Louis Keiffer and I decided to give the Sea Scouts a "man overboard" drill. Louis, unannounced, jumped overboard. I threw him the life ring with about 100 feet of line attached. He grabbed the ring while I was holding the other end of the line. The line tightened before I could turn it loose, and I was snatched overboard. We thought the boys would never turn around and pick us up. We never gave them another "man overboard" drill.

Snapper Fishing

The Coast Guard finally permitted private boats to go offshore during daylight hours, provided the boat carried large identification numbers hanging from the rigging. We decided to take some of the Sea Scouts snapper fishing offshore from Fernandina. We left on a Friday afternoon after work and headed down the Intracoastal Waterway. Darkness overtook us before we made Fernandina. We met a northbound oil barge with a tug boat. The boys thought we were in Fernandina and wanted to tie up to the barge.

The Fernandina lighthouse was, of course, blacked out, but we made our way into Cumberland Sound, where we found a Portuguese shrimp boat anchored. As we approached, the fisherman could be seen running about the deck shouting at us. We circled the boat and finally understood that he was telling us not to run over his anchor line.

We finally made our way into the Fernandina harbor and headed for the city dock. As we approached the dock, we found that it had been converted to a Coast Guard base. We were not supposed to be running at night, so we made a quick turn and tied up alongside the shrimp boat. The next morning we got a funny look from the Coast Guard patrol until one of the crew recognized me.

We cranked up the engine at 6 a.m., motored out to the snapper banks, fished a while, and headed back to Brunswick. We docked at our dock in Terry Creek at 7 p.m. The engine had run for 13 hours continuously.

Four Scouts and Christmas 1944

A few days before Christmas 1944, Louis Keiffer and four Sea Scouts ran the catboat up to Savannah. They called me at work to tell me they had struck a submerged piling as they went through the drawbridge at Thunderbolt. They asked me to come and help bring the boat back that night so we could haul out the next day and repair the broken plank. They had slowed down the leak so the 2-inch handheld bilge pump could handle it.

I borrowed my father's car, along with a gasoline coupon, and drove to Thunderbolt. One of the boys drove the car back to Brunswick while we headed down the Intracoastal Waterway. As darkness fell, we continued running, picking up channel markers with our spotlight. After passing several markers, the light beam shone out about 20 feet and bounced back off a blanket of heavy fog.

We had a chart, a compass, and parallel rulers. However, none of us had a watch. We plotted a course from marker to marker and hit several right on the nose. Finally we missed one and couldn't tell whether or not we had overrun it. We broke out the lead line and put one of the boys on the bow to sound. He sounded quite a while until on his last cast the lead didn't splash. It just went plunk into a mud bank. We were all relieved, so we backed up and anchored for the night. During the night, we heard a Navy plane flying around in circles. We learned later that the plane crashed off St. Catherine Island.

The next morning just after daylight, but while the fog still lingered, we heard a boat blowing its foghorn as it made its way northward. Our boat was painted gray so the crew of the other boat could not see us anchored off the channel. We would ring our bell and the 100-footer would stop and several crew members would run around the deck trying to spot us. Finally they would move ahead slowly. We'd ring the bell again. They would stop, look, and listen, then creep ahead slowly. Eventually they worked themselves beyond the sound of our bell.

Later that morning, Christmas Day, the fog lifted and we found that we were anchored within sight of the channel marker we'd missed the night before. We headed south at full speed. Later that afternoon, we passed a dredge and asked the time. It was 4:30 Christmas afternoon.

As we entered the Altamaha Sound we saw the fog bank moving in off the ocean. We took a bearing on the river running by Doboy Island just before the fog caught us again. We kept going and found the entrance to the Frederica River just before darkness fell. Running in the fog and darkness we ran from one side of the river to the other until the Frederica River drawbridge loomed up about 50 feet ahead of the boat. We made a sharp turn to the left and eased back to the dock now used by the St. Simons Boat Club. After mooring the boat, we walked to the Olsens' house and asked them to call our families. They had heard nothing from us for a day and a half. Mrs. Olsen offered us some Christmas dinner, which was most appreciated since we had eaten very little on our trip down. We learned later that the Coast Guard Reserve had sent a boat out to look for us. However, when the fog came back in they had turned around and returned to St. Simons.

We hauled the boat the next day and repaired the broken plank. However, we did not make any more long trips.

CHAPTER EIGHT

U.S. Coast Guard

United States Coast Guard

James D. Paulk
Courtesy of Robert Paulk

Doree Avera
Doree Avera is J. D. Paulk's granddaughter.

RECOLLECTIONS OF JAMES D. PAULK

My grandfather, J. D. Paulk, was commissioned during World War II to serve as commanding officer of the southern half of the coastal region known as the Sixth Naval District. This group of Coast Guardsmen had to patrol the beaches of the barrier islands off the coast of Georgia and as far north as Hilton Head, South Carolina, and to the south along the eastern coast down to Jekyll Island and Cumberland Island.

The Coast Guard sent down to the Sixth Naval District a large group of the most beautiful Tennessee Walking horses. The problem was that these horses could not walk or run very well on the beaches. My grandfather had grown up out in the country and was raised on a working farm and knew that the best horses for the swamp and marsh were found right on the barrier islands. These horses were known around Brunswick as marsh ponies. My grandfather persuaded the Coast Guard to let him capture and train some of these ponies. They could take the uneven land, severe weather conditions, and long hours of hard service and still be strong and healthy.

So these men patrolled the Georgia beaches on these wild, but now completely broken in marsh ponies. Just for fun during their rest times, the men would have horse races over on Cumberland Island. If you made a bet on my grandfather, you were sure to come out a winner. He used to be called the king of horse-racing when he was a teenager because no one could out-ride him.

The Coast Guard was part of the U.S. Navy and had the important task of operating an information system by means of beach patrols, picket boat patrols, and lookout watchtowers. So the guarding of America's shores became a joint Army-Navy-Coast Guard-FBI operation. The FBI had to be given evidence of attempted landings along the coast. The Coast Guard was given the additional job of surveillance of the local small craft operating in home waters. This included fishing and pleasure boats. Some of these boats had already been taken over for patrol duty by the Coast Guard. Special ID cards were issued to fishermen and other boatmen by the Coast Guard so these men could continue to work. And, just as important, the Coast Guard had the responsibility of rescuing survivors of boating accidents. In other words, the Coast Guard beach patrol was organized as a special agency to be the "eyes and ears" of the Army and the Navy, to guard the coast, not to repel invasion.

In January 1943, the blimp base in Brunswick was opened. Blimps began patrolling the sea lanes for submarine detection. As shown by Burton Vice, the Coast Guard began to replace the soldiers who, along with civilian volunteers, had filled a void and performed a vital service in the interim.

On July 25, 1942, the following was sent out from headquarters: "These beach patrols are not intended as a military protection of our coastline, as is the function of the Army. The beach patrols are more in the nature of outposts to report activities along the coastline and are not to repel hostile armed units."

The vice-chief of Naval Operations informed the commanders that "the beaches and inlets of the coasts would henceforth be patrolled by the Coast Guard whenever and wherever possible.". . . Army and Navy intelligence officers organized a close liaison with Coast Guard Intelligence, which still continued to operate as a separate command but under Navy direction.

The Sixth District had its own problems. Sand dunes and swamps, long sandy beaches and rocky areas, inlets and rivers were complicated topographical areas. This is where those marsh ponies could and did help the men patrol the coastal regions. Boats, Jeeps, trucks, horses, and dogs were used by the Coast Guardsmen to keep the coast protected. By the end of the first year, 2,000 sentry dogs and 3,000 horses were actively used in patrol duty. The men had special uniforms, which were quite formal. Also issued to the men were canvas leggings, cavalry boots, peacoats, rain gear, thermal underwear, and insect protection gear.

The Georgia coast has 14 barrier islands from Savannah to Fernandina Beach, Florida. The Brunswick area had the most activity. On April 8, 1942, two American ships were sunk off the coast by the German commander Kapitaenleutnant Reinhard Hardegen in U-boat 123. This attack brought the war close to our homes on the Golden Isles of Georgia.

On nearby Jekyll Island, the millionaire landowners of the Jekyll Island Club were told to leave for their safety. The beach patrol moved in. Horses were brought over by barge from Brunswick and housed in the stables of the Jekyll Island Club. The patrolmen were now living in the servants' quarters. Sam Altman of Brunswick, serving under my grandfather, was stationed on Jekyll. The millionaires never returned to Jekyll after the war.

Some of the material for this report came from *Prints in the Sand* by Eleanor Bishop, Pictorial Histories Publishing Company, Missoula, Montana, 1989.

Burton Vice

Until I enlisted in the U.S. Coast Guard, Iowa, Kansas, Missouri, and Nebraska had been my worldly travels. Early in 1943, I was transferred to Hilton Head, South Carolina, to the Mounted Beach Patrol Training Station. At that time, the only way to get to Hilton Head was by boat from Beaufort, South Carolina. After training at Hilton Head, I was sent to Fernandina Beach, Florida, to help build a barracks for the mounted beach patrol at the north side of Fort Clinch. A crew for Cumberland Island was being formed as the men from the training center completed their course. I was picked for the Cumberland Island Patrol.

Our patrols were on the beach covering both Big and Little Cumberland. We took care of plane wrecks, patrolled the beach, and monitored radio calls on land, sea, and air. We always were in contact with Brunswick, St. Simons, Hilton Head, Jacksonville, and Fernandina.

When we arrived at Cumberland Island, our first stop was at Dungeness (the Carnegie house on the south end of the island), which we used for a watchtower. The barracks were the old maintenance workers' two-story, wooden-frame buildings, which were in great shape. We prepared the stables for our horses and admired the cars that were kept at Dungeness.

Work details were sent to the respective posts to prepare them for use as soon as possible. Also, guard duty was assigned to places like the tower at Dungeness. What a beautiful mansion! The pool house and what equipment was left in it got a good share of our off-duty time. We used the exercise equipment quite a bit if the weather wasn't too hot. Mostly we swam. What fun to see how far we could swing over the water on ropes trying to go across the pool from one end to the other without falling in!

The Dream and The Queen

Two private boats were used for transportation to Fernandina: *The Dream* and *The Queen*. *The Dream* docked at the Cumberland Sound wharf and *The Queen* docked south of the castle (Dungeness) at a boathouse on Beach Creek that could only be used at high tide. We used *The Queen* if *The Dream* was being serviced or was out at the time. We never used the St. Mary's waterway. In case of emergency, the Coast Guard would meet us with a patrol boat. Some of these boats were converted civilian boats.

An elderly seaman with a crippled leg whom we called Captain John was the captain of *The Dream*. Captain John and his wife lived in a cottage north of the dock where *The Dream* was moored. A part-time helper usually ran *The Queen*. The overseer of the island was a gentleman named Mac Laren. Mr. Mac and his wife lived in a cottage north of the stables and the building used by the beach patrol. He drove a Ford pickup and his companion most of the time was a big black dog. Where you saw Mr. Mac, you also saw his dog.

Equipment and Communication

The United States Coast Guard trans-substation on the island had a Jeep, a re-con car, a weapons carrier, and a six-ton truck for heavy hauling of grain, hay, etc. Our communication system on the island, other than the radio for outside business, was an Army telephone system. We had a line installed behind the dunes on the beach from each post to the Dungeness post since that was the headquarters of the officers in charge. Each post had a different ring except in case of an emergency.

High Point and Little Cumberland

High Point was at the north end of Cumberland. This post not only had horses but also used sentry dogs on patrol. Once in a while we'd have a ball game or some kind of a get-together at a post. Other than that, we didn't see each other until we would go on liberty, have some deliveries to make, or attend a service class at the post.

Little Cumberland was the hardest post to get to and from. You had to cross Christmas Creek when the tide was out. At high tide, no go! There was a Jeep to use, but once it was on the island, you couldn't get it off since it had to be loaded upon a barge. We never got to see the lighthouse that was located on the north end of Little Cumberland. I think there was only one building on the island and that was used for barracks.

Plum Orchard

We were removed from Dungeness to Plum Orchard, another Carnegie estate. Our barracks was one of the buildings that had been used by the maintenance people. We used the laundry building and any of the equipment in it that we needed to wash our clothes. Standards then were a lot different than they are now. But laundry tubs and wringers were better than wringing by hand. Buckets had to be used to carry the water and we had clotheslines for hanging the laundry. The water system filled the supply tanks, swimming pool, and house supply by means of a ram. I've never found out what made it work. At night when it was still, you could hear a sound—*kaboom, kaboom, kaboom*—real soft and steady. What fun we had swimming in that indoor pool! This was the only part of the mansion we were allowed to use.

Duckhouse

Time came for us to move to the Duckhouse. What a difference from Plum Orchard, where there were beautiful flowers, lawns, laundry room, nice two-story barracks, windows with screens, and an indoor swimming pool! Now we had a shack with no screens, no pool, only sand dunes and the horse and saddle, horse-drawn weapons carrier, two-wheel ammo carts, and 50-gallon drums for hauling water for drinking and cooking. We drove a sand point so we could get water with a pitcher pump for watering the horses and plants and taking showers. Also, we had to use it to wash our clothes. Now we crossed the sand dunes and a swamp to get to the beach for our ride to Dungeness to catch a boat to Fernandina, Florida, for liberty, to go on patrol, or to go swimming. We couldn't ride on the beach if the tide was in, so we took the main road.

At the north end of Duckhouse was a little room that had a sign painted over the door which said, Armory and Radio Room. Across the porch from the radio room and on a sand dune, we had a walk-in freezer for our refrigerated food. This unit and the radio batteries were run by a gasoline generator. We received and sent out mail on the liberty run. Our emergencies were sent out by radio. Army engineers built us a big lookout tower on the beach. The radio was then moved to the tower. Our call letters were "Man X-Ray Item 2." The armory wasn't moved so all the rifles, submachine guns, and side arms stayed at the Duckhouse.

A wooden sidewalk was made over the sand dunes east of the house, making it easier for us to get over the hill to reach the stables, take showers, go to the beach, or wash clothes. Since this worked on the dunes, we made a walk across the marsh so the snakes and alligators didn't bother us so much going to the beach. Diamondback rattlers, cottonmouths, and coral snakes were watched for very closely, but I don't recall anyone having been treated for a snake bite.

On Thanksgiving Day 1943, all the wives of the men based on the island came out to the respective posts to have dinner with us. The Coast Guard brought them out from Fernandina and picked them up that evening, returning them before dark. The Red Cross and Salvation Army paid us a visit at Christmas time, bringing us New Testaments, gloves, scarves, watch caps, cigarettes, and good wishes.

Wrecks and Strandings

Two of us stood watch on the beach and/or at Dungeness Tower. One hot day, a fighter plane and a twin-engine Marine Beechcraft, hedgehopping over the island, crashed into the marsh. Air-Sea Rescue out of Jacksonville was notified, and since we reported the crash, we were instructed to locate anyone onboard the planes. We were ordered not to touch the bodies other than tie a line so they wouldn't be washed out into the channel when the tide came in. When we found them, we were in mud and water up to our knees. When the Air-Sea 83-Footer got there, we were in water up to our chest. You can think of a lot of things in a marsh besides you and the guy you have tied to you. I was from Nebraska, and one of the guys that we found in the wreck was from Bayard, Nebraska.

One thrill we had was on a very, very dark night after a heavy storm at sea. A very large object began coming ashore and was reported per procedure. Then came the thrill. We took up positions behind the dunes and began challenging. No answer. Whatever it was just kept on coming. Happiness came with the daylight when, to our delight, we discovered it was a Navy barge that had broken its anchor way out at sea. All that was on the half-size floating football field was an empty nail keg and a scoop shovel. A week later, the Navy tugs, at high tide, took it back out to sea.

How Do You Communicate When You Can't Use Morse Code?

A twin-engine SNB-2 Navy radar sub chaser radioed that it had lost power on one engine and was having trouble with the remaining one but was trying to make it to shore. That was about the center of Cumberland Island. Sure enough, about halfway between Plum Orchard and Stafford, the pilot landed in a pasture close to a timberline on its east side. The plane was okay and the crew had no problems other than one well-equipped plane that didn't have any flying power.

Now I can show you how great a sailor I was at that time. Soon after the plane was down, we arrived at the landing sight. A blimp from Cecil Field came flying over us looking at the plane. They were sending me Morse code and I could neither receive nor send it. As a last-ditch effort the crew wrote a note, put it in a paper cup weighted down with an orange, and dropped it to me. The note read, "If you are from Cecil Field hold your hands over your head. If you are not, where are you stationed?" Well, I couldn't send them an answer because I didn't know where the plane was from. I began talking to them by using tree limbs to spell out what I knew. After a while, with my "shorthand timber answers," they waved and left. Two days later a crew of mechanics from Cecil Field came out with two engines and a maintainer and replaced the engines. The maintainer made a runway in the field and flew the plane off without a hitch of any kind.

Later, but at different times, two fighter planes crash landed on the beach just east of Dungeness. One was at high tide and he got too close to the dunes. The plane looked like you had opened a car door. The pilot unhooked his safety belt and just walked back up the beach to Dungeness to get help. He had a bruise on his arm and a scratch on his leg. The plane was a loser at that stop. The other fighter came out even better than the first one. He landed farther down the beach toward the jetty. His plane had only a broken oil line, which was replaced. The plane was flown back to Brunswick where it was based.

Animal Experiences and Entertainment

Every once in a while one of us would swim out to a shrimp boat and the crew would give us shrimp, crabs, fish, or any seafood that they thought we could use for dinner. Had there been a shark in the area, he might have had his own ideas about fish dinners.

Deer

One day some of the guys were out roaming north of Dungeness and found a dead doe and her fawn. The fawn was nearly starved to death so they brought him back to the barracks and what a pet he made! He lived in the barracks like a dog. He would sit by the table and beg for food. He loved toast, anything sweet, and especially green vegetables. He would go up the stairs by himself, but we had to carry him down because he was afraid he'd fall As he got older, he would leave early in the morning after breakfast and not show up until supper time. He'd stay all night and do the same thing the next day. After a while he would leave and be gone two or three days. Then he'd be gone for a week. After a while, he left for good. If we ran across him or happened to see him in the woods he'd come up to us, but he never came back to the barracks that we knew about.

Watch Out for the Gator!

During mating season, bull gators will travel from one pond, lake, or marsh to another. Their temperament at this time is very short and mean, so don't think they won't let you know what they intend to do! On our way from Plum Orchard to High Point to pick up the liberty one pretty morning, we happened to discover one of the large bulls coming down the road. We were in the weapons carrier, which is pretty well protected with large, heavy-duty bumpers. We stopped, thinking he would get out of the way. Instead he grabbed the bumper and tried to shake the vehicle. We finally backed up and drove around him. Later we checked the bumper and he had marked it real well with his teeth.

Another time, one of the men was out in the marshes and came back dragging a small, three-legged young gator. Several of us were standing around trying to figure out how it had lost its leg. The fella that brought the gator in weighed between 180 and 200 pounds. He was just touching the gator with the toe of his boot while we were talking. We told him, "You'd better stop kicking him." He was going to get bit if that gator got tired of his nudging. Since it was cold weather and the gator was sluggish, he didn't move too much. All of a sudden the guy was on the deck. The gator bit through his boot. Thank heavens for heavy combat boots! He didn't even mark the man's foot! Old "Three Legs" was returned to the marsh as the nature study on strength and loss of limbs was over.

Hogs: Did We Solve Our Problem?

A couple of the men penned up one of the wild sows as we had lots of slop to feed her. In a few weeks she began to look more like a hog you would have on a farm back home. Not only was she getting fat, but we were getting a litter of little pigs. She gave birth to five of the prettiest little pink pigs you ever saw. Now we were on the wrong side of the problem-solving system. There were too many mouths to feed so we had to turn her loose. Now we really had a mess since they wouldn't leave. The second mess was when they found shelter underneath the Duckhouse, which was open on the west side. Everyone soon learned how cats and dogs feel when fleas infest a place. I'll bet you can still find a couple somewhere at the Duckhouse.

Some of the horses of World War II were of good blood and could show some speed if raced. We had a couple of good times testing out old remounts against good breeds of stock. Usually we created our own entertainment—swimming, reading, writing, softball, exploring, fishing, and just "chewing the fat."

In closing, we never had anything to report that could have been harmful to the island or mainland in a serious way. A couple of bodies of American pilots washed ashore. We happened to be the ones who found them, but we were never told what happened or why. Guess it wasn't any of our business.

Charles Howard Candler III

The fear of German U-boats kept our family from going over to Cumberland during 1942 and 1943. Our summer home remained unused. However, the Georgia State Guard Boat Unit, composed of boats and personnel from the area, continued to operate up and down the inland waterway, taking supplies to the Army and Coast Guard who patrolled on all the islands from Cumberland to Savannah.

After the submarine menace was over, we were once again allowed to go over to Cumberland. The Georgia State Guard Boat Unit was disbanded, and many of the personnel joined the Civil Air Patrol, either as pilots or observers. The Army and Coast Guard continued to patrol the beaches until well after the war was over. Then my brother, my cousin, and myself, teenaged hellions that we were, proceeded to tear down or otherwise "dismantle" the barracks and lookout towers on the north end of Cumberland!

Lookout Tower

Catherine Warren Dukehart

My view of the war was from Cumberland Island in Camden County. I'm not sure which year, but there were four Coast Guard posts situated up and down the beach. These were manned by members of the Coast Guard from various American cities. They patrolled the beach on horseback, and we persuaded them to let us ride.

The Coast Guard men stationed on the island lived in our caretaker's house. The horses were stabled in wooden buildings on the edge of the sand dunes. We would invite all of them to visit us at High Point where we played records and danced. We were 13 or 14 years old, and my girlfriends loved this! We hoped the war would last forever! One of our Coast Guard friends found an old phonograph record, "Dinner for One Person, James," which we played endlessly.

Our yacht was painted gray and our captain, Olie Olsen, went to serve his country with her in the Georgia State Guard. He saved many seamen from the two tankers torpedoed off the coast of St. Simons. He was a hero to me! Several years after they were abandoned, the lookout towers in the sand dunes remained as reminders of the war but were now the props of great imaginative adventures for the children playing on them. The stables were burned down by my daring cousins.

Charles B. Daniel

The Coast Guard was on St. Simons Island before the war, and its primary station was located on East Beach. It was a search station. Early in the war the Coast Guard patrolled the beach and the coast and assisted the Navy when any planes were down.

United States Coast Guard Station
East Beach, St. Simons Island, Georgia

Fred Heinold
U.S. Coast Guard
Courtesy of Fred and Evelyn Heinold

Fred Heinold

In 1941 I was single and living at home in Winthrop Harbor, Illinois, in the northern part of the state at Lake Michigan, and was working in Waukegan, Illinois. In November 1941, I went to Chicago to enlist in the U.S. Coast Guard and was sent to the New Orleans, Louisiana, area for boot camp training. When that was completed, I was sent to the U.S. Coast Guard Station at St. Simons Island, Georgia, by way of Charleston, South Carolina. I think there were six of us whose last name began with the letter H who came from Charleston to Brunswick, Georgia, by bus and were met by someone from the station at St. Simons Island. It was night time and very dark. I well remember the ride across the five wooden bridges from Brunswick to St. Simons and wondering "where in the world are they taking us?"

As a motor machinist, my duties were at the beach as well as at the boathouse on the Frederica River. We all took part in many jobs, including watch duty in the tower and other work and training. In 1942 I had gotten leave and was traveling by bus home to Illinois. When the bus arrived in Walterboro, South Carolina, there was a message that my leave had been canceled and that I must return to the USCG at St. Simons. That was when the ships had been torpedoed off our coast and all leaves were canceled. Of course, we were involved in the rescue operation.

After serving three years, I re-enlisted for three more years as the war had not ended. In all, I was in the Coast Guard for six years. I was discharged in 1947 when my tour of duty was complete. After the war I had no desire to return to Illinois to live. I had married Evelyn Wallace, a St. Simons girl, and had become used to the winter weather here.

Military Installations

CHAPTER NINE

St. Simons Naval Air Station

Charles B. Daniel

The biggest thing happening on St. Simons Island was the airport, which had been taken over by the Navy.* Early in the war, fighter planes began to arrive as the airport was being converted into a fighter training base. The airport entrance was off Airport Road about one-eighth of a mile south of Demere Road. I can well picture the guardhouse and the sailors saluting.

Since we lived about three-quarters of a mile from the Navy airfield, we could hear almost everything that went on and see a lot of it from our house. I remember how impressed I was by the first planes to arrive as they were the Grumman F4F3s, which had fought in the Pacific in some of the early large battles such as Wake Island and the Pearl Harbor attack. These planes were considered no longer fit for combat duty and were shipped back to be used for training while the industrial complex got geared up to build more. There were about twelve to fifteen F4F3s early in the war. On any particular day about eight of them would fly. Every day at 5 a.m. you could hear them starting the various planes, seeing how many they could get ready to run for practice and training missions that took off as soon as it got light. In addition to the F4F3s, there were other airplanes: the F6F Hellcat, which was built by Grumman, the SBD Douglas Dauntless Dive Bomber, and the TBF Grumman Avenger, which were torpedo planes. Also early in the war, there was the Brewster Buccaneer, which was another somewhat obsolete dive bomber.

Some of those early days of fighter training were very exciting. For each day's training exercise a plane towing a target would take off after all the other planes. It would tow a target like a chute at the end of a long rope. Occasionally the plane would not get high enough and the target would get caught on the telephone or electric wires or a tree. The plane would fly around while the rope whipped and cracked near the ground without its target. Early fighter training at the Navy base occasionally included mock dogfights within sight of the shore with the North American P51 fighters from Moody Army Air Force Base at Valdosta, Georgia.

One specific crash I remember occurred on the Sea Island Golf Course property. The plane was one of the original Grumman Wildcats that had been sent back from the Pacific for training duty. It crashed and was almost covered up in the mud. Of course, they always guarded them, roped them off until they somehow lifted the planes out and took them back to the base. Another plane crash early in the war occurred very close to the old Christ Church Rectory on Demere Road. A plane called Volti Vengeance tried to take off on the shortest runway at the airport and was not able to clear the oak trees at the end. Two men were killed and a large fire resulted. There were daily occurrences of different types of mishaps at the air base, but most were not serious. I recall the first time a brand-new B25 Army bomber visited the St. Simons airport. This was before we had made the bombing run on Tokyo. What a beautiful plane that was and how large it looked!

The function of the airplane base on St. Simons slowly changed from a fighter training base to a support operation for the Combat Information Center (CIC) School at the King and Prince. This school was under construction and they were getting ready to bring in a lot of people in early 1943. That probably was the primary training operation for St. Simons for the balance of the war with support from the planes at the air field.

* *The Brunswick News:* July 14, 1942, "Airport taken over by Navy Department - Order of U.S. Court received here and officially transferred at ten o'clock."

T.R. Walker

T.R. Walker
Courtesy of Mrs. T.R. Walker

The only reason I went into the Navy was because a buddy that I had gone to high school with (in Eastman, Georgia) was being drafted into the Army. I said, "Ah, heck, let's join the Navy." We went to Macon, Georgia, to enlist and they sent us to Jacksonville, Florida, to get our training at the naval air base there. They told us that if we took the same thing we'd probably stay together the whole time. Because I didn't register, the U.S. Recruiting Service thought of me as a deserter. When I was in the Pacific in 1944, I was still receiving letters about that.

About three o'clock on the Saturday morning we broke boot camp, they called this little group of men over here, and this little group, and this little group until there were six of us left. They told us that if we didn't go to trade school, we would go to this island where there "ain't gonna be no women; ain't gonna be no liquor." We got in a van that headed to St. Simons! That was August or September of 1942. At that time I was an apprentice seaman in the Navy.

When we arrived, there was a little dirt strip for the CAP at the airport. All the rest was trees. There wasn't even a barracks at the naval air station. We stayed at a motel, and the officers stayed at the King and Prince Hotel. When you turned to go to the King and Prince, there was a nightclub on the corner called The Anchorage. Once in a while it was off limits to sailors. To the north of the base there were only a few houses until you got to Frederica. I'm not sure but I think the government built some houses back up north of the airport for the servicemen. I was married in 1941 so my wife came down and stayed on the island. She had a friend who had several houses on the street where Wynne Gables was located. My wife was in charge of these rental properties for her friend.

There was a Catholic church up Frederica Road. A friend of mine named Pohl, a yeoman first class in the regular Navy, liked to go out and party at night and get "all lit up." Whenever he came in he wouldn't go to bed until he'd gone to that priest, confessed, and got forgiveness. Then the next morning we'd go and beg him to get out of bed because being in the regular Navy, he knew how the station was operated. Most of the fellows coming on the base at that time were new recruits and really didn't know about keeping records and all, but this guy Pohl did. He practically ran the station.

Lt. J. G. Dillon was my officer. He was an engineer. Together we'd go out on the field at night where the airstrips were being built. He'd get on the bulldozer for a while and I'd tie chains on the trees. Then I'd get on the bulldozer and he'd tie chains. We'd pull up those old oak trees where the runways are now.

Lt. Dillon stayed at the King and Prince because he was an officer. One night the non-officers were planning a beer party. There were seven or eight of us. However, Lt. Dillon wanted to be included in our party. Someone said, "Lt. Dillon, you don't mingle with enlisted men. You are an officer." But Dillon said, "Boys, I've got lots of beer in my station wagon. Meet me at the pier." When we got to the pier, Dillon said, "Walker, you and me are about the same size. Let's change uniforms." We did and it wasn't 10 minutes before the shore patrol came. Of course, they carried Dillon and me back to the barracks. The next day the skipper called me in and said, "Well Walker, I hear you want to be an officer!" I said, "No sir, that was liquor talk." He said, "Well, weren't you in an officer's uniform?" "Yes, sir." Then he said, "I want to tell you something. If it wasn't for the enlisted men, we wouldn't have a navy. After this, if you and Jack want to change uniforms, you'd better go where Lt. Shore [patrol] can't find you."

Did you ever hear of George Bush? The former President of the United States? St. Simons Island Naval Air Base is where he took his flight training and it was while I was stationed there.

The weather was very changeable on the island. When a squall came up the planes were routed to Jacksonville or to airports in the Carolinas. The fog played havoc with flying and we lost several pilots. In the fog, they'd overshoot the field, get over the water, start to bank, the wing would dip in the water, and they would crash. Some of the pilots we recovered. Some we didn't. At that time, I was drawing flight pay and I'd have to fly. One plane would pull a target and the other planes would shoot at it for practice. At times I would go up with the pilot when he did his target practicing as part of my flight time.

I was in transportation, and besides keeping up all the vehicles, it was my outfit's responsibility to unload the barges of gasoline that docked at Gascoigne Bluff on the Frederica River. The aviation gasoline was pumped from the barges into the gasoline trucks. We'd empty the gas truck into the storage tanks on base, then go back and get another load. This was done around the clock. We set up huge spotlights at night on the bluff. Trucks were running up and down that oyster shell road for over 24 hours each time.

The tanks in which the gasoline was stored on the base would build up moisture. This moisture in the gasoline made it very dangerous to use in the aircraft, so periodically we pumped this gasoline into 55-gallon drums. In those days we had coupons for rationed automobile gas. The guys on the base, however, were able from time to time to get this "watered" gasoline for their cars. It may have been illegal, but the gas didn't go to waste. The skipper, or commander, of the air base was Commander Thomas. He had an old 1937 Ford. It had mechanical brakes that were always needing repair. Of course, he had a Navy vehicle to drive and kept the Ford in the shop on the base. At that time, I didn't have a car. He'd always want me to keep his brakes up, and I got to use his car whenever I wanted. Whenever I'd use it, he'd give me some gasoline coupons.

Leaving St. Simons

When I left St. Simons in 1944, I was a motor machinist first class. I went first to Norfolk, Virginia, and stayed there about six or eight weeks. I came to find out my orders were lost. They had fallen behind a desk. I was supposed to be in Fleet Air Wing Nine. By the time I got to Quonset Point, Rhode Island, Fleet Air Wing Nine had already gone to North Africa. Everyone in that unit was wiped out. That file behind the desk saved my life.

I was in a plane crash in Quonset. After I got out of the hospital, I transferred to a submarine base in Ft. Lauderdale, Florida. I went by train, and my wife, who had come up to be with me when I was in the hospital, rode with me as far as Jesup, Georgia. I worked on a submarine at Ft. Lauderdale for five or six months. Then I was sent to Boston, and from there I went to the Pacific. I was there four or five months before they dropped the bomb. I was on a repair ship near Okinawa when the bomb was dropped. My ship was in and out of the Leyte Gulf when the A-bomb was dropped on August 5, 1945, on Hiroshima and on August 9, 1945, on Nagasaki.

A Surprise Meeting

When I got out of service I decided to join the Georgia State Patrol. I went to Atlanta and the colonel said, "Well, let me introduce you to the major." I walked into the major's office and the colonel said, "This is T. R. Walker." The major said, "Well, I'll be a so-'n-so.....Walker!" The surprised colonel said, "You mean you know each other?" The major, who had been in the shore patrol, said, "Yes, we were the ones who christened St. Simons to the Navy!"

Lee Vincent Howe

I was born in Kansas and in 1942, at the age of 22, joined the U. S. Navy, Aviation Cadet, V5 Program. After pilot and pre-flight basic training, I went to the naval air station at Corpus Christi, Texas, for advance multi-engine training. On October 27, 1943, I was commissioned ENS USNR and designated naval aviator and ordered to the naval air station in Lake City, Florida, for operational training. Due to excessive student load and lack of operational aircraft, I was further ordered to the naval air station on St. Simons Island. I reported there, December 20, 1943. While on a training mission, I crashed in St. Simons Sound but lived to tell.

Orvin Eggen

October 11, 1944, found me bound for a naval air station at St. Simons Island. This was for some S. M. Radar Gear Training of Carrier type. We happened to arrive at a bad time. It was hurricane time for Georgia and most of the south coast. Some damaging winds were up to 40 to 50 miles per hour. We enlisted men were left to huddle in our wooden barracks while the officers were quartered in brick and stone hotels that the Navy had commandeered.

"The Navy took over the St. Simons airport. I applied for a position and was given the job as chief telephone operator."

Virginia Dean Foster
Telephone operator for Southern Bell on St. Simons

Going to the Lutheran church in nearby Brunswick, I befriended a Norwegian family, the Olsens. On October 31, 1944, my wife, Helen, came down for a visit and stayed with the Olsens. I got special permission to stay off base, so I used to walk the two miles to the Olsens' house.

At this base we learned to work with radar and its controls over aircraft. We actually used real planes. They would fly out over the ocean and we would practice locating them and then track them in simulated air attacks.

On November 12, 1944, we left St. Simons and went to Miami to await assignment to the next school.

Helen Ann Eggen

Orvin met the Olsen family at St. James Lutheran Church in Brunswick when Mrs. Olsen invited him home to dinner and then offered to have me come down from Detroit, Michigan, to visit with him. I remember the Olsen girls taking us to an orchard, seeing the ocean for the first time, Orvin walking early in the morning down this country path, and Mrs. Olsen telling him he didn't have to be afraid. Mrs. Olsen and I became very good friends.

There was a hurricane while Orvin was stationed on St. Simons Island. All the big shots at the station moved to town [Brunswick] and the rest had to stay there. I guess it was pretty scary.

Having Orvin in the service was hard. I gave up my home, and our son, Jerry, who was only nine months old at the time, and I went to live with my parents.

Frances Postell Burns

I worked for the U.S. Post Office on St. Simons Island for 25 years. When the war started and the Navy got established at the naval air station, it set up its own post office. My main job during the war was at the naval air station post office on the island. Janet Brick and I worked there. One of us had to go down to the main post office, where Mrs. Everett worked, get the mail, and bring it back to the substation in a truck. Of course, one of the sailors did all the work. Coming back from getting the mail one day I could see the sky real well, and I said, "There must be a hurricane out there somewhere." He looked at me and said, "How do you know?" They didn't give any weather reports or anything at that time. I said, "Just look at the sky." I had been here all my life and could tell. One came near us. After the war was over I went back to the post office on St. Simons.

John Gragg

Tyrone Power, the movie actor, was stationed at the naval air station on St. Simons. He was a Marine pilot. While he was stationed there, the girls used to take off as soon as school was out and wait until he got off at 5 o'clock so they could get a glimpse of him.

One Sunday, we were riding around on East Beach. It was a group of us boys and one of them had his father's car. Jack Lang was also in the car. A little boy, the son of a naval officer stationed at the naval air station, ran out from behind a car as we drove down Bruce Drive. We didn't see him and struck him. We thought that he was dead. It scared me to death. One of the guys riding in the back seat jumped out. The little fellow was bleeding from his mouth and nose. We dared not touch him. His father heard the brakes screeching and ran out of the house, picked him up, and got in our car. The boy driving the car was too sick to drive, so someone else got in the driver's seat and drove to the naval air station. The boy's father was in civilian clothes and the Marine guard pulled his weapon to shoot because we didn't stop at the gate. However, when we stopped, he got out, identified himself, and we were rushed into the infirmary. Thank goodness the boy was only unconscious.

W.H. Pool, Jr.

When it was my time to be drafted, I knew I didn't want to be in the Army and the Marines was too macho for me. The Navy appealed as the "cleanest" branch of service, so I joined it in January 1945. For boot training the Navy sent this Georgia boy to the Great Lakes near Chicago. It was the year of the big snowstorms. There was so much snow that the only good thing about it was that the obstacle course was literally lost and we didn't have to run it during training!

How I Got into the Hospital Corps School

When we arrived, we were given a series of aptitude tests. Near the end of our training, we were called in and questioned as to where we would like to go. Evidently they thought I had enough sense to go to school because they asked me if I would like to. I said, "Sure!" Then they asked what kind of school I wanted to attend. I said, "Well, you have all my tests, what would you suggest?" They replied, "How about hospital corps school?" I had never had any interest whatsoever in medicine, but I said, "Sure. That sounds good."

So I ended up at the hospital corps school in San Diego, California, stationed at the site of the San Diego Exposition and literally housed in a huge Aztec temple. There were 1,200 of us living in this one-room edifice. A company of 100 filled one row of bunks down the length of the building. It was unbelievable, but they needed a lot of hospital corpsmen.

I didn't like the California weather either. Every night we took a blanket and went to an amphitheater, which at one time had had an organ in it. The organ had been removed, and a large screen stood in its place. We'd all sit out there with our blankets wrapped around us and by the time the movie was over the only thing showing was our eyes.

While I was in corps school VE day occurred, but it made little impact because all our training and orientation was not toward Europe but the Pacific. They just made an announcement over the intercom and we went back to class to continue our training. When Roosevelt died, that was a much bigger deal for the school. I finished in the top 10 of my class, so when it came time for us to ship out, I got first choice where I wanted to go for my "internship." One of the options was the naval hospital in Charleston, South Carolina. I said, "Yes!" That was an area I could relate to.

Our Cross-Country Trip to Charleston

However getting to Charleston from San Diego turned into a zoo. The troop transport train car we boarded had rows of bunks stacked three high and we filled the whole car. We went from San Diego to San Francisco to hook up with a train heading east. However, we missed our connection in San Francisco. For the next week they hitched our transport car to the end of anything (train, that is) going east. Some trains had a dining car. Some didn't. We would stop at a station and they'd buy stacks of boxed food and pass them out when we needed to eat. There were no bathing facilities on this car. Once in the middle of Texas, they informed us that lunch would be in an hour. We lined up and went into the restroom at the depot to wash off. We also washed our T-shirts and hung them up to dry. Since it was so hot and dry, by the time the lunches were served our shirts were ready to put back on. We also washed off a few other things, too! Primitive living! I thought we'd never get through Texas, much less to the East Coast.

After a week we finally got to Charleston, where I completed my internship. On arrival we were put on a roster. Whenever a request came into the Navy for a corpsman, the next person on the list would take that assignment. If my name had just happened to be different, I would have gone to Guam, but as my name came up there were openings for corpsmen at several naval air stations in Florida and on St. Simons Island, Georgia. I chose St. Simons.

Naval Air Station, St. Simons Island

The naval air station on St. Simons was a very interesting base. Sailors out of boot camp came for six weeks' radar training. Old, "worn out" planes were used to fly patterns for tracing by the radar trainees. After a group finished the training, it was sent into the field. Immediately, another class came in. Sometimes the station would be crawling with Navy "brass" as they came for a one-week course. Sometimes other personnel would come in from the field for retraining. The base was continually changing its emphasis, depending on what school was going on at that time. Those of us who were there permanently were only a small crew.

We had a 12-bed infirmary and mainly treated minor ailments. Sick call was held every day. Dr. Gossom was the doctor stationed there. Our medical group consisted of 12 corpsmen, one nurse, one medical officer, and one dental officer. Anyone with a serious problem was transported in the ambulance to the naval hospital in Jacksonville. We

Medical Corpsmen at the St. Simons Naval Air Station
On the steps of the infirmary.
Front row, second from left:
Dr. Donald Gossom
Middle row, second from left:
Nurse Undine Cleveland
Back row: Frank Coleman
Courtesy of W.H. Pool, Jr., M.D.

Standing beside the ambulance.
Hospital Corpsmen W.H. Pool, Jr. (left) and Frank Coleman
Courtesy of W.H. Pool, Jr., M.D.

also had a car and if someone needed a specialist, such as an ophthalmologist or dermatologist, we drove to the various clinics in Jacksonville. As to serious injuries, it was my personal observation that on the base were a lot of cars and one motorcycle. Almost every weekend we patched up someone who had been injured while driving that "damn" motorcycle. They would fall and scrape the whole side of their body or break an arm.

It was rare to have more than three patients in the infirmary. Occasionally, the doctor would hold someone to be watched for 24 hours who may have had a bad laceration. We did have an epidemic of food poisoning when all the beds were filled. Some were put on the floor. Everyone was throwing up and had diarrhea. That was a bad, bad scene and all of us were on duty.

One thing we didn't have to get used to on St. Simons was the sulfur water. The base had a purification system. The secretary at the infirmary, a long-time resident of St. Simons who lived at Frederica, brought her water from home. She didn't like the purified water because it didn't have any taste. The food basically was good. Everyone complained about it because that is what we were supposed to do. But we brought our food over to the infirmary, and "doctored" it up. We also had the advantage of getting more since we had patients to feed! Most of the time we cooked our own breakfast instead of going to the mess hall. We had a little room out back and our bunks were in the infirmary.

Those who were assigned to the infirmary had to go out in the ambulance and sit near the runways just as part of duty in case a plane had trouble. Occasionally they did. The worst thing I remember was a plane that came in and crashed. Not a "crash" crash, but the landing gear collapsed as it landed. The plane spun around on the ground, and they were able to get the pilot out before the plane caught fire. Nobody was hurt. They just pushed the plane to the side and the next plane came zipping in. I thought if I'd been a pilot, I'd never take off again after seeing that.

VJ Day occurred while I was on St. Simons. I remember clearly because at that time I didn't drink, so I agreed to stay on duty and hold down the fort at the infirmary as my cohorts went to town and celebrated.

General Dwight D. Eisenhower's Visit

After the war, Eisenhower and his wife came for a vacation at the Cloister. He was coming by air and since Mamie didn't fly, she came by train and arrived before her husband. This was a big deal for our little base. A memo went out that if we had to be out that day, we had to be in proper uniform. In the infirmary, we were alerted and on call. The maintenance crew came out the week before and painted all the little picket fences and gates. The base looked spick and span for Eisenhower, who zipped in and a week later zipped out. I'm sure he didn't notice all this, but we did get a letter from him after he was back in Washington expressing his appreciation for our hospitality.

Because the war was over, people began to be discharged. Having come into the service relatively late, I was one of the last to be discharged. My responsibilities in the infirmary increased as the staff decreased. Eventually I was in charge of one half of the infirmary. The main reason was the reduction of staff, but, as Dr. Gossom was well aware, I had become interested in medicine. Part of my responsibility was completing reports and sending them to Washington. Since I signed Dr. Gossom's name to all these reports, I was afraid he'd sign something going to Washington and they would kick it out as a forgery!

Patients at Sea

Sometimes we made an occasional excursion offshore to pick up a patient in a passing ship. If a freighter had someone on board who was sick but didn't want to put into port, we went out in the decommissioned PT boat, met the ship, transferred the patient, and took him to shore for treatment. The first time I went out to sea to pick up a patient was the first time this "dry land'" sailor had ever been to open sea. There was a fair wind blowing at the time. For a while we had the barrier islands to protect us, but when we got out into the ocean we started going over these big swells. I was sitting on top of what had been a gun turret on the PT boat. All of a sudden we went over this big wave and under the next one. Luckily, there was a pole there that I grabbed. Otherwise I would have been swept overboard.

There was an old PBY Catalina on the base. It was a large airplane with bubble windows on each side. A call came in that someone on a private yacht had had a heart attack and fallen overboard. The medical officer wasn't there so they asked me to go. We took off in this big ol' bird . . . weird airplane. When we spotted the yacht I was so excited and goggled-eyed I was hanging out in one of those bubbles watching everything. Finally as we were just about to land someone hollered, "Stupid, hold on!" I sat down, held on, and braced. Thank goodness I did because when we hit the water, it was like running into a brick wall. I would have been thrown all over the place. It was just *wham! wham! wham!* as we hit the tops of those waves. We finally settled down. We inflated our raft, rowed over, got the patient, and hauled him onto the plane. I knew he was dead, but I wasn't a medical officer so I couldn't pronounce him dead. All the way back to St. Simons I had to give this dead man artificial respiration until the medical officer could declare him dead.

Once a seaman on a Coast Guard cutter had suspected appendicitis. The cutter was on its way back in, but to save several hours, we were sent out in the PT boat to meet the cutter and transfer the patient. It was night, and after we were near the point where we were to rendezvous, we suddenly realized that here we were in the Navy and no one onboard knew Morse code. The signalmen had all been discharged. A ship came into view. We started receiving all these signals and didn't know if it was the boat we were to meet. One guy onboard who knew a little about Morse code tried to flash the message, "If you have somebody sick on board, signal 'yes'." Evidently they didn't understand us and kept going. Finally the cutter came from the right direction. We picked up the patient, hurried back in, and flew him to Jacksonville. He recovered in spite of us.

My Choice

Being in the Navy was my choice. I never regretted having served in that arm of the service, even though regimentation and the military are not my thing. I hated hats and was always losing my sailor hat. Whenever I'd get some place, I'd take it off and leave it. I finally went over to the PX and bought a dozen to have on hand. When I got out of the service, I'll never forget meeting my parents at the railroad station in Atlanta, getting in the car, taking off my little sailor hat, pitching it in the back seat, and saying, "I don't ever want to have another hat on as long as I live."

CHAPTER TEN

U.S. Naval Air Station Glynco, Brunswick

**U.S. Navy Blimp
USNAS Glynco**
Courtesy of Victor Aloisio

Ruth Croft Kent

The German U-boat menace made the protection of the Atlantic seaboard shipping lanes a high-priority project in Washington, D.C., during the summer of 1942. Establishing airship operations along the coastal shipping lanes off the coast of South Carolina, Georgia, and Florida became an urgent part of that project.

In the summer of 1942, a site was selected approximately six miles north of Brunswick, Georgia, for the proposed Naval Air Station, Glynco. Construction began in September of that year, and the station was commissioned on January 25, 1943. During the war years, Glynco served as an integral part of the anti-submarine network. Throughout the thousands of hours of patrol flown by squadrons based at Glynco, not a single airship was lost while on convoy duty during World War II.

Charles B. Daniel

In addition to the air base on St. Simons, in early 1943 construction started on the blimp base in Brunswick, the function being to house approximately 10 to 12 blimps that would patrol the sea lanes offshore for submarines. Every morning the blimps headed out with the west wind blowing from the land. They would head to the shipping lanes. Normally they would return about dusk. Sometimes during the winter when the wind would blow out of the northwest, the blimps, not being very fast, would not get in as early as normal. Occasionally at midnight you would hear them struggling against a hard wind to get back to their base.

Clyde Shepherd

We were working at Robbins Field outside of Macon when we heard about this mysterious job the Navy was going to have on the coast. But in those days war was going on, and everything was a deep secret. Actually, my father went to Washington a lot, and he and Carroll Griffin wanted this mysterious job. We finally got the job, and then found out what we had. It was this little ol' job on St. Simons Island at

McKinnon Airport. There was already a runway there. We were very disappointed.

Then we got the contract for the blimp base in Brunswick because Carl Vinson was on the Military Base Committee and he was a good friend of my father's. We had built what they call Georgia Air Depot in Macon, Georgia, which was in Vinson's district. He saw that we had done a good job, and when the job came up in Brunswick, it came to us. My father's firm was the W.C. Shepherd Company. The blimp base was actually built by a company called Shepherd and Griffin. W. C. Shepherd and Griffin Construction Company was the legal name on the contract.

The war was on and steel was under allocation, so we had to build the blimp hangers out of structural timber. The radio tower, which I climbed one time and was, I think, 700 feet high, was also made out of structural timber. The timber was Oregon blue fir. Fire posed a hazard so the timber was impregnated with a fire retardant I believe may have been calcium sulphate.

One interesting thing about those timbers was what they called timber rings. When you bolted the timber together there would be rings that fit one timber into another. One ring went between the two and then the bolt tightened up between that. There was a man in Atlanta who sold us those rings. He got rich. The people who sold the scaffolds also made out real well. The scaffolds were put together so that people could get up there and put the timbers together with the timber rings. Robert and Company out of Atlanta was the architect. They came along and made plans after we started building. That's the truth about it. We were always way ahead of them.

Blimp Hangar Under Construction
Scaffolding by Safeway Steel Scaffolds, Atlanta, Georgia, 320 ft. long by 34 ft. deep by 120 ft. high supporting box girder weight of approximately 500 tons.

These were cost-plus jobs, but they weren't cost like you might think. They were the cost of the work plus the fee and the fee wasn't like cost plus 10 percent. You bid when they gave you the job. They negotiated the job and they paid you a fee. No matter if it cost twice as much or half, you got the same fee. It's always been that way—a cost-plus. We got modest fees for those jobs.

At first I lived at the King and Prince Hotel while we worked at McKinnon Airport. There were no tourist people there and the military boys all ate mess. There was only one restaurant. We could go to the Frederica Yacht Club on the weekends, which was a treat. Then we got the job at the blimp base, and I moved to the Oglethorpe Hotel. I had a great big room in the back. I was there by myself with none of our people because it cost too much. You could go to the Lafayette Grill across the street, but you couldn't get in the "dad-blamed" place. Mrs. Jones ran the dining room, and you'd have to wait and wait and wait. While I lived at the Oglethorpe, Mrs. Jones always somehow or another got me in. The hotels were packed, but they couldn't raise the rates because there was price fixing. I stayed there until I went to Brazil to build four bases there. I was the boss' son, but I had managerial duties. I wasn't but about 27 or 28 years old. We had excellent people to work with.

Our time frame in building the blimp base was "as fast as you could," but then everything was on a fast time frame. We had a good commander, Lloyd. They ran roughshod over the architects and everybody, but in all due respect, they had too much work. We sent in reports, of course, but Bu-Docks [the Bureau of Yards and Docks] had people there. We spent the money and then had to verify everything that we had spent. There was a brilliant Jew, Manny Seltzer, who more or less ran it, although admirals came and went. As to who handled the security while building the blimp base, the military had people at the gate. I think they were just people who were on our payroll. Hell, I rode a horse all through there. There were no fences probably until we started building the hangers.

Our construction workers followed us around. Camp Stewart in Hinesville, Georgia, was a bigger job that we got before we got all the other jobs. That probably was about 1938. The war hadn't started. Everybody came to town with no place to stay. I lived with a family who had set aside two rooms and a bath. They were compassionate Christian people. The man was Colonel Frazier, and his children developed Hilton Head Island.

When we started Camp Stewart, I think there were ten thousand people working there at one time. They camped out in the woods. They drove from Macon or wherever, would work the 40 hours, get four days, and go back home. And they weren't making that much money. There just was no money. When we built Camp Stewart, they paid off in cash and had to bring Brinks trucks up there. When the Depression was on a lot of those people wanted their money to buy groceries. Probably a lot of them never had a bank account.

I went back to Brunswick 10 or 15 years after the war to see the blimp base when the hangers were going to be torn down. The timbers impregnated with fire retardant had ultimately led to the destruction of the hangers. The moisture, humidity, and heavy dew in Brunswick settling on the timbers caused the calcium to gradually leach out. There was a crust on the timbers which looked like salt cake. The timbers began to dry rot. We entertained some proposition of tearing them down but didn't fool with it. It was dangerous.

Rudolph Capers
Interviewed by Dexter Kimsey

Rudolph Capers was 28 years old when he started working at the blimp base in Brunswick in 1942 while the Shepherd and Griffin Construction Company was building the base. His daddy, a carpenter at the base, owned an automobile, and they drove to work together from Darien, Georgia. Since they had defense jobs, C gas coupons were issued to them. Each coupon entitled them to five gallons of gas.

Rudolph worked 40 to 48 hours a week earning 62 cents an hour at the beginning with gradual increases in pay. The first summer he worked with mosquito control, spraying ditches and any place water was standing on and off the base. This was accomplished with a pressure hand-pump sprayer containing diesel fuel. He doesn't believe there was any insecticide mixed with it. The diesel was stored in 55-gallon drums.

"There were two blimp hangers at Glynco that could house six football fields. It would rain in the hanger when the sun was shining outside!"

Ruth Croft Kent

After summer ended, he worked as a painter's helper cleaning up, distributing supplies, and driving men to their work area. Later he became a carpenter's helper, working in the warehouse loading and distributing materials and driving workers to the job site.

Two blimp hangers were built on the base. They were wooden with concrete floors. He recalls four blimps being housed in each hanger but there could have been six. He remembers one death: a sailor who was hanging on to one of the lines dangling from the blimp held on too long. He had to let go and hit the asphalt.

German prisoners were housed in barracks enclosed by a fence with barbed wire on top. Eight to 10 of the prisoners were carpenter's assistants, and Rudolph got to know some of them quite well. They were friendly young men, and he would buy tobacco and cigarettes for them. One German, Adam, could speak English very well, and Rudolph communicated to the rest of these workers through him. Once he saw one of the prisoners crying like a baby and asked him why. The prisoner said he did not know if any of his family was still living.

John A. Fahey

Flying airships out of Naval Air Station, Glynco, Georgia, during World War II on patrols often lasting 16 to 20 hours was always an arduous and taxing responsibility. By 1943 most of the U-boats had moved out of our range to the middle of the Atlantic Ocean. Despite the lack of contacts, we still had to be vigilant during the entire flight to keep U-boats out of the shipping lanes where in 1942 they sank so many Allied merchant ships. The tension was rarely broken on long flights, often flown in extremely bad weather, but on one day my crew was shocked, amazed, and amused by a strange sight when we made our landing approach to the naval air station. The ground handling officer who directed the 30 sailors who grabbed our blimp's lines was fully dressed as a Barnum and Bailey Circus clown. We learned later that our fellow officer's father was a real circus clown and Chuck had decided to break the monotony for returning flight crews. He succeeded to the nth degree. Fortunately, even though thoroughly distracted by his outlandish attire, none of us crashed the airships that day during our landings.

Don and Helen Merrill Franks

HELEN JOINS THE WAVES

For young women to join the Navy in 1942 took guts and determination. In Denver, Colorado, with orders in hand, she boarded a Pullman train headed for Iowa State Teacher's College. The facility had been taken over by the U. S. Navy for the training of new women enlistees. The Pullman arrived in Cedar Falls on the morning of December 15. It gets very cold in Iowa in winter and 1942 was typical. During boot training the regimen of marching plus classes all day in Navy history, language, and all the other "basics" was not easy for anyone, especially in the freezing climate. But friendships were quickly made as Helen found three other gals from the West: Mills from Idaho, Mitch from Nebraska, Jeff from Washington State.

After completing boot training, this group of four was transferred to Lakehurst, New Jersey, the Navy's headquarters for the then little-known and expanding lighter-than-air [blimp] programs.

Their assignment was to become well trained in matters of weather. Actually they became aerographer's mates, who work in meteorology and assist the officers in charge of weather forecasting. Helen and her shipmates learned to encode and decode the weather information as it came and went through the teletype machines; how to identify cloud formations; read an anemometer (to measure wind speeds); calculate the dew point, sunrise, and sunset; work a theodolite; and prepare weather maps. The six-month course was completed in three because those trained in weather were in great demand by the rapidly expanding U. S. Navy fleets. After training, Helen's orders were to report for duty at the Naval Air Station Glynco in Brunswick, Georgia, by May 1, 1943. She was not at all familiar with the location of this assignment, but her duties were to serve the weather office and to assist the station in providing competent weather information to the flying personnel of Zeppelin Patrol Squadron 15.

When Helen reported for duty at Glynco, arrangements had to be made to accommodate the women. In the great wisdom of the Navy, the King and Prince Hotel on St. Simons Island served as home for these first WAVES [Women Accepted for Voluntary Emergency Service, the Navy Corps for Women] until a separate barracks was constructed on the base. Women in the Navy did more than increase the number of "Navy Men." They were like a fresh breeze that came from the sea. At least it seemed so to many of the war-weary men who returned from sea duty. Spirits were raised as were standards (not so much cussing).

DON: SEA SCOUT TO QUARTERMASTER

When Don Franks entered the rigid discipline of Navy boot camp, the very first chief petty officer he met asked, "Any of you boots ever been a Sea Scout?" As an enthusiastic boot, Don shot his hand in the air.

"Okay," said the petty officer, "you teach the other 124 men in this company to tie a square knot and show them how to wear their neckerchief properly." Then he added, "Take these 10 men out onto Lake Michigan in that whale boat over there and bring them all back." Don carried the rooster flag in the final inspection and pass in review when his company was selected the best recruit company in the battalion.

After routine testing for skills and aptitudes, Don was informed that he could choose any of the service schools. By now he had met Elmer, who became his buddy and who was given the same choice. Don and Elmer agreed that they preferred a "deck rate" on a ship as opposed to below-deck assignments. Having made the choice, the two were shipped out to Rhode Island for training. The Morse code, semaphore, maps, navigation, deck seamanship, all good things Don had learned from his scouting experience, were in the curriculum. Don and Elmer worked hard and upon graduation were rated in the top 10 percent of their class. Quartermasters were a much-needed rate in all the Navy. Now came time for Elmer and Don to part. Don put two dollars' worth of nickels in the jukebox at the Blue Moon Tavern in Newport to play "Elmer's Tune." Drove most of the customers out of the place that night. QM3/c Don Franks went to the N. Division of the USS *Ranger* (CV-4), home-ported at Norfolk, Virginia. QM3/c Elmer Flaa went to the PT boat school that trained John Kennedy and the rest of our famous PT boat crews.

Don at Sea

Don declined the opportunity to stay stateside and teach the new class to follow him in quartermaster school. He chose sea duty on an aircraft carrier and went to North Africa with his shipmates and loads of U. S. Army Air Force P40s (fighters). The invasion of Allied forces at Casablanca, Morocco, took place while he celebrated his nineteenth birthday in November 1942. Everyone was too busy trying to get to his own next birthday to notice Don's.

Several of these trips across the cold North Atlantic convinced Don to agree to transfer to ComAirLane, as if he had any choice in the matter. They didn't tell him he was to report to the commander of the Naval Air Forces in the Atlantic Fleet. But with two other third-class petty officers, he found himself in Georgia, looking for a U. S. naval station that had not yet been built. When they got off the train from Norfolk, Virginia, wearing their winter dress blue wool uniforms, they found they were in Brunswick, Georgia. It was warm for March even in the South, and they were not prepared for what was to be their future home in the delightful semi-tropical climate. They asked directions to the Glynco Naval Air Station, the name assigned to the base when it was commissioned one month earlier. Without getting sufficient information from the railroad personnel, they were advised to go to the post office to learn the location of their destination. The kindly postmaster, seeing these three sailors carrying their sea bags and hammocks in their hot winter uniforms, told them to get on the next Greyhound bus heading north and get off at a place where there are "some very important-looking Marines guarding something. Maybe that's the place . . . just 10 miles north."

The Blimp Base

The three found their assignment, reported onboard, and were welcomed into a new men's barracks and onto the blimp base. They looked out the windows of the large barracks and saw no airships or aircraft of any kind. A landing mat was laid out, but there was nothing on it. There were not many station personnel and even fewer assigned to the squadron with Don and his friends. Their squadron was designated a Zeppelin Patrol Squadron to be numbered 15 (ZP-15), as others of this same type were being formed to patrol the entire east coast of North and South America. Their purpose was to hunt down German submarines.

It didn't take long to look over the facilities. The men's barracks, the administration building, a mess hall, and BOQ (bachelor officers' quarters) were the first to be in use. No hangers, no recreation hall. Most of the activity revolved around the administration building. The new station skipper, Captain Tony Danis, was housed with the squadron skipper, Cdr. R. C. Gossom. The officer of the day station, the aerology office, and the small chart house were all in close quarters. It was like being on a ship again. The cooks on the base shot wild pigs, and fresh

**Administration Building
USNAS Glynco**
Courtesy of Phyllis Steinmann

meat was available. Not so with the water! The water along the coast has a sulfur taste., so the Navy cooks served Coca-Cola at most meals.

By the end of March 1943, a blimp arrived on the station. With some 34 other enlisted men, Don began training to qualify as a crew member of the new K-type 350-foot helium-filled Goodyear (LTA) aircraft. Now training (mostly by experience) was to be conducted by the officers who had completed "lighter than air" training at the naval air station in Lakehurst, New Jersey. These officers were the top-rated naval aviators who had been at sea on carriers or who had just finished their flight training and received their gold wings. They had some training flying these blimps, but not much. Mechanics of all kinds learned about aircraft engines; radiomen learned how to dispatch and receive messages in the air. Most of the men returning from sea duty had to be made into "air dales" or aviation rates.

Don, one of only two quartermasters on the base, found himself in the chart house to assist First-class Quartermaster Fisher in drawing charts for each scheduled flight. He actually assumed a dual role. He was assigned to flight crew and kept the navigation equipment, the charts, manuals, and flight logs of the crews. He worked long hours over some of the charts and became proficient in their many uses.

Don Meets Helen

Just outside the chart house was a helium tank used for filling the weather balloons. One bright day while Don was laying out a # 3 patrol on a chart of the Southern Coast of the U. S., he saw this attractive aerographer's mate filling a weather balloon. Without thinking of the consequences, he mentioned to Chief Fisher that he would sure like to have a date with that very "ship-shape" third-class petty officer. Chief Fisher stepped out into the passageway and told Helen that "a young guy in there would like to have a date." She said, "Okay."

While Helen was busy in the aerographer's office, Don was on a rigid flight schedule. Time as well as money for dating was very limited. Don had taken out an allotment of $75 per month to be sent by the paymaster to his father for the expenses advanced him for his college education. When his father advised him that he had satisfied his financial obligation, Don was very happy. Now he could spend some money on Helen, like a sailor should when he finds a girl he really likes.

Don made every excuse to see or be near Helen, who was really not interested in a smart-alec sailor who had not even learned to dance. One excuse was to borrow the dictionary in her office. Helen, with more than a few opportunities, dated others. However, Don and Helen did have time together for going to the beach and the movies and for taking long walks among the short palmettos and tall pines, talking about their families. Times were very uncertain for all. Associations were made. Good times memorialized. Things were done without much concern that they would last.

Engagement and Marriage

Still not knowing how to think about the future, Helen and Don talked of marriage. Don knew he was in love, war or no war! He had been carrying an engagement ring around for a while. On Christmas Eve 1944, he and Helen had a date to see the movie on the base as Helen was scheduled to go on watch later that night. He intended to propose to her that evening. Even though he had fallen asleep in his bunk and was late to pick up Helen for the movie, he did ask the question. She accepted.

They took the steps needed to get permission from the Navy, the church, and others. Helen borrowed a white uniform and scrounged up all the other things a bride needs. Her bridesmaid was her bunkmate and fellow aerographer, Floss. Don had the chief of the aerology office stand with him, and he and Helen were married March 16, 1945, at the Episcopal Church in Brunswick. After the ceremony, the wedding party met for breakfast at the Oglethorpe Hotel. Then the couple took the bus to St. Augustine, Florida, for a two-day honeymoon.

The Navy proved to be the one big obstacle for this happy union. Time together was regulated so it was no small chore to schedule their time together. When on duty, Helen remained with her shipmates in the WAVES barracks. Don kept with his flight crew, eating and sleeping with the men as before. When on flight status, the men were required to remain on base the night before their flights. Flying a blimp was different than other flying. Early take-offs were necessary to allow for the K-ship to be "on station" (some 300 miles out to sea) before dawn in order to pick up the surface ships that were in convoy.

Don and Helen took bus rides to the nearby beach, followed by dinner, and found that a vacation-type hotel almost became their home. For a while, it worked out well, except for the expense. Finally they decided to rent a room in a private home, maybe with kitchen privileges. The local newspaper provided a list of homeowners who had facilities available for couples in need of housing. Helen and Don stopped in front of a spacious two-story white frame home at 1108 Union Street in Brunswick. On the front porch, a wonderful Southern lady seemed to be waiting for them. "Do you need a place to stay?" she asked. "Oh, yes. Do you know of some place close?" was their quick response. After a short visit and a chance to get acquainted, they learned that this lady and her husband had a daughter who was with her Navy husband. They also had a son in the Navy. Their name was Holden, and they missed their family and welcomed some Navy company, offering Helen and Don the opportunity to share the upstairs part of their large home, including the kitchen downstairs. What could have been better? A very lovely place to call home when they could arrange their time away from duty, two weary sailors had found a restful place.

The success of the Allied forces were by 1945 being recorded all over the world. On April 12, 1945, less than a month after Helen and Don were married, President Franklin D. Roosevelt died. Vice-President Harry S. Truman found that he could direct the world's conflict to a conclusion, and by golly, he did! He told everyone where the buck stopped.

Young Parents

Not long after Truman became president, Helen's Navy medical examiners advised her that she and Don were to become parents. What does a young unsuspecting and very inexperienced sailor say to his wife when she gives him the word? His response, "Oh, boy, I sure didn't have that in mind, did you? What do the Navy regulations say about that?"

It did not take long to find answers. The Navy, in those days, could not provide for women on active duty who were having children. It was fine for men to become fathers, but not for the women to become mothers. Helen's discharge on May 8, 1945, read: "Under Honorable Conditions." Just like that she was no longer a member of the greatest navy the world had ever seen. But she certainly had done her part proudly as an aerographer. Don and Helen were lucky they had a home with the Holdens, and Helen could spend her time there on Union Street.

The War Winds Down

After V.E. Day, the war effort shifted to the Pacific Theater. By summer 1945, the need for any further German submarine hunting was greatly diminished. Flight schedules were reduced and East Coast operations were closing. Transfers of personnel to the Pacific Theater were coming in daily. Don found he was needed in an experimental squadron at the naval air station in Lakehurst, New Jersey, the center of all lighter-than-air operations. When orders came for his transfer, Helen went to her home in Kansas until Don could find suitable housing in New Jersey.

The atom bomb of August 6 was followed by the ending of the hostilities in the Pacific on August 14. November 5, 1945, Don was released from active duty. Even though he had a good opportunity to stay in the Navy, Helen wanted to be away from the Navy. He took a detail from the naval air station to the U. S. Navy Separation Center at Lido Beach on Long Island. Don got his battleship discharge, his separation pay, and a letter from the Secretary of the Navy, James Forrestal.

Don writes: "My U. S. Naval Aviator's flight log reminds me that I first met and flew in the ZNP K-34 on March 29, 1943, from U. S. Naval Air Station, Glynco, near Brunswick, Georgia. The flight lasted 14.6 hours and began a long tale of some 100 flights (993.7 hours) during 1943, 1944, and 1945. I was quite proud when we learned that of the 90,000 or more surface craft escorted by these blimps in the Atlantic during the war, none was lost to enemy action."

Helen Merrill Franks

As a Yankee in the Deep South for the first time, I had a lot to learn. I wasn't aware of the geographic differences since I was born and reared in a small town in southwest Kansas. I had traveled out of the state only a few times before enlisting in the Navy in November 1942. The previous year three girls with whom I worked and I had taken a trip to Missouri, Kentucky, Tennessee, and Arkansas. That was my only encounter with the Southern culture, though it was only a brief exposure.

My arrival in May 1943 at Navy Glynco near Brunswick was my first experience with separate entrances to stores, separate drinking fountains, and segregated restaurants. On a bus trip to Jacksonville several of us stood all the way from Brunswick even though there were vacant seats, since those were reserved for blacks. In places where we were allowed to go, such as Sea Island and St. Simons Island, there was no visible sign of segregation.

**WAVES Basketball Team
USNAS Glynco**
Front row, center:
Helen Merrill Franks
Courtesy of Helen Merrill Franks

The WAVES on the station were about evenly divided as far as their geographic origins were concerned. Much time was spent "shooting the breeze" about how things were where we came from. One of the four of us in our cubicle in the barracks was from North Carolina and had been reared mainly by a Negro mammy. My bunkmate was from Greenwich Village, New York, and, in spite of our cultural differences became a good friend. The fourth WAVE was a "Cape Codda" from Cape Cod, Massachusetts. It took me a while to learn the dialect. Living together in such close quarters, though our duty hours were varied, required considerable patience, tolerance, and understanding. For the most part, we got along well.

After I married Don, we were able to find housing in a large house in Brunswick on Union Street. The Holdens, whose home we shared, became a sort of surrogate family, sharing kitchen privileges, grocery shopping, and such. The beaches were what I most enjoyed. The hurricane of 1944 and a fire in a blimp hanger were two memorable happenings. Oh, I forgot to mention the odor from the pulp mill. My home in Kansas was one-half mile from a sugar beet factory. The smell was different, but reminiscent!

Phyllis Rhoades Steinmann

There are a number of vivid memories from my stay in Georgia. The old Oglethorpe Hotel, the crab cakes and shrimp cocktail, the children who sold boiled peanuts on the bus, the young woman who worked at the bakery and always stuck extra goodies in the sack, the fancy restaurant on St. Simons where a date took me and there were no prices on my menu, the small white wooden Methodist Church where I went when I was off on Sundays and no one but the minister ever spoke to me. I remember riding the bus to Sea Island to the Cloister, where they allowed us to use their swimming pool for 10 cents, which was for the towel.

Once I was going to Orlando to visit my brother who was in service. I had to get going early to catch the bus to Orlando. It was still dark. I saw a vehicle coming with big lights on it and thought that it was the bus. It stopped. It was a truck with a guy hauling shrimp. He asked where I was going. I said, "Orlando." He said, "That's where I am going. I'll take you there." He did, and bought my breakfast when we stopped. He was nipping on the bottle a little, but we made it and I was not harmed.

Speaking of hitchhiking, once I went to Jacksonville with two other girls to shop. One of the girls got it on her mind that we should hitchhike home. We did and were picked up by an elderly man, who blessed us out for hitchhiking. He was a senator.

I was in the WAVES two years. Three months I was in the Bronx and three months in Lakewood, New Jersey, training to be an aerologist. Then I was stationed at the blimp base in Brunswick for one and a half years. There were only four women who worked as aerologists. We worked on shifts: two days from seven a.m. until noon, two days from noon till midnight, and two days from midnight until morning. Then we had two days off. Our job was to track the weather. Information from the more than 100 weather stations in the East would come over the teletype coded in groups of five numbers. Each group had a meaning, such as wind direction, velocity, cloud cover, kinds of clouds, rain, fog, and thunderstorms. We then took this information and placed it in a space about the size of a dime on the map where the particular weather station was located. This way we outlined a front. Pilots needed to know what they were flying into.

We had a map of the United States that measured about 3x4 feet. The weather stations were marked by numbers from 200 to 900. As the decoder read the information sent in from these stations, we entered it on the map in the proper place.

Releasing Weather Balloon
Courtesy of Phyllis Steinmann

Measuring Direction and Angle of Ascent of Weather Balloon with Theodolite
Courtesy of Phyllis Steinmann

This is the way it looked before we started: O

This is the way it looks when finished, except smaller.

We had to be able to put a dime over it and not have any part of it showing. There were nine different things we might be required to put inside the circle:

○ ◐ ⓛ ◔ ◑ ◕ ◉ ⊖ ● ⊗

The line coming out of the circle could be any of the 16 compass points. The lines coming out of the wind barb were read just twice as many as put in and could be 1 to 18. There might be any one of the 99 symbols where the ∞ is, which represented the present weather conditions. There were nine possibilities where you see ?; nine (9) more where you see w and nine more where you see v; each one different. Any one of seven symbols might go in where you see R. The ↖ in the upper left might be one of eight different directions, all depending on what the decoder read out. There were eight possibilities where the ✓ is. We had to locate the stations and enter all the information and do them at the rate of four stations a minute or faster. That was too fast for my Southern brain and fingers to work.

Recording Instrument for the Anemometer which monitors the wind velocity
Courtesy of Phyllis Steinmann

Homing pigeons used to communicate with base from blimps out on patrol
Lucy Torres, Pigeon Instructor
Courtesy of Phyllis Steinmann

We also sent up weather balloons. During the day we sent up black balloons and at night white ones with a flashlight that would reflect on the white. At night, we followed these balloons with the field light. We could get the velocity and direction of the wind. Every hour we observed the clouds, the number and kinds. On the ground we had instruments that recorded the wind velocity.

The crews of the blimps would take carrier pigeons out with them on patrol and send messages back to the base via the birds instead of by radio. Once I went up in a blimp. It was like being in a rowboat on a bumpy sea. We went sideways and up and down . . . a rocking motion. We flew so low we could see the people on the beach. I got seasick from all the motion.

The hangers at the base were 10 stories high. They were so high that a special ditch was built below the eaves to catch the rain water off the roof. The ditches were about a foot wide and 18 inches deep. Train tracks led into the hangers and when the box cars brought in supplies, they looked like miniature trains. They were so small in comparison with the building.

The 1944 hurricane I remember vividly. PBY planes were sent up from Miami because of the hurricane. By the time they were settled in, it was too late to fly them any place else to avoid the hurricane. They were stored in the huge hangers. There was so much rain with this hurricane that the rain gauge, which held 10 inches of rain, was full and running over. We had to continually go out and make observations. It was during this hurricane that my brother visited me and we couldn't go anywhere.

F. H. Torkildsen, Jr.

I Didn't Know It Was That Far!

Earl McQuaig lived over in Darien and was chief electrician out at Glynco. Seems as if one weekend the officer on duty called to say some construction lights on top of one of the blimp hangers were out. Earl said it was just getting daylight when he drove in the gate of the base. This dental officer was coming out the gate at that time. He said, "Earl, where are you going?" Earl said, "I've got to go on top of one of the hangers to change a construction light." The officer said, "Can I go with you?" "Yeah, if you feel like you can climb," said Earl. "Oh yeah, I can climb." I don't remember how the ladders were in there, but you had to climb up and across a platform. Earl said when they got halfway or two-thirds of the way up they had to walk along a gang plank before they walked out to the outside of the hanger. Earl said this fella was chewing tobacco, and he said, "Oh, wait a minute." He took the plug of tobacco out of his mouth and threw it.

Earl went on up and changed the construction light. He said the dentist followed him on out. When they came back, got down on the catwalk, and were walking along, Earl's foot hit a block of wood that had been laying up there and knocked it off. It hit the ground. The dentist looked down and said, "God almighty, I didn't know it was that far. Do you mean to tell me my plug just now hit the ground?" Earl said he almost fell off the catwalk, laughing like crazy till he was give out.

Elder Robert L. Atkinson, Jr.

CHANGING LIGHT BULBS

I went into military service during the last of 1941 and returned to St. Simons in 1946. After getting got out of service, I got a job at Glynco as an electrician and was working there when the hangers at the blimp base were demolished. My electrical work at Glynco included putting lights in the red lights and the beacon light on top of the hangers. My buddy worker and I put in three bulbs. The bulbs rotated and when the last one burned out we had to go up to the top of the building and replace the bulbs. It took us about half a day to get there. I would crawl up there, go up, across, and up and across. Then I would go up from the inside, get to the top, and open the trap door. Next, I would go on the ramp with the railing and walk on up. I got a little itchy up there, figuring the wind would blow us off. But on a calm day, I could see all over the way over to St. Simons.

The roofers were pretty skilled fellows. We called them riggers. They had ropes tied to them that were attached to the building. They patched the roofs and looked for leaks on the hangers. They would jump, swing out, and land with their feet on different parts of the roof. They checked those roofs from one end to the other. The blimp hangers were all wood with a concrete foundation. When they were to be torn down, a demolition team came in, planted sticks of dynamite on strategic pillars, set them off, and the hangers came straight down.

The wood from the buildings wouldn't burn. You could pour gasoline on it and set it afire, but the wood wouldn't burn. It was fireproof. I saved a piece of timber when they were hauling it away.

Launching Liberty

CHAPTER ELEVEN

Shipyards

This One Tells Its Own Story
Courtesy of Georgia State Archives

In September 1941, the U.S. Maritime Commission entered a contract with the Brunswick Marine Construction Corporation of Brunswick, Georgia, to build four harbor tugs for the Navy.* After the beginning of World War II, it began an expanding ship-building program. The foundation for this program was the Liberty ship, which was called the "Ugly Duckling." The Maritime Commission was in charge of the ship-building program, and the new War Shipping Administration (WSA) was in charge of recruiting former seamen, training young men to man the ships, and transporting supplies and materials for the war effort.**

Another contract with the Brunswick Marine and the U.S. Maritime Commission was signed March 26, 1942.*** This contract was to construct the New, or South, Shipyard and to build 30 cargo vessels (Liberty ships). Engineering and groundbreaking were begun April 1, 1942, by contractors Daniels & Company and engineers Sireene & Company. They began construction of the yard by agreement with the landowners while the Maritime Commission was in the process of acquiring the land by appraisal and condemnation.**** A war was on and time was important.

The Brunswick Marine had laid the first keel for a Liberty ship by July 1942 and by January 21, 1943, had laid keels on all six ways at the South yard but had launched no vessels.***** The Maritime Commission authorized the taking over of the Brunswick Marine contracts by J. A. Jones Construction Company as of February 1, 1943.***** The first Liberty ship was launched on March 13, 1943. Liberty ships and the Merchant Marine were the backbone of the war effort. The people on the home front, working day and night seven days a week, building those ships were essential in keeping that backbone strong.

* U.S. Maritime Commission letter, Dec. 14, 1942.
**ptEncyclopedia Americana*, Vol. 18, pg. 363.
***U.S. Maritime letters - Mar. 26, 1942 - Bwk. Marine entered (Facilities) contract to build 30 cargo vessels (Cargo Contract).
****U.S. Maritime letters - April 16, 1942, and May 5, 1942.
*****U.S. Maritime letter - Jan. 21, 1943.

Charles Gowen

About 1939, the Moxham family, a client of mine, purchased the Brunswick Marine Construction Company and started building some tugs for the U. S. Maritime Commission. When the war started, the government wanted a shipyard in Brunswick. Moxham started building the shipyard, which was built on the old AB&C terminal at the south end of Brunswick. Moxham found out it was too big a task for him so the government got the J. A. Jones Construction Company in Charlotte, North Carolina, to take the job.

Edward (Pete) Frith

In 19 and ohhh . . . I can't tell you the exact year just off the top of my head, but two northerners, Egbert Moxham and Rex Thompson, came down to Brunswick and negotiated a contract with the U. S. Maritime Commission to build four tugboats. They put up the enormous sum of $35,000 to build the shipyard . . . Moxham $25,000 and Thompson $10,000.

They settled on the original site of the old Brunswick Marine. It had been a small operation for hauling out shrimp boats and small craft on the railway, scraping the bottom of boats and making repairs, and working on engines. It had been a small operation, but it was just right. Moxham and Thompson also purchased land around the site . . . about 15 or 20 acres.

Example of Modern Equipment
Brunswick Marine Construction Co.
Courtesy of Georgia State Archives

Their first contract was with the Maritime Commission. That was when I became acquainted with them for the little part I played in it. Egbert Moxham came to the Downing Company, which was liquidating its assets. I was the last person there, left to dispose of the equipment that was salable. Mr. Moxham came by himself in that big slouch hat he always wore and wanted to buy some typewriters. He didn't know anything about typewriters and neither did I. He bought all the typewriters we had.

Moxham called me up and said, "How about coming to work for me? I like your style." "What will I do?" I asked. He replied, "Well, you'll be the assistant comptroller." I said, "I don't think so. I'm vice-president here of a dying business. I want to be the comptroller." He said, "Let me check it out and I'll call you back." He called me back and said, "Well, the man we brought down here from the North to be the comptroller has agreed to be the assistant comptroller. You can be the comptroller. You know, I took those typewriters you sold me back to the office and every one of them fell apart. That's when I decided that I wanted a man working for me that could outdo me in a trade." I went out there feeling very important and Egbert Moxham to me stood higher over any man's shoulder than anyone I had ever met.

When we launched our first tug, it was a big "to do" in Brunswick. The name of the tug was *Port Wentworth*. We had built a ship and we had launched a ship! I believe half of Brunswick was there for the launching. Seemed like it anyhow. George Reels, my old boss at the Downing Company, added the only tragic note. He came out there as he always did . . . walking like he was running. He came trucking across the marine railway where they hauled out the shrimp boats, his foot slipped, and he fell and broke his hip.

The Brunswick Marine then got the contract to build Army cargo ships. Daniel Construction Company came in and built the yard with six ways at the south end of Brunswick. Moxham and Thompson went over to the new yard and started constructing Army cargo ships— Liberty ships. They fell behind in their production and the Maritime Commission said they were not meeting their schedule. I don't know the exact phraseology to use to say this, but we'll say "relieved of their duties"! So they went back to the little shipyard, the original shipyard. I never went to the big yard. I stayed at the old yard. Moxham had left a man to manage the old yard. He came with a big reputation and accomplished nothing.

When you work with the Maritime Commission you have a lot of paperwork. Each week we had to list how many people worked, how long they worked, and what was accomplished. We also had to list all our costs for reimbursement. The Maritime Commission had to look at our costs and had the privilege of throwing out any it didn't approve of. Each year the Maritime Commission sent one of its New York auditors to inspect all costs. Once when the auditor was at the Brunswick Marine looking over the costs, a company official disagreed with him. I was working in the back office and they were in the center office. All at once I heard this commotion. Things were being thrown around, falling . . . or something. I ran up there to see what was happening. The official had knocked the auditor down and was astride him pounding him in the face. I knew which side my bread was buttered on! So instead of pulling him off the auditor, I got down and held the auditor's feet so he could do a good job of beating him up. The Maritime Commission didn't know anything in this world except what was on paper. It got its paperwork, but it didn't know the heart and soul of the work that went on there. It didn't know the characters. It didn't know Egbert Moxham and it didn't know Rex Thompson.

F. H. Torkildsen, Jr.

THE OLD THREE-HOLER

When World War II started, the Brunswick Marine still had the old three-holer outdoor toilet right on the dock where it had always been. (Of course, at that time, it just employed men.) I happened to be sitting in there one day when this fella came in. He looked like he was from middle Georgia as far as the way he looked and talked. He had on one of those short coats and wore overalls with the straps on them. This fella hurried in and when he took his short coat off, he laid it down on the bench (seat) next to him. When he finished, he got up and started to throw his overall strap up over his shoulder. The hook caught his coat and dropped it right down through the hole. The tide was out and when you looked down you could see that the edge of the water was in the middle of the hole. He said, "I've got to hurry up and get my coat. Man! I've got to have it! I've just got to have it!" I said, "Wait a minute fella. You don't want that coat. Look at what it is laying in." He said, "Naw, I want the coat. I've got to have it. My lunch is in the pocket." He went down and got it.

I made it a point at lunchtime to see what in the heck he had for lunch. When he unfolded the newspaper around his lunch, the first thing he pulled out was a baked sweet potato. He peeled that thing. You can imagine what it looked like and he was going to eat it.

William H. Brown

The Brunswick Marine Shipyard, now owned by Mr. Egbert Moxham and Rex Thompson, had just received the contract to build four harbor tugs for the Maritime Commission. My brother, Bob, had completed one year at Georgia Tech. During the summer recess, he had an operation and did not recover in time to return to Tech in the fall. So he went to work for the Brunswick Marine Shipyard in late summer or early fall.

Bob helped Captain Sparre, an elderly ship carpenter, lay out the lines of the tug on the floor of a former church located in the 200 block of Dartmouth Street. Bob's one year at Tech proved a big help to Captain Sparre in laying out the lines from which to make wooden templates or patterns. From these they cut out the steel plates.

About this same time, the Brunswick Marine Shipyard secured the contract to build Liberty ships. It is my further recollection that Bob helped on the construction of the new shipyard. They finally built the yard with six ways. Bob then became the foreman of # 5 way until he left to join the Navy, rather than be drafted into the Army. He served the remainder of the war in the South Pacific on a naval repair ship. I believe it was a converted Liberty ship.

After the spring quarter of 1943, I graduated from Emory in Atlanta. I came home and went to work in the new shipyard on the platens, laying out steel plates from the wooden templates. [At this time the new shipyard was under the auspices of the Brunswick Marine. J. A. Jones Construction Company took over the new yard at a later day.] This wasn't very interesting for a recent college graduate. I asked to transfer to the # 5 way as a shipfitter's helper. A partially completed hull was under construction there. They assigned me to a shipfitter, Mr. Echols, a farmer from Patterson, Georgia. We worked the second shift from 4 to 11 p.m. Mr. Echols had all morning to work on his farm. He then rode a bus to the yard and worked 4 to 11 p.m. We weren't the most efficient workers. After a month or so working in the hull and breathing the welding fumes, getting overheated, and then getting chilled from the night air, I continually suffered from strep throat. Therefore, I decided to give up shipfitting.

It was my recollection that there were about 16,000 people employed (I didn't say working) in this shipyard. This number was about 1,000 more than the 1940 population of Brunswick. Apparently the yard did not have competent supervision to handle a group of inexperienced workers (farmers

Launching of the Westore
U.S. Maritime Yard, Brunswick Marine. Picture taken from a blimp.
Courtesy of John A. Fahey

and recent college graduates) this large. Also I heard that there was a shortage of steel materials, which further assured that this yard would not meet the Maritime Commission's schedule for delivery of completed ships. I have often wondered who might have been responsible for the shortage of the steel.

Interesting Stories

With that large number of employees, there were bound to be some interesting stories. Like the one about the office worker who asked the newly classified carpenter who was hammering away, "What are you making?" Without hesitation, the carpenter replied, "$1.20 an hour."

Then we heard about the fellow who lined up every day to check out pushing a wheelbarrow full of short blocks from the carpenter shop. Every day the guard on the gate would tell him he couldn't take those blocks home. So the fellow would dump the blocks and continue with the wheelbarrow. After several days, the guard stopped the fellow and said, "I know you are stealing something. What is it?" The fellow answered, "Wheelbarrows."

This is a true story. One afternoon a new tack welder was assigned to our hull. This fellow was from Clayton, Georgia, and had never seen a ship. He climbed the stairs, looked up and down the 441 feet of rusty deck, and said, "Hits a terrible pile of iron to float in the water."

One afternoon as Bob and I were riding our bicycles to work for the afternoon shift, my right knee hit my lunch box. The lunch box hit the front wheel of my bike, knocking the wheel crossways. I went over the handlebars on the rough pavement, which skinned me up considerably. I proceeded to the yard and went to the clinic. While waiting on the nurse to check my wounds, I heard another nurse taking some information from a fellow who seemed to be suffering from malaria. She asked where he lived. He said, "Fargo, Georgia" (which is on the edge of the Okefenokee Swamp). Next she asked him what his occupation was. Apparently, he didn't know what "occupation" meant, so she asked him, "How do you make a living?" The fellow said, "I ain't never made 'arry one."

It was always a treat to go out on a Liberty ship for its sea trials. The trip lasted most of the day, and a very good lunch was served. I was fortunate to make one such trip. The ship was scheduled to leave at 8 a.m. At that hour the deck lines were taken in and the ship began to drift away from the dock. Griffith (Diddy) Taylor was supposed to be onboard as a recorder in the engine room. He was late arriving and, as I mentioned, the ship was drifting away from the dock. I looked around, found a small heaving line, threw it to him, secured the line to a cleat, and Diddy swung over the ship and made it. Speaking of sea trials, one ship went out one winter day and a heavy fog came in. In fact, it was so thick they couldn't find the channel, so the ship had to anchor for the night. The Coast Guard had to carry food to the crew and passengers because they were only supposed to eat lunch onboard.

After J. A. Jones took over the yards, things began to move more rapidly, and several records were set for delivery of ships. There was a lot of pressure on all employees to meet certain deadlines. I remember standing on the bridge and looking down at the mast house. There sat a one-gallon can of paint that had been spray-painted to match the color of the mast and the mast house. The painter just didn't have time to move the can.

FARMING - ACCOUNTING - TIME KEEPER

After my retirement from shipbuilding, I thought about farming, after having listened to Mr. Echols talk about his farm. However, I soon realized that I had about as much talent for farming as I did for shipbuilding. About this time, Pete Frith at the Brunswick Marine offered me a job in the accounting department. I accepted. However, bookkeeping and accounting were not my line of work either. I remember Pete Frith spending a hectic morning looking for $8,000 on the Navy contract that I had posted to the Army account. Shortly afterwards, he offered me the job of yard timekeeper, which I readily accepted. He was most grateful to have me leave the accounting office.

We soon discovered that some workers would get a friend to punch their time cards. My assistant, an elderly gentleman, Mr. W. T. Price, started standing in the clock house each morning to be sure every man punched just one card. Apparently, the former timekeeper had also been selling moonshine on the side. It took several weeks for me to convince his customers that I was not in that business.

The timekeeper had to keep up with the hours each man worked and the time spent on different jobs. This was a tricky task since the men would work on both Navy and Army contracts during the day. When I started, it concerned me that I might miscalculate the hours due the men. However, it didn't take long for me to learn that even if some men couldn't read or write, they could figure their time on the back of their pay envelope with a pencil stub. If I made a mistake, they quickly brought it to my attention.

Bow Sections and Freighters

The Brunswick Marine had a Navy contract to build the bow sections for landing crafts. These sections were barged up to Charleston, South Carolina, to be assembled on the hulls being built there. The Navy changed the specifications on the thickness of the steel from a light-weight to a heavier steel. Mr. Moxham told the Navy it would cost more to use the heavier steel. The Navy said, "Okay, tell us how much more." I was given the task of checking the additional time required. I made the analysis and found that it was less time consuming to use the heavier steel. Mr. Moxham wasn't very happy with my analysis.

The company also had a contract at the same time to build three small freighters for the Army Transportation Corps. These bow sections had to be lifted by two steam-powered cranes, moved slowly to the ways, and lowered into position. One afternoon, as the two cranes were lowering a bow section into position, something happened. The cables on one crane slipped, causing the bow section to fall and pull both cranes down with it. Steam and soot covered the yard and workers fled in all directions. The operator of the crane jumped, fell to the ground, and broke his hips. As I mentioned, my assistant was an elderly gentleman who walked with a limp due to severe arthritis. When the dust settled, I looked around for Mr. Price. He was not on the yard. In a few minutes I saw him limping back down Bay Street. He had run halfway to town!

Mr. Moxham called me to his office, gave me $10, and asked me to go downtown and buy him a pair of coveralls so he could go out and inspect the damage. The only pair that Schreiber's had in stock was white. I brought them back and gave them to Mr. Moxham, along with the change from his $10. He took one look at the white coveralls and said, "I can't wear those things out on the yard. Everyone would stop working just to look at me." He threw them in the closet and went out in his good clothes.

The company provided me a clerk to write up the time slips. We had a field office on the yard. One morning I came to work wearing my Coast Guard Reserve uniform. We had been on duty in St. Simons Sound Sunday night listening for submarines that might be on the surface recharging their batteries. We had trouble cranking the engine on the picket boat, so I was late for work. I approached the field office through the window in the end of the field office. I saw the clerk at her desk. I walked down, opened the door, and entered but could not see the clerk. Finally, she crawled out from under her desk. She had been up to Fort Stewart that weekend. Her soldier friend told her he was going to marry her. When she saw my khaki uniform, she thought the soldier had arrived. Apparently marriage wasn't what she had on her mind that weekend.

Mr. Moxham's older son, Egbert Moxham, Jr., called "Bud," worked in the office. He would periodically come out to make an inspection. Bud sometimes wore a bow tie with a four-in-hand tie in the same pattern in lieu of a belt. One day a welder quit. When I delivered his severance check, he asked if I could cash it. I cashed it and he gave me $2 with instructions to go buy Bud a belt.

The company completed construction on the three Army freighters and three Navy yard oilers (small tankers). After the Army

Navy Yard Oiler
Navy had taken delivery of this Yard Oiler as there are sailors on the decks.
Courtesy of Charles Ragland

and Navy vessels were delivered, the war was winding down and there were no more contracts available. Bud designed a steel-hulled fishing trawler similar to those used in New England. The trawler was built and sold. However, no other trawler sales were made. Finally, the company closed out the marine work and created Concrete Products Corporation to build porex and precast concrete roof slabs. This proved to be rather profitable until the business was bought by W. R. Grace Company. W. R. Grace operated the business for a number of years and then sold it to some local investors who operated it for a number of years. The business was finally closed and the property was eventually acquired by the Georgia Ports Authority for an expansion of the port. The Moxhams returned to New York, but Rex Thompson and his family remained in Brunswick.

Karl Meschke

In the summer of 1943 when I was 14, I got a job at J. A. Jones Construction Company as a messenger. I delivered requisitions and other correspondence throughout the shipyard. We were paid the princely wage of 43 cents an hour. Toward the end of the summer, however, a woman from the U. S. Department of Labor came on the scene and forced J. A. Jones to terminate all of us who were under the age of 16 in spite of the severe shortage of workers.

During the summer of 1945, I worked at the other shipyard, Brunswick Marine Construction Company, as an outside machinist apprentice at 86 cents an hour. This yard was located at the foot of Dartmouth Street and built seagoing tugs and yard oilers for the Navy.

Brunswick Marine Construction Company actually started the large shipyard at the south end of town, but the War Production Board took the responsibility of managing the yard away from them supposedly because of poor management. Some say that it was politically motivated in that J. A. Jones Construction Company was well connected in Washington. Brunswick Marine was given the much smaller job of building the YO's and tugs. These were considered more in line with the company's capabilities.

The yard oilers were relatively small vessels used to supply fuel to ships moored in a harbor or some protected area. They would transfer oil from permanent storage tanks to the seagoing ships. They had their own engines and would come alongside a ship and deliver oil to their tanks. Several years later when I was in the Navy, I encountered one of the YO's we had built.

Main Entrance to Shipyard (above)
Courtesy of Charles Ragland

Looking across the platens (above right)
In background ships are under construction on the ways.
Courtesy of Georgia State Archives

Charles E. Ragland

Within a few weeks after Pearl Harbor, the announcement was made that Brunswick and Savannah would be building Liberty ships. I came back to Brunswick in February 1942, and ground was being cleared along the Brunswick River. The Brunswick Marine was going to operate the yard and build the ships, although everything was the U. S. Maritime Commission operation. The yard was built by Daniel Construction Company. It did the actual building of the buildings and the ship ways, roads, and everything involved in operating the yard. As it built the yard and completed one section, the government expected the Brunswick Marine to start building ships on the completed section.

I arrived and applied for a job as a photographer since I'd had some experience in that area. I was in charge of photostating the work that was going on. The personnel building, where the darkroom and lab would be, had not even been built. They put me to work driving a station wagon part of the time. Even though there was a small first-aid station on the yard, there were injuries that required hospital attention such as accidents to the eyes from welding. I drove people to the hospital as well as driving to town to get supplies and meet people who were arriving on the train.

One morning, the sign above the gate had been changed from the Brunswick Marine to the J. A. Jones Construction Company (February 1, 1943). The U. S. Maritime Commission had canceled the contract with the Brunswick Marine, giving the reason that it wasn't moving fast enough. The government was expecting the various parts of the yard that had been completed to start building immediately . . . from the keel of the ship to laying it out in parts. The government just wanted to see those things being done. It thought that the Brunswick Marine was too slow, so it took the yard away and put J. A. Jones in. Things began to move rapidly before very long.

As each ship way was finished, the government expected to see a keel laid for the next ship and to see people out there welding steel. When there was a war, ships were needed to get the supplies overseas. You can't fight a war without a constant source of supplies. The government was extremely fussy and upset if no progress was being made. Before my darkroom was completed, they had me making photographs. I used another darkroom and also did some developing

Above: Cranes hoisting pre-fab sections to deck of Liberty Ship

Right: Hoisting of bow of Liberty Ship

Courtesy of Charles Ragland

at my house to get prints made. The pictures were being sent to Washington to show the amount of work that was being done on each ship way. Before very long, all six ship ways were built and you would see down the line from # 1 way all the stages of the building.

Not only did they want photographs of the progress, but they used photography as a method of instruction. The instructional work was being set up by someone I always called Max. He set up all the programs for teaching the workers how to perform certain tasks. There were photographs showing each step in welding, laying out the steel, putting in steam lines, pipefitting, et cetera. Most of the workers who came to work at the shipyard did not know anything about shipbuilding. Many were farmers. They had to be taught by seeing each step of their particular job. That was the quickest way to get them trained. As the first ships were built, it seems as if I spent a lot of time each day photographing various things that were being done so that the photographs could be used as directions for the next ships to be built.

It was a tremendous effort on the part of everybody to get those ships built so fast. From the time the first ship was launched, the race was really on to see how quickly another one could come off the ways. Ships were always launched on the high tide, even though it was in the early evening. Instead of waiting until the next day after the launched ship had been towed by tugs to the outfitting basin, you would see a gasher crane on each side of the vacant ship way moving in the steel for the keel for the next ship. It was just a matter of a few hours that a ship way did not have a ship at some stage in building on it. It took a really good training program and excellent coordination among the departments to make something like this work.

The government hired Chris Vironides and some musicians who were part of the New York City Symphony Orchestra, which had been started during the Depression days to give musicians in New York a job. They brought about 20 of those musicians down to Brunswick with Vironides as the director. They played music during lunch, at launchings, and in concerts for the public at the Memorial Auditorium.

It was all part of the effort to help make life a little more pleasant for the people moving in from all parts of the United States.

I think one of the things that impressed me most about the shipyard days was the attitude of the people. There were some who did not put their best into it, but the vast majority did. I remember seeing a woman walking across the road to the shipyard. She had just been notified that her husband had been lost in action. These people just didn't go home and cry and quit. They came back to the yard and worked their job. They worked with vigor because to them building those ships could help them feel they were doing something to end the war that had cost them their husbands, brothers, or boyfriends.

The Liberty ships were always taken out on a trial run before they were delivered. I went on several trial runs. Some of the tests were to run in figure eights to check the steering system and to test running full speed ahead and full speed stern. The guns and other Navy equipment were tested by naval personnel stationed at the shipyard. All of this was done in the course of a day. They would leave in the morning and be back at the dock in the afternoon. The Navy had PT and other boats giving security on the trial run. The ship would go out beyond the St. Simons Sound buoy to practice the maneuvers. When all the outfitting and tests were completed, the ships were delivered and put into service.

Part of my job was to take care of the newspapers that wanted stories about the shipyard. Everything that was released had to get clearance through one of the executives of the U. S. Maritime Commission, like Mr. Dranke. Mark Pace, a young man who was a writer, tended to the writing of all the articles and worked closely with me on the photographs. (No news media photographers were permitted to take pictures at the yard.) Probably on a special occasion, such as when a well-known personality was christening a ship, newsreel photographers were allowed. It was my task to make the photographs that the wire press wanted. Mark would give me a list of how many prints were needed, and we would mail these to various newspapers throughout the Southeast. This publicity was always an important part of each launching. It gave the people a good feeling to know that what they were doing was being read about in their hometown newspapers. One Christmas the workers at the yard agreed to give a free day of labor on Christmas Day. They did it for the people who needed the ships. I was out at the yard photographing the workers as they talked with Mark. We sent out hundreds of photographs of people working. It was truly a wonderful experience.

There were always a lot of people being terminated and a lot of people being hired. It was the policy of the company not to give anyone leave for anything. If someone had a problem, such as a death in the family, the company would terminate them but tell them that when they were ready to come back to talk with one of the interviewers and be reinstated. I guess it was simpler than trying to keep up with who would be coming back and who wouldn't. They simply terminated you. The company knew how many welders were needed, how many shipfitters, and how many carpenters. They had a running tally each day and knew if they needed someone to fill a place. It was a terrific task, keeping enough people on that yard to keep it working.

During the summer months, ice was scarce. I remember people lined up in front of the old Glynn Ice Company on Cochran Street all the way back to Union Street, which was about six blocks. People didn't get mad and upset. They were considerate of each other. We were all in a united effort and we acted very civil. I look at people today and think about the problems in the 1970s with the gasoline shortage. People displayed a more selfish, pushy attitude than in the days of World War II.

The people cooperated. There were people who rented out spare rooms. If you had an extra bedroom, you were asked to call a certain number and let them know so that they could send someone over. Many times the bedroom was rented to two people working at the shipyard on different shifts. One would sleep in the daytime if working the night shift and the day-shift worker would sleep on the same bed at night. It was an attitude of "how can we get this job done?" and they did it.

There was a down-hill effort after the Germans were defeated and speculation about how long the war would last with Japan. The shipyard had been given a contract that when it completed the 90 Liberty ships to go ahead on another ship that was a little over 300 feet. She was a diesel-powered ship instead of steam like the Liberty ships. The government wanted 10 of these ships built. Equipment and engines had already been brought and stacked up in the buildings at the shipyard. It was sold as scrap iron when the war with Japan was over. We had geared up to be in the war a while longer. Of course, when the announcement of the atom bomb came, we all knew it was over then.

At the shipyard, some of us knew that some special weapon was being built. We had heard about a project that a Mr. Groves was managing, which was the Manhattan Project. In fact, Mr. and Mrs. Groves came to Brunswick when she christened one of the Liberty ships.

Superior Court Will Soon Have Woman Reporter

The Brunswick judicial circuit is to have a new court reporter beginning March 1, and it will be a woman. Judge Gordon Knox, who is here today holding a non-jury session of Glynn Superior Court, announced while in the city that Miss Ruby Johnson, of Hazlehurst, had been appointed official stenographer to succeed M. E. Wood, of Baxley, and she will assume the duties of the officer Saturday.

Mr. Wood, it is understood, recently resigned and after March 1 will devote all of his time to the practice of law in Baxley. He has served as reporter of the circuit for many years.

Miss Johnson, it is stated, is well qualified for the position. She has had considerable experience to legal stenographic work. While there have been women stenographers in other judicial circuits in the state, and while there are now said to be one or two, this will be the first time a woman has ever served as stenographer of the Brunswick circuit.

The Brunswick News 1942

Ruby Johnson Shane
Interviewed by Mary Lee Childs

Ruby Shane's maiden name was Johnson. She lived in Hazlehurst, Georgia, graduated from Hazlehurst High School in 1937, and worked as a clerk with several public officials in the Jeff Davis County Court House. She was the first woman court reporter in the Brunswick Judicial Circuit. A court reporter's job was tiring, requiring long hours of typing notes, and was stressful because everything had to be accurate. But Ruby learned how to organize and plan her time and activities. She worked with all types of cases; at that time, there were very few divorces. Hardly ever did you see a woman in the courtroom. If fact, the jurors were all men. Traveling by trains, or waiting for them, and taking a travel iron to make badly wrinkled clothes presentable were part of the experience. She was a court reporter for about

Fab Shoppers Give Praise to Their Able Ruby Johnson

We would never forgive ourselves if we permitted this last issue of the *Mariner* to be published without us expressing our deep appreciation to "Jonie." Ruby Johnson, better known as "Jonie," formerly served as Court Reporter for the circuit for Judge Gordon Knox, resigned that position in order that she might contribute her part to the war effort. May 1942 found her starting her employment with this Yard. She worked for several departments for short periods.

On June 1942, she was assigned to the Fabrication Department. Starting on that date she became a member of our Fab Shop family and from then on she has sparked every movement sponsored by the Fab Shop. Jonie has always taken it upon herself to personally see that the Fab Shop was 100% on Bond deductions. She has toiled many long hours selling bonds, pleading with workers, urging and smiling in a most determined manner, concentrated on what drive was in progress, giving freely of herself that the quota might be reached and passed. She sponsored the Fab Shop basketball teams and it was her quiet, energetic force that kept those teams together...never too busy to lay aside her work in order to help others...whether it was individual problems, USO Work, Yard activities, bond drives, Red Cross campaign, National war fund drive, or her own basketball team...Jonie was there. We shall long remember you, Jonie, words are futile, but you can well believe that with each handshake and each good-bye, there goes a silent prayer that life will be good to you. Your unassuming smile, your untiring effort, and you will remain deep in our hearts.

Signed: Supervisors and employees of the Fabrication Shop

two years when she realized that court sessions were diminishing and accepted a job with the first company to build ships in Brunswick.

Ruby was staying in the beautiful Oglethorpe Hotel for a court session when the Washington VIP's came to set up a shipyard and let a contract for the building of ships. They needed someone to record their meetings, and the manager of the hotel recommended Ruby. At first she was with Mr. Moxham at the Brunswick Marine, but Ruby has stated that it was much more fun to work with the Jones company. She thoroughly enjoyed their association. Ruby began working for the shipyard in September 1943. She worked for Mr. Hall in the fabrication shop as office manager, personal secretary, and leader for almost everything that went on in the shop. She stayed until 1945, when the war was over and the shipyard dismantled.

Ruby didn't consider this time as a sacrifice but more of a duty. She was happy to do anything she could.

Willie Moore

I was born in Warren County, Georgia, but raised mostly around Atlanta. When I was nine years old, my daddy walked out on us and that put me in charge of things. We run a share farm for a couple of years with a man called Charlie Stubbs, who was a mean man. I left and went to a little place called Norwood, Georgia, and butchered there for about five years for a Mr. Flanders. Then I went to Warrenton and cut meat for a fella by the name of Mr. Lane. Then come this time when I had to go to the Army. I was drafted and went to Fort Benning, Georgia. About that time J. A. Jones had started a subcontract with the Government. I was a little carpenter, a jock boy [jack-of-all-trades]. So I was drafted to this defense work. I first started out in Augusta at Fort Gordon as a carpenter and I got to be a leader. We left there and went to a place called Goldsboro, North Carolina. We built a blimp hanger. We went from there to Hampton, a little place in South Carolina. We built an ammunition dump there. That was one of the most beautiful things I have ever seen in my life . . . the way that thing was built. We was running Jeeps and all that underground. Trees was growing on top of it. That was one of the strictest places. You couldn't carry nothing in there. When you got to the gate, you had to strip everything.

We left there and went to the capital of South Carolina, Columbia. We built a little hospital at Fort Jackson. Then we went to a little place called Blackstone, Virginia. [Fort Pickett Military Reservation is located there.] We went then to Greensboro, North Carolina, and built a beautiful hospital. That's a beautiful place. We used to go down and watch people make cigars. We stayed there a long time. All this time I was working for J. A. Jones. They subcontracted all this from the federal government. That's the only way I could stay out of the Army.

When I left Greensboro, I came here [Brunswick] on the 6th of February 1943. [J. A. Jones took over the shipyard February 1, 1943]. Had a pretty hard time when I came here, you know. We was mostly all black. They had the shipyard going at that time. We had to go to school for six weeks. I knew dimensions and all that, but I didn't know anything about steel. I had never put steel together. The school was called a Boilermaker's School. We had to learn how to weld overhead, underhead. We had blueprints, just like laying out this house . . . everything. We read those books about how to handle steel . . . how to bend steel, how to burn, how to chip, how to weld, but you had to still do it with your hands. Whether you was a shipfitter or not, you had to learn it where you can tell the man what to do. I can talk about the inner bottom more than anything because that was my job.

When we got through with that, I called Jones, that was J. A. Jones' son, 'cause they didn't have a place for us. We met with the commissioners and the union of the boilermakers. We had finished school and they had to give us a place. They had to give us a job. We were already skilled laborers. They didn't have any blacks in there. They didn't have anything but common laborers here.

When we left Greensboro, we had all our credentials. I was a leader man. I brought 12 men here with me and I went to school. We went back to the commissioners and boilermakers, and they said, "Well . . . what we are going to do . . . we are going to give you the graveyard shift." They put all of us on the graveyard shift. We done such a good job that after about six months everything come into place. We started working all together.

I was a leader man at that time. I didn't know anything about a ship. I started on the inner bottoms, the first thing of the ship. That's down in the ship. That's starting it off. They got so many parts going this-a-way and that-a-way . . . all had to be sealed off. I had a chipper, a welder, two laborers, and an iron man. The man would come out and give me the paper for what the men would do that night. That was my job. On the inner bottom, I had to put the seal on it because any air or anything would cause a leak. I had to crawl all through them bottoms and put soapy water on all those welds, let it sit, and, if it leaked like that, I had to take a marker and mark it. The welder had to come back in and redo it. We worked on the ground in the open before it went on the way. My wife worked in the fab shop. That's how I met my wife. She had a good job in the fab shop. If I needed a dog or some clamps—we had them named and all those things had to be numbered—that's what she did.

Let me tell you something . . . we had so many people that didn't know anything. If you were white, you could get by pretty good. I had to train a white person but learned all up and down that, I hate to say it but it's true, the white boys I trained was better than the black boys. I tried my best to figure it out but I couldn't. Here comes a boy right off the farm. He's got a saw, a square, and a hammer. That's all he's got. I know he don't know nothing. So the man says, "You think you can handle him?" I said, "Yes, sir, I'll take him." First thing I do is sit down and talk to him. "We don't have no lying . . . no nothing," I say. "We go strict by the book. We go by the blueprint. I can get along with you if you can get along with me. I'm no better'n you are. I'm just a little more experienced than you. We'll work together." I didn't have any trouble with them. I told them if they made a mistake, "Maybe I forgive you this time. Make another one, you're gone!" They didn't allow you to make any mistakes. Building a ship is something else! People don't realize how careful and how many things you have to do to not make mistakes.

I worked in Brunswick until they got through building the ships [when the war began to wind down]. I tried to get out then because I wanted to get married, but the next thing I knew I got a letter saying, "Come to Charleston." That was with the federal government. I was at the shipyard in Brunswick from February 1943 until I was sent to Charleston, South Carolina. J. A. Jones was out of it then. I was with the government. [He had to satisfy military time.] The ship we built in Charleston was 925 feet long. You could get lost on it. It was five stories. The ships we built in Brunswick, we could put them inside the ones we built in Charleston.

I sot the foundation for the machine guns. I'm the guy that sot the track. Everybody can't do that. They had to be plumbed. You had to do it just right. That was in Charleston. You have to be a master shipfitter to take on the jobs I had then 'cause they didn't put just anybody on that gun rack. We put the hull together. You had to weld it. Then you had to chip it off and then weld it again. It's a lot of skill in that. If a man made a bad weld on the outside of the ship, rather than have it chipped off we burned it off. A burner was very important. A chipper . . . everyone was important. Everything fit into place.

We were very much serious about what we were doing. Just about everybody was on edge with the war going on. The only thing that ever got me in my work was in Goldsboro, North Carolina, when we were building the blimp hanger. I saw a man fall from the top to the bottom. The hangers were wooden. Blimp hangers were 200 feet in the air and had a three-foot ledge all around the edge. The superintendent came out there one day while we was eating dinner. When he come, he got them glasses [binoculars] looking everywhere. He happened to spot a man up there. He said, "Willie Moore." I said, "Yes, sir." "Who is up there on that thing?" "I don't know. I don't think any of my men are that crazy!" Sho 'nuf, it was one of my men. He was asleep on that three-foot ledge. . . 200 feet in the air! So the superintendent say, "That's one of your men." I took the loudspeaker and said, "Come on down here, Sam." We got all those wenches and he could get in the bucket and come down. He come on down. I said, "Sam, I am sorry. You went to sleep at the wrong time, the wrong place, and the inspector here. I ain't got no other alternative than to fire you." The inspector explained to me, "That's true, mister. If that man fell we would have to pay for him. Willie, you can't have a man like that." They fired him that minute. Didn't give him another day.

Here [Brunswick] was one of the safest places I had been. We did have one man on the work dock that fell. He didn't die. We didn't have any accidents down there (shipyard) much. Most we had down there was flash burns to your eyes. We had nurses sot up there so if you got a flash you went in, stayed there about two to three hours. They would treat your eyes.

When they dropped that bomb . . . when VJ Day come, I thought I could get out. I went to the office and they said, "No, you got to do another six months." Two weeks from then I got a notice. I think the notice read, "You are still in for six more months." I was in Charleston about 20 months.

All through the war I was over blacks and whites. Just like I said, so many of those boys come in there and I know they needed a job. They came in and didn't know nothing. I let them work. If they made a mistake, I tried to get there first and help them. The truth is I can get along with white boys far as obeying. I never had no feedback from them. My boys feedback sometimes. I had to fire one who talked back. We didn't have time. We had ships to turn out.

I got married just as soon as I could come home after VJ Day. After the war I went into contracting and building houses. After a long while doing that, I opened a dry cleaning plant. I run it for 14 years, right here in Brunswick . . . the Acme Dry Cleaners. I was about the first black boy that opened a filling station in this county . . . Amoco filling station on Gloucester Street. This Sea Gull Hotel, the first black hotel, I was the man that ran that. I sold cars for Ford Motor Company. Only black person that sold cars and he let me write them up. I sold a lot of cars for James Gould! The war was really good to me. It put me in a position to do a lot of things I don't think I would have accomplished if it hadn't been for the war. That's why I worked so hard to educate my kids.

Norma Jean Strickland Martin

My family moved to Brunswick from Waycross, Ware County, Georgia, in January 1941. My father had quit farming and taken a job as a salesman in Brunswick. I entered Miss Sapp's fourth-grade class at Sidney Lanier Elementary School. In 1941, Glynn County had four elementary schools: Ballard, Arco, Purvis, and Sidney Lanier. Sidney Lanier was the newest. I had come from a two-room school in Ware County and Sidney Lanier was beyond anything I had ever seen. It was great!

When President Roosevelt addressed the U. S. Congress after the December 7th attack on Pearl Harbor, Miss Stallings, the principal at Sidney Lanier, broadcast the president's speech over the intercom to all the classes. In June 1942, we moved back to my grandparents' farm east of Waycross. My father was working in Waycross when they started hiring people at the shipyard in Brunswick. He and my mother drove to Brunswick, applied for work at the shipyard, and both were hired in 1942. My father worked as a timekeeper and my mother was a chauffeur/driver for the shipyard. Mother's job was to make mail runs to the post office and trips to the shipyards in Savannah and Jacksonville for parts. She and the five other women drivers also chauffeured Maritime Commissioners and other dignitaries who visited the shipyard.

I had to stay with my grandparents near Waycross until January of 1943 because my parents couldn't find a place for us to live until some of the new subdivisions were built. When I moved back to Brunswick, it had changed so much I could hardly believe it was the same place! The south end of Brunswick where the garbage dump had been was temporary housing and parking lots for the shipyard. On the north end, the woods along Fourth Street had disappeared and barracks-style apartments, called Goodyear Park, and subdivisions of single-family homes had gone up.

We found a house in the new subdivision of Brunswick Villa. My mother worked days and my father worked nights so one of them would always be at home with me. We had a three-bedroom house and rented one of the bedrooms to people who worked at the shipyard. Many people around Waycross and Jesup worked at the shipyard but never moved to Brunswick. They shared rides to work every day.

When the Waycross highway bridge over a creek on the west side of the Satilla River burned, some said it was sabotaged. That was probably only a rumor that started because hundreds of people drove across the bridge every day to work at the shipyard. The rumor about sabotage ceased when, within a matter of days, a temporary bridge was in place and work at the shipyard was not interrupted.

I remember the air-raid drills and the blackouts and how afraid I was that the shipyard might be bombed when one of my parents would be working. I would go with my mother to pick up my father at the end of the night shift and we would wait for him in the administration building. Sometimes we would go back and watch the sorting of cards on a tabulating machine. There was always a big sign at the main gate to the shipyard that measured the sales in each war bond drive. One that I remember was of soldiers raising the flag on Iwo Jima. As the bonds were sold the flag on the sign would move up. Everyone invested in war bonds and dreamed and made plans about what they would do with all the money they were making at the shipyard. When movie stars came to Brunswick to promote the bond sales, they would have rallies in front of the Oglethorpe Hotel. I remember how small the movie star Veronica Lake looked standing on that huge, old Victorian porch. I remember the flags with blue and gold stars that families hung in their windows. A blue star represented a serviceman and a gold star represented a serviceman killed in action.

On D-Day, June 6, 1944, I was the only one with my grandparents at their farm near Waycross. My uncle, my grandparents' youngest son, was a paratrooper in the 82nd Airborne. When we got up that morning, we heard over the radio that the Allied invasion of Europe had begun and that the 82nd Airborne had dropped paratroopers behind enemy lines. My grandparents knew their son was in the midst of the war and they didn't talk much that day. We just listened to the radio and they prayed. In all I had three uncles in the army. One served in Alaska and Germany and was seriously wounded in Germany. Another served with General Patton in North Africa and Italy. The third was in the 82nd Airborne. They all returned home!

I was in the eighth grade when President Roosevelt died. It was announced in our class at school and some of us cried. President Roosevelt was the only president we had ever known. When Germany surrendered there was a big celebration in Brunswick. There were so many cars and people on Newcastle Street you could hardly move. People drove their cars up, down, and around the four blocks of Newcastle between Mansfield and G Streets, honking their horns and shouting. People on the sidewalks were singing and dancing. When Japan surrendered there was another big celebration on Newcastle Street, but there was also an air of sadness because people had received word that the shipyard would close.

The shipyard closed soon after the war ended, and many of the people who came to work in the shipyard stayed in Brunswick. They had nothing to go back to and many found jobs in Brunswick. My family stayed and my father worked as desk sergeant for the Glynn County Police.

Mary Kramer Farrell

Our family moved to Georgia from Massachusetts in January of 1943. We arrived in Brunswick and immediately decided St. Simons was the place to live. We were at the Guale Inn until Mom could convince a cottage owner to open up his summer cottage. My dad worked for the Berkline Furniture Company in Agawam, Massachusetts, just outside of Springfield. The company had been given a contract to supply hatch covers and other wooden items for the Liberty ships. I don't know where the hatch covers were made, but I think I heard Dad speak of an assembly line, which I feel meant they were made in Brunswick. Dad was superintendent of the frame shop in Massachusetts and was in a supervisory capacity in Brunswick. In later years, I did see cocktail tables (for restaurants) made from the hatch covers.

Marjorie K. Wilder

My husband was from Georgia. I came from Alabama. At the time the war started, we were living in Cleveland, Tennessee, where my husband was employed by the TVA. When the shipyard was built in Brunswick, they sent recruiters out to all the neighboring states' labor offices looking for people to work in the shipyard. My husband went to Brunswick in March of 1943. He was a burner in the shipyard. He beveled the edges of the ship [hull] till it was razor sharp. Then the welders would come in and fill that in. That was what held the hull together. There were only two men that I knew of that could do that work. I do know that is what kept my husband out of service. He was called up four times and deferred each time.

I went in as an electric welder. When I started, I went to school, trained to be a welder, and went on the yard as a tacker. I worked for a while there, then went back to school and went in as a production welder. The first production job they gave me was shaped like a big hollow stump. That's what the anchor chains went around. It took eight yards of triple welding to fill that thing full. If you were a good welder you could do it in eight hours. That was the hardest night's work I ever pulled! Then I worked on the bulwark rails. On the upper deck I did overhead welding and I worked on the gun decks. My shipwright was a black man from Pascagoula, Mississippi. My shipfitter was from Mobile, Alabama. There were two other men who were shipfitters and they, too, were draft age but 4F. One of them was a Mr. Mixon and the other was a Mr. English. My leader man was Mr. McKenney from Blue Ridge, Georgia. I worked in the fab shop from May 1943 until June 1944. My youngest child was born in September of 1944.

We lived in the Gordon Oaks Apartments when we first moved to Brunswick. Gordon Oaks was about one and a half blocks from the shipyard. The shop was one and a half blocks from the water front. The boats went right off the ways into the shipping channel. I have stood in the back of the fab shop and watched the rain in stormy weather come in over the ocean. It looked like it was rolling. Sometimes afternoon tides would be so high that certain sections of the fab shop had to shut down.

I enjoyed my welding. That was the prettiest work I ever did in my life! The method of welding today is entirely different. We did our welding in the fabricating shop. We built the parts that went in the ship and they lifted them onto what they called a gurney that ran on railroad tracks. They had an attachment on the back that would lift up and carry the parts. In constructing the upper decks of the ship we put in what I called "sleepers." It was like building a floor. We would brace them with pieces of iron called "dogs." The shipfitter placed the sleepers down exactly where he wanted them. Then the tacker, the person that was under the shipfitter, would come along. You went down the immediate seam—right in the center—with a 3/4-inch welding rod. Then you went just above it again but it overlapped. Then you came below it and when you got through you brushed it. You could see every color of the rainbow! Sleepers were about eight to ten inches wide. That welding wasn't on one side. It was on both sides. Anything on that ship would break before that seam.

There was a whole row of welding machines, and they had what we called "leads"—a rubber hose. The leads would reach the entire length of that fabrication shop. We had to pull them across while we worked. When shifts changed, each person had to wind their leads over those machines. We used 1/4-inch and 3/4-inch welding rods. When we filled in the bulwark rails, we used the tiny, tiny rod. That was the hardest work on the ship because the rail itself was not the same metal that the rest of the ship was. When I welded my first bulwark rail, it got bigger instead of filling up, but all of a sudden I got the hang of it and just filled up the hole. That's what held the bulwark rails together.

I wore coveralls, had a helmet, and wore safety shoes that had steel in the toes. I wore glasses and, because of my eyes, they had to get me a helmet with unusually dark lenses in it. That was the first time I ever worked on Saturday and Sunday. I was brought up that on Saturday we got ready for Sunday. On Sunday we did nothing but go to church and Sunday school. If we needed anything for Sunday we either got it Saturday, did without, or waited until Monday. During the war when I went home for a visit, my aunt said, "You mean to tell me you are working on Sunday?" I said, "The soldiers are fighting on Sunday." I felt like God would forgive us because without the ships we were building they couldn't do their job.

The Liberty ships were equipped with guns. I would say the gun deck was about eight feet high. You had to climb a ladder to get to the top of them. They were square, about as big as a small room. The guns sat in the middle and rotated. I did the welding. People thought they didn't carry guns, but they were very well equipped with them. On the section I worked there were three guns.

I never went out on the water. I stayed in the fab shop and welded parts that went into the ship. We worked on the hull, too, before it was taken out to the ways. There was one thing I had to tack or weld to the hull that I could never figure out what it was for. It was fastened to the floor with a piece that went on the ship. I called it a "shelf" because I didn't know what else to call it. I laid flat on my back and welded the shelf to the piece of metal. Then it was fastened to the floor of the ship. I asked Mr. McKenney one night and he said, "I haven't got time to talk. You've got time to weld. Now let's get to it."

Every person I worked with came from another state with the exception of Mr. English, Mr. Mixon, and Mr. McKenney. They were Georgians. Two girls in our crew came from Ocala, Florida. Two of the shipfitters came from Mobile, Alabama. Most of the people in my section were people that had been with other shipyards and knew what they were doing. They had little stalls where they taught us. There was a group of little stalls down the side right after you went in the gate of the shipyard. There was a desk, a welding rod, and some pieces of iron. You stood them up, put them together, and welded. The lady that taught me made it look so easy. I picked up the welding rod and did the same thing. I had to chisel the rod loose from the piece of metal. It was a quick training session of one week. Then I went on the yard and tacked for about three and a half months. I got mad at the shipfitter I was working under and threatened to quit. They sent me back to finish my welding. I took one week of production welding. After you get the hang of it, it is the simplest thing in the world! So the rest of the time I was in production welding and loved every minute of it. I worked the four to eleven shift.

My Journey to Brunswick

One of our children had started school in Cleveland, Tennessee, before we left for Brunswick. I had shipped the furniture from Cleveland to Brunswick in March. My father's health deteriorated suddenly and they called me home. That was the reason I was so late getting to Brunswick.

My father died May 1, 1943. I left my home in Albertville, Alabama, the next weekend to go to Brunswick. I got to Rome, Georgia, with no problems. We had a dinky little bus that didn't go any further than Rome. I sat there one whole day waiting to get a bus to Atlanta. Finally they went to the shop and came out with a bus that I think must have come out of Noah's ark. It was pouring rain when we got into Atlanta. I finally managed to get a bus to Hamilton. Two tires blew out! We sat there two and a half hours waiting for a bus to arrive. Well, I had bought my ticket in Albertville where they had routed me all the way to Brunswick on Trailways. I had never been down there and did not know what to expect. Come to find out, Trailways did not go to Brunswick. So when I got to Macon I spent a night there trying to get a bus and trying to get my ticket straightened out. I guess I would have stayed in Macon for the duration of the war if it hadn't been for an Army officer and his men waiting to get out of Macon. He got my ticket changed for me.

The bus finally pulled in about 11:30 that night and I got on. The only reason they let me on was because I promised to stand up. My three little children were also standing. Just as we were pulling out, this young soldier came running up and hanging onto the door. The young man was crying. He said he was on his way to Florida. His mother was dying and he was trying to get there. The driver said, "I can't take you. I'm full." I said, "Let me take my kids. I'll get off and you can have my place." The driver said, "Well, if you don't mind scrounging him in, he can ride too." That's the way we rode from Macon to Savannah. I stood up every step of the way. My oldest child was seven, one was five, and the other was three. The three-year-old was the sleepy head of the bunch. The little fellow would stand there and weave back and forth sound asleep. The soldiers took pity on me, took their jackets, padded the overhead racks, laid the three children up there and they slept.

When we got to Savannah, I was tired! Well, the driver got me a seat on the bus that was coming down from North Carolina. We got just out of the main part of Savannah a little piece and this young woman was standing on the side of the road with two small children by her side and one in her arms. There was another lady with her. When she got on the bus I offered to hold the baby, but she wouldn't let me touch her. The mother was standing there trying to balance herself with the baby. I asked her where she was going, and she said, "Darien." It sounded like it was down the road a little piece (60 miles) so I gave her my seat.

I got into Brunswick that afternoon. It was Mother's Day and one of the hottest days I ever saw in my life! I was mad, I was tired, and there were black gnats by the "blue million." I walked across the bus terminal and could feel the floor planks giving under my feet. Brunswick was the most rundown town I ever saw in my life! The houses needed painting, needed roofing, and I thought, "Heaven above! I have come to the place God has truly forgotten."

Brunswick

Brunswick was very much alive! There were 75,000 people there, including the shipyard workers and the soldiers. It was like a circus, really and truly. They had nice shops—Gordons, Guarantee Shop, Kress, and Altmans. That was the first time I ever saw women wearing shorts and slacks. It was so hot my husband said, "Why don't you go to town and get yourself a pair of shorts?" I said, "Would you let me wear them?" He said, "Yeah." So I got some. The next time we went uptown I said, "What are you going to do?" He said, "I'm going up to Gordons." I said, "What are you going to do there?" He said, "I'm going to get you a pair of slacks to wear over those shorts."

The government had built the Gordon Oaks Homes on Norwich Street between the hospital and the shipyard. I had a block and a half to walk to work. In June of 1944 we moved to the Goodyear apartments. They were five or six miles from the shipyard on US 17 out past the Hercules Powder Plant. A bus came around and picked us up. We had tokens for fare.

Sugar, meat, and shoes were rationed. Yardage was not. Clothes were not—if you liked what they had. I was working at Belks in Cleveland, Tennessee, when the war came. When they knew everything was going to be rationed, the manager of Belks gave the employees the right to get as many pairs of shoes as they wanted and thought they would need for some time to come. Well, I got enough shoes for my children that I didn't have to buy any for them during the war except just some sandals every now and then and for myself. I got my husband several pairs. I sent my shoe coupons to my sister-in-law because she didn't have enough coupons. She sent me her meat coupons because they had their own meat. Gas was unheard of. I have driven many a mile and bought black market gas tickets and hunted black market cigarettes. Cigarettes cost 20 to 30 cents a pack, depending on the brand, and gas was 15 to 20 cents.

I Want Some Gas Coupons Now!

We had a Buick with running boards on it. How far back does that go? 1935? 1936? My brother, who was a soldier stationed in California, was due to come home on leave. He had written and said, "If you get any time off, save your gas coupons and come home while I am there so that I can use your car. I will get you the gas to go back home on." Well, I hoarded every ticket. We walked every where we went. If I went to town, I walked.

I went late one afternoon, had the car serviced, and filled it up with gas. The next morning when we got ready to leave, the car wouldn't crank. My husband got out and looked. The gas tank was dry . . . There wasn't but one person in the city of Brunswick outside of my husband who knew what I had done. I knew what had happened and where the man lived. (He was my husband's nephew.) I told my husband. "Just be quiet." I walked down and knocked on the door. He came to the door. I held my hand out. I said, "A.V., I want some gas tickets." He said, "I haven't . . . " I said, "I want some gas tickets and I want them NOW! If you ever touch my car again, you will wish you had never heard of me." I got the gas tickets. He had come to the house and drained our car until there wasn't a drop left. They had to put gas in the carburetor before they ever got that thing cranked!

Female Welder
Courtesy of Georgia State Archives

The Lard Story

Lard, which was the primary thing we cooked with back in those days, was also rationed. There was a small grocery store in Brunswick and I had gotten acquainted with the people. I bought things there and the man started letting me buy lard. I would get a three-pound carton of lard every month. My friend, Bobbie Thomson, said to me one day, "I sure do wish I could get a carton of lard." I told her to come to town with me and see what happens. (You would have to have known her to really appreciate the story. She was a little bitty thing, barely 5 feet tall, and she might have tipped the scales at 95 pounds.) Well, we went in the store and bought some groceries. The grocer always had the lard wrapped in three-pound packages stored under the counter. He laid mine up on the counter. Bobbie asked him, "Do you have any extra lard?" The grocer replied, "No, ma'am, I don't. I can't get enough to supply my regular customers." She stood there, looked at him for a few seconds, and didn't say anything. In a few minutes she said, "Well . . . I can't make you sell me lard, I can't make you tell me you have any lard, but I can tell you this . . . there'll be plenty of lard in hell to fry you merchants with!" That man had the funniest look on his face for a few seconds. He never said a word as he reached under the counter and handed her a carton of lard. From then on, as long as we both lived in Brunswick, we didn't have any problem getting lard.

The day President Roosevelt died, I'll never forget what I was doing. I was getting ready to go to work and was fixing supper for the kids and Jim when he came in. I was at the sink slicing potatoes for French fries and had the radio on. (There was no such thing as television.) Every Sunday afternoon they had a black choir in Brunswick that sang the prettiest songs. I always listened to them. All of a sudden the radio shut off and the announcer said that the president of the United States was going to come on. I was listening and it was President Truman. He announced the death of President Roosevelt. People, including me, who had never met the man cried. The only president the working people ever had was President Roosevelt . . . and President Truman.

The years I spent in Brunswick were the saddest in my life. So many of my relatives were in the war. My brother was 17 years old. He was in the war, but his health was no good after he came back. I had a nephew who was wounded and was a complete paraplegic. He was Gordon Scott from Chattanooga. He was in the book *Who's Who in the South* because of his work with other paraplegics. He instigated the wheelchair places for the crippled. At night if we turned on the lights our shades were drawn and fastened. If we had the radio on it was low. If we went uptown and the air raid siren went off, we would get under the nearest tree that had the most moss so there would be no sign of movement—no shadows. Brunswick itself was black.

When J. A Jones closed, people just disappeared. Brunswick became a ghost town. We moved to Ball Ground, Georgia, the last of April 1945, and my husband went to work for Bell Bomber on Highway 41 in Marietta. He worked there till the day the armistice was signed. I was out in the backyard when I heard bells and whistles begin to ring and blow. Well, the radio had already told us that Japan was almost ready to give in, and when Mr. Truman dropped the atomic bomb, that did it!

Women work side by side with the men
Courtesy of Georgia State Archives

The thing that burns me up now is that people want to sweep the war under the rug. The man who is in business with my grandson in Douglasville, Georgia, was standing there talking one day. I don't know what brought the subject up, but just out of a clear blue sky Blake said to the man, "My grandma was a welder during World War II." The man whirled around and said, "You welded?" I said, "I sure did!" He started talking about it and Blake said, "You know if we were to go to war today like it happened then, how many young men do you think would volunteer?" In Cleveland, Tennessee, in 1941, I couldn't walk down the street for men that were volunteering to go to war.

Several years ago I was in Mobile, Alabama, and toured the ship and submarine in the bay. After the tour I was standing on the deck and a sailor was there. I said, "I wish this ship could talk." He said, "Why?" I said, "I would love to hear the stories. This is what I did during World War II. I worked on ships." He turned around to me and said, "You mean to tell me . . . " I said, "Yes, I was a welder." Even today it still brings tears to my eyes to think what those boys went through.

Lucille Richardson

Well, my friend called me and said, "Richard, you should go up there to the post office and put in for a job." So I put in for one and was told to be there Monday morning ready to go to work. [This was the period when they were recruiting people for the shipyard.]

The job was at the shipyard in Brunswick. So I went to Brunswick on Monday. I rented an apartment in Dartmouth Homes, right off G Street, and lived there 18 months. My husband, Joe, came and joined me after a month and a half. He didn't have much work here [Marietta, Georgia]. He worked for the WPA and decided he would go to California and get a better job. He got a good job out there, but then he wanted to come home. We tried to get him to transfer, but he didn't do it. He come home. Because he quit his defense work in California to come to Brunswick, they wouldn't let him work at the shipyard. He got a job with O'Quinn's in his clothing shop on Newcastle Street in Brunswick.

I was a welder at the shipyard. Well, when I first went there I was hired as a tacker and I tacked for shipfitters. I tacked for three days. What is tacking? . . . Hit it so it stays there [touch the metal with the welding rod so that the metal stays in place until it is welded]. Then I was put on welding. I went to school every night for six weeks. We had a supervisor and each person had a piece of metal to work with. Every week he would give me a different type job to weld, and when six weeks was up, I had my training. I got top pay from then on . . . for 18 months. I had never welded before in my life. Never touched it, but now I could weld anything I wanted to.

We was in a contest with the Mobile shipyard, and Crew, a black girl, she did more footage than anybody. We gave her all the footage she could make footage on [all the welding she could do in a certain period of time]. And she got it. We won the contest!

Women who built ships for America
Courtesy of Georgia State Archives

I have a girl and a boy. The girl was two and the boy was four when I was in Brunswick. My husband worked during the day, and I worked from 4 p.m. to 11 p.m. He saw after them at night while I was working. Well, I tell you what, if a lot of them men had to work as hard as I did, the war would have been won a lot quicker. There was a man that worked right next to me, and he worked just enough days to keep out of the service. He worked three days and laid out two. I worked! I would work a lot of Saturdays. I made time, time and a half and double time on Saturday and a lot of Sundays.

O.J. Cason

During the summer of 1943, between my junior and senior years in high school, I worked at the shipyard in Brunswick. I lived in Waycross but had a sister living in Brunswick. She and my brother-in-law let me stay with them. I was fortunate to have an uncle who was the foreman of the outside machinists. The outside machinists installed winches and were also responsible for making sure the lifeboats were okay. My job was to keep man hours. It involved seeing and keeping a record of what each man or group of men did during the day.

One incident that happened I will never forget. We had to take the lifeboats out to check them so as to make sure everything was intact. Four of us took the boat and went toward Jekyll Island. The tide was out and we ran aground. We pulled most of our clothes off, got out, and tried to get the lifeboat into the water. No luck! So we sat there until the tide came in. There were three men and one boy that were cooked from the sun. One of the men was rather sick for several days.

I saved about $700 that summer since I was able to work some overtime.

Betty Lou Moore
Interviewed by her daughter Colleen Moore Sellers

Welders
Betty Lou Moore (left),
Polly Jefferson
Courtesy of Colleen Moore Sellers

Betty Lou Moore moved to Brunswick July 4, 1943, with her husband, Louis, and four children. She was 34 years old and had trained as a nurse in Dallas, Texas, prior to her marriage but had not worked outside her home since her marriage. She applied at the J. A. Jones Shipyard on July 5th and began welding classes on July 6th. She first thought of applying for a job in the infirmary but then found out the welders made more money.

The shipyard ran seven days a week around the clock, and that's how everybody worked. She made 40 cents an hour while in classes for six weeks, then became a tacker for 90 cents an hour. After about a month of being tested and observed, she became a first-class welder and made $1.20 an hour on the 4 p.m. to midnight shift. Her husband, Louis, was powerhouse operator and first-class electrician on that shift. She cleaned house, washed and ironed clothes (everything was starched and ironed in those days), and cooked a large meal every day so the children would have supper then they came home from school.

She worked on flat surfaces, overhead surfaces, on scaffolds, and on ladders. Someone asked her one day why she was doing that when she didn't have to work. She replied, "I have a brother who is in the Army, and I'm doing my part to win the war and bring him and all the other boys home." She got a piece of steel in her eye one day, and it took quite a while to heal, but she didn't miss one day's work. A doctor in the infirmary at the shipyard treated her. They usually had one or two doctors and several nurses on duty all the time.

While she was doing housework, her husband would get the groceries and the ice for the icebox. He would also pick up things for neighbors, since not everyone had a car. At the grocery store, they would let you buy one pack of cigarettes along with your groceries, and he had a strong smoking habit. Also, in the mornings while doing her housework, she came into contact with some of her neighbors in the war-housing project where they lived.

In January of 1945, the shipyard sent several of its people to Oak Ridge, Tennessee, to work on a special project. Louis was one of these people. He gave his wife a telephone number but warned her not to use the number unless something happened to one of the family. His uncle Wiley Burch of Omega died, so she went to the Emanuel Homes Recreation Building and called the number. No one in the war-housing projects had a telephone. A little while after she returned home, a man came to the door, identified himself as a member of the FBI, and asked her why she was calling that particular number. She explained where her husband was working and that it was an emergency. When the atom bomb was dropped in Japan, Louis and she were very surprised that he had been working on the atom bomb project.

Betty Lou quit working in May of 1945, and the family moved during the summer to the Gordon Oaks housing project in the south end of Brunswick. It took quite a while to completely demobilize Brunswick and tear down all the wartime housing projects, but eventually everyone either went back to where they came from, some to farms, some to other jobs. But many people stayed in Brunswick and found jobs, started businesses, and helped Brunswick become the bustling little city that it is now. Louis went to work for the Hercules Powder Company and stayed there until he retired in 1970. Betty Lou never worked outside the home again, except for a few months at a local pants factory. She had a new baby in 1948 and continued her life as a busy housewife and mother.

Mary Lee Childs

In August of 1943 I had graduated from the University of Georgia and accepted a job in Brunswick with my high school friend Ruby Johnson, who was secretary for Mr. Hall, superintendent of the Fabrication Plant at the shipyard. My college friend Willene Flanigan and my sister, Maxine Beall, quickly followed me to Brunswick. Both of them worked inside the ship on the ways. I was asked to interview new employees for the plant. I felt bad for the men who were leaving the farms because I wondered what they would do after the war.

I worked seven straight days a week for the first three months. I felt very strange about that because I was always accustomed to going to church on Sundays, but I could still go on Sunday night and did so. My sister, Maxine Beall, Willene Flanigan, and I lived in one of the war apartments through arrangements made by Willene. I was in Brunswick only six months. Our apartment was about a mile from downtown Brunswick, and we would lug our groceries back to the apartment. We took turns by the week for everything we did . . . buying groceries, cooking, cleaning the kitchen and large room. This large room served as a bedroom, sitting area, and washing and ironing area. The apartment was built for two with two large single beds. Since we were three, we turned the mattresses crossways and made the original king-size bed. Yes, we even took turns sleeping in the three spaces on the bed! Fortunately, we never ever had a cross word. Willene and I would just walk off and leave my sister, Maxine, when she walked too slowly for classes that we took in blueprint reading. It was a requirement if we wanted our pay increased. My sister and I joined Mr. Jake Langford's basketball team. He had been my coach in high school. Maxine was very good and went on to receive some awards.

The work at the shipyard was done in three shifts. We were fortunate to have to work only the day shift. I was told that housing was so scarce that some of the apartments were used by three separate shifts for a place to sleep. We often went to the movies and would see the latest war information, as well as some war-related movies. The lines were long because there was not much else to do. Most of the people were as poor as we were and had no cars. Even if they did have a car, gasoline was very limited.

After working six months, I was given a week's vacation and flew out to Corpus Christi, Texas, to see the boy I had been dating for more than three years. We ended up getting married on April 26, 1944. It was the day he was commissioned and received his wings. I tell him now that was the day he got them "clipped."

Arthur L. Manning

My family moved to Brunswick from Jesup in 1930. By the time the war was in full swing, my two brothers and one sister had married and moved out of our rambling two-story rented house on Norwich Street. I was the "baby" of the family and lived with my mother and dad. My father worked at the North Shipyard [Brunswick Marine]. We took in many boarders and knew quite well the term "hot bedding." People were commuting to work daily at the shipyards from Jesup and beyond. Brunswick was overcrowded, jumping from around 15,000 to 75,000 seemingly overnight.

When I was 16, I got a summertime job with the J. A. Jones Construction Company, where Liberty ships were built. I became a welder messenger. My job was to visit the six ships under construction on a daily basis, find the welder foreman, and keep time and attendance records for payroll purposes. I would then go back to an office under the bow of # 3 way and make out the daily report for the general supervisor. I was paid a phenomenal $39 a week! More money than I had ever heard of (in 1944).

When school started, I worked after school at Cassidy's Radio Shop as an apprentice repairman. Radio parts were hard to get. We often could not get a particular tube, so we rewired the circuits, putting in new sockets and substituting any tube we thought might work. Often we unwound defective transformers and hand-wound them back with new wire to make them work.

I had German ancestry, though quite some ways back. Our beloved English teacher, Jane Macon, asked if anyone in the class knew the three German national anthem names. I raised my hand and replied "Horst Wessel," "The Wacht Am Rhine," and "Deutschland Uber Alles." She looked me straight in the eye and said, "Young man, I hate German people."

At Glynn Academy, we had the machine shop foreman from the shipyard teaching machinist courses. Equipment was provided by the shipyard. This man built a scale model of the Liberty ship engine in our classroom, all machined from metal. It ran off compressed air and developed 120 horsepower! Every Thursday, we were treated in the school auditorium to a real classical concert by Christos Vironides and his orchestra. All worked at the shipyard.

Accidents at the Shipyard

My next older brother was a welder leader man at the J. A. Jones yard. He recalled going out on a shakedown of a new Liberty ship. They had deck guns. Being untrained, the gunner raked the deck with gunfire. I remember a painter falling to his death just a few minutes before a ship was launched. He had been painting the ship's name on the bow and fell off the scaffold. I also saw a welder electrocuted in a ship's inner bottom. He had been using a work light on an extension cord. He banged the bulb on a bulkhead screw, reached to unscrew the bulb, and died instantly.

Another welder was inspecting a cofferdam, a room about midship used as ballast. They would fill the cofferdam with water when needed to make the ship ride heavier. The cofferdam was filled with water and he was inside at the time. An uncle of mine was welded in the watertight inner bottom of a ship by accident. Fortunately, they heard his frantic banging and rescued him before it was too late.

I recall two other shipyard accidents. Under each ship way, there was an electrical switch panel that controlled power to that ship. For some reason unknown to me, these power switches were open blade types mounted on a panel with a manual handle. The blades were exposed. At each shift change, the CP operator cut power to each way, and the oncoming operator switched power back on when he came on duty. One operator was electrocuted as he grabbed an open switch blade instead of the handle on the switch. The other accident happened when a welder was working just under the top deck adjacent to a hold. He fell off the scaffold all the way to the bottom deck (about 40 feet), landing on his head on a manhole bolt use to batten down the ship's inner bottom inspection hatch cover. Of course his head was demolished.

Identification tags
worn at launching of
S.S. Thomas B. King
Courtesy of Gloria Smith Ramsour

Dyson Flanders

The last ships we turned out during the war at the shipyard in Brunswick were diesel powered. They weren't like the big old steam-driven motors we had before. They also had a refrigerated compartment in the back for carrying supplies. They were much smaller ships, about half the size of the Liberty ships, but were much faster. They were being used to go from island to island in the South Pacific.

In the back where the pipes went around the refrigeration, there was what was called a void space. There wasn't much room in that area for anyone to get in and wrap the pipes. They had two of the skinniest men doing this work. When they found out I could do it in one day, where it took them one and one-half days, every weekend during school I'd go down to the shipyard and through that void to put the asbestos around the pipes and glue it on. I was a senior in high school, only five feet, and weighed about 115 pounds, so I slide through there and that freed up two men to do something else.

Susan Brown

One of the things that I remember about the war was the Liberty ships that were being built in Brunswick. I worked at Tait Floral Company, and each time a Liberty ship was launched, we had to make a red, white, and blue bow with gold letters on the streamers to put on the champagne bottle to christen the ship. It was my job to fix the ribbons and also to make orchid corsages for the lady dignitaries. I was never privileged to see any of the launchings, but I felt that I had a small part in the war effort.

Above: Mrs. Alfred W. Jones christening the Liberty Ship, S.S. Howard Coffin
Dorothy Torres (left), Mrs. Alfred W. Jones, Mona Douglas
Courtesy of Sea Island Archives

Above right: Launching SS Samselbu
from one of the six ways at the Brunswick Ship Yard. Note the stages of construction of the Liberty ships on the remaining five ways.
Courtesy of John A. Fahey

Elizabeth Reu Johnston

One time I had the privilege of going on a Liberty ship after it was completed, but before it went down the ways. I was captain of the Pirates Club that year, and the ship being launched was named *Howard Coffin*. Mr. Coffin had promoted the organization of a group of high school girls to dress up in pirate costumes and pretend to attack the Cloister Hotel on Sea Island when it was opened. He was a very wealthy man connected with the automobile industry in Detroit and founder of the Sea Island Company.

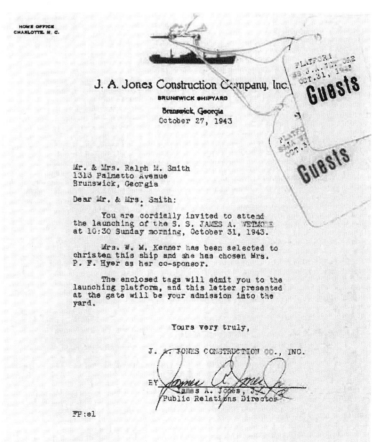

Right: Invitation to the launching of S.S. James A. Wetmore
Courtesy of Gloria Smith Ramsour

Since Howard Coffin was instrumental in starting the Pirates Club, we were invited to attack the ship. We dressed up in our costumes, took our daggers and swords, and at the crew's invitation boarded the ship. They were nice enough to show us around and feed us lunch in the galley. It was the most subdued group of pirates you have every seen, because we were young enough not to have been accustomed to being surrounded by men and all on the ship were men!

After lunch we left the ship and watched Mrs. Alfred Jones, whose husband was president of the Sea Island Company, christen the ship with a bottle of champagne.

Tug Guiding Liberty Ship Just Launched
Courtesy of John A. Fahey

Launching crew getting Liberty Ship ready to slide into Oglethorpe Bay
Courtesy of Georgia State Archives

Carl M. Rooks
Interviewed by Colleen Moore Sellers

Carl Rooks, age 20, came to Brunswick on December 16, 1944, as a member of a naval gunnery crew on one of the Liberty ships. The Merchant Marine ran the ships. The Navy crews took care of the guns and stood watch around the clock. The young men stayed at the Glynco Naval Air Station near Brunswick for two weeks while they waited to board their ship.

When the ship sailed from Brunswick on January 2, 1945, it stopped first at Savannah, then Baltimore and Boston, where it picked up wheat, two locomotives, two tenders, and two gliders. At Halifax, Nova Scotia, it picked up two more locomotives and tenders, which had been saved from the shipwreck of another Liberty ship. The gliders were on deck and were torn up during a storm in the North Sea. The ship carried this cargo to London, England, a trip of 21 days, and stayed there for two weeks before returning home for another cargo of wheat.

While in London, the Navy men lived on their ship, taking turns at liberty in London and duty on the ship. Carl got lost one night in London when the V2 bombs were being dropped by the Germans. He located a London bobby, who told him where to catch the bus to the Victoria docks. He walked the beat with the bobby until time for the bus.

The second cargo of wheat was carried to Naples, Italy. They arrived there the day the war ended in Europe. The people in Naples unloading the ship had been in such hard straits from the war that they would try to steal the wheat. Carl noticed one man who had on two pairs of pants that were tied around the ankles. He had hidden about a bucket of wheat between the pairs of pants. Carl let him go, but the man at the gate caught him and made him put it back. They stayed on the ship in Italy for about two weeks and again took turns for duty and liberty. On the way back to the United States, the men did not have to stand guard every night the way they did on the way over.

Carl stated that the food on the Liberty ship was excellent. In fact, it was the best food he had the whole time he was in the Navy. One of the Merchant Marine mess boys on the ship was a local boy, Tom Horton, who was about 17 or 18 years old. Tom became a Glynn County magistrate in later years. The home base for the naval crew was New Orleans. The men were paid $60 per month plus their keep.

Carley Zell

After war was declared in 1941, the J. A. Jones Construction Company received the contract to build Liberty ships in the shipyard at Brunswick. Jones was an outstanding contractor from North Carolina. Emil Kratt was the president. A contract for the cafeteria at the shipyard was awarded to four of us: Arthur Houston, Norman O'Donnell (C&S Bank), John McGee (later worked with Frank Horn), and me.

I was picked to head the operation. I went down to Miami and put an ad in the Miami paper for a manager. About 20 people answered the ad. People with sleek mustaches, the heads of private clubs, and finally toward the end of the evening, a chap wearing a sweat shirt, perspiring a great deal, and with tattoos on his arm. I thought to myself as he rode up, "There's a fellow that straw bosses in Brunswick would give their right arm for." His name was Chuck Woodard, a hard-working person. He was hired!

Then it happened that McGee and Houston decided the operation was not big enough for the four of us. O'Donnell and I bought them out. O'Donnell was in Savannah, so Marvin Dobbs and I operated the Magnolia Cafeteria at the shipyard. It was a huge undertaking. We had a total of 365 employees and 12 stands on the various parts of the shipyard so that we could serve meals 24 hours a day. The contract with the government provided that our profits would be limited to 5 percent, but no limit was placed on the prices we could charge. At that time we possibly were the second largest industrial cafeteria in the world. The head of Chrysler Corporation had one on the West Coast.

There were 16,000 employees at the shipyard. Occasionally some of them, primarily those that were always looking for something easy, complained about the food making them sick. Chuck Woodard would take them into the big icebox and ask them what food upset their stomach. They would point out this or that. Chuck would eat four or five mouthfuls of it and say, "Is this the food that poisoned you?" We never had any legitimate lost-time accidents due to food in the history of the cafeteria. We had carloads of prime meat from the West. We had fish in every Friday from the Fulton Market in New York. The only way in the world we could possibly fail would have been to have had a six-foot seven-inch someone at the door to hit them over the head with a baseball bat.

One of the highlights of the operation was during the Christmas holidays. The workers agreed to work without pay on Christmas Day. We at the Magnolia Cafeteria agreed to furnish food without anyone paying for it. Needless to say, that was a mammoth day's business. We distributed more pies and cakes than we did in any week-long affair. It was a credit to have the government say we were one of the finest cafeterias anywhere in the U.S.

Emil J. Kratt (left), General Manager, John D. Pellett Assistant General Manager Brunswick Shipyard, J.A. Jones Construction Company
Courtesy of Allen Pellett

We had outside activities called canteens, which Ray Johnson managed. Ray came here with a background of working for the Steven's Company, the people entrusted with selling soft drinks, hamburgers, hotdogs, and other food to all the sporting events. He decided to go back to Texas and resigned from his job.

Albert Crews was working for a laundry. We lived at 1810 Oak Avenue, and he would deliver the laundry to us every morning with a big "buck" smile and a grin on his face. One day after Ray left, Albert came in and I said, "Albert, do you know anything about cooking and preparing food?" He said, "Oh, yeah." I said, "Where?" Albert said, "CCC Camps." "The hell you say," I exclaimed. He got the job. He was on the job only three or four weeks when my partner O'Donnell called up and said we had to fire Albert. I asked, "Why?" He said, "Listen, Jimmy Jones, son of J. A. Jones, says he is not big enough for the job." I asked, "Can't we wait until I get home?"

In the meantime Albert and Jimmy became just like this [he held up two fingers side by side]. Jimmy wouldn't buy toilet paper without asking Albert personally. Albert had the job with the canteens. Over the years Albert Crews was my very closest friend.

Poke McHenry
Jacksonville Times-Union *columnist Vic Smith*
Friday, March 28, 1986

BRUNSWICK BEAT 'EM ALL IN SHIPBUILDING

JACKSONVILLE BEACH - The current fracas between our country and Libya has turned thoughts of Ralph Blackwell of Jacksonville Beach to the days of World War II and the epic achievements of the old Brunswick Shipyards.

The yards were abandoned at the close of the war, and very little physical evidence of them remains. But the memories will never die as long as any of the more than 16,000 men and women who made history there survive.

In another life, they had been lawyers, actors and prizefighters, bankers, jockeys, farmers and baseball players. Barbers, beauticians, golfers and artists. Chicken raisers and moonshine makers.

At the shipyard, they were the machinists, the welders, the helpers and the tackers, the riveters, the pipefitters, carpenters, plumbers and shipfitters, the leader men and quartermen and foremen and engineers who built the Liberty ships.

Some of them were too old or too young or otherwise unfit for active military duty. Some of them couldn't even read or write. But they could learn and they could work and they were solidly dedicated to doing their part in the overall war effort.

They built more Liberty ships in one month than any other six-way yard ever built, before or since. A six-way yard is where six ships can be built simultaneously.

To lay the keel and deliver in a single month one 441-foot ship requiring the fabrication and assembly of 3,500 tons of steel, among other things, is a feat of heroic proportions. Six such ships—one per way per month—would have been fabulous.

To produce seven in one month from six ways was just unbelievable, but the men and women in Brunswick did it in December 1944.

"It was something that could never be duplicated, said Ralph, who was foreman on Way 3, which delivered one of the seven ships on Dec. 4 and the seventh on Dec. 30.

In that fateful year of 1944, when Germany began tottering under the ever-growing might of the Allies, 53 Liberty ships slid down the Brunswick ways. This was tops in the area; Jacksonville and Panama City delivered 51 apiece and Savannah 44.

On Dec. 16, 1944, the Germans launched a savage attack on the advancing U. S. First Army and sent it reeling backward in what became known as the Battle of the Bulge. Many American soldiers were trapped and faced possible extinction.

The plight of these soldiers weighed heavily on Ralph and fellow workers.

"Our boys over there battling for their lives won't have any merry Christmas," Ralph said one day at lunch. "Why don't we show them our appreciation by working Christmas Day for nothing?"

The idea was greeted with wild enthusiasm all through the ranks of workers. Nearly 1,200 of them reported for duty and put forth extra effort, and the materials they used that day were donated by suppliers. All bosses shed authority and took up tools on that day. Buses furnished free transportation, and the cafeteria served free turkey dinners. It was a magnificent, spontaneous outpouring of patriotism that drew raves of approval from servicemen all over the world.

The law wouldn't let them work for nothing, but the company agreed to give each worker a separate check for the day. The workers then endorsed the checks over to the federal government for the war effort.

The total amounted to $16,080 (wages were a tad lower in those days), and J. A. Jones Construction Co., builder of ships, donated a matching amount.

Ralph was one of a foursome chosen to go to Washington, D.C., and present the checks.

"Those people who worked at Brunswick were just the finest," Ralph said. "They never failed once to give everything they had every hour of every day. They were proud of what they did, and justifiably so."

Ralph, 69, was born in Maysville, Ga., and grew up in Atlanta, where he attended old Tech High School. His blueprint training there provided an invaluable base for a lifetime of shipbuilding experience.

He and his family moved to Jacksonville in 1961 and he was employed in Jacksonville shipyards until retirement about four years ago.

The Brunswick Mariner

HIGHLIGHTS OF THE YARD'S CHRONOLOGY

From February 1942 when the contract was signed to build Liberty ships at Brunswick, the shipyard has come a long way. It has achieved national and international fame and acclaim. It has received new contracts before its existing contracts were completed and it swept in goodwill by its support of bond, Red Cross, and war fund drives.

On April 1, 1942, the first ground was broken, and J. E. Sireene Company and Daniel Construction Company were underway with the gigantic job of building the shipyard. By May 9, they had the mold loft open for business where work began on the Liberties. On July 6, 1942, the first way was put into use and the first Liberty ship from the Brunswick yard began to take form. Last construction on the ways took place shortly after VJ Day in 1945.

On February 1, 1943, the J. A. Jones Construction Company took over the operation of the shipyard and a new general manager, Emil Kratt, took the reins.

The first launching came March 13, 1943, when the *James M. Wayne* hit the water, watched by a crowd of many thousands. The last launching came on August 23, 1945, when the SS *Coastal Ranger*, the 99th ship, was christened at a night launching.

The highest figures of employment at one time were approximately 16,000 with over 2,000 women employed.

Award ceremony of the Maritime "M" to J.A. Jones Construction Company, Brunswick, GA
Front row (l to r): Edwin Jones, James Holland, G.M. McIlhenny, James Gould, Admiral Vickery, J.A. Jones, Emil Kratt
Courtesy of Allen Pellett

The greatest honor to come to the yard was the Maritime Commission's Gold Eagle pennant for continued meritorious production awarded March 23, 1945. Preceding this final honor, the Commission had awarded the maritime "M" on January 15, 1944, for outstanding production achievement. For 1944, the Brunswick yard topped this entire area in delivery. For its extraordinary safety record in 1944, the yard was awarded the distinguished Service for Safety Award given by the National Safety Council. Prior to this acclaim, it won the Sixth Naval District Pennant for having the lowest accident frequency rate and was adjudged the nation's safest shipyard under U. S. Maritime Commission contract.

Morale Campaign
made use of signs, public address system, rallies, contests, suggestion boxes, and distinguished visitors
Courtesy of Georgia State Archives

By over-subscribing seven bond drives, the yard bought a total of five B-29s for war in the Pacific. On Christmas Day 1944 all the workers agreed to give their earnings, which was $16,000 to the Seaman's Fund. The yard matched the fund.

Among distinguished visitors who came to the yard in its three and one-half years of activity have been Admirals Howard Vickery, Emory S. Land, Jules James, William Glassford, and Anthony McFall; Governors Mellville Broughton, Greg Cherry of North Carolina, and Ellis Arnald of Georgia; Presidential candidate Thomas Dewey; Postmaster General Frank C. Walker; General Leslie Groves, overall director of the atomic bomb project at Knoxville, Tennessee, and General J. S. Bragdon. Female glamour came to the yard in the persons of Mrs. Doris Duke Cromwell and Mrs. R. J. Reynolds, Jr. Storybook hero visitor to the yard was the famed Dr. Corydom Wassell, the U.S. Navy captain who evacuated his wounded men from Java.

Seven thousand two hundred housing units were built for workers who came to build ships at Brunswick, and five new school buildings were added to the existing facilities.

Glimmerings from the Past

CHAPTER TWELVE

Stories From the Home Front

Glynn County was transformed when World War II became a reality. Thousands of people came to build the shipyard, ships, and military installations. Because of the human influx, schools became overcrowded and housing projects sprang up on vacant lots. The latter part of 1942 and all of 1943 were the years of transition. Brunswick changed from a sleepy community in the middle of the Great Depression to a fast, productive citizenry working toward a common goal...to win the war!

With intense purpose and patriotism, the people pulled together. Homes were opened to ease the housing shortage; sweaters were knitted for the military; bandages were rolled for the Red Cross; volunteers supervised the USO; sacrifices were made to work in war industries; soldiers, sailors, and marines were welcomed in private homes; and civilians responsibly performed military obligations and protected the coast until the military moved in.

Materials were essential for war. Our troops had to be armed, transported, fed, and clothed. Items became scarce and rationing was instigated. Even needles and pins were in short supply. There were no new automobiles or refrigerators for the duration.* Old-fashioned iceboxes were still in use. Scrap-metal drives were initiated. An article in *The Brunswick News* states that Dr. J. W. Simmons donated the iron fence around the family cemetery plot.** Simmons is quoted as saying, "The ones in couldn't get out and the ones out didn't want to get in, so what's the use?" Cuffless pants became the style to save material. Silk for ladies' hosiery was used for the construction of parachutes until nylon could be manufactured and tested for this use.

Rubber went to war. Tires were rationed and patches upon patches on inner tubes were the norm. Scrap rubber became tires, gas masks, overshoes, and other items for the military. Gasoline rationing had families walking. The black market infiltrated Glynn County. For those willing to pay the price, rationed or scarce items could be found.

With the influx of people, public health was a vital part of the war effort. The concentrated areas of Glynn County's defense plants and military installations caused an increase in venereal diseases. Eating facilities springing up overnight to feed the masses taxed the health department inspectors. Rapid construction and growth demanded close inspection of water treatment and sewerage facilities. The fog machine for mosquito control became a familiar sight, and an intensified rodent control was conducted to check the spread of typhus fever before it reached epidemic proportions. Glynn County was fortunate to have Dr. Millard E. Winchester as head of the Health Department. His pioneering work with venereal disease and typhoid fever was recognized worldwide.***

Yet amid all of this change, day-to-day living, loving, working, growing, and exploring persisted. Today those who were children, teens, and adults during that period in history reminisce and share their experiences.

*The Brunswick News - September 24, 1944 - "No New Autos Until Six Months After the War Ends."
**The Brunswick News - August 17, 1942.
***See appendix.

Malcolm Seckinger

"Tell us about the spy!"

I was 10 years old on January 2nd after the war started. I don't know who came up with it or who all was involved, but in the dormitories behind the Mark Carr homes, it was determined that one of the tenants was a spy. So a group of us boys got together and watched his every movement for several weeks. We took turns keeping surveillance. We were going to be heroes and turn him into the FBI. We never did. It was just a game to us boys, and we lost interest as time passed.

We also did other spying. We would tell our parents that we were going to spend the night out in someone's yard. We spent most of the time carousing around the parks and the boulevard spying on lovers. They would line up along the boulevard in cars and wait for a car to move so that the next could move in. It was a pretty good rotation system. Really interesting to us boys who were just reaching puberty! The ground down "lover's lane" looked like it was vulcanized! The yard at the USO on Union Street was in the same rubberized state. All the Coast Guard guys would meet their sweeties at Hanover Park, which was along my paper route.

We made spending money selling parched peanuts to the workers who were building the war projects. They would buy all that we could parch. Then after the war projects were built, we made money walking the railroad tracks picking up pine lighter knots that fell off the Hercules Powder Company trains. We sold them to the people who lived in the projects to light their stoves; all the projects had coal stoves.

My family moved to the south end of Albany Street, only six blocks from the shipyard. At that time the only block on Albany Street that was paved was by Lover's Oak. When they at last built sidewalks, the one in front of our house was about 10 feet from my bedroom window. People were on the sidewalk at all hours of the day and night as shifts changed at the shipyard. There was the constant sound of people walking and talking. I just knew someone was going to come through my window.

Daddy was an air-raid warden and had a little tin hat. During drills, only persons with civil defense designation were allowed on the streets. I walked up and down the streets with him making sure that the shades were pulled.

Close neighbors Mrs. Reu and Mrs. Gillican were plane spotters at the tower at the country club. They had code names. We went with them often to help them see the planes. One day we went out with

Farmer in the Dell *(tune)*

We'll buy our stamps today;
We'll buy our stamps today;
Heigh - O - America
We'll buy our stamps today.

It's Liberty for aye!
It's Liberty for aye!
Heigh - O - America
We'll buy our stamps today.

Mrs. Gillican, whose husband was an avid golfer. Their son, Charles, and I went out on the golf course and picked up these spikes that had a handle on them. We called them "commando knives." One day we went to show Mr. Gillican our knives and when he saw them he said, "That's where all the 'T' bars went!"

The headlights on the cars were painted half-out, making it hard for people to see clearly. We made a dummy and covered it with catsup. As people drove down Union Street at night we would throw the dummy up on their windshield. It's a wonder someone didn't have a heart attack! During the war, everyone dressed up and walked up and down Newcastle Street at Halloween throwing confetti and soaping the store windows.

Two girls whose fathers had stores on Newcastle Street would see who could buy the most savings stamps. If one bought a large amount one week, the other bought a larger amount the next week. At first they would buy a few stamps to put in their stamp book. Then they would buy a whole stamp book. Finally, they would buy a whole bond! I remember gluing the soles on my shoes. As I was walking to school I'd scrape my toe and they'd start flapping. Then I would have to tie a piece of string around my shoe to hold the sole on.

Mrs. Vickers would take a group of us boys to St. Simons around Demere Road to the airport, which was occupied by the Navy. There was a junk pile that we could get to where they put all the scraps of airplanes and airplane parts. Needless to say, we rummaged through the pile and took home "souvenirs." I got to go on a shakedown cruise of one of the Liberty ships. We went out 25 miles. I didn't eat anything onboard because I got seasick.

I remember when the Army took over Mr. Olsen's boatyard in Brunswick (on Terry Creek by the St. Simons Causeway). The Army was bivouacked close by, at L Street in front of the Hercules Powder Company. One time Mr. Olsen had the Lutheran Church Men's Club out to the boatyard for a fish fry. After they finished, the men walked out on the dock so Mr. Olsen could show them one of the boats. When they started coming off the dock, the soldiers who didn't know they were there stopped them and kept them there. It was about three o'clock in the morning before they could be convinced who they were. Mr. Reu, who was the plant manager for the Hercules, was among the group and the soldiers wouldn't even let him off to use the telephone.

It was unbelievable that in four years' time they could take all the woods in Brunswick that were here, build a shipyard from scratch, build all those housing projects from scratch, train all those people, and turn out over 100 ships. The amazing thing is that all the "able bodied" men had been shipped off to war. And to top it all, they had to train all those people who came in off the farms and had no experience in any stage of shipbuilding. To be so unprepared, it is hard to believe what not only Glynn County but also this country did in four years.

Michael C. Reu

I remember selling roasted peanuts to the people building war apartments near our house . . . going to school in the afternoon and going to the movies in the morning. I remember friends made when their parents moved in with the shipyard who moved away in 1946. I remember when President Roosevelt died . . . but who was Harry Truman? I remember being afraid of the Dirty Japs.

I had lots of interest in war planes. We would sneak onto the airbase on St. Simons to get pieces of broken planes. Bicycles were scarce, and I was thinking about selling mine but decided not to. It was used to get me around Brunswick, where I discovered couples having sex day and night in Hanover Square (how close dared we get before they bothered to pay any attention to us?); to deliver *The Brunswick News*; or to visit the USO nearby and antagonize the sailors and soldiers. I remember there were few fireworks on the Fourth of July and was amazed when I ordered fireworks from a comic book in about 1944 that they actually arrived.

Being eight to thirteen years old was a good age to be during World War II. Having never been eight to thirteen years of age before, it seemed normal.

Benny Frank Brown

My father, a sharecropper, took my mother to a doctor in Collins, Georgia, one hot summer day in 1940. The doctor stated that my mother had an arthritic hip and could best be treated by sitting in salt water daily. I don't know why my father and mother chose Brunswick over Savannah, but I'm glad they did. I suppose it was my father's choice, because my parents divorced in 1941, and my mother moved to Savannah.

December 7, 1941, was a day my father and one of my aunts chose to visit my uncle, who was a career soldier at Camp Stewart, Georgia. On our return trip to Brunswick, a flagman at a bridge broke the news of Pearl Harbor to us. I remember being surprised that we were not already at war. Radio and the movies had certainly allied us with the British and Chinese.

After this the shipyard seemed to magically appear overnight. My relatives left the farms and moved to cities—Brunswick, Savannah, and Augusta—to work in shipyards, defense plants, and all-war related efforts. I remember people sleeping in our apartment in shifts. My father worked in the shipyard in the daytime, had a "hillbilly band" at nights, and delivered mail on the weekends to St. Simons and Sea Island. My aunt delivered the mail on weekdays. I don't know when my father slept.

I started selling the *Atlanta Constitution* in front of the shipyard in '44 and '45. I got up at 4:30 a.m., rode with Mr. Barnes to meet the train at 5 a.m., and arrived at the shipyard between 5:30 and 6 a.m. for the shift change. You could follow the progress of the war each day by looking at the diagrams on the front page. Arrows were used to denote the Allies; the rising sun or a swastika were used to symbolize the enemy.

One weekend, we took a trip back to the "country." Outside of Jesup was a prisoner-of-war camp. As I recall, Italians were there at first and later Germans. I remember, too, going to St. Simons to see the anchored ships that had been torpedoed by German U-boats.

World War II, as horrendous as it was, enabled my parents and their relatives to escape the poverty that the Civil War had heaped on them. I was the first person in my father's family to graduate from high school since the Civil War. Prior to that war, there were lawyers and professors in our family. Wars bring on so much change.

Neal G. Gale

I, like my father and grandfather before me, was fortunate enough to be born in and live my life in Brunswick, Glynn County, Georgia. The Great Depression of 1929, which began about two years after my birth, left our nation and Glynn County in a state of economic decline that we hope will never be repeated. We were fortunate that my father had a supervisory job at the Hercules Powder Company, one of the principal employers in the county. Unfortunately, he died in 1936 of influenza. My mother had been a school teacher and was able to find employment in the school system. As a small boy, I felt that we were well-off because nobody in town had much.

My productive economic life began when I was 10 years old: I bagged groceries all day on Saturdays for 50 cents. When I was 11, the minimum age, I was able to get a paper route and make $2.50 a week for delivering the *Florida Times Union* seven days a week beginning at 5 a.m. At 14, things changed dramatically. I got a job as usher and doorman at the Ritz Theater for $5 a week. Many heads of families in Glynn County didn't make much more than that in 1942. Then came the war!

Two shipyards came to Brunswick. In early 1943, at the age of 15, I was able to convince the personnel officer at J. A. Jones Shipyard that I was 18. My first weekly paycheck as a shipfitter third-class was $42.60. I didn't know there was so much money. During the next year and a half, I was promoted to shipfitter first-class and with overtime made as much as $82 per week. Just as I was getting used to being wealthy, I went in the Navy and was paid $42 per month.

Life in Brunswick during the war was very exciting for a big teenager who could pass for 18 and had a pocketful of money. The problem was where to spend it; there were few things for sale. An automobile was out of the question for there were none and little gas to run them on, even if you had one. Being an entrepreneur type of individual, I managed to spend it all and, after the war, started college dead broke and working for peanuts again at menial jobs.

Frank Schopfer

The early Forties were a turning point for our family. To me, it was an era of great adventure. It was about a week away from my twelfth birthday on December 7, 1941. I knew something momentous had occurred, but I could not foresee the changes that would take place in Glynn County and Brunswick.

I was born in an old house about six miles from Brunswick. It would be stretching things to say it was "Georgia Cracker Architecture." We had no electricity, running water, or indoor plumbing. Eventually power lines found their way out to our part of the county, and, lo and behold, we had electricity just like the town folks! There were no close neighbors, and I had no other children close by to associate with as I grew up. So it was really a shock when I started first grade at Ballard Elementary and suddenly was in the midst of all those kids from Sterling, Thalmann, and other far reaches of the county. I only mention this bit of background to show how insulated we were at that time from the things that were going on in town. We would go into town maybe two or three times a month and always on a Saturday. I never knew what it was like to go to town on a weekday, but Saturdays were red letter days!

As with all of us in our generation, I came along during the Great Depression, and for us, it really was a depression. My mother used to say that steak was 10 cents a pound, but we didn't have the 10 cents. Even coming up with three cents to mail a first-class letter was hard to do. We were never hungry, though, as we had a cow or two to milk and we grew a lot of stuff in the fields. My father considered himself fortunate if he could work two or three days a week, but all that changed after Pearl Harbor.

Going to town, as I stated before, was a big thing. If you were fortunate enough to park in front of Kress, your trip was a success. My dad drove a Model A Ford and we would sit in it and watch the people pass by on Newcastle Street. There was a blind man who would walk up and down past Kress playing a guitar with a tin cup affixed to it for donations. He would walk to the curb on Gloucester Street, stop for a while, and then slowly stroll past Kress again. I was always amazed at how he could do this, but I'm sure he had the paces memorized. Another fascination to me was to listen to the old Portuguese gentlemen as they sat on the park benches along Newcastle Street talking, although I understood not a word they said. Now they are gone, and although I'm sure some of their descendants are living, you don't hear Portuguese spoken on the streets anymore.

Later on as the war progressed, I remember the truck convoys loaded with troops going past our house for hours at a time. How I wished that I could ride along, too. To me it seemed as if they were having a wonderful time as they waved and shouted at us. I have often wondered how many of them ended up in North Africa or perhaps on the beaches of Normandy. One day a convoy was coming by, and, as usual, I was at the side of the road watching and waving. For the most part, the troops were waving back, but for some reason to me they didn't quite look like the troops I had always seen before. An MP Jeep came along and stopped in our driveway to direct traffic. I nerved myself enough to ask one of the MPs what outfit this was. Imagine my surprise when I was told they were German prisoners headed for Florida. By George, here I was in Glynn County and I had seen them with my own eyes! My day was doubly made when, to my delight, a hat blew off one of the men and landed in the ditch. I retrieved, kept, and wore that hat for many years, but, alas, it disappeared, along with all my comic books, which would be worth a fortune if I had them today.

The blimp base was built in response to the submarine war off the Georgia and Florida coasts. Sometimes the blimps would come low over our house and I could see the crew members in the gondola. I would wave to them and they would respond likewise. That was heady stuff for a young fellow, and naturally I thought how great it would be to be up there with them. Of course, the shipyard was built and thousands of people came here to work. Even my mother worked at the shipyard and my father became fully employed. Nothing was ever the same after that. You had to stand in long lines to go to the Saturday night westerns at the Ritz Theater. Due to the housing shortage, people were living in their cars. A lot of public housing was built by the government during that period.

Wanting to be patriotic, my mother signed on as a volunteer aircraft spotter. Her assigned station was the forestry fire tower located at Arco. Her first day on duty meant that she would have to climb to the top of the tower, which she managed to do without mishap. Let me just interject here that my mother is not an off-the-ground type of person, so to get to the top of the tower was a feat in itself. However, coming down was a different thing altogether. Once she started down the steps, vertigo overtook her and she just couldn't move. Two men finally had to go up there and retrieve her. Her days as an aircraft spotter were over.

As a young child, I would go to the area that became the blimp base. That particular part of Glynn County was known as Freeman's Rest and was populated mostly by black families. One story that my mother tells is about a black friend of hers known as Aunt Rachel who lived there. When Aunt Rachel was married she was a young girl about 16 years of age and her husband was much older . . . in his forties. He went by Uncle Son.

One day Aunt Rachel was sick and had to stay in bed while Uncle Son left to do his daily work. While in bed Aunt Rachel heard a commotion in the rafters over her head and to her horror saw a rat snake coiled around a rat. In the ensuing struggle, both the snake and the rat fell down on the bed, where upon the snake proceeded to finish the rat off and begin ingesting it. When the rat was swallowed, the snake stayed on the bed digesting its meal. It was still there when Uncle Son returned and managed to get it out of the house.

Ruth Konetzko Daniel

My husband (Mel Daniel) had a plumbing business that was established in 1882 by his father, Moses Daniel. Moses Daniel had five sons. Three were plumbers. The business stayed open until 1980. That is when I retired. Both brothers who had continued the business had died. Our shop was located on Grant Street between Floyd's Barber Shop and the old National Bank Building in the square facing Newcastle Street.

During the World War II, we were very busy doing private work for owners who had people rooming in their homes. We had difficulty getting supplies, especially brass and other pipes. Prices skyrocketed during that time. Everybody was needing the same thing. It would take months to get a certain part, especially from the Wilbur Reed Brass Company, which was in Wisconsin. We also had trouble getting help because everybody went to the shipyard.

So many people flocked into Brunswick. There were just a couple of hotels in Brunswick, the Royal and the Oglethorpe, but the people opened up their homes. The grocery stores were busy. On Friday mornings between eight-thirty and nine o'clock they all got their groceries in. Washing powder was in great demand, as was sugar. I shopped three grocery stores to get washing powder. My sister-in-law Gwen had a baby, and my sister-in-law Mary usually went with me. I made three stores in 30 minutes to get each family a package. I'll never forget the standing in line and the hurrying.

We had a large church structure (St. James Lutheran) but very few members. Many Lutherans moved in to work at the shipyard. Servicemen also attended our church, and we would invite them to dinner. It was the only time they got into a home. We had a lounge for the servicemen in the parish house of the church. They could come there and read. I remember the blackouts—how we sat in the dark and listened to the radio. I remember the night of D-Day when they landed in Europe. Church bells rang and the Hercules whistles blew. We all went to church about three or four o'clock in the morning. We even got Mama up and took her with us.

Hanover Park has a fountain, which is still flowing and is kept up very well. They use to have different plays and music in the park for the people during the war. They say that if you ever drink from the fountain in Hanover Park you will always come back to Brunswick. Everybody pulled together during the war, even the strangers who came to work. There wasn't the crime at that time like it is now. Everybody was for the country.

Eugene T. Davis

My mother, brother, and I lived on a small farm about 92 miles west of Brunswick (Pearson). When my brother turned 17, he decided to join the Navy. Since I was only 10 years old, my mother and I could not manage the farm. My two oldest brothers were already working at the J. A. Jones shipyard. My uncle and aunt bought a boarding house at 1528 Reynolds Street and let my mother and me move into the two-story house they had rented in Arco. We inherited a couple of boarders in the deal.

We lived close to the pulp mill, and it took me a while to be able to tolerate the foul smells coming from it. Another adjustment that I had to make was drinking the sulfur water from the school fountains. I attended Arco Elementary School on Ross Road and took a lot of pride in buying savings stamps and taking part in collecting paper to contribute to the school for the war effort. I remember our school winning the chance to fly a special flag for collecting the most paper or selling the most savings stamps.

Arco band
Left to right: W. W. Wages, James Ray Clark, (unknown), Marian Wages, Betty Spivey, Lester Wages, Buddy Spivey, Bob Meyers, Harold (Casey) Jones, Billie Bird Wages, Bobby Huff, Fred Earl Wages, W. G. Thigpen, (unknown), C. C. Huff, and Eugene Davis' bass horn (without him).
Courtesy of Eugene Davis

Mr. Bill Wages, who lived on the same street as we did (Ash Street), had organized a small band called The Arco Band. I was given the opportunity of taking lessons from him and playing the E-flat bass horn. We had the opportunity of playing at several Liberty ship launchings. It was very exciting to sit on the platform at the bow of those massive ships where all the dignitaries participated in the launching ceremonies.

It was a very sad day at school when President Roosevelt died. I particularly remember our sixth-grade teacher, Ms. Louise Connally, who was also the principal, crying and some of us joining her with our tears. VE Day was a more joyous day, but we expressed our regrets that President Roosevelt didn't live to see it.

In June of 1945, my uncle and aunt decided that they wanted the Arco house back, so we had to find another place to live. Since my brothers worked at the shipyard, we were able to rent a two-bedroom brick war apartment in the 700 block of Albany Street (Gordon Oaks Apartments). This move made it possible for me to be nearer to the shipyard and get a better understanding of the number of people working there by watching the number of cars that traveled up and down Albany Street at shift changes. As I look back, I see these war apartments as being really energy efficient, even by today's standards. Each apartment had a built-in coal bin just outside the back door, and the hot water was generated while you were cooking your meals on the coal stove. A coal heater, located in the center of each apartment, also served well to keep the living room, bathroom, and two bedrooms warm during the winter months.

Living near the shipyard let me witness the mass exodus of shipyard workers on VJ Day. This day, the swing shift (4 p.m. to 12 a.m.) passed south on Albany Street going to work; but as they reported to their respective work stations, the announcement was made over the PA system that the war was over. Most of the workers reporting to work turned around and went back to their cars to go back home. This meant that the northbound traffic in south Brunswick was very congested for a good while, but the horn blowing and yelling from passing cars was impressive. When the traffic from the mid-afternoon rush cleared and dusk approached, I could see trucks and trailers loaded with furniture heading west on Albemarle Street turning north on Albany Street. It was almost as if I would hear them saying, "The war is over! I've done my patriotic duty! I'm goin' home!"

I was one of the ex-farmers left stranded in Glynn County, which meant that I had to develop most of my cherished friendships with native Glynn Countians. My hangin' around Brunswick might have created some frustration for Ms. Jane Macon during my senior year in high school because she never seemed to be able to figure out why she had not taught my mother, father, grandmother, or grandfather! [Miss Jane Macon was a beloved teacher who taught several generations of many families. In the 1940s she was the senior English and literature teacher at Glynn Academy High School.]

Eugene Davis
with E-Flat Bass Horn
Courtesy of Eugene Davis

Marie Way Lang
Marie Way Lang's ancestors came from Dorchester, England, to Dorchester, Massachusetts, in the 1600s. When the witch hunts began, two of the three Way brothers decided to go south. One brother settled in South Carolina and the other went to Midway, Georgia. The South Carolina Ways are her ancestors. She married Hubert Lang.

My husband's father started the Lang Planing Mill in Brunswick. When my husband came back from World War I, very few jobs were available. The Atlantic Refinery Company announced it was building a million dollar plant in Brunswick and needed someone to hire the labor to do the job. My husband applied for the job and was hired. At the completion of the refinery, many people came to Brunswick to work, and the Lang Planing Mill, which had been suffering through the Depression, was then able to continue and my husband went to work for his father. During World War II, the mill was checked by the government on what was being sold and how much was charged for it. Very soon, the government used the Lang Planing Mill as an example on how to operate as its prices were very fair.

On the Sunday that the Japanese bombed Pearl Harbor, my daughter Lillian Marie and I were playing golf at the Brunswick Country Club. As we approached the club house, we could hear the radio very loud (that was, of course, before television), and we wondered what the pro's wife was listening to because we knew she was hard of hearing. When we got into the room, it was full of people, and we then heard, as they repeated it over and over, that the Japanese had bombed Pearl Harbor. We rushed home to tell the rest of the family. My daughter Mary was spending the night with Judge Cogdell's family, and she tells that when the news came over the radio Judge Cogdell became very serious and talked to the girls about what war meant.

As soon as the U. S. declared war against Japan and Germany declared war against the U. S., the wheels of defense began to roll. People came into Brunswick from all over the South to work, and there were very few places for them to live. It seemed strange when soon a

Rationing Board was in place and you had to apply for stamps for gasoline, sugar, and many other things that we had always taken for granted. When the J. A. Jones Company had the full-fledged shipyard in place, it was amazing to see crowds of people who were out on the street day and night. Schools were very crowded .

The shipyard published a newspaper, *The Brunswick Mariner,* every week. I was a file clerk in the welding department and wrote articles about our departments. I also wrote articles about our son, Hubert, Jr., who was in the Navy on a minesweeper in the South Pacific. He saw duty all over the Pacific and in Saipan.

We also had a huge blimp base. The large blimps became a very familiar sight to everyone as they patrolled the ocean day and night. German U-boats did attack ships off our coast. Women gathered at churches to roll bandages, and when news was released about the deaths of several young men in our area, the whole town grieved and worked harder than ever in the effort to defeat Germany and Japan.

Ralph Bufkin

My family moved from Windsor Park in Brunswick to Bruce Drive, East Beach, St. Simons in 1940, and we lived there throughout the war years. I was nine years old. A group of the neighborhood kids and I were at the Coast Guard station on Sunday afternoon, December 7, 1941, when word came through about the attack on Pearl Harbor. The rest of the day was spent listening to the radio for more news. Over the loudspeaker system at Sidney Lanier Grammar School the next day, we heard President Roosevelt's address to Congress, asking for a declaration of war.

STRICT SECURITY MEASURES

Almost immediately, strict security measures were adopted due to the war, including the closing of the beach from sunset to sunrise and patrolling by the Coast Guard on horseback. They later used Jeeps and trucks. Supposedly, anyone found on the beach during darkness would be shot on sight. No lights were to be visible, so blackout curtains were used for windows and doors, and porch light bulbs were removed. In addition, the top half of car headlights were painted black. There was an air-raid siren located at the corner of our street. C. M. Ward was the air-raid warden, and air-raid drills were conducted frequently. Some of the residents became aircraft spotters, identifying and reporting all aircraft observed. Most of these measurers were relaxed as the war progressed.

Rationing of food, gas, shoes, and tires was soon enacted and pretty much prevailed until the war's end. Because of the influx of so many people for the shipyard and the U.S. Navy facilities, our few grocery stores could not handle the demand for food. Many times my mother would drive to Jesup or Waycross for groceries. During the war, my mother and other ladies met to make bandages for the Red Cross. Everyone had a victory garden to help ease the food shortage. There was no physician on St. Simons at that time, and my father, a dentist, served as an emergency medical officer for the Coast Guard.

My contribution to the war effort was through the Boy Scout troop where we had metal foil, newspaper, and scrap-metal collection drives throughout the war.

OTHER RECOLLECTIONS

Several ships sank in early 1942; the light from a ship on fire illuminated the beach at night on one occasion. The torpedoes and gunfire could be clearly heard and rattled our windows and dishes. Later, depth charges or bombs dropped offshore could be heard and felt. One of the results of the sinkings was a lot of oil on the beach, which would be covered by blowing sand and if stepped on in the summer could blister your feet. On another occasion the beach was littered with many whole dressed turkeys. [On the night of April 8, U-boat 123 sank the SS *Esparta*, a United Fruit Company cold-storage motor ship.] The torpedoed tankers were salvaged and anchored off the St. Simons pier. The holes were large enough to have run in a couple of locomotives side by side. These ships were sunk in water so shallow that when they rested on the bottom, water came only to the main deck. Both ships went back into service.

A small group of us were at the Coast Guard station when they towed in a lifeboat from a sunken ship. As I recall, there were four or five seamen aboard, mostly in their underwear and with blistered skin and lips from exposure and possibly fire. We discovered the lifeboat and a large sealed aluminum can of Hershey's chocolate kisses, which, because of chocolate shortages and rationing, we thoroughly enjoyed eating! The Coast Guard boys kindly invited us kids to eat dinner with them on several occasions. They always had meat and butter.

In addition to building Glynco Naval Air Station, the Navy took over the King and Prince Hotel and used it as a radar school. Two radar towers were erected there. The Navy also took over McKinnon Airport on St. Simons. Aircraft there were used to train airborne radar operators and to provide aircraft for students at the King and Prince to track. On one occasion, about five twin Beechcraft trainers ran out of fuel because of miscalculation of winds. They ditched near St. Simons. One that ditched in the St. Simons sound was piloted by Lee Howe, who married Mary Jane Everett, daughter of "Dutch" Everett. On another occasion, a USN plane taking off from St. Simons on runway 15 struck some tall pine trees in the backyard of Christ Church parsonage, crashed, and burned, killing both pilots. A crowd of us were on Demere Road watching firemen trying to put out the blaze. When ammunition started cooking off from the fire, everyone scattered.

Whenever USN aircraft were operating offshore, the Navy dispatched crash boats in order to pick up survivors in the event a plane went down. In the summer, the crash boats, which were PT boats with two instead of three Packard V-12 engines, would swing close to the pier with their huge wakes so that we could dive off the roof of the pier into their wakes. The Navy also erected a radar tower on Jekyll. A few sailors and the island caretakers were the only inhabitants. A group of us Sea Scouts went to Jekyll on a Coast Guard auxiliary boat and were allowed to sleep in the hotel under the caretaker's supervision. Everything was left as it was when the members of the club left before the war. What luxurious furnishings!

In 1942, the U.S. Army held maneuvers on St. Simons. There were Army anti-aircraft gun emplacements with soldiers manning the weapons. There was a 50-caliber machine gun and a 20 MM cannon unit in the empty lot behind our house. There were probably a total of 10 such units on East Beach alone. There was a heavy anti-aircraft unit just off the East Beach causeway on the hard sand. Later, there was a firepower demonstration in front of the casino, where they fired all size weapons from 30 caliber on up to about 77 MM at towed targets, using tracer ammunition. Very impressive. These maneuvers lasted about a week.

St. Simons School

The St. Simons Elementary School was built during the war. Prisoners of war, mostly Italians and some Germans, were used to construct the building. They were bused and trucked in each day from a camp, I believe in Wayne County. The prisoners were very friendly and would spend time with us and tell stories about their homes and service. Only a few spoke good English. They had been captured in North Africa.

A Final Recollection

For three summers during the war, I delivered Western Union telegrams on St. Simons for Donald Doyle. On numerous occasions, I had to deliver telegrams about wounded, missing, or killed in action servicemen to their families, some local people and other families who stayed on St. Simons when their husbands at Glynco or St. Simons had been transferred overseas. I remember having to deliver, first, a wounded in action and then later a killed in action telegram to the J.C. Strother Hardware store next door, about their son J.C., Jr.

Franklin M. Cloud

My family lived in Pittsboro, North Carolina, when World War II was declared. My father's job with the local GM dealer soon terminated because no new vehicles for civilian use were built due to material diverted for our war efforts. My mother's job was not affected because she was a registered nurse. There were three children, my older brother, C.A., my younger sister, Betty, and me. On September 22, 1942, my father obtained a security job (senior guard) at Camp Butner Army Base near Durham, North Carolina, about 30 miles from Pittsboro. Due to the rationing and shortage of gasoline, he moved to Durham alone. In those days people often worked seven days a week, so he was rarely off to come home. On March 31, 1943, he transferred to Camp McCall near Southern Pines, North Carolina. After a few months there, he obtained a patrolman job with J. A. Jones at the shipyard in Brunswick, Georgia. This was to last for the duration of the war. Mother visited him there and liked what she saw, and plans were made to move shortly after the school year ended in Pittsboro in 1943.

War Apartment Living

When the time arrived, we four caught a train to Sanford, North Carolina, and arrived in Thalmann, Georgia, the next day. My father met us in our 1935 Chevy and drove us the 19 miles to Brunswick. We stayed temporarily in the Mark Carr homes at the south end of Union Street near the shipyard. These were efficiency one-room war apartments. Our request for larger quarters was already being processed. We moved right away to 3558 Gordon Oaks Apartments, which were located between Third and Fourth Avenues on Albany Street, the same street where Lover's Oak is located.

Our Gordon Oaks apartment had two bedrooms with a shower and toilet. The cookstove was designed to burn wood or coal. The water heater was an uninsulated galvanized tank designed for a fire to be built in the bottom when one wanted hot water. Both these appliances heated the apartment too much for use in the summer. There was a single wood or coal heater near the bathroom and bedroom doors for winter comfort heating. I used to go to the railroad track a few blocks from the apartment and gather up splinters, which sifted from the box cars hauling pine stumps. We used this wood to start the coal fires and, sometimes, to heat the water in the tank. Most of our showers were taken with cold water, which was a great relief from the heat of the summer. We were not accustomed to modern conveniences and I don't remember a great deal of suffering from heat or cold.

Our life in Gordon Oaks Apartments was very exciting. From our apartment at shift time we could see great numbers of people come down toward the shipyard, while an equal number came up the street from the shipyard. We were only about three blocks from the shipyard and the noise of heavy cranes transferring steel, riveters shooting rivets, and the public address system were heard 24 hours a day. We got accustomed to the noise and action past our house and they weren't a big problem.

A place to stay within walking distance of the shipyard was hard to come by. Many converted sheds and garages to apartments and some with large homes turned them into boarding houses. Granny Butler on Fourth Avenue and Mrs. Cope at the corner of Fourth and Albany Street ran boarding houses. Mrs. Cope also rented her garage for a while. People were without air-conditioning, and some had outdoor toilets and poor living conditions.

A Different Lifestyle

We all entered a very different life style . . . from the sleepy rural town in North Carolina to a boom town on the Atlantic Ocean with mild weather and palm trees. One of the most impressive sites in Brunswick was the Oglethorpe Hotel on Newcastle Street. The Ritz Theatre was located on the north end of Newcastle Street and another movie theater, the Bijou, was on the south end. Down past the Bijou on the left was a bowling alley. I later got a job setting up pins there. They required me to get a social security card. (There's no record of my earnings withheld at social security.) My brother and I both had paper routes with *The Brunswick News*—at age 11 for me and 13 for C.A. C.A. was very good at it, but I could never seem to make any money.

The soldiers and sailors from the military installations in the county could be seen on weekends enjoying their liberty in town. There was a USO club for the servicemen located on Union Street. This large house provided dances and other services for all branches of service personnel. The speed limit was 35 mph during World War II in order to save tires. These tires were made of synthetic rubber and of poor quality. Shipyard commuters often had flats on their vehicles. It was a common practice to install a thick huge patch, called a boot, to cover holes in the tires. Gasoline for our car could only be purchased with rationing stamps. Our car had an A sticker, which was the least number of gallons allowed per month. The car sat for many days without use, and my parents walked to work and we walked to school. When school started in 1943, I attended Wolf Street School, a school constructed for the increased attendance of defense workers' children. In the sixth grade, I joined the band and played the coronet, then later the baritone horn. In the seventh grade, I moved to Prep High, where I completed grades seven and eight.

During the war period, my father and mother never got any vacation or time off from work. My father worked shifts and my mother, a registered nurse at the Brunswick Hospital on First Avenue, was on call 24 hours a day. My mother gave anesthesia in the operating room at the hospital. Many of the yard workers were injured or killed on the job. While in Brunswick, we got our first telephone so the hospital could get in touch with my mother. Our telephone number was 770-R.

When the war was over, the yard stayed open only a short while. My father and most others were soon out of a job. A great hurried exodus began and the population of Brunswick dropped dramatically. The Mark Carr Apartments on Union Street soon became a ghost town, and families also left Gordon Oaks, but not as fast. My father got a new job in Tallahassee, Florida, with an auto dealership. However, during the war years, my folks had saved to purchase a farm in North Georgia. The decision was made to relocate to the farm and not go to Florida. We left Brunswick in 1949, all except C.A., who stayed to finish high school at Glynn Academy, graduating in 1949. C.A. still remains today in Brunswick.

C. A. Cloud, Jr.

My family came to Brunswick in June of 1943. My dad was in the security force at the shipyard and was transferred to Brunswick by the J. A. Jones Construction Company from Camp McCall, North Carolina. We followed him to Brunswick and had to live in a one-bedroom war apartment in the Mark Carr Homes complex. We only camped out there, so to speak, for a week. We were approved to rent a two-bedroom Gordon Oaks apartment, # 3558 in the 300 block of Albany Street.

My mother went to work the next day at the old Brunswick Hospital at 1129 Norwich Street as a nurse anesthetist. Dr. J. B. Avera and Dr. Burford interviewed her and put her right to work. She was the only one that put you to sleep for operations and surgery, or to deliver a baby, and was on 24-hour call until about June of 1949. She worked hard for little pay. I remember the second day I was in Brunswick. I was walking downtown on Union Street. A kid met me on the sidewalk in front of the Baptist Church and said to me, "I'm gonna knock your block off!" Never having seen him before, I said, "OK, let's get at it." He backed down and left apologizing. I later found out he had a mental problem.

I remember long lines at the movies and other stores. You couldn't get many manufactured goods like radios, bikes, and bike tires. My mother used to buy groceries at the Community Super Market by the old hospital, and she often complained that the newcomers were treated differently by local merchants. Cokes and candies were many times saved under the counter for local residents.

I delivered sale flyers in the Mark Carr homes. People slept in shifts and when I would go up on the porches to place a flyer on or behind the door, the occupant many times would be lying mostly unclothed on the bed trying to sleep. Those apartments had only one window and one door. In the summertime, they were like a steam box. There was a complex built to make life easier for the shipyard workers. It had a movie theater, dispensary for medical needs, a snack shop, library, post office, and pool room. There was a similar facility in Goodyear Park (Goodyear Homes). A 35-mm movie was made of a lot of the activities at the shipyard, such as beauty contests and other events. It was left in the old Ritz Theater. Frank McCullough, the manager, showed it to me. I have often wondered what happened to the film footage.

Viola Carswell Daniels

A lot of men and women worked as domestics for the millionaires on Jekyll Island. A lot of the men served as golf course caddies. To get to Jekyll, they had to catch a boat at the foot of Mansfield Street. When the war started, the millionaires were not allowed on Jekyll so these people were out of jobs. Many went to work at the shipyard. During the war I taught third grade at Risley Elementary School. School at that time was carried on in shifts due to the increased population. The building at H and Wolf Streets was used for classes.

During the years of World War II, my family included my mother, my niece and my brother who lived at another residence. My mother took in boarders. She furnished a place to stay and meals for shipyard workers. Our living room was used as a bedroom during that time and the other two rooms were rented out. A ceiling was put on the amount of money a person could charge for boarders. One of the boarders was from Waycross and later we were married.

There was war housing for the blacks out near the ball park by the Hercules. The Buggs Center was near for their recreation. In the Arco area was another war housing for the blacks. All the houses were built the same. They were little without any eaves. The Buggs Recreation Center and Selden furnished places for entertainment. [Selden, located in the area near the Palmetto Cemetery in Brunswick, was a private high school for blacks. A recreational area for blacks was also located there. St. Athanasus, the other private school for blacks in

Elizabeth Wilson, Mrs. Daniels' niece, lived with her. During the war as a student at Fort Valley College in Fort Valley, Georgia, she remembers sending straight pins, safety pins, and screen wire for doors to Brunswick. She could find these materials in Fort Valley, a small town.

The Brunswick News, March 12, 1942

NEEDLES AND PINS BECOMING SCARCE

Needles and pins, which have always been plentiful and purchased at nominal prices, are becoming scarce; in fact needles are said to already be off the local market, while the scarcity of pins has been noticed.

Housewives did not realize the needle supply was so limited until they started out to purchase them. Today, it was stated, it is doubtful if more than a dozen packages can be found anywhere in the city.

The pin shortage is expected to become equally as acute in the near future, it was stated.

Brunswick, was located a stone's throw from Glynn Academy.] The male membership at the First African Baptist Church was limited because so many had been drafted into the military service. There were two grocery stores in the downtown area, Piggy Wiggly in the 1500 block of Newcastle Street and the A&P on Mansfield Street. During the shipyard time, the building at I and Wolf Streets was built by Mr. Walter Brown and purchased by the Boilermaker Workers for business and recreational purposes.

Joyce McGill Campbell

CONGRESS DECLARES WAR!
These headlines were the largest and boldest I had ever seen in *The Brunswick News*. It was December 8, 1941.

When World War II started, I was in grammar school and when the war ended in 1945, I had just entered Glynn Academy High School . . . 10 years old when the war started, 14 when the surrender was officially signed. My oldest brother, Floyd, was the only one in our large family old enough to enter the service. He had worked at the Hercules for a year after graduating from Glynn Academy, then entered Oglethorpe University only to leave at the beginning of his second year to join the Navy, where he became an aerial photographer. He was first sent to the Banana River Base in Florida, then to California. Later he was stationed aboard the USS *South Dakota*, the flag ship of Admiral "Bull" Halsey, where Floyd served as his personal photographer. Among the official photographs for the Navy records were the very graphic pictures of the kamikaze (suicide) pilots from Japan who crashed themselves onto the deck of the *South Dakota*. Although my brother brought copies of these pictures home after the war, I never saw them. He was stationed aboard the USS *Missouri* and was present and took most of the photographs at the actual surrender of Japan to General MacArthur. While we do not have a set of those photographs anymore, he presented a complete set to Glynn Academy. [No one at Glynn Academy or the Glynn County Board of Education is aware of these photographs. It is suspected that they had been stored in the basement of Glynn Academy and were thrown away in later years with a lot of other materials that were damp and showed evidence of having been chewed on by small rodents.]

I remember V-Mail, the little blue, thin folded-over one sheet notepaper that servicemen used to write home. While Floyd tried to edit the letters himself of anything that could be compromising, occasionally we would receive one of the letters with blacked-out places, which the censor apparently thought might contain information that could be useful to the enemy should they get hold of the letter. We had no idea where Floyd was, as was the case with most families with men in service. We could only write to him, which we did copiously, through his name and serial number to an APO in New York. To me, it seemed miraculous that through that source our letters actually reached him.

My father worked for the Atlantic, Birmingham and Coast Railroad, which ran from Brunswick to Atlanta. We first lived on Dartmouth Street in Brunswick, but before the war we moved to the

Hail! Hail! The Gang's All Here (tune)

Hail! Hail! The stamps are here!
Got to fill my stamp book.
Got to fill my stamp book.
Hail! Hail! The stamps are here!
Got to fill my stamp book now!

country. In the country my dad was closer to his work where the AB&C Railroad crossed the then Seaboard Railroad. I remember the "troop trains" as they passed, overflowing with troops who put their heads and arms out the windows, waving to everyone they could see. I also remember the convoys of Army trucks on the highways and the need to pull over to the side of the road as they passed. Because we were taught as children to be patriotic—and this certainly was reinforced during the war—I was filled with pride when I saw our troops on the move in their convoys. Even during the war, we would take our picnics over to the wooded area near the pier on St. Simons. I remember the many planes and blimps flying overhead, constantly patrolling our coast. Also, the oil slicks by the pier on St. Simons many times prevented us from going into the water. This was apparent when the two oil tankers were torpedoed off the coast but also every time a Liberty ship was launched. I heard, though it may have been a rumor, that a submarine had actually been blown up near the coast of St. Simons.

In my eighth-grade class, I was responsible for taking orders for savings stamps, collecting the money, and sending the order in. The 25-cent stamps were green and the 10-cent stamps were rosy red. When the stamps were returned, the students would paste them in their books. They were accumulating $18.75, which entitled them to a $25 U. S. Savings War Bond.

Even though my father worked full time for the railroad, he loved farming. So we had a full-fledged farm. At the same time, he set aside a small plot for the children to raise a victory garden. It was part of the war effort for people to be encouraged to grow their own vegetables, thus providing for their own food and allowing more foods to be sent to our troops, which were our first priority. I remember the rationing of gas and tires. No cars were manufactured during the war as the automobile plants were turned over to the manufacture of tanks, Jeeps, and whatever else was needed for the war. Every piece of wire and metal that we got our hands on we put in our scrap box. It was a simple matter to remove both ends of the tin cans, flatten them, and put all the pieces into the scrap container, along with whatever else we could accumulate, and wait for the "scrap man" to come around. We always felt so good when we had lots of scrap metal when he came.

One nostalgic note was the cannon that was facing a small park across from City Hall that was donated to the scrap drive. In a sense of patriotic duty our community donated that cannon.* Perhaps that very thing helped to save a life. We had no elastic to speak of and I did like elastic in my underwear. Since it was not available, we had little strap ties on the sides of our underwear. That was fine until one of the straps happened to break.

My sister assisted in hosting at the USO. A dance was sponsored for the officers stationed at the King and Prince Hotel on St. Simons. My future brother-in-law met my sister at that dance and told her that very night that she was the girl he was going to marry. He was from California and had been fortunate to meet a sweet Southern girl. They have been happily married for many years.

*Read John Morris' account of what really happened to the cannon.

Tramp, Tramp, Tramp (tune)

Stamps, stamps, stamps,
my book is growing,
Growing fuller every week.
Soon our sales will hit a peak.
We are helping week by week,
Give the nation power
and hope for VICTORY!

PATRIOTISM

The movies were a great source of news in the newsreels that accompanied feature films. Also the extras featured movie stars striving to get people to buy bonds and stamps. Patriotic songs were sung in assembly at school or at any meeting we had. Of particular importance to me were George M. Cohan's "Over There," "White Cliffs of Dover," and all the songs involving the branches of service. These continued to keep our spirits up and make us believe in what was going on. One of my brother's best friends, John Whittle, who had lived on Prince Street, was killed during the war. As long as he lived, my brother never forgot John.

Our question in those days was not whether or not we would lose the war. We were simply told, and we believed it firmly, that we could not and would not lose the war. So it was a matter of how soon it would end and how soon we would win it. Bear in mind that we children as well as adults felt the full confidence in our leadership to win this war. President Roosevelt; Winston Churchill; Generals Marshall, Omar Bradley, Patton, and Eisenhower; and Admirals Halsey and Nimitz and many others were in the forefront so much and seemed so capable that we had confidence in their abilities to take us through.

DEATH OF ROOSEVELT AND END OF WAR

When I heard the news on the radio of Roosevelt's death in Warm Springs, I raced to the backyard to tell my mother. She, I guess, felt like a member of the family had died because she started to cry. While I knew she and Dad had great respect for this man, perhaps it generated in her a little fear of what the outcome might be because of his death. Nevertheless, Truman assumed the helm, brought the Manhattan Project to fruition, ordered the dropping of the atomic bomb on Nagasaki and Hiroshima, and thus brought the war to an end. We had won! The actual signing of the surrender wasn't until September of 1945.

The bombs had been dropped. Men and women began their journeys home! I have since heard criticism of that decision. I disapprove of that criticism altogether because the Japanese had been sufficiently warned. We had weapons that were really phenomenal, and in order to save American lives those bombs had to be dropped on a nation whose leadership refused to believe this could happen. However, that began fears of nuclear warfare, which have been quelled somewhat by some of the truces that have been signed. Since the *Missouri* remained in Japan for some time, my brother was able to bring all of us girls many silk outfits that the Japanese people made. Floyd had been deeply affected by what he had seen and spent a year at home recuperating after that trauma before returning to college at UCLA in California. Being stationed on the West Coast, he had come to love California and spent the rest of his life there.

After the war when the G.I. Bill was passed and veterans could attend college at government expense, we had a few older classmates who returned to Glynn Academy for that required diploma. I had a terrific crush on one of them (who shall remain nameless), but even I was aware that the difference between a 17-year-old high school girl

"We mailed care packages to my father and relatives in England. Fresh fruit coated with melted paraffin was especially appreciated."

Eleanor Smith Gathright

and a 21-year-old military veteran was quite vast, so the crush didn't survive. However, at the age of 20, I did marry a 24-year-old ex-Marine who, incidentally, had received his college education under the G.I. Bill.

In the Augusta area I have two friends who were directly involved with the war. One is from England and the other from Germany. Their stories of what they suffered and survived are quite incredible . . . the terror of bombings, air raids, bomb shelters, and having to hide from the enemy. Both had to do without so many things we still had. All in all, we were very fortunate in this country because our major belief was that we would win the war. The enemy did not reach our shores even though they came close.

Karl Meschke

My dad was an area warden. I remember at least one Civil Defense blackout drill conducted in Brunswick when he was somewhat dismayed at the lack of concern exhibited by some of the neighbors. There was a persistent rumor that one or more local residents supplied diesel oil and other supplies to German submarines by shrimp boat. The Glynco blimp hangers under construction stood out on the skyline, particularly from the causeway. They were reported to be among the largest (some said the largest) wooden buildings in the world at that time.

Glynn Academy dropped inter-high school football in 1943. The official reason given was gas rationing and the difficulty in traveling to other cities for games. A much more plausible explanation was that Coach "Red" Adams was called to active duty in the Navy and the only available replacement could in no way control a group of rowdy seniors who would graduate in 1944. Fortunately for the succeeding classes, football was reinstated in 1944 when Coach Page was hired. Even in 1944, however, the team had to travel in private cars to the first couple of games. This was discontinued when one of the players had a wreck on the way to Valdosta and another of the drivers (not a player) got drunk on the way home. It was suddenly decided that gas could be made available for a school bus to transport the team after all.

Several boys our age did some tree planting during the war because no one else was available. The trees were planted on Brunswick Pulp and Paper land in 1944 by Billy Meyers, John Morris, Chip Daniels, one of the Fendigs, and me. Like so many others, we planted a large victory garden in a vacant lot on Magnolia Avenue. We grew corn, tomatoes, beans, onions, cabbage, peas, and cucumbers. We supplied many neighbors with fresh vegetables, and my mother spent hours canning the surplus.

A hurricane hit Glynn County in mid-October 1944. This was long before they named hurricanes after either women or men, so it had no official name, but it did considerable damage. The storm added an extra six feet to high tides and broke loose a Coast Guard boat from the station on Gascoigne Bluff on St. Simons Island and beached it next to the recreation building at Howard Coffin Park in Brunswick. They had to bring in a dredge to refloat it. The Navy apparently knew that the storm was coming and evacuated the blimps and planes. Most civilians had very little warning, and I remember that we went to school at 9 a.m. only to be sent home within an hour or so. Trees were blown down, roofs were blown off, power was off in some areas for a couple of days, the Glynco hangers were damaged, and many parts of the city were flooded. Some of the areas where the temporary war apartments were located did not have adequate drainage and suffered from high water.

Gun Cotton Cordite

During the war the Brunswick Pulp and Paper Company actually produced some "gun cotton" cordite for conversion to explosives. Gun cotton, or cordite, is made by treating cellulose with a mixture of nitric and sulfuric acids. Before World War II, it was made almost exclusively from cotton linters (hence the name) but they became scarce and substitutes were sought. Wood pulp is a somewhat cruder form of cellulose than cotton, but it was found to be satisfactory if the nitrating process was modified. The baled pulp was shipped from Brunswick to another location and converted. It is my understanding that it was not a major factor in the production of this explosive but was a wartime expedient.

John B. Morris

I remember long before Pearl Harbor riding my bicycle to the south end of Brunswick (we called it the Sugar Docks then), going aboard a Japanese freighter that was loading scrap iron to take back to Japan (for later use against the U.S., I imagine!), and talking with some difficulty with a friendly seaman who gave me some printed material—all in Japanese! I wrote in my diary on December 7, 1941: "The dirty Japs attacked Pearl Harbor today. We will get them!"

A German canon on big wheels sat as a monument to World War I in the public square near the intersection of Newcastle and Mansfield Streets. Sometime during World War II it was taken off its pedestal with some ceremony and was supposedly sent off to be melted down for the war effort. The war had ended when I next came upon it all mixed in with debris on some vacant lot near Gloucester Street and the waterfront. It never made it into the war effort!

I was a member of a junior Civil Air Patrol group. I don't recall what we did, but I was proud of my khaki uniform, complete with a cap and an Army-style belt buckle! I remember going on my bicycle down the alley behind the Edo Miller Funeral Home and looking in with dismay at the charred bodies that had been picked up from a submarine-sunk Allied freighter. (Actually, I didn't hang around long enough to be sure whether these gruesome remains were friend or foe!) I was thrilled to go on the trial run of a Liberty ship at the Brunswick Shipyard because of a very friendly gentleman whose name I've forgotten. The J. A. Jones Construction Company had fully taken over the old Sugar Dock area and had its enormous gantry cranes up in the sky quite visible when one would drive as far as one could without security clearance at the south end of town.

"The cannons that were landmarks on the front lawn of the Strachan residence on St. Simons were donated to the government for scrap metal."

Eleanor Smith Gathright

SEA WALL

The seawall protecting the King and Prince Hotel was built early on during World War II by the U. S. Navy, which had taken over the hotel as housing for the officers of the Radar Training Station located at the St. Simons Airport. Without it the hotel would probably have been lost to erosion. While stone has been added subsequently, the Navy-built wall is still the main part of the tidal defense there.

NAVAL AIR STATION

I worked one summer at the post exchange at the St. Simons Naval Air Station where the radar training took place. My menial job was at the lunch counter—preparing huge vats of egg salad, forming hamburger patties, and making other tasty morsels! During this period my mother was employed as a secretary in one of the base offices and we drove over from Brunswick to work each day.

BEAUS

I remember being favorably impressed and liking two of my mother's beaus who came calling at our home in Brunswick (my father had died when I was a baby). One was a master sergeant from Camp Stewart, and he had an elegant antique convertible car I liked to ride in. At another period, there was the Marine Corps major who had me visit him for several days at Paris Island, where I became convinced I wanted to grow up to be a major in the Marines! I think Major Fuller was later lost in action. My sister, being five years older than I, had visits from gentlemen friends in the service. They would sit out on our front porch whilst I remained hidden behind the drapes of some nearby window!

HOMING PIGEONS

I raised homing pigeons in our backyard at 1103 Egmont Street, having been guided in their care by Sidney Nathan. After the war, the Navy at the Glynco Naval Air Station gave me a lot of pigeons they no longer needed. During hostilities they daily took a cage with two homing pigeons to the Brunswick waterfront so that shrimp boats that had no radios could send messages back about submarine sightings.

REV. LEE A. BELFORD

I was sad when the rector of St. Mark's Episcopal Church in Brunswick, the Rev. Lee A. Belford, went off to war as a chaplain in the U.S. Navy. He had been an important influence on me in my impressionable early teens . . . and many years later it meant a lot to me that he was a participant with me in a church-sponsored civil rights witness in Mississippi in 1961. Lee had been designated to serve as one who most likely would not be arrested . . . so that, as in earlier years, he once again was my pastor, visiting those of us Episcopal clergy who were in the Jackson City Jail. Finally, I remember when Franklin Roosevelt died in 1945 while the war was still going on. I was in tears . . . never having known any other president.

James (Sonny) Miller
Sonny Miller's father owned Edo Miller Funeral Home in Brunswick.

On December 7, 1941, I was lying on the floor reading the funnies when my dad heard about Pearl Harbor. I didn't understand why all at once all the young men were gone and there were only kids, women, and old men. I worked at the Edo Miller Funeral Home and saw the workers at the shipyard sleep in shifts with each having his own bedclothes. I saw this on many of the ambulance calls.

They sank a German submarine and brought to my dad some letters they found that were written in German to see if he could read them. He was born in Germany, but he couldn't read them since he left Germany when he was seven years old. He got Philip Kulman to read them. The FBI was involved in this investigation. On VJ Day, my uncle burned a casket on Newcastle Street. It set the asphalt on the street on fire but nobody cared.

Julian Cason

I have lived in Brunswick and on St. Simons all my life. During the war, my mother took in boarders, mostly kin, from nearby farm areas. My dad worked for the Brunswick Pulp and Paper Company and was a volunteer airplane spotter. I remember climbing the fire tower (110 feet high, I believe) where Dad would record all aircraft flying within our range of vision, with type, direction of flight, time, etc. Some of the things I remember most are the rationing of various items, such as shoes, sugar, tires, and gasoline. I also recall the tremendous lines at the Ritz Theatre, which was open around the clock for a short while during the war years. The blackout curtains, air-raid drills, and 9 p.m. curfew cannot be left out. It still amazes me when I recall all the temporary housing that was thrown together, seemingly overnight, while the Liberty ships were being built almost as rapidly.

Bill Spaulding

I was born and raised in Brunswick. After high school graduation in 1948, I went into military service and did not return to Brunswick to live. At age 11, I didn't fully recognize the impact on my family and their lives that World War II would have. My eldest brother had joined the Marine Corps in 1939 and was in service at the time of our entry into the war. My other brother, older than I, enlisted in the Navy immediately after the attack on Pearl Harbor.

Air-raid drills were immediately begun in all residential and business areas. We had air-raid wardens assigned to each residential block, and their duties were to make certain that all houses were blacked-out during these practice sessions. All curtains were drawn and all non-essential lights in the house were darkened. All street lights in Brunswick had a shield installed on the east side of the light to prevent light from shining towards the ocean. All auto headlights were painted black with only a small rectangular opening in the middle of the headlight. This

Battle Hymn of the Republic (Tune)

I can see the bombs and bullets that our bonds have bought today. They will help defeat the Axis and their vicious, wicked ways. So we cannot cease our buying or our working night and day, We've got to win this war!

was to prevent excessive light escaping into the night sky. I was a volunteer aircraft spotter. I was trained to spot enemy aircraft (German and Japanese) and was assigned specific daylight hours each week to go up into the forest fire spotter tower between Arco and Dock Junction and look for enemy aircraft. This was sponsored by the Boy Scouts. I rode my bicycle from home to the fire tower.

With the torpedoing of the two tankers off the coast of St. Simons, the beaches were closed until the oil and human remains could be cleared. Cars were allowed to drive on the St. Simons beaches in those days, and the entrance onto the beach was on the right side of the pier. All car traffic and swimming were suspended for a few months. One of the tankers was towed and anchored in the sound between St. Simons and Jekyll Islands. A friend and I would sail out and inspect the tanker. The starboard side of the bow had a gaping hole that we could almost sail into, but didn't.

The rationing of gasoline and tires cut heavily into the amount of traffic in Glynn County. We had a 1935 Chevrolet and used it only on special occasions. Most all other occasions we walked or rode bicycles. This was a time of self-sacrifice and most of us age 11 through 14 were in the same boat and didn't mind the difficulties. Rationing limits, the best as I remember, were two pairs of shoes a year, two tires a year, one pound of sugar per month for each family, one pound of coffee per month, limited meat, and limited can goods. Even though candy bars were not rationed, they were very hard to find.

War bonds were the area where civilians could help the war effort. Buy bonds! In school, we could buy war bond stamps each week Hollywood stars would travel the country promoting their purchase. Veronica Lake, a big name in Hollywood in the early 1940s, included Brunswick in her tour. The whole city turned out to see her. One drive to help the war effort was for aluminum. Every citizen was asked to donate all aluminum for the war. My mother donated all her aluminum pots and pans and I remember how proud I was of her for this.

Some friends and I would hitchhike to St. Simons during the summer months of 1944-1946. We would ride bicycles to the toll house on the causeway, park our bicycles in the grass, and walk across the toll bridge. Pedestrians were charged 10 cents. After paying our toll, we would hitch a ride with the first car that would stop. Auto traffic was slow due to gas rationing, and many times it was slow going in order to swim at the beach.

Hollis Cate

Because of the war and the influx of people to the shipyard, I met the girl (Mary Boone) I was to marry several years after the war. There were many others who met and married under the same circumstances. In 1943 there was no organized high school football. But we did play six-man football. I remember going to Darien to play the team from MacIntosh County. We played our home games on the field behind old Prep High School. The six-man format was a direct result of the war. In 1944 Glynn Academy resumed regular football.

I associate many songs with that time: "I'll Be Seeing You," "Kiss Me Once and Kiss Me Twice," "Don't Sit Under the Apple Tree," and "This Is the Army, Mr. Jones." There was a sadness about them, a focus on lovers separated by the war. The Andrews Sisters belted out many of them. After they recorded "Drinking Rum and Coca-Cola," the sale of rum went up manyfold across the country. I also remember the song "Lucky Strike Green Has Gone to War" (Lucky Strike was a brand of cigarettes).

The car headlights were painted black half way down . . . and "save that tinfoil" . . . gas rationing stamps were pasted on windshields . . . not much sugar: "put in one teaspoon and stir like hell!" . . . even leather "went to war." What a time that was! A blink of the eye in terms of history, but I'll never forget it.

Thora Olsen Kimsey and Sonja Olsen Kinard

A STORY SHARED

A story was related to us about a utilities transmission engineer whose territory included Brunswick. One day when he was in Savannah he received a call to go to Jekyll Island immediately. A cable had been cut. He and his assistant had portable two-way radios. They hooked up a two-way radio in their truck and headed for Brunswick. At that time, the English were using radar rather successfully. The Germans were trying hard to get it. The Americans had radar but in a very crude form. At that time, the extent to which radar could be used was to locate a ship "in line" but not to tell how far it was. To get that information required triangulation. Radar points were set up at Mayport, Florida, and Jekyll Island and Tybee Island, Georgia. The middle one at Jekyll was where the cable had been cut. The cable, of course, came back and tied into a telephone line.

Jekyll was in the engineer's territory, and it was his responsibility to fix the section on Jekyll. Therefore, he and his helper went down to set up one end of it. His helper set up what was called the "land line" on the Brunswick side. A man who had been cutting right-of-way for many years had a barge/lighter that was secured to carry the radio equipment to Jekyll. At that time there was no bridge to Jekyll. The engineer and the captain of the barge left in the late afternoon for Jekyll. By the time they reached the Jekyll dock, it was totally dark.

At Jekyll, the captain and the engineer unloaded the equipment onto the dock. As he would be working in the marsh, the engineer was dressed in rough clothing. Engrossed in the technical aspect of his mission, he started walking up toward the location of the radar point. As he was stumbling in the dark, he felt cold steel on his neck. It was a guard. The engineer, afraid this was a trigger-happy G.I. who was going to shoot his head off before he could turn around, put up his hands. His clothing, the fact that it was night time, and no one knew he was coming made it look like he was a saboteur. This radar point on Jekyll was one of the most secretive things that the government had at that time. He finally talked the guard into letting him put his hands down. When he started to identify himself, he realized that he didn't have any identification on him . . . and he was not in uniform!

East Side, West Side (Tune)

War bonds! War bonds! All around the town
The banker and Mrs. O'Grady's income up and spending's down!
But when the war is over, me and a few million more
Will have more spending money than we've every had before.

At last, he was able to convince the others who had joined the group to go with him back down on the dock. He showed them the equipment and what he was going to do. They actually helped him to install with the main line the two-way radio so that he could communicate with the mainland. In about two or three days, the construction department came and laid another cable.

In the early part of the war, the Hercules Powder Company was making components for explosives while continuing to manufacture naval stores from crushed pine tree stumps. During the war, business ballooned, doubled or tripled. The utilities company had an old PBX (exchange) to take care of all the telephone lines at the Hercules, but then it grew so rapidly and they had to do something in a hurry. The utilities company had to move in with the latest telephone equipment. It was called a step-by-step office. It is not used anymore, but in those days it was the best thing available.

There was another person in Brunswick who served in a supervisory capacity for this installation, and both were at the Hercules often to see that it was wired correctly. While this was going on, it was natural that the Hercules workers were interested in what they were doing. As they drifted by the installation during their lunch break, some would ask, "What are you people doing?" One particular fellow was more interested than others. The telephone people recalled the guy coming by and asking questions that were more technical. It was obvious the guy was smart and knew something about electronics. He impressed them and came more often than the others. Each time he wanted to know more and more. All of a sudden, he didn't come by anymore. They figured he had gotten drafted and thought no more of him.

Red Light District?

One Monday on one of his trips to Brunswick, the engineer, as usual, was traveling with a construction crew. They would do what they called "cruise the lines" to locate problems. Just south of Savannah there was a Bamboo Garden. Across from the Bamboo Garden was what in those days was called a tourist court. They had about six or eight rooms where you could sleep. Their telephones were what were called "farmer lines" with as many as eight people on one line (party lines). There was a telephone in the office of the tourist court, and on the outside was a private pay telephone. Anyone could use this pay phone. As the crew came along on this particular day, the telephone pole, which was right by the entrance, had a red light near its top. It looked like someone had put it up there to guide folks to come into the tourist court. That light was an "unauthorized attachment," not allowed because it was a hazard to any telephone man who climbed the pole. If it had been a 110 volt, the linemen could get shocked. The crew knocked the light off and proceeded to Brunswick. They spent a week in Brunswick. Coming back on Friday, they noticed the red light was on the pole again. This time, they knocked it off and took the light with them.

The next morning, the big boss of the utility called the engineer into his office in Savannah. He was introduced to a stranger who started by saying, "I know that you are a loyal citizen," then went into stating the engineer's age, how long he had been with the company, and many other things. But the information he was conveying that caught the engineer's attention was when he told him he had a radio-telephone license #_____. Not a soul in this world knew that number at that time except the federal government and the Office of Strategic Services (OSS), predecessor to the CIA.

Then the man asked the engineer point-blank, "Would you tap a telephone line if you felt it would be to the benefit of your country?" Since 1929, that was a cardinal sin at the telephone company! You did not tap telephone lines unless you had a court order. The engineer knew this. With his boss standing there, he didn't know what in the world to do. Finally he said, "I think I am entitled to know why you asked me that question." The man said that he was with the OSS. He added, "We know a man out at the tourist court who works at the shipyard in Savannah is making a lot of calls to New York. We think that he is reporting the ships going out as they go down the ways." Then the OSS man laughed and said, "The next time you go by that telephone pole, don't rip that red light off. There is, we think, a spy staying in one of the cabins near the pole. There is a little hair wire up the back of the pole. You keep coming along and knocking it off. The light is nothing but a bluff. It isn't even hooked up. The idea is that if anybody sees the little wire, they will think it is just to the red light to guide people to the tourist court. But that hair wire is a tap into the telephone line and every time you go by you are tearing it down."

The reason that the OSS man had known so much classified information about the engineer was because at one time the engineer had worked with the OSS in Augusta. The OSS was monitoring the phone calls of the man at the tourist court. Every time he called, he called a different pay station. The contact in New York moved around from place to place. In the meantime, the spy started calling Jacksonville pay stations. Finally, a surveillance was put on a suspect in Jacksonville and a record was obtained of the pay stations he used. The suspect was a bellhop at the Seminole Hotel in Jacksonville. He was the same guy who had asked all those questions at the Hercules in Brunswick.

The crux of the whole thing was when the spy, a German, finally got the last or most important communiqué from the suspect in Jacksonville. The Germans were sending in a rubber-bottom boat from a U-boat with four men to land in the Mayport area. They were coming in at night. The suspect had been signaling from the top of the Seminole Hotel to German U-boats. He was to supply two cars for the four men. The Germans did not know it, but there were more soldiers waiting for them to come in than you could shake a stick at. The Germans came in on the boat but were not arrested. The OSS wanted to find out what it was all about. The four German saboteurs who had landed were on a mission to poison the water supply in New York City. When they got ashore, they split up and left in two cars. One car went up the coastal highway to New York and the other went into Alabama and up that way. The idea was that if one was caught, the other could get through. What they didn't know was that by tapping them, the OSS knew who the guy in New York was and had him under surveillance. When they arrived in New York, they all were arrested. There was never anything mentioned about this because the government didn't want anyone to know.*

THE BLIMP BASE

The engineer was often at the blimp base in Brunswick. Once he saw a little plane take off and land inside the hanger. The hangers were very large and held from four to six blimps. The blimps patrolled from Mayport, Florida, to Savannah looking for the German U-boats that lurked along the Eastern Seaboard. Many ships had been sunk, but most before the blimps were put into service.

Patrolling in a blimp could at times be boring. They were very slow-moving aircraft and could not outrun any enemy craft. They did carry depth charges, but they were offensive crafts, not defensive. Once north of Brunswick and south of Savannah the crew on a blimp saw a German U-boat that had surfaced. It was having mechanical difficulties and could not submerge. It was a sitting duck. The crew on the blimp immediately took position to drop depth charges. The mechanism jammed and they couldn't drop anything. They were shot down by the Germans, but not before they got a radio message off. A destroyer based in Savannah was dispatched to the area where the submarine was and, according to the engineer's story, captured it intact. No one ever talked about it. His understanding was that the U-boat was taken to Savannah and then to Charleston. The U.S. military was extremely glad to get the sub intact.

SHIPYARD

The shipyard was the biggest thing that ever happened to Brunswick. The problem was that it was wartime and they had a war schedule. Things had to get done yesterday. When the telephone company went in to put in communications under normal conditions, engineers visited the site and drew plans. Usually, it was a long, drawn-out, detailed job taking all the specifications into account. The same with the power company. But all of a sudden, the shipyard was being installed, and they were saying, "Everybody get down here right now and do the job." So what the engineer did was get a tractor with a big subsoiler type plow behind it with a cable reel. They just took out across nowhere putting the cable in. Normally you had drawings and knew where the cable was. Nobody knew where the cable was except the engineer and his crew. It was all right and it worked. However, after the shipyard was there for a while, the cable went open.

If something goes wrong with a wire on a pole, it can be seen, but if the wire is underground that is another problem, and a bigger problem if it is open. If the wire is in a sheath, the engineers can tell when the wires get crossed because it can be measured and located. However, if the wire was open, there was no way to measure it. To top it off, if was under the J. A. Jones shipyard. This young Thomas Edison, however, had designed a capacity measurement device. Sending out his crew, they were able to measure the capacity between the wires. He hadn't missed it very far.

* The *Atlanta Journal* -July 12, 1997 "Obituary of Dallas Mobley" - Dallas Mobley was an FBI agent during World War II. "He made the arrest of George Dasch, one of several German spies who landed on the east coast by submarine, buried their uniforms in the sand and went to New York, purportedly to poison the water supply." This statement verifies our contributor's story.

Frances Stewart Smitherman

I was from Miami, Florida, but Dad had a farm in Quitman, Georgia. He decided to go to Quitman and farm, so he sold his house. The Depression came and he didn't have the five hundred dollars that he owed on his property. The bank was going to take his stock and everything. Daddy asked this old tenant farmer, "You got five hundred dollars?" "Yeah, I sure do, but I need it," the man said. "Do you want everything I have . . . lock, stock and barrel?" Daddy asked. Daddy sold the land to the tenant farmer. The bank said, "You can't do that." Daddy said, "I can. It's done!" You see, there was a catch in the deed that said you couldn't sell the timber until the land was paid off. If Daddy could have sold the timber, he could have saved his farm. That's the way the bank got the land every time. They got the deed from the bank and the bank was really mad about it. The tenant farmer became rich when the Depression was over. He could sell the timber off the land because it was paid off in cash.

I was six years old when we moved from Quitman to Brunswick during the Depression. Mother had a brother who lived in Brunswick. An aunt by marriage had this little house, and we lived there with her. Dad was able to keep his car. He made the back end of it into a truck. He bought vegetables and peddled them until he got a job at the Hercules. Then we moved out to this little farm on the Darien Highway.

When World War II started, they built the blimp base right across from us. It was not a mile from our house. Blimps and airplanes flew right over our house night and day and made a lot of racket. I saw some prisoners of war inside a barbed-wire fence at the blimp base. They were good-looking men! A German submarine was blown up about six or seven miles off St. Simons. I remember planes were flying over our house one night and we heard the bombs hitting, but we didn't know what they were. You know, water carries sound and Dad owned up to half the river behind him. The only reason I knew about it was because my sister-in-law's daddy went down to get whatever was useable off the ship. The men were dead.

You couldn't walk down the street in Brunswick for the sailors. They would walk up to you and ask you for a date. I wanted to date, but my dad wouldn't let me. I was too young.

Working for the Telephone Company

When I was 16 years old, I quit school and went to work for the telephone company. I used to catch the Greyhound bus into work. We had to wear a band on our arm and sign an oath that we would go to work regardless of whether we were bombed or not. Because aircraft information went through phone lines, you often had to disconnect someone in the middle of a conversation to allow the aircraft information to get through. They didn't have all the modern equipment they have now. You got fired and fined ten thousand dollars if you listened in on a conversation. The telephone company bought a Liberty ship. The employees paid for it. They took the money out of my check because I signed up for it. Everyone at work did that.

Tangled Blimp Lines

We were sound asleep about two o'clock one morning when a blimp got too low and its lines got tangled in our pecan trees. You've never heard such cursing in all your life! The lights were shining all through our house and Daddy was afraid they were going to knock our house down. A blimp is a big thing! It was about three hours before they got the ropes loose. I don't know how. All I remember is all the lights and cursing.

Why Did You Shoot My Wing?

I remember a little red plane that looked for fires used to fly over our house. It flew so low the noise would knock the shingles loose and scare our chickens. One day Daddy got the shotgun and shot a hole in the wing of the plane. The plane landed over in the field and the man said, "Why did you shoot my wing?" Daddy said, "You are shaking shingles off my house and scaring my chickens." The man said, "I won't do it any more if you won't shoot at me any more." Daddy said, "That's a deal!"

London C. Roberts, Sr.

My brother and I were born in the house that my dad and uncles built on the corner of Norwich and Seventh Streets in Brunswick in 1924. The house is still in use but has been moved to a new location. After building our home, my father became a painter and for several years worked for the Sea Island Company. In later years, he formed a business of floor laying, sanding, and finishing. Prior to December 1941 he bought a new red Chevrolet sedan delivery truck for his work and it cost a whopping $995. I was not quite 12 years old when the Japanese bombed Pearl Harbor on December 7, 1941. I remember the family gathering around the radio and listening to this horrible deed. When the shipyard was built in the Brunswick harbor, my dad got the contract to sand and finish the huge room called the lay-out room. It was tremendous. I helped after school and on weekends because help was hard to find.

Brunswick was wall-to-wall people with the shipyard working 24 hours a day. After the war got into full swing and factories converted to making war products, candy, cosmetics, and other items became scarce. Due to the lack of sugar, my mother substituted syrup for sugar in her coffee. I always loved Hershey bars and pineapple, but I could never find any. When they built a huge mess hall at the airport on St. Simons, my dad got the job of sanding and finishing that room. I was helping on that job also, and one day I saw some candy bars in the PX. I asked a sailor who was helping with the floor work if he could get me some Hershey bars. He got me a box of 24. I thought I had gone to heaven!

Mary Ann Whilden Moore

At the beginning of the war, Brunswick was a sleepy little village, hard hit by the Depression. With the war and the coming of the J. A. Jones Shipyard, however, Brunswick's population exploded. There were so many workers that the banks could not handle all the payroll checks that needed cashing. The merchants began handling the overflow. Every Friday morning Daddy, who owned Whilden's Shoe Store, got $3,000 or more from the bank, and every Friday afternoon we cashed checks until late in the evening. There were such throngs that Momma and I stood at the front door until the store reached capacity, then we locked it. The rest waited patiently for their turns.

Everything was in short supply and there wasn't much for the workers to spend their money on, but they all wanted to buy something . . . socks, handkerchiefs, hosiery, billfolds, shoes, anything. My grandmother sewed men's boxer underwear from flour sacks or whatever cloth she could find. We sold as many as she could make. The workers were on shifts, so there were people on the streets at all hours. We lay in bed listening to the "Your Weight and Fate" penny-scale go *ding-ding-ding* all night long. Most commodities were diverted to the military, and to civilians, they were rationed: sugar, coffee, gasoline, meat, leather shoes. An interesting alternative to leather shoes was made with cloth uppers and soles of wooden dowels sliced lengthwise and glued on the bottoms. Those shoes did some interesting things when it rained.

There was never enough capacity of services for the workers. All the schools went to double sessions, morning and afternoon. I loved the afternoon schedule. I could sleep late, play until noon, go to school with my chums for four hours, and still have time to listen to my favorite serial programs on the radio.

The newcomers who worked in war-related industries were of all types . . . good and bad. A little girl was reported missing, and half the population, it seemed, turned out to find her. Cars were parked everywhere around a field or wooded area. Men were walking in lines so as to cover all the area. Daddy took Momma and me there. He helped search but made us stay in the car. Somebody found the girl, who had been sexually assaulted and murdered. Some things don't change.

A young man brought a war souvenir into downtown Brunswick one day. It was a hand grenade. He took it into Floyd's Barber Shop next door to our store and was tossing it up in the air and catching it. The barbers panicked and ordered him out. He left and walked on down the sidewalk. When he reached Cohen's Department Store, two doors down from us, something went wrong. The grenade exploded and blew out the entire front of Cohen's store and damaged windows up and down the street. The mannequins in Cohen's window looked like they had been in the war. It was amazing, but the young man lived. Of course, his hands were never the same again.

The shipyard built Liberty ships, which hauled war materials to the war zones. Merchants who bought war bonds were invited to a maiden voyage of one of the ships. Daddy went, but I don't think he enjoyed it much, especially the food. He was seasick all day! When near the end of the war President Roosevelt died, ordinary people on Newcastle Street had tears running down their cheeks. As a child, I had thought Roosevelt always would be there. Momma and I were in the Fox Theater in Atlanta when the war ended. The lights came on and the announcement of VJ Day was made over the public address system. We all stood up and cheered. I don't recall anyone watching the rest of the movie. We went out on the street where buildings had emptied of people who were dancing with joy, and we joined in. Thank God it was over!

Mildred Jenkins Kicklighter

My dad, S. O. Jenkins, came to Brunswick in 1929 to open a restaurant and tourist cabins. He built a garage with a filling station next door to it. I was born on the spot where our business is still located (4262 Norwich Street) and have lived here all my life. This used to be Highway 17 and the main route to Florida.

The word that comes to mind at the mention of World War II is *fear*. The men were going to war and the women were going to work. I was 10 years old in 1941 and afraid that my dad would be called to go, but because I would have been alone, he was deferred. My after-school job became selling cold drinks and cashiering in our station. It was my job to stick the gas ration stamps on sheets so that we could buy more gas to sell. The shipyard workers stopped for gas and cold drinks after work. We also cashed checks for them. The city bus ran from Dock Junction to town every 30 minutes. Most everyone went to town on Saturday. A movie for a dime was a real treat.

Jacqueline Baumgartner Walker

The years 1941 through 1944 bring many memories of my childhood between the ages of six and ten. My parents, Jack and Miriam Baumgartner, owned the Parmelee Restaurant in the 1500 block of Newcastle Street in Brunswick near the Ritz Theater and the pool room. Some of my earliest memories of Newcastle Street were singing with the Salvation Army in the park. My parents worked day and night in their restaurant because it was one of the few local restaurants in that area that could serve the shipyard workers and the military bases. Many wives of servicemen worked for my parents so that they could be near their husbands while they were stationed at Glynco. The Lafayette Grill, Rogers' Drug Store, and Denny's Bar were other restaurants that were nearby.

Our family home was at 304 Albany Street and the shipyard was just three blocks away. The trains ran day and night behind our house. My father's three acres of land behind our home was confiscated by the federal government for the rest of the war for the sum of one dollar per year, and "war apartments" were built on this land. During the hurricane of 1944, many families came into our home due to the flooding of their apartments.

Downtown Brunswick, Georgia
Corner of Newcastle and
Gloucester Streets
Courtesy of Georgia State Archives

At the Sidney Lanier School, the children were taught every patriotic song of each military service. Pictures of Roosevelt, Stalin, and Churchill hung in our classrooms. I cannot keep a dry eye to this day when I sing "God Bless America" or "The Star Spangled Banner." My first-grade teacher, Miss Lois Bowen, used to bring us candy treats from her father's country store. I am sure that I join hundreds of Brunswick-area folks with memories of candy shortages, blackened headlights, clear flashlight bulbs painted with red fingernail polish for Christmas tree decorations (no more German ornaments available), and rationing coupons for shoes, sugar, butter, and meat.

One of the greatest childhood memories of those years was when our family received a Gold Star for our window because my mother's brother, Erin Parmelee, was killed in the Navy battle of the Coral Sea. Perhaps the one great impression that I remember was on display under the large oak tree in the middle of Gloucester Street between Rogers' Drug Store and Holiday's Drug Store. It was a one- or two-man German submarine that had been captured off the coast. It made all my fears of an enemy invasion so real.

Gloria Smith Ramsaur

Before my daddy, Ralph M. Smith, and mother were married, Daddy spent his summer vacations training with the cavalry at Fort Bragg, North Carolina. After they were married in 1932, Daddy continued to train with what he called the Home Guard. During World War II he was a member of the Georgia State Guard.

Blackouts began along the coast of Georgia. These were signaled by an air-raid whistle. Daddy would have to change quickly into uniform and report to the armory. When those whistles blew, I remember Mother would say we had just so many minutes to have the house in total darkness. We stayed in complete darkness until an all-clear whistle blew.

One night two oil tankers were torpedoed off Sea Island. Eventually one was towed to the Atlantic Refining Company docks on the Turtle River. My parents went out to see it. That day Dad brought home a piece of shrapnel from the German torpedo. Our three sons used it for show and tell when they studied World War II in school. Mother stated how the crews of the tankers were rescued and brought into Brunswick, how they were fed, clothed, and given housing by local officials. She has often told us that she had been sewing the night the ships were torpedoed and had left a spool of thread on the mantle.

**Above left:
Schrapnel from one of the oil tankers torpedoed off the Georgia Coast.**
Tanker was towed to the Atlantic Refining Company Docks where Ralph Smith obtained the schrapnel.
Courtesy of Gloria Smith Ramsaur

**Above right:
Civil Defense Arm Bands, Ration Book and 1930's radio**
Courtesy of Gloria Smith Ramsaur

The next morning the spool was on the floor—knocked off by the vibrations of the explosions, she has always believed.

Marjorie Few Mitchell

I was 11 years old on that fateful Sunday afternoon when we received news of the bombing of Pearl Harbor. I was in Ward's Drugstore on St. Simons Island when the announcement came on the radio. I don't remember any particular emotion other than shock. The war per se didn't involve me to any great degree. I had no relatives who were called to serve their country and the side effects, such as rationing and blackouts, were only minor happenings in my world. One of the most poignant memories was when we were having bond drives locally and Veronica Lake, a popular movie star of that time, was to be in the parade. I had missed band practice that week and I was not allowed to march with the band in the parade.

My grandparents owned a music store in Brunswick, and I remember my grandfather's telling about a man who was working at the shipyard. He was a Georgia farmer who had never had much cash to spend and now he was making a huge amount of money. He came in the store and bought the most expensive guitar in the store. Then he proceeded to take it outside and wrap it around a lamp post. He said he had always wanted to do that!

Marvin Bluestein

Marvin Bluestein was in the amphibious forces in Europe during World War II. He later went on a destroyer and was in the carrier force in the Pacific. His father, Benjamin, was from Russia and was born into the bakery business in Europe. He came to Darien, Georgia, because he had a brother there. Marvin's mother, Sadie, and Benjamin met and married in Darien. They moved to Brunswick about 1916 and opened a bakery.

My parents owned the Vienna Bakery at 1616 Newcastle Street in Brunswick. Their bread was named "Aunt Betty's Bread." My dad had passed away many years before World War II, and my mother ran the bakery. My brother and I worked there. The shipyard was just being

The Brunswick News, March 3, 1942

Vienna Bakery
1616 Newcastle St.
Phone 376

WE DELIVER

Delicious Raisin Bran Muffin,
doz..20c

Potato Doughnuts, a real treat
doz..20c

Devil Food
Layers..25c

Devil Cup Cakes
doz..30c

Hot rolls... twice daily
doz..11c

Hot Breads, 6 o'clock each
evening..11c

built when I went into service. My brother was there about a year after I went into service and experienced some of what was happening at that time. My mother use to write and tell me about it.

The war had quite an effect on the bakery. The amount of material (sugar, flour, gasoline, etc.) my mother could get for the bakery was based on five previous years of volume. Then they rationed her a percentage of that. Of course, the population of Brunswick grew from fifteen thousand to sixty thousand plus. People use to call her at night trying to get bread and pastries. People actually got mad at her because she did not have the bakery goods for them. So she got in touch with the people in Washington, told them her problem, and they arranged to get her a considerable amount of rationing coupons to ease the situation. It is interesting how she went about this. My mother always believed in going right to the top. She went to Abe Nathan, who was her lawyer, and asked him to make a phone call. He was a little surprised. He said, "Call? Why don't you make your own phone call?" She said, "I want you to call President Roosevelt." They put in a call to the president. They didn't get him, but they got some man in the White House. She explained her plight to him and that call brought immediate results. She got lots of rationing coupons.

Agnes Maddison Floyd

My family moved to Brunswick sometime in the 1920s. My father worked for the Gulf Refinery and traveled from Savannah on an oil tanker as a marine engineer to Texas and other points. He began working at the Hercules Powder Company in the late Twenties and our family moved to the Urbana area to be near his work. I was born in 1930, and the family had moved to the south end of town. My father had obtained transportation by that time.

During the war years, my father was the president of the Rationing Board and had to make decisions when people applied for extra ration stamps for medical or other reasons . . . these could be for gas, sugar, shoes, tires, or other items. This was a voluntary position and the clerks that were in the office were paid. My father continued his job at Hercules and had to car pool and pick up other workers. Women became a part of the Hercules workforce. One sister and one brother worked at the shipyard in the summers. One sister was a junior hostess at the USO on Union Street, but I was too young to do any of these things.

We lived on Union Street and had a big screened porch. We could sit on the porch night or day and see hundreds of people walking to and from work as the shifts changed at the shipyard. My mother converted two upstairs bedrooms to an apartment, and we had a couple from Virginia with a little girl live there until the end of the war.

The circus grounds on the corner of Union Street and Second Avenue were converted almost overnight with wooden war houses . . . one-, two-, and three-bedroom units, also a business center with post office, stores, library, public telephones, auditorium, and movies (almost a small city). This complex was named Mark Carr Homes and covered the area from Second Avenue to the shipyard. Most workers did not own cars, and bicycles were hard to find. I had a bicycle when I was 11

Old Gray Bonnet (Tune)

Wear your old gray bonnet with an old feather on it,
Then to Uncle Sam you can say,
Because of my bonnet with the old feather on it,
I can buy a bond today.

years old and was lucky to get it. We always walked to school. I remember the air-raid drills and the air-raid warden coming and knocking on our door because light was shining through the space between the drapes. They were not closed all the way.

Before the war you could go to downtown Brunswick and know everyone you saw. After the war began, you could go to downtown and not know anyone you saw. The downtown movies were shown night and day for the workers. We could not go to the beaches due to gas rationing and patrols by servicemen. We swam in the salt water creeks in Brunswick. We had a cousin who lived in London, England. At one time they were evacuating children, and we expected him to come and live with us. The blitz subsided somewhat, and he did not have to come and stay.

Mary Miller

My war work sounds anything but glamorous as I kept my job as a teacher in Jacksonville, Florida. So many teachers went into the armed forces or took better paying jobs in war work that it was almost impossible to keep schools open. The teachers who remained in the classroom had larger classes and extra responsibilities. Also, after school we volunteered for various tasks, such as hostessing at the USO at night.

Knock Hell Out of the Little Red Box

On Saturdays, I volunteered for the Red Cross Motor Corps. To serve, we were required to take a course in motor mechanics, which was taught by the owner of a large filling station where repairs were made on cars. We learned to make minor repairs such as changing tires. Most cars had a little red box under the hood which made a connection with the horn. Horns had a way of suddenly starting to blow. We learned how to stop them. It was simple! Open the hood, take off a shoe, and knock hell out of the little red box! Once when my car horn was blowing, I followed instructions with hood up and shoe in hand, but alas, there was no red box on my make of car!

I was assigned an ambulance in which I took various workers on errands for the Red Cross. Several times I took workers to perform the hardest job, that of notifying relatives of soldiers killed in action. We had mock air raids at night. My assignment was to pick up victims and deliver them to the hospital. We used dark red lipstick to cover the headlights and drove in almost complete darkness. Civilians kept off the streets.

Knitting was something else teachers could do. Everywhere we went, we carried our knitting. When I had coupons enough to get gas to go to Brunswick on weekends, I got yarn from the Red Cross there. Mrs. Ralph McCrary (Louise) and her sister were in charge. Our work of knitting sweaters, helmets, and scarves helped to fill the local quota in Brunswick. These Jacksonville activities were repeated in every town, in Brunswick and all small and large towns throughout the United States.

Rationing Board

When summer school vacations came, I went home to Brunswick and volunteered to be a clerk for the Ration Board. In the beginning, it was a small operation. Guy Hacket was the first head of the Brunswick Rationing Board, and Mrs. Mabel Tyson and I were the first clerks. The first summer, work was not heavy, but by the second summer more articles were rationed and a larger staff was required. Guy had resigned and been replaced by Mrs. Sereno (Grace) Norton. An office had been officially opened on F Street in one of the rooms under that side of the Oglethorpe Hotel and it remained there until the end of the war. Every summer during vacation, I worked there as the turnover was large and substitutes for sick leave or vacations were needed.

Ration boards were formed by having a board member for each commodity that was rationed. There was a chairman of the commodity with four or five helpers. Workers in the office were called clerks. Applications for the product were obtained at the office, filled out, and turned over to the panel. Members of the panel looked them over and wrote on the application the total number of coupons allotted. The clerk counted out that amount, placed it with the application, and gave the coupons to the applicant. People seldom got the total number they wanted. The clerk was present, but the panel was not when the applicant picked up the coupons. It was the clerk who was blamed and who received much abuse from the applicant when his allotment was short. One day when I went home for lunch I was really fed up and I said, "I'm tired of hearing Goddamn." My father, a perfect gentleman, said "Where did you hear that?" He insisted that I quit, but I stuck it out until the war ended.

I made enemies. A prominent businessman had asked for coupons to take his son to Chattanooga to enter school and was refused. He was furious. I said, "Why don't you put him on the train that goes directly from Brunswick to Chattanooga? He would love that and being with other boys going there." The man never forgave me as long as he lived for ever thinking his son would ride a train. Somehow he got the coupons. The man who processed the pulp mill applications accused me of lowering his application. An owner of a filling station often kept coupons out on delivery of gasoline, collected them, and sold them at a good profit. We learned a great deal about people on our jobs. My experience gave me great admiration for the British, who endured rationing for some eight years after the war and still offered their coupons for sweets to tourists.

Alice Melvin

Waiting and Rationing

The first thing that comes to mind is waiting in line for everything. Our sleepy little town suddenly had hundreds of people move in from everywhere to work in the shipyard, Hercules, and the pulp mill, to mention a few. In the grocery stores, especially the meat market, you had to pick a number and wait until your number was called to be waited on. Meat was rationed by being issued little red

Tokens, Gas Rationing Card and Stamps, and Food Rationing Books belonging to Mr. and Mrs. Ralph M. Smith
OPA, Office of Price Administration
Courtesy of Gloria Smith Ramsaur

numbers about the size of a dime. These and other tickets for rationed goods were issued by a board, which was located in the basement of the old Oglethorpe Hotel. You entered on the F Street side.

Nearly everything was rationed. What wasn't rationed was hard to find. Shoes that were not made of leather weren't rationed. I remember buying a pair made of a yellow linen-like material with wooden soles that would bend. We saved our shoe coupons to buy for our two little girls. I sewed a lot for the girls, and you had to be at the store when they got the material in to get any that was nice. Cloth wasn't rationed, but you had to wait in line for it. There were a couple of years that no new cars were made and no electric refrigerators. If you didn't already have a phone you were out of luck.

We did most of our grocery buying at Lovett's Grocery on Gloucester Street. Sometimes we would trade at the Community Market across from the old hospital. I don't remember if sugar was rationed, but it was hard to get. I was at a friend's house, and she had somehow gotten several five-pound bags of sugar. It was so hard she had to bang on one of the bags with a hammer to break it up. Silk hose were very hard to find. My husband, Red Smith, worked at the Oglethorpe Hotel, and some men came in selling silk hose. He bought several pairs and every time I put one on they broke out in runs all over. That was before nylon hose.

My in-laws lived on St. Simons and we went over quite often. The bridges on the causeway had boards that went clackety-clack when you drove over them. We were always stopped at the toll house and our car trunk was searched. I never knew what they were looking for. The shore patrol [Navy] did the search. Men in uniform didn't have to pay, and one of my brothers-in-law always said, "Alice, let me drive. I get a kick out of driving over that road and not paying." After years of using the causeway I guess he did feel that way.

When the shifts changed at the shipyard you couldn't get across Union Street for the traffic. A big building was built on Third Avenue and Union Street called Mark Carr Cafeteria. It was always busy. Rooming houses opened everywhere there was a house available. Rooms were rented to more than two people. Ones that worked at night slept in the bed in the day and the day shift slept at night. This doesn't sound true, but people who owned rooming houses know. Brick apartments were built all over town. They had wood-burning cookstoves and old iceboxes that had to have block ice. If you went to Glynn Ice Company to buy ice, there would be a long line of cars waiting.

A lot of the one-room apartments were built of wood. My friend Ina Hawkins came from Baxley to work in the shipyard and lived in one of the green one-room apartments that were built from Third Avenue south to the shipyard gate. Ina and her sister went to school to learn welding. She was paid 68 cents an hour while in school. Then she went to work in the yard. She was raised to number-one welder, put on

"I remember stamp books for each family member . . . meat, shoes, gas, tires . . . being unable to get stockings. The older girls put makeup on their legs and drew a line down the back of their legs with an eyebrow pencil to look like a seam. (In those days, all stockings had a seam down the back and there were no pantyhose.)"

Eleanor Smith Gathright

the platens, and raised to $1.27 an hour to start. Her sister had the most footage in welding and was chosen to sponsor the first Liberty ship; Ina was co-sponsor.

Ina described the one-room apartment. There were long buildings with several apartments in each with centrally located wash houses with wash tubs and rub boards (no washing machines) for the renters. I guess the first ones there got to wash their clothes first (by hand). In the apartment she had a hot plate with an oven to cook on. When she got off work at 11:30 p.m., she would walk the 20 or so blocks to the movies at the Ritz Theater. Some people would go to the movies and stay all night to have a place to sleep.

The Oglethorpe Hotel was a very busy place. Mrs. Gardner, the owner, had the old ballroom on the south end of the hotel remodeled into a club with a circular bar, a bandstand, and a live orchestra at night. The shore patrol patrolled that area all the time. My husband was the bartender, along with Arthur Deloach and, sometimes, Jack Gardner.

After a ship was launched it had to go out in the sound for a trial run. We use to go down to the pier on St. Simons and watch them come in. My brother-in-law, Joe Smith, and his friend Joe Reddish were chefs on these trial runs. One time after they got offshore, a very dense fog rolled in and they had to wait to get back in.

Dororthy Deaver Fiveash

Brunswick was always my home, and I lived there until I married Charlie Fiveash. I graduated from Glynn Academy in 1942 and worked for the Housing Authority during the war. There were a lot of farmers who thought they could make a lot of money working at the shipyard, so they came to live in Brunswick. There was no housing. The government took over all the empty lots in the city and put up some brick housing for the people. The houses had cement floors and wood stoves to heat with and cook on. I worked in one of the project's offices collecting rent. After the war was over, the government tore down the housing and gave the lots back to the people who owned them.

Ralph O. Dorris

My family was living in Nashville, Tennessee, on December 7, 1941. My father, Harry Dorris, was a builder. Building materials went to support war efforts, so my dad worked on government building contracts. We stayed six months in Hot Springs, Arkansas, and in Laurel, Mississippi, where I learned about cotton picking!

Dad went on ahead to Brunswick in the summer of 1943 to find housing for the six of us when he worked at the shipyard building Liberty ships. Mother and us four boys arrived on the Greyhound bus with each of us carrying two or three bags. Due to gas shortages, there were very few cars. Buses and trains were the primary mode of transportation.

We were a church-going family and soon found our way to McKendree Methodist Church on Norwich Street. The pastor refused to allow the youth to have dances or non-religious activities in the social hall, so many of us in summer months attended dances that were chaperoned in the basement social hall of Xavier Catholic Church.

Since we had lived inland all our lives, swimming and the beaches off St. Simons, Jekyll Island, and Sea Island were attractive activities. Only one problem . . . none of us could swim. It wasn't long before my dad missed his four sons at lunch on a Saturday and found us on a dock taking turns throwing or pushing each other off the small dock into the water. (This was not far from the famous oak tree where Sidney Lanier penned "The Marshes of Glynn.") Dad lined us up, marched us across what is now Highway 17 to the pool at the Community Recreation Center, and signed us up for swimming lessons.

My family lived in Emmanuel Homes, which were new. There was a community center in the war apartment complex, and many youth and family activities were held there. As founders of the Fun Club, we had birthday parties, dances (music furnished by phonograph records), and Scout meetings. It seems the influx of new residents from all over the country during the war years served to benefit Glynn County. The concept of today's Sharing and Caring Program could easily have started here.

In the middle 1940s big bands were the rage. Our senior class enjoyed the nationally known band of Sammy Kaye. Did we ever "swing and sway" with Sammy Kaye!

In 1946 on graduating from Glynn Academy, I enlisted in the Army Air Corps and was able to benefit from the G.I. Bill. I chose to go to Tulane, not Georgia Tech as my dad wanted me to do. He wanted me to join his construction company, Dorris-Green Construction Company, which built the Glynn Academy High School Stadium and some of the first post-war motels, and remodeled downtown Brunswick.

William L. Holt

The only living quarters available in Brunswick in late 1943 or early 1944 were those little two-bedroom brick "war apartments." The hot water tank depended on the wood cookstove, and heat was supplied by a potbellied woodstove in the living room. It rained a lot and was very cold.

The stump train went into the Hercules about a block behind our house on a siding, and some of us boys would jump on the empty cars and throw off scrap wood to burn. I jumped on a moving box car one day and my foot went through the ladder and hit the turning wheel. I thought for sure I had lost a leg. I was much more careful after that.

We moved to Albany Street, and there I met Dan Spell, who became my best boyhood friend.

My first view of the ocean was at St. Simons, and in later years, all of us kids spent a lot of time over there at night. Some of us boys were in Sea Scouts, and Mr. Keiffer was involved in it with us. He made a big impression on me with his mechanical ability. School was

"My dad was the general manager of the Brunswick Pulp Mill. He thought that gas rationing was going to interfere with his getting to work. So he got a horse. One day he rode the horse out to the mill to see how long it would take. He never had to use it."

Betty Ann Gaynor Lundberg

all right, but I was not motivated. I really didn't apply myself. I realize now I could have really done something if I had.

Life was pretty good but tough up to this point. Then the war ended. There was shouting in the streets, and everyone was happy. Then the most insecure days of my life began. The shipyard was closed, and you couldn't beg a job. Our family had some savings and war bonds. Unemployment was 52-20, that is, 20 dollars a week for 52 weeks. Everything was cheap, so we did all right. Post-war conditions made a great impression on my mind, so every job I had after I grew up had to have security to it. About the time I entered high school, I got a job at Walker Grocery in South Brunswick. It was a good job, and I made 35 dollars a week for six days; the going wage for men was only about 50 dollars a week.

My father still couldn't get a regular job. He built a few houses for people, and I subsidized our budget some. We didn't starve. I guess there was no welfare then or my father was too proud to apply for it.

Raja Potts Bell

Living in Glynn County during World War II was one of the most memorable times of my life. My mother, daddy, brother, grandparents, and an uncle did indeed migrate to Brunswick from Pendergrass, Georgia, in 1943. Everyone, with the exception of Mother, worked in the shipyard. We lived in the long, long buildings that were identical in appearance. The only thing to differentiate one from the other was the number of your complex. We had lived on a farm in Pendergrass, and I was thrilled to death to have so many playmates. In the country all you had were brothers, sisters, and cousins.

I was a precocious child. What I didn't do or didn't think of couldn't be done or thought of! I had never had a birthday party per se; of course, I'd always had a cake with candles and my family, but never a party like the ones I was invited to in the "city." I had been to two or three of these parties and taken a gift to the honoree. My devious mind began whirling. I had no idea how long our sojourn in this great paradise would continue and, being an Aquarius, I decided to take the bull by the horns and become a Cancer. So in the hottest part of the year, I decided to have a birthday party. I told no one of my plans. I simply went up and down the street inviting everyone to my birthday party that afternoon.

I wasn't scared. I had no thought as to what mother would say or do. I gave no thought to refreshments or lack thereof. I simply wanted to get some presents, and indeed I did! My mother did not embarrass me in front of my little friends. She could have wrung my neck, I'm sure. She simply put us in the car (a coupe with a rumble seat) and went to town to get ice cream cones. Now to Mother and me, an ice cream cone was an unheard of treat. The place we came from didn't even have electricity. We had an ice man who came by once a week and sold blocks of ice for our icebox. I don't remember anyone being surprised or disappointed that we had no cake. We were too thrilled to be eating an ice cream cone and riding in a rumble seat. Going anywhere in a car was a treat. When we lived in Pendergrass we rode to town in a wagon.

Needless to say, my biggest surprise came when the children returned to their homes. Be done with niceties, as in mother tanned my derriere . . . she beat my butt to a fare-thee-well! I thereafter was happy and proud of my January 29th official birthday. I have no idea what effect my untimely and unplanned birthday party had on Mother's budget. I'm sure it wreaked havoc with the ration coupons and everything else Mother had to contend with. I don't even remember where the coupe came from, whether it belonged to the family or whether Mother borrowed it from a neighbor.

I do remember the shipyard workers rode to work in the back of a truck that came by to pick them up. I also remember the metal lunch boxes and the hard hats. Brunswick had a distinct odor [pulp mill] . . . an odor I thought I'd forgotten until we traveled through Louisiana one year in route to Dallas, Texas, to see our son play college football. I'm talking about 30 years here. That whole state smelled like Brunswick!

A Wild Boar!

One weekend we went on a picnic out on nearby St. Simons Island. We had an enjoyable day until late afternoon. A pig that had probably been watching our family and waiting for our scraps got a little impatient and came tearing out of the woods. You guessed it, he ignored Mother, Daddy, and my little brother, Larry. He headed straight for me. This time we were in a four-door vehicle, the kind where the doors opened from the opposite of today's cars.

Mother had already gotten in the car with Larry. Daddy was loading the picnic paraphernalia, and I was, as usual, nosing or dawdling around. Here comes this ferocious pig with a horn sticking out of his nose. This young'un was scared speechless. Everyone was yelling, "Jump in! Shut the door!" I was doing my best. Closing that car door would have been a major feat for an adult; for a four-year-old it was an impossibility. Yep, you guessed it. I fell out, and Daddy ran over one of my legs. No, it wasn't broken and I wasn't disfigured. It just slowed me down for a bit and gave Mother a rest.

Conch Shells

Never having seen the ocean before, the seashells were quite a fascination for us. Once we had gone to the beach and picked up what were, I've since learned, conch shells. No one knew these things were alive! We brought them home, and Mother placed them on the ironing board to dry out. Imagine our horror and fright when in the middle of the night these creatures began to crawl off the ironing board and hit the concrete floor. It scared the daylights out of us. So much for those pretty shells!

Elizabeth Reu Johnston

I remember so well the day that we heard about Pearl Harbor. It was Sunday afternoon, and someone called my daddy to tell him about it. He reacted much the same way he reacted later in being told of the death of each one of his parents—complete shock. I don't suppose anybody in the United States ever thought we would actually be under attack, but the United States whipped itself into good shape as fast as it could. One way it did was by bringing in and encouraging the regular or ordinary citizen to depths of involvement that would be hard to match today.

We were to see many changes in Glynn County. One change was the shipyard that was built at the south end of Brunswick where there had been beautiful wooded parks and a few rotting docks. Most of it was deserted. I remember going down there one time and finding a lot of rosin barrels that had been stacked up for years. My piano teacher had a daughter who took ballet, and she wanted some rosin to put on her toe shoes so she wouldn't slip when she was in her recital that night. I remembered the rosin barrels so I rode down there on my bicycle, climbed over some fences, and broke off a piece of rosin that had dripped out of the barrel and gotten very hard. I took it back to her . . . so I know that there was nothing much at that end of Brunswick before the shipyard was built.

Thousands of people moved to Brunswick to work the three eight-hour shifts building the Liberty ships. The shipyard never closed down. People came from the mountains, the country, and all the surrounding states to make money and to help the war effort. The changing afternoon shift was like a sea of people moving down Union Street, Albany Street, and every street that went towards the southern end of town. Immediately after that you had the people going home from the previous shift, so there was a period of about two hours when the sidewalks and streets were completely full of people. It was like an ocean wave coming toward you and then receding. You tried not to be outside at that time. You hurried to get home from school and off the streets before they went to their shifts. They didn't mean you any harm. There were just so many, many people. Some did make a few catcalls. That was the first time I heard a wolf whistle.

The south end of Brunswick, which had beautiful towering oak trees, became filled with housing projects quickly put up—sort of like large efficiency apartments. They were built out of wood and all looked alike. I was puzzled as to how people found the right doorway, but, I suppose, they had some landmarks.

My daddy was general manager of the Hercules Powder Company in Brunswick, which had been converted into a defense industry. Being an honorable man, my daddy would not use his gasoline rationing C card for anything except business. He would drive his car to work or to meetings about business, then he would drive it home. It would be in the garage until he had more business to attend to. I remember walking to church with my dad on Sunday nights because he would not use his car. That was not a war-effort activity. Actually, now that I think back about it, I really cherish those moments because it was the time I had him all to myself. My mother had to stay home with my brothers. I didn't care a thing about going to church at night, but I didn't mind it because I was with my daddy. We would walk all the way to church and walk all the way home. It wasn't that far. He was a big man, and when I was walking with him I really had to trip along to keep up with him. He never acted as if I had to rush, rush, rush.

His work was very time consuming. He was gone a lot during the war because his plant ran for three shifts. It never closed down. I didn't know what work they did at the Hercules. All I knew was Daddy was a very firm boss. Anybody who quit his plant and went to work at the shipyard would not be able to come back to the plant. Apparently he was losing a lot of workers who thought the grass was greener on the other side. One day when I got home from school a rather pitiful man was sitting on the front steps. I didn't know what to do. Did I walk around him, go in the back door, or what? He was not frightening. He spoke to me and said he wanted to see my daddy. I said, "He's not here." He said, "Well, I was one of those fools who quit the Hercules to work at the shipyard. I want to come back." I thought, "Oh, good!" so I went inside, telephoned my daddy, and told him about it. He said, "No." He kept his policy. That man went away with a great disappointment.

SCHOOL DAYS

The war made a lot of difference to me personally because of a certain little girl who came down from the mountains of Tennessee. She was a typical pasty-faced, freckled little girl of Scot-Irish descent. She came to Brunswick with her family so her daddy could work at the shipyard. She probably had to live in one of those wretched little apartments somewhere. She was used to being outside and being able to have visitors from her place on the mountain. She did not like being in Brunswick, and I did not like her being in Brunswick. The reason was her last name started with "R" and my last name started with "R." Her name came just before mine, so in all those classes where we were divided alphabetically I was separated from my particular friends whose names began with O and P. She got my place! I had to go off and be one of the first ones on the roll of the other classes, and I resented it. This girl did not know how I felt. She used to kind of cozy up to me and show me poems she had written. Bless her little heart! She was so homesick for Tennessee, but all I could think about was how she had knocked me out of my place. It wasn't much fun. My friends and I would walk home together, and they would talk about things that had happened in their class. I would have been there if that little girl from Tennessee had not been there.

The worst thing that happened at school was in the ninth grade. We had a wonderful teacher named Miss Brock. She was so good at what she did and so pleasant to be with. Her class was too big, so what did they do for a solution? They hired this incompetent old man. He didn't know what he was teaching or how to teach it. They gave him about eight to fifteen students and I was one of them! Well, I could tell after being in Miss Brock's class that the man was not covering the same material that she was covering at the same time. Besides, I didn't like being separated from my friends. I, somehow, was in a class where most of the students were not college bound. They were delighted to be in the class! When he walked in the door, we had to stand up by our desk and put up our two fingers for "V for Victory" because his son was in the Army and he wanted us to be conscious of that.

As far as teaching us first-year algebra, he was a sorry disappointment! Not that I was so crazy about algebra, but even I could tell I wasn't learning what my friends were. When we had a test, he would give us one problem! If you could work that problem, you got a 100. If you missed some part of the problem, you didn't get a failing grade, which had always been the case . . . not in his class! No! If you missed just a little bit of the problem then the "old man" would give you an 80, 90, or 95.

After my mother heard about this for several weeks, she decided I was right. So she told my daddy, who was president of the Board of Education at the time, that he had to go tell Mr. Langston, the principal, to move me back to that other room. My daddy wouldn't do it. He said, "No, she will stay where they put her." My mother said, "Well, you will have to teach her first-year algebra next year or she will never be able to keep up." That's what he had to do!

The next year I had an excellent teacher, Miss Bernice Tracey. Miss Tracey faced the facts and divided her second-year algebra class into two sections, those who had had Mr. C. and those who had learned first-year algebra. If you worked your head off, which I did leaning over my daddy's chair at night, you could after the first semester start making A's with Miss Tracey's help. You had to learn first-year algebra in half the time and then try to catch up with the second-year algebra class.

Men and Women in Service

They had a radar school at the King and Prince Hotel on St. Simons Island, and some of the men who were Naval officers were very dashing. They came to our church (St. James Lutheran) and to Luther League, our young people's group. Pauline Torkildsen was one who opened her arms to everybody, and these people were included. She went around and picked all the young people up at their houses and took them home. I was lucky to be old enough to meet with them on Sunday night. I thought it was the most wonderful and glamorous existence.

There was a seaman in the Coast Guard who came to church. His name was Arthur Laurenson, and he was from Wisconsin. My mother saw how homesick he was so, she asked Arthur if he would like to come and have Sunday dinner with us. He did. He seemed to like being with us and liked Mother's cooking so we had the experience of getting to know him. One time he brought a friend with him named "Spunky." They were shipped out to the Mediterranean. Arthur wrote to me one time long after he had left that Spunky had been killed. His ship had gone down in the Mediterranean.

In our family my brothers were too young to be in any kind of service and my daddy was in the war effort with the Hercules. I had a cousin, Bill Way, who went into service. He wanted to be in the Air Force and fly, but they wouldn't take him because his blood pressure went sky high every time he went in to pass the physical from Infantry to the Air Force. He never got to fly with the Air Force, but he became a glider pilot, which was far more dangerous. Once the gliders landed, he had to be a ground fighter. He was in England and flew in connection with D-Day. He lived through the war and resides on St. Simons. Corrine Way was a WAVE and was trained as a physical therapist. My mother remembers that Corrine finally was in charge of all the physical therapy work for the Navy. She went from hospital to hospital training or supervising other people.

James A. and Mildred Prentice

We were living in Leesburg, Florida, when my husband received a telephone call from the shipyard in Brunswick to come and teach welding. The shipyard was under construction at that time. We moved to St. Simons on June 9, 1942, with our three children, Barbara, Jimmy, Jr., and Linda. We rented the Roll-In Cottage on Bruce Drive on East Beach. Behind our house were sand dunes, which are no longer there.

My husband was a welding foreman out on the ways at the shipyard. He was on different shifts: 7 a.m. to 3 p.m., 3 p.m. to 11 p.m., or 11 p.m. to 7 a.m. He was in a car pool as gas was rationed. We had blackouts at night and had to have the curtains drawn. When we went to Brunswick to the doctor or grocery store, we were stopped by soldiers who searched our car on our way across the causeway. We had to pay toll . . . 25 cents per car and 10 cents per passenger. In June of 1944 our fourth child, Johnny, was born.

I remember when we had a storm [1944] and the Coast Guard told us to leave the island. I packed our 1939 Plymouth and we got as far as the entrance of the causeway. The soldiers stopped us because the causeway was covered with water . . . We were afraid to go home because the roads were covered, but when we got home everything was high and dry.

My husband and my brother had a shoe shop at the pier. A barber shop was in front. They had a contract with the Navy to fix shoes. They did this work between shifts at the shipyard. My brother was in the Marines and was wounded on Guam but came home. Those were happy and scary days for us. The boys thought they were fighting a war to end all wars.

Times have really changed. The pier has changed so much. Where Roberta's is now was Everett's Grocery Store. The 4th of May Café is now where a garage and filling station were. The new casino was built. Our sons, Jimmy and Johnny, taught swimming there. My husband ran the movies at the old casino. After the war, we bought a house on Broadway with war bonds and are still there. Now our children live all the way from Seattle, Washington, to St. Augustine, Florida.

Betty Brown Alexander

My mother, sister, and I came to Sea Island to stay with my grandmother, Mrs. Edward C. Bruce, in the summer of 1941. My father, an officer in the Army Reserve, had been called to active duty and was sent to Washington to be trained as a censor. He was assigned to the

Panama Canal Zone to establish censorship offices. We expected to join him there, but on December 7, 1941, when the Japanese attacked Pearl Harbor, all plans for sending dependents overseas were canceled.

My mother decided she would like to join the war effort and at the same time be closer to my father in Panama. We moved to Miami, where she worked for the censorship office. She knew Spanish and was able to read much of the Spanish mail that went through Miami. The Germans had spies in Latin America, and it was important that the mail be censored. Later we moved to Havana, Cuba, and Tegucigalpa, Honduras, where my father was military attaché.

I returned to Brunswick in the fall of 1944 to join the junior class at Glynn Academy, as my parents thought it advisable for me to graduate from an American high school. I spent the first year with my aunt and uncle (Charles D. Bruce) in Brunswick and the second (my senior year, 1945-46) with my grandmother at Sea Island.

Memories associated with the war include going with my grandmother to the St. Simons casino to take cakes to serve to the soldiers who came on weekends from Camp Stewart. As her cottage was on the beach, we had to be very careful about having the windows covered at night with dark shades. Because of the shortage of gas, I often spent the night in Brunswick with friends when I had extra-curricular activities and had to miss the school bus. I often look back and think how kind they and their families were to put up with me so much.

Patricia Brown Novak

I was in and out of Glynn County during the years 1941 through 1945. When asked about early times, I usually refer to my original application for government employment, the form that requires the applicant to list every address and place of employment since birth. It has proved helpful.

From September of 1941 until February of 1942, I lived with my grandmother, Mrs. Ed Bruce, Sr., at her home on Sea Island, as my parents were involved in a move from Ohio to Miami. An interesting fact that I recall is that sometime during the war, Grandmother moved from her house on 28th Street, which was then remote and probably required more gas to get to than she was allowed. She settled for a number of years in a house on the beach and later built her own home on Bruce Drive on East Beach on St. Simons.

We lived in Florida for several years during the war while my father was stationed in Panama as chief of the Censorship Office there. Because my mother sometimes worked the night shift in a censorship office in Florida, Betty and I had experience in taking care of ourselves more than is usual for children of that age, which was one consequence of the war.

Among my recollections are blackouts (which seemed mysterious, but sort of adventurous, too). I also remember different tags for gasoline and foods that were rationed, especially sugar! As an aside, I remember when we had the "gasoline crisis" a few years ago. Some young people born long after World War II said, "They can't do this to us!"

In May of 1943, my family moved to Havana, Cuba, where my father was assistant military attaché. In February of 1944 we moved to Tegucigalpa, Honduras, where he was an Army attaché to the embassy. We lived there until January 1947, so we celebrated the end of the war down there. An unusual fact I remember from Honduras in those years is that some of the stores were "blacklisted" because they were owned by Germans or people who still had relatives in Germany.

I was just a child during the war, but I did marry a fellow stationed at Glynco in 1960 when it was still a naval station.

Thorwald A. Pearce

I was born October 1, 1931, in Wilson County between Seville and Pineview, Georgia. Our family moved to Brunswick in 1943. A combination of bad crops and low prices for products were the basic reasons for leaving the farm. On the way to Brunswick, one of the trunks blew open, and my baby sister's clothes were blown out for miles. We couldn't get Daddy's attention enough to stop the car, so she started life in Brunswick with the clothes she had on her back.

The first area we lived in was Emanuel Homes. The Georgia National Guard on Norwich Street was the meeting house for the people living in the homes. I remember going to a movie there, also waiting in line there for the ice truck. My baby brother was only four or five years old when we left the farm. We did have a time with him! We had to escort him to the "woods." It took a long time for him to get used to indoor plumbing.

We were living at 201 Wolf Street when the big storm [1944] came through. Our house was a good four to five feet off the ground. I can still see the salt water up to within six inches of the floor. I also remember seeing pictures of row boats down town by the Bijou Theater. It seemed as if there were miles of cars across the street with just the tops clear of water. There was a parking lot at the shipyard under water, too.

On Saturday, it was nothing for people to be lined up two or three blocks to see Lash Larue, Sunset Carson, Tom Mix, and Johnnie McBrown, just to name a few. Rob Steele, the first movie star I can remember seeing, was also big in the Forties. That was in a tent put up in Seville, Georgia. The movie ended with Rob and the leading lady sitting on a log used for tying horses. As they started to kiss, they fell backwards, dangling by their legs, embracing as the movie ended!

Saving and Bailing Scrap Paper

I was in Mrs. Farr's class at Sidney Lanier Elementary School. Some of my classmates were Betty Price, Jimmy Paulk, Jimmie Peerson, and Clair Pickren. All of us were into saving paper for the war effort. While we lived at 201 Wolf Street, Dad went back to Wilson County and brought his hay baler to Brunswick to bale the scrap paper that was being collected for the war effort. It was set up in the city barn or the building where repairs to city equipment were made at that time. There was a two-man operation already in service. It was built in such a manner as to have half above floor level, half below. Paper and cardboard were placed into it, packed down by hand, then a ram-like apparatus forced all the cardboard and paper down into the area below the floor. You finished the bale at floor level. It was fairly easy for one individual to move this type of bale around. The hay baler was different. A gasoline motor was used to operate it while the in-floor type used an electric engine. The gasoline baler was faster. Dad was authorized to use city dump trucks to pick up the paper. Dad worked for the City of Brunswick a long time before getting a job at the fire department.

Carl Smith

We came from Douglas, Georgia, in Coffee County, where there were very few jobs to make a living. My father was a farmer and a carpenter. I was 13 years old when my family moved to Brunswick in 1942 to work at the shipyard. My father was a shipfitter, and my mother worked in the tool room. I had three sisters, and the oldest went to work at the shipyard. I entered the sixth grade at Sidney Lanier Elementary School. Moving to Brunswick was an adventure. I was an ol' country boy and I had never been anywhere before. I had never ridden on a train until we took the Gallberry Special from Douglas and arrived in Brunswick at the train station located behind the Oglethorpe Hotel.

In Douglas, my main stay for money for the Saturday movies was to sell scrap metal I collected. Movies only cost 15 cents. I would get my money's worth at the movies by going in the morning and staying all day. Flash Gordon was a favorite. Then there were the cliff hangers that would keep you coming back each week . . . but for me only if I had sold enough scrap metal.

In Brunswick, I headed shrimp for 25 cents a bucket and had a newspaper route. I also sold boiled peanuts at the shipyard gates. My mother would boil them, and I would bag and haul them in my wagon. When the shift changed, people grabbed bags so fast. They were in a hurry and didn't wait for change. Back then, just the opportunity to work was the important thing. We didn't care how much it paid. People were proud and talked about how much work they could do in a day's time.

Before rationing, we didn't have enough money to buy goods ...when rationing started, we had the money but couldn't get the goods. Back then, to rob or steal was a stigma that people didn't want to be known for. We could sleep with our doors unlocked. No one bothered anything. We were also glad to see company come to the house. It was a time when life was a lot simpler.

Charles Gowen

Superior Court Judge C. B. Conyers, an older lawyer, was practicing by himself in Brunswick when I joined his firm in 1925. We practiced together until Judge Conyers died in 1945. His nephew, Chris Conyers, graduated from Emory circa 1937 and practiced with us until 1939, when he decided there was going to be a war. Chris wanted to get into the Navy Air Corps, so he joined in 1940 and trained at the Naval Air Training School in Pensacola. Chris was in the Caribbean, out of San Juan, for most of the war.

When World War II started, Judge Conyers and I were the only ones in the firm. Judge's health wasn't very good so it was pretty much all mine. After we went to war, Albert Fendig, who was my brother-in-law, was in the Navy and was called up. I agreed to look after his law practice while he was gone. Soon after that, Bernard Nightingale, a lawyer in Brunswick and a city attorney, went off to war in the Army. I agreed to act as city attorney for him while he was gone so he could get his job back when he came home. I spent most of my time during the war doing the work of three lawyers. General practice in Brunswick at that time, anything that had a fee with it, was attractive to lawyers.

GLYNCO

In addition to my other duties, Judge Conyers had been county attorney, and since he wasn't able to handle it, I was doing that work. Hal Friedman called and asked me to come to the courthouse. He said a Navy man was there. A commander had been sent by the Navy to locate a blimp air station in the Brunswick area. It looked like the easiest place to get land in one group was where Glynco (FLETC) is now because Union Bag owned all the property. They got it from Brunswick Peninsula Company, which had been there before. We sat down and talked. The commander said, "All right, we will go ahead with it." Must have been spring of 1942 because it was when the German submarines were sinking ships off the Georgia coast. Blimps would be the answer to that because they could get on top of submarines and bomb them. With a blimp station near Miami, one in New Jersey, and one in Brunswick, the Eastern Coast was covered. They built those big hangers out of wood because metal was being used in the war effort. They got the timbers from the Pacific Coast in Oregon. I know one workman fell off the top of one and was killed when he fell to the concrete.

The government sent in not only the Naval aviators who were flying the blimps but also a substantial support group who took care of Glynco and handled all the work and business. They had a lot of WAVES there who were in one of the dormitories. There were several thousand military personnel at Glynco.

BUS SERVICE

The government wanted a bus service operated between Brunswick and Hazlehurst to bring workers into the shipyard and take them back home because there wasn't any place for them to stay in Brunswick. We got the job of operating these government buses. They sent down some buses built out of old automobile carrier trailers that had been used to haul automobiles to dealers. Well, they enclosed them and had seats for 50 to 60 people. Packed them in pretty well! The buses arrived, but they didn't have any way to open them from the inside. We refused to use these buses until they fixed it so the people inside could get out. They operated for two to three years. There were other bus services operating towards Waycross and others toward Savannah. There was shipbuilding in Savannah so the buses didn't go very far because Liberty County was nearer Savannah.

Arley Fiveash, Carley Zell, and I had formed a little bus company to run out to Glynco when Glynco was being built. The buses we operated were some old school buses. They had a lot of common laborers putting in runways and cement foundations. The man who had the contract for the work at Glynco said if we would get the buses going, he would guarantee us we'd make some money out of it. "But," he said, "you have got to do two things. You've got to cash their checks and sell them tickets for the next week before they spend all the money and can't get back to work." We had to get about $25,000 to $30,000 in cash from the National Bank and cash the checks for those coming in. If they spent all the money that weekend they couldn't get there on Monday.

One amusing story—I was cashing checks and selling bus tickets one Friday afternoon when the workmen at Glynco got paid. This black man came in, and while he was getting his check out of his pocket a condom fell out. I said, "You're about to lose your equipment there, friend." He said, "Yeah, but that's not the worst. You know I tried to get my money out of my pocket in church and another one fell out."

An interesting thing at the end of the war about the buses that we operated for the government: We had a contract to run them and they paid us. They agreed to hold us harmless where we couldn't lose any money on them. Could even make some. It ended up that we had a few thousand dollars' profit. I wanted to get clear of it. We tried to get the government to come down and check us out. I got Dick Russell (Georgia senator) to get after them. He finally got a man to come down. The man walked in and said, "You know, they don't know how to handle this. They have had similar contracts all around the Gulf Coast, Pacific Coast, and Atlantic Coast. You are the only ones that made a profit. Everybody else lost money and they want the government to reimburse them." The fellow surveyed the operation. We had the books for them to look over. He said, "Now we don't want to rush through this. I'm going to retire in 60 days and I don't see any reason to start anything else. We will just take it easy." We finally got cleared and got out of it.

The Navy took over the airport at St. Simons and used it as a naval station. It took over the King and Prince Hotel. A lot of naval aviators came back to the United States for rest and recreation. They went to the King and Prince for three things—it was a nice place to rest, their wives could come and join them, and the radar school gave pilots the latest thing in radar operation.

The government sent the Marines to Jekyll, and they took over the island. They patrolled the beaches because German spies, who were later apprehended in Ohio and electrocuted, had landed in Florida. They were expecting German submarines to put saboteurs ashore, so the beaches were patrolled. A German sub surfaced at night and sank one of the tankers off Little St. Simons with shellfire. The people on Sea Island heard the shots and could see it. There were several tankers torpedoed. One sank off Cumberland that stayed there and made a fishing drop for a while after the war.

Jack Hice started a cafeteria in Brunswick on Newcastle Street between F and Gloucester that did a flourishing business. Jack was a genius. He could think up the best things to make money—like Sea

Pak. He started that. As soon as it got moving, he lost interest. He may have started the shipyard cafeteria or was talking about it. Carley Zell got a cafeteria man to come in as a partner and they operated the cafeteria built by J. A. Jones. Albert Crews was an employee for the shipyard cafeteria. Then Carley formed a wholesale house that was located at the foot of Gloucester Street down where the ACL Railroad Freight Depot had been. They could get most anything they wanted in the way of supplies for the shipyard.

Rosie, the Riveter

Labor unions made an awful lot of money. Everyone who worked at the shipyard had to join the union. About half of the shipyard employees were women. They did a tremendous amount of work and did a good job. They were called "Rosie, the Riveter." We use to laugh about it because after they were making big wages, one of the first things a lot of them did was get a divorce. That was the first time women could afford to get a divorce. It was a rapid change in the economy. A lot of people made money. During the war, Vance Mitchum, a lawyer in Brunswick, didn't have many criminal cases . . . mostly police court. He had a good secretary who could draw up petitions. I think an uncontested divorce case was one hundred dollars. Each time court met Vance would have 50 or 60 of them. He did real well.

It was a great thing when they launched the Liberty ships. After a while it got to be a pretty ordinary thing, they were running them off so rapidly. They had six ways. As soon as one was launched, another was started. The day the invasion of Europe [D-Day] took place I was on one of the ships on a trial run just outside of the Brunswick Bar. We got what little information there was on the ship radio.

Paul Patterson

Before the war St. Simons, Sea Island, and Jekyll Island all had very wide Daytona-like beaches. There was a ramp at the pier that permitted access to the beach by car. In those days automobiles were allowed to drive on the beach . . . very slowly of course. I used to ride the running board of my grandfather's (Paul Morton) car.

Early in the war a shipyard for the construction of Liberty ships was built in Brunswick. This necessitated having the Corps of Engineers dredge a channel to allow the ships to make their way from the launch area out to sea.* This was certainly a priority project due to the intensity of the war effort. There were, however, some side effects. The new channel immediately caused very heavy erosion to take place, first on Jekyll and St. Simons and later on Sea Island. On Jekyll, hundreds of feet of land were eroded into creating what has since been called the "Jekyll Roots" due to the exposed roots of the felled trees. On St. Simons the effects were drastic. The beach eroded down to a low-tide only situation, and quite a few houses that formerly sat well back in dry dunes now found themselves with their piling foundations in the water at high tide. Several were lost to the waves. The newly built King and Prince Hotel was eminently threatened. Fortunately, the Navy had commandeered the hotel for use as quarters for officers. Seeing that it was about to be undermined or swept away, the Navy built a seawall in front of and down both sides of the hotel, which caused the hotel to be saved but consequently situated on a manmade peninsula. We all heard that the channel was to be maintained for the duration of the war and then be allowed to return to its natural state so that the shoreline might be reclaimed. Well, that never happened, and to this day our beaches continue to be victimized by World War II.

* *The Brunswick News* - June 23, 1942 - "Big Dredge Pumps 1,000 Yards Hourly."

Beverly Wood Hart

My grandparents settled in Brunswick from Barcelona, Spain, via Massachusetts, Philadelphia, and North Carolina. Both of my parents were born here, and except for college and a couple of years living in Atlanta, I've lived here ever since. My mother, sister, and I lived in a big old Victorian house on Egmont Street. (My father died when we were in grammar school.) I remember Mama drawing the heavy draperies at the long windows at the sound of a siren, which meant an air-raid warning was in effect and everything had to be blacked-out.

Mama [Elvera Torras Wood] was a superb pianist. She was chosen to accompany Metropolitan Opera tenor Giovanni Martinelli, who gave a benefit performance at Memorial Auditorium for the war effort. I rolled bandages for the Red Cross and attended dances at Fort Stewart in Hinesville. We drove there by bus with my aunt, Josephine Torras Harwell, chaperoning. I also attended dances at the radar school, which was located at the King and Prince Hotel on St. Simons. Those were romantic times for a teenager who could not really comprehend the seriousness of the war.

Brunswick's population exploded with people coming to work at the shipyard as evidenced by the lines which stretched two blocks or more of people waiting to see a movie at the Ritz or Bijou Theaters. I remember seeing women standing in line with work clothes covered by fur coats. I assumed they were making some money but had little time to get it all coordinated!

The Pirates Club [a service organization of high school girls organized by Howard Coffin, developer of Sea Island] gave a Bundles for Britain Ball. President Mona Douglas was sent here from Scotland to live with her cousins, Alex and Judy Houston, until the war was over and it was safe to return home. Again, we had fun doing something that, I hope, helped the war effort.

Scarlett Blanton Rickenbaker

I graduated from Glynn Academy in June 1941 and worked in the plotting room (maps, little boats, submarines, and planes) for the Civil Air Patrol. I wore a uniform and was picked up before light every morning by Jeep. Very exciting for an 18-year-old. I also did airplane spotting from the rooftop of the King and Prince compound and rode my bicycle to and from home. Later, I was a junior draftsman at the shipyard in Brunswick for several months. This was great because there were a lot of young guys doing the same thing! At 19, I took off for art school in New York City, coming home on holidays and summers for three years. So I was in New York when the war was over.

Elizabeth (Betty) Brown Carpenter

I worked at the shipyard as a junior draftsman with Helen Scarlett Blanton. We didn't know what we were doing and sketched things on blueprints with no idea at all how to correct a blueprint. We held our breath when they christened a ship and it started down the ways. My mother did a lot of things for the war effort. On Saturdays people brought cakes to our house to take over to St. Simons on Sundays for the soldiers. Can you imagine a dining room table covered with cakes that were not made from mixes? Those soldiers were so young and lonesome. The director of the USO boarded with my mother, and there were dances and activities held at the Shelander house on Union Street. My brother, Brewser, made the highest grade in our district but couldn't enter the Air Force until he gained 20 pounds. Mother bought a lot of ice cream and made a lot of milkshakes. He just barely made it.

My mother happened to be having lunch at the Sea Island Yacht Club on St. Simons (next to the Coast Guard Station on the Frederica River) when the survivors of the torpedoed oil tankers were brought in to the Coast Guard Station. She told me how terrible it was. The sailors had been in the sun in salt water covered with oil beside a burning ship for so long the whites of their eyes were red.

The most terrible thing that everybody experienced every day was reading the casualty list in the newspaper. Brunswick was so small, we knew just about everybody, so there was often a familiar name. The three that come to my mind are Rupert Blount, John Whittle, and Lloyd Poppell. There were many more.

My cousin, Julia MacPherson, married Cliff Powell, a chemist at the Hercules who was chosen from among young chemists all over the United States to go to Oak Ridge, Tennessee, to build the atomic bomb. They were told only that what they were working on would end the war. None of the wives knew either and were playing bridge when the announcement came about the bombing of Hiroshima. The wives, who were in Oak Ridge also, said, "This is what they've been working on!" Julia's brother was an officer at the Nuremberg war crimes trials.

Clara Marie Gould

My father, James D. Gould [commander for the 23rd District of the Georgia State Guard], was in the car business and had no cars to sell. He would go to Jacksonville and buy used cars to sell. I went to Wesleyan College in Macon, Georgia, and traveling on the train to Macon was like being in a sardine can. There were so many soldiers on the trains that we had to stand up most of the way. We had to take our food and clothing coupons with us. I remember saving up enough to buy a pair of shoes. I remember going to a christening of a Liberty ship. There were several speeches made, bands playing, and always a lady to man the champagne bottle. We had a house on St. Simons not far from the King and Prince Hotel where the Navy ensigns were stationed. In the summer, until the house was rented to the Moxhams who were with the Brunswick Marine, we girls would make big signs and hold them up facing the King and Prince. We hoped the ensigns would see them. The signs said things like WHAT ARE YOU DOING TONIGHT?

Vivian Overstreet Lemmond

When the war started, I was 14 years old. My step-father had died when I was 12 years old, and Mother was left with two children to support. I remember that it was very rough financially. When the shipyard started up in Brunswick, she opened up a hotdog stand to help feed the multitudes that descended on the area as the shifts changed. I can remember seeing people lined up for half a block to get sandwiches for lunch or dinner because they were too tired to go home and cook. I also saw tents, huts, trucks made into campers, and other make-do shelters that the people were living in until some housing could be built. That's when all those war apartments were built.

People came from farms and places where they had never worked a factory job before. I had an older cousin who came to live with us and worked as a riveter at the shipyard. She always had her hair tied up in a bandanna for safety purposes. Later on my sister went to work there. We lived near the blimp base and always had to keep light from showing through the windows at night. I can remember the black cloth curtains drawn. Also, the car headlights were painted across the top half to keep from being seen from the sky. Tires were impossible to buy or find, and many, many times, I remember blow-outs and flats while trying to get to or from someplace.

I remember riding my bicycle to St. Simons Island with a friend and getting burned to a crisp all in one day. When I was able to drive Mom's car, we could go down a ramp at the pier and drive directly on the beach and park. I remember the day that FDR died. I went with some friends down on the beach and couldn't get the car started to get off the beach before the tide came up. Finally a policeman came and helped by towing the car up the ramp.

One summer I worked on St. Simons at the Golden Isles Hotel in the dining room and roomed at a boardinghouse near the pier. The King and Prince Hotel housed all the young officers. We called then "90-day Wonders." I dated one or two of them. That was a fun summer.

Thora Olsen Kimsey

The lifeline to the mainland for island residents was the Fernando J. Torras Causeway. Five wooden bridges, two of which were drawbridges at either end of the causeway, spanned the rivers, which wound their way through the marshes. The bridges in 1941 were the original wooden bridges built when the causeway opened in the summer of 1924.

From Gascoigne Bluff on the Frederica River, I had a special view of activities within that small area of the island. Only three families lived there-the Edwards (Mr. Edwards was the overseer of Hamilton Plantation, now Epworth-By-The-Sea), the Estes (Mr. Estes ran the Sea Island Nursery), and our family, the Olsens. From this location I often watched yachts cruising the Inland Waterway as they headed south for the winter season and north for the summer. It was fun to recognize some of the same yachts each year. Three blasts on the ship's horn signaled the bridge tender to open the drawbridge.

Jew Town, a black settlement, was about one and a half miles from our house. The Frederica River was the scene for frequent baptisms of Jew Town church members. We often came home from church and saw a group gathered at the water's edge dressed in white robes. We hurried to the river to listen to their singing and watch the baptisms.

After the United States entered World War II, the boats in front of our house became mainly tugs and barges. Going "outside" in the sea shipping lanes could mean danger from German subs. I remember the barges would shine lights along the edge of the marsh at night to guide them as they slowly inched their way along the dark river. My two sisters and I shared a bedroom, which overlooked the river and had eleven windows. We could lie in bed and watch the play of lights along the riverbank. It was eerie yet exciting.

Mr. Chitty and Mr. Rowe, the bridge tenders at the Frederica River drawbridge, opened the center span to let boats through. It was a lengthy procedure to watch and seemed so very long if you were in a hurry to get across the causeway. The bridge tender closed the first gate and slowly walked to the other end of the span to close the second gate. He took the large metal pipe, the key, and inserted it into the lock found below an opening in the center span roadbed. The bridge tender pushed against the waist-high pipe handle with his arms and body and walked counter clockwise in a circle until he unlocked the bridge. He inserted the key in the other opening and turned it to open the bridge. To close the center span the procedure was reversed. It was a very slow process. Though we were at war and it was rush, rush, rush, one could not be in a hurry when the bridge was being opened! They did this procedure in all kinds of weather all year long. We could not deny the amount of traffic that crossed the wooden bridge during the war because the clattering of the boards as the vehicles moved across could easily be heard at our house. During the war when barges and tugs plied the Inland Waterway, the bridge would be opened for several hours at a time to let the barges through and then closed to allow automobile traffic across. People had to be patient.

Part of the activity and scenery on the Frederica River included the Coast Guard boathouse, the Wee Scot Dock, and the Sea Island Yacht Club Dock, located just south of the toll house where the bridge tenders stayed. The Wee Scot Dock, which once moored Wee Scot sailboats, and the Sea Island Yacht Club Dock, which once moored luxurious yachts, now moored government boats.

A guardhouse to protect the docks was built by the short oyster-shell road leading to these docks on the southwest end of St. Simons Island. "Mex," a Coast Guardsman, was often on duty at the little

Sea Island Yacht Club (foreground)
Sea Island Boat Club (background)
on the Frederica River at
Gascoigne Bluff
Courtesy of Sea Island Archives

guardhouse. Mex was part Indian and his parents were missionaries to the Indians in Minnesota. He had joined the Coast Guard because he saw an ad that showed horses and he liked horses. (The coastal patrols on the islands used horses to patrol the beaches.) At times he came to our house and my brother taught him math. When Mother became very ill and was in the hospital, we often came home from school to find Mex washing dishes and sweeping the floor. Mex wrote several letters after he left for Savannah, but we never knew where he went after that.

Convoys of Army trucks bringing hundreds of soldiers to the beach on the weekends were a familiar sight. We saw them headed to St. Simons as we were going to church in Brunswick on Sunday morning. Sailors were always hitchhiking to and from St. Simons and Brunswick, and we always gave one or two a ride. Sailors and Navy officers came to church, and many became good friends. It made us smile to see a young Navy officer standing in front of the church with a box of Rinso washing powder in his arms waiting to give it to Mother. Occasionally to our delight, they brought us some chewing gum or candy. Mother usually invited them to our home to dinner. Some servicemen not only came to Sunday dinner but also stayed for supper! Many became regular guests, and Mother kept in touch with them for years after the war. While our older sister was in college, my younger sister and I moved out of our bedroom so a sailor's wife could come and be with him before he shipped out.

Mother and many of our relatives knitted khaki and navy blue woolen, V-neck, sleeveless sweaters for the war effort. The soldiers Dad knew who came from farms sometimes tended our victory garden. Mother had a pressure canner for canning the vegetables. We were always having people visit us and have meals with us. Once I thought an Army officer's son would never get his fill of corn on the cob grown in our garden!

After they torpedoed the tankers, I remember seeing Ivory soap floating onto the beach along with other items and thinking of the ad

"Ivory Soap . . . It floats." The articles cluttering and dirtying our beaches and the crippled, torpedoed tankers anchored near the pier brought the war very close to us. The Solomon Islands and Philippines were unfamiliar names and places we had to learn and locate on a map. Soldiers and sailors, blimps, Liberty ships, and masses of people--the things that were foreign to St. Simons and Brunswick a short while before--became the reality of World War II.

Our brother went into the Merchant Marine after graduation from high school in 1944. I remember the vacant spot in our family, but it couldn't compare to those families whose loved ones never came back. I was 12 years old when the war started. It was a time of intense patriotism and pride for our country and everyone pulled together. I will not forget the people we met and the lives touched and changed because of the war.

Sonja Olsen Kinard

I was eight years old when World War II started. We lived on Gascoigne Bluff, just north of the Frederica River Bridge on St. Simons Island, Georgia. Our house, a two-story redesigned garage that my dad had improvised after our house burned down, overlooked the old Sea Island Boat Club docks.

On April 8, 1942, Mother picked me up after school instead of my riding the school bus. I was in the third grade at Sidney Lanier Elementary in Brunswick. I can't remember if Mom told me about the ships being torpedoed, but as we crossed the Frederica River Bridge, we saw a group of men sitting huddled on the ramp of the Coast Guard Station wrapped in gray blankets and covered with oil and dirt. At the toll house at the end of the bridge on St. Simons, Mother pulled the car across the road onto the grass. Dad came up accompanied by the captain of the tanker *Baton Rouge*. Dad had on his khaki pants and shirt, and the captain was dressed in a khaki one-piece jumpsuit. Both were dirty and greasy, and neither had shaved for several days. Two words had been added to my vocabulary during the early part of the war: *saboteur* and *survivor*. When I saw my dad, I said to him, "Dad, you look just like one of the saboteurs" (meaning survivors).

The captain of the *Baton Rouge* gave Dad a number of articles from the tanker, such as the large life ring with the ship's name on it, the ship's bell, the compass, and many other things. Most of these are in the possession of my brother. After the ships were torpedoed, I remember the oil-scarred beach on St. Simons, but the beach was also cluttered with crates of oranges, cabbage, and other vegetables. I even remember seeing a mattress. I always thought that the food came from the oil tankers, but after starting on this project, I discovered that a refrigerated boat that contained food had been torpedoed by the same U-boat 12 miles southeast of the St. Simons buoy.

Because of the influx of people to the area, the schools were overcrowded. When I was in the fifth grade, they had the first elementary school on St. Simons in one of the church camps on East Beach. I started school on St. Simons that year with Mrs. Fraser Ledbetter as my teacher. I boarded the school bus at the Frederica Bridge and rode the school bus that came from Brunswick to St. Simons every morning. Since I had to catch the bus so early, I was transferred back to Brunswick. (My sisters and brother and I were always the last to board the bus in the morning and the first off in the afternoon when we went to school in Brunswick.)

Sidney Lanier Elementary in Brunswick operated with two shifts daily, 9 a.m. to noon and 1 p.m. to 5 p.m. I had to attend the first shift because the school buses were scheduled for Prep High and Glynn Academy High School, which went until 3 p.m. At the end of the first semester, those who attended the first shift switched to the second shift and vice versa. First semester, Miss Collins was my teacher and second semester, Miss Sawyer. Three teachers in one year! Also three different sets of classmates. Between one and three o'clock, I was free to wander anywhere around the school. No one kept tabs on me. I usually went into Miss Gautier's room and helped her. At least she was nice enough to let me come in and I didn't disrupt the class as far I knew.

Living on the Frederica River and the Inland Waterway provided many sights. However, I do remember when the naval air station on St. Simons needed to be supplied with gasoline. A tugboat pulling a couple of gasoline barges docked at the long county dock in front of our house. Gasoline trucks traveled day and night back and forth on the oyster-shell road beside our house. At night, huge portable spotlights were set up as they pumped the gasoline into the trucks. Our bedroom was on the river side of the house, and the light shone through our eleven windows. The noise of the trucks traveling to and from the dock and the roar of the pump engine lasted all night long and into the next day.*

* In gathering the recollections, I met the former sailor, T. R. Walker, who was in charge of this detail.

Woodie Angela Estes

During the war, my daddy planted our victory garden at the Sea Island Nursery on Gascoigne Bluff, and we supplied friends and family with fresh vegetables. Mother canned any surplus vegetables. Since gas was rationed, Mother and I went to Florida for my physical therapy for cerebral palsy on the Greyhound bus. The buses were crowded, and the servicemen had priority seating. However, some were compassionate and allowed Mama and me to precede them so we could sit together.

I remember we were invited when Mrs. Alfred Jones christened the Liberty ship *Howard E. Coffin*.

My brother-in-law, Rupert Carr, was stationed at Fort Stewart and assigned to the transportation department. When he went overseas, he was a driver for General George Patton. On returning home, he had some interesting stories to tell. His wife, my sister, Nova, and their children lived with us while he was overseas. After the war, my mother, as manager of the Flower Shop on Sea Island, met many famous people. General Dwight Eisenhower was extremely charming when he came to pick up corsages for his guests. When Alben Barkley, vice-president to Harry Truman, was on his honeymoon, Mother arranged the flowers for their room. Sarah Churchill, Winston Churchill's daughter, was married on Sea Island in the Alfred Jones home. Mother was called in to decorate the house for the wedding.

Frances Bankston Manor

With the mention of Fort Stewart, my memories ran rampant visualizing the convoys of trucks filled with soldiers coming to the beach for recreation or maneuvers. We lived on St. Simons Island where Sea Gate Inn is now. The water's edge was much farther away then. We had a wooden walk from our porch to the beach that passed over dunes, sea oats, and sand spurs. In the dunes the Army had dug gun placements and installed enormous guns and sandbags. Every day a soldier was positioned along this route. I was a fifth grader, and you can imagine how impressed and concerned I was.

We had our beachside windowpanes darkened with heavy green window shades so enemy subs were unable to see the house. Street lights didn't exist. The King and Prince Hotel, located near us, was bachelor officers' quarters. The military were friendly, and we ran in and out freely, especially in the wrought-iron stairwell area that is now the dining room on the beach side. That stairwell is concealed now with all the alterations and drastic changes.

My dad worked at the shipyard in Brunswick. My brother, Byron, joined the Navy. There were six children in my family, and I certainly understood all the rationing stamps and tokens for grocery items such as sugar, shortening, shoes, and gasoline. School had two sessions a day. I remember having to go in the afternoons (1 p.m. to 5 p.m.).

Living on the beach really exposed us children to the tragedy of the two oil tankers that were torpedoed off the coast. We believed the worst!

Jack Conyers

We arrived in Brunswick in 1943 and found living quarters in Brunswick Villa. Mother did not like living there and being that near the stinking pulp mill. Every possible living space was occupied in Brunswick and St. Simons. The only place we could find on St. Simons at that time was an old-abandoned fishhouse that smelled mightily of fish in the front area but had living quarters in the back. We moved in. Mother, always being an industrious soul, set to work cleaning the front of the fishhouse with Clorox and scouring pads to get rid of the odor. She then converted it into a bedroom, which she rented to a Navy officer and his wife. Renting rooms to officers and their wives was a big deal, and many lasting friendships were made. We finally moved into a house on Beachview Drive that not only had two bedrooms to rent but also a bedroom for me. It was the first time I had a bedroom of my very own.

I remember a Beachcraft plane that crashed in the ocean. The Navy used it for radar tracking by the officers training at the radar school at the King and Prince. A young boy, Jack Parmelee, actually swam out to the crashed plane and helped hold the people above water until they could be rescued. One airman was killed immediately, one later died of injuries, and two others were saved.

I was old enough and independent enough that when I couldn't sleep I would get up and go for a walk. One night I got the bejeepers scared out of me. I was walking the beach and met a sailor patrolling the beach with a rifle and bayonet. We mutually scared each other all to hell and gone. I don't know if they had an alert or if he was on a regular patrol of the beach. I was just as big as he was. He said, "You scared me half to death." I said, "I'm sorry." Needless to say I didn't do much night beach walking after that.

A very traumatic experience was seeing a woman's body washed up on the beach. A WREN (Women's Reserve of English Navy) had taken a plane to Miami from England. The plane crashed and her body washed ashore. The Coast Guardsmen were trying to pick the body up off the sand. It was a gruesome sight. The body was severely bloated. Her back was essentially gone. The only thing holding the top half and the bottom half of her body together was the flap of skin of her stomach. The stench was awful!

I had a terribly embarrassing experience one day when I went to see my Uncle Bill Conyers, who was a bartender for Henry Cofer. A sailor was bemoaning the fact that he was unable to locate any girls. I said,"Shoot, there are lots of girls around here." Innocent . . . gosh I was innocent! He said, "Well, I sure would like to meet some." Uncle Bill, just chuckling up his sleeve, let me go. I tried to introduce him to a girl who lived at Wynn Gables. She knew me, and it was terribly embarrassing to her because here I come with this horny sailor to introduce him to her. She was not at all prepared, but she handled it very nicely. The sailor fairly quickly realized the awkward social situation and went on his way.

The first job I ever had was setting up pins in the four-lane bowling alley at the Casino. I made good friends there, especially my black friend, David Ingram, and learned many lessons about the facts of life from setting up pins with David. During the war outside wrestling matches were held in downtown Brunswick, and my dad took me to one. They had a wrestler named Roland Kirchmeyer. These men were too old to be in the military and earned their living wrestling.

I well remember the hurricane of 1944. They sent us home early from school on the school bus. Now that was a trip! Mr. Carswell, the mechanical drawing teacher, was driving the bus. The waves were washing across the causeway, the bus was losing power, and we were going slower and slower. As we were coming off the Mackay River bridge, a Navy truck was coming toward us. The stakes on one side of the back of the truck had blown loose and were flapping in the wind. They hit the bus and shattered the windows in the rear. Mr. Carswell panicked and yelled, "Is everyone all right back there?" I guess it was the first time I heard a kid cuss a grown man. A boy's voice from the back of the bus yelled, "Goddamn it. Keep this bus going. I'm all right!" Once we got onto St. Simons it wasn't too bad, and Mr. Carswell was able to make his deliveries. My brother had sent me a helmet liner, which I was wearing. It was like a knitted hat. As I backed off the bus into the wind that hat blew straight off my head and sailed away!

Because our house was sheltered from the main force of the wind, we were able to sit on our porch that evening and watch the radar equipment at the King and Prince blow apart. I was fascinated by a large, thick wire cable that had torn loose and was swinging back and forth in the wind. After the hurricane had passed us by, my friend Dan Cody and I got in inner tubes and floated from my house almost to the pier looking at the damage.

Fishing on St. Simons was superb during the war. I remember going to the pier when the trout were running. You would find people standing hipbone to hipbone fishing. Everybody was catching trout! When you didn't have as much meat as you might want, this was very important. Once while standing on the pier I remember seeing a school of mullet as wide as a street swimming towards Brunswick and disappearing from view.

We moved to St. Simons in June so everyone thought I was a summer resident. I tried to tell them that I lived here. I went down to the pier every day . . . pretty lonesome. I would occupy my time fishing and would come home with a mess of yellowtails. Mother thought that was the cat's meow. I didn't like fish so she would cook me hotdogs.

Thomas Gignilliat

I remember coming home in the late afternoon on December 7, 1941, turning on the radio, and listening to a steady stream of newscasters describe the bombing of Pearl Harbor. I really think my dad had expected it to happen, but I do not think anyone was really prepared when it did happen. The war definitely changed the lives of all St. Simons residents. My family moved to the island when I was a few weeks old, so we had been there for a while when the war started. Our lives and lifestyles changed from that of a small close-knit community where everyone knew everyone else to that of a teeming mass where you really did not know anyone except old friends. This was brought about by the conversion of Malcolm McKinnon Airport into the St. Simons Naval Air Station and the huge build-up of the Coast Guard from the lighthouse and a small surf station to numerous other types of operations, including the shipyard and Glynco Naval Air Station in Brunswick. Once the war was over the old life never returned, so it must be assumed that it was "killed in action" during the war.

Before the war, and for some time after its start, one thing that I do not remember changing was the fact that Mr. J. C. Coleman of the Glynn County sheriff's office was the one and only law enforcement officer on the island. At some point during the war, they added additional officers to assist him. We must have been pretty law-abiding citizens to get by with one officer for so long.

I rode the school bus to Brunswick for grammar school and junior high. While attending school in Brunswick, I took money to school every week to buy savings stamps that were glued into a book.

When the book was filled, it was turned in for a war bond. Also, during these times we had scrap drives for metal, rubber, and many other materials.

During the war, the County Casino was the general meeting place for the young crowd. Whether you needed a book from the library, wanted to attend a movie, bowl a few lanes, get something from the soda fountain, or dance, the Casino was the place to go. I seem to have spent a lot of time dancing on the open-air dance floor to the big band sound coming from the jukebox.

My summer vacations were spent working for McKinnon Oil Company at the gas station on St. Simons. By the end of the war, we were really creative at repairing flat tires. Due to rationing of gas and tires, a number of people were not doing much driving, which was good since most tires and tubes were running with patches on top of previous patches. Gasoline was rationed by classes of need, and one of my jobs after the station closed at night was to take the meter readings from the pumps, the cash from the register, and the gas coupons and see if they balanced. A lot of the gasoline sold locally during the war, regardless of tradename, was hauled from the old Atlantic Refining Company in Arco. Gasoline in those days sold for 22 cents a gallon, 24 cents for ethyl.

My mother had ration books that were good for one thing or another. It seemed that everything was rationed, but you had a book for every member of the family, so it was not that bad for us. My mother's parents owned a farm in South Carolina, and every time we went up there, we came home with a carload of meat and canned goods. They raised their own beef, pork, and chicken and had a spare barn that was filled with home-canned fruits and vegetables.

After the activation of Camp Stewart, the Army deployed anti-aircraft artillery to St. Simons for maneuvers. These units convoyed down from Camp Stewart, dug holes to position their guns and equipment, and maintained surveillance of the air space. When their tour was completed, they would remove their equipment, fill in the holes they had dug, and convoy back to Camp Stewart. Shortly after they departed, a new unit from Camp Stewart would arrive, dig out the same holes, and position their equipment.

For months during the early part of the war, it seemed that German submarines roamed at will along the Georgia coast. There were numerous sinkings up and down the East Coast. The survivors were brought ashore the next day. I have seen some strange items washed up on the beaches from these ships. Most of the ships were tankers, so naturally a lot of oil made its way to the beach. One morning, the beach was littered with mattresses and oranges. Then there were frozen turkeys all over the beach. After the air station opened there were always Marines and sailors trying to catch rides from the pier to the air station and vice versa. Almost everyone would give them a ride. Many of the Marines had returned from Guadalcanal and were guards at the air station.

One thing made possible by the war was that you could get your driver's license at age 15 instead of 16 years. On my fifteenth birthday, my dad took me to the Georgia Highway Patrol in Brunswick to get my license. The officer gave me a written test, graded my test paper, and started to fill out my license. Thinking I was being cheated, I asked if I was not supposed to have a driving test. He informed me that he had been watching me drive for three years and really did not think I needed the test!

My uncle, Gene Gignilliat, moved with his family from Atlanta to Brunswick during the war so he could go to work in the shipyard as a welder. It was probably one of the best jobs he ever had. The wages were good and the work was steady. The shipyard was a 24-hour-a-day, seven-days-a-week operation. I do not remember them ever shutting their yards for anything until after the end of the war.

This one is not about St. Simons or Brunswick but is in the general area. There was a Japanese community of farmers living south of Darien that had been there for some period of time. Shortly after the start of the war, they were relocated in interment camps. They were there one day and gone the next. I do not have any idea what happened to them later, but I do know that they never returned.

W. L. Wilkes

My family moved to St. Simons Island, Georgia, in 1936. I attended Glynn Academy High School in Brunswick and graduated in 1941. We rode the school bus daily to Brunswick. We had one large bus for the south end of St. Simons and a smaller one for the north end. During summers and after school, I worked at odd jobs. I caddied at the Sea Island Golf Course and worked for three different electricians as a helper. I worked mostly for Elmer Webb, who owned Webb Electric Company. Mr. Webb was a role model for me and taught me a lot about values and hard work. When he worked at Camp Stewart, while it was under construction, I went and lived with him and his wife in Ludowici, Georgia. When he went to work at Moody Air Force Base in Valdosta, I also went with him.

While I worked for Webb Electric Company, we were hired by an Italian family who had leased the Shelander house on Butler Avenue to install an elaborate short-wave radio antenna in the attic. They said they had fled Italy to get away from Mussolini, and they wanted to keep in touch with their families. Sometime after the two ships were sunk off St. Simons, towed into St. Simons Sound, and anchored, the FBI questioned Mr. Webb and me at length about what we knew about this Italian family and their actions. They suspected that they were communicating with German U-boats and arranging for refueling them. I never did know what happened to the family or what the FBI found out.

Selective Service, or the draft, was started in 1939 or 1940, and troops stationed at Camp Stewart started to visit St. Simons in large numbers for R&R weekends. They would camp in Neptune Park in tents. We had some exciting times with the troops because they were at "Swamp Stewart" and isolated for weeks at a time. When they came to St. Simons, some of them were pretty wild. For a while during this time in the summer, I worked for Brantley O'Quinn. I rented motor scooters and bicycles, drove a taxi, and operated a pool room for him, so I came in contact with a lot of soldiers!

My best friend, Bobby Lewis, and I decided to join the Navy. We went to Jacksonville to enlist. For some reason, probably my small size, I did not pass muster, but Bobby was accepted and later was called to serve in the submarine service. His sub was sunk off the Philippines on December 8, 1941. He was captured and sent to a Japanese prison camp where he died of malnutrition and tuberculosis five or six months before the islands were liberated.

My father and other older men joined the Home Guard on St. Simons. They trained at Redfern Field and used the old hangers as their base. They drilled and marched with wooden guns. They were block wardens and air-raid wardens and were assigned guard duty. The Coast Guard patrolled the beaches on St. Simons as well as kept up radio surveillance. Some Army troops from a small unit stationed in Brunswick helped patrol the island. Jekyll and Cumberland Islands were patrolled by horse patrols.

After the Home Guard stopped using the hanger at Redfern Field, Mr. Jim Kent converted it to a skating rink, and that is where I met Moonyeen Brown, who became my wife. I worked a short time at the Hercules Powder Company until the shipyards were constructed.

The Georgia Power Company could not get treated poles or copper wire, so they used iron wire, which rusted in the salt air, and untreated poles that quickly rotted. I found out about this soon after the war ended and I started my career with the power company. We had to replace all this equipment.

I registered for the draft in February 1942, enlisted in the Navy in late 1943, was called to active duty on January 10, 1944, and reported to Bainbridge, Maryland, for boot camp. My brother, Clyde, also enlisted in the Navy, and we both served in the Pacific. He was on an LST (Land-Sea Transport), and I was in a beach battalion and was in the Okinawa landing. I was discharged at Memphis, Tennessee, on January 17, 1946, and returned home to a calmer Glynn County and a wonderful place to live. Three of my sisters married men who were stationed at the St. Simons Coast Guard Station.

My father-in-law, Hoyt W. Brown, Sr., served in World War I, and the ship that he served on was sunk. Early in World War II, he was active in the draft and ration boards and was a leader in establishing the USO in Brunswick. In 1942, he also enlisted in the Navy and was in the North African campaign and the landing in southern France. In World War II, his ship was sunk off North Africa. He was sent to the Pacific, where he served on a troop ship that was sunk in the Okinawa landings. When he returned home, I told him I didn't want to go fishing with him in a boat.

My brother-in-law, Hoyt W. Brown, Jr., graduated from the Merchant Marine Academy, enlisted in the Navy, and also served in the Pacific. Bill Feeney was stationed at the Army camp in Brunswick that was located on the Hercules Powder Company property at L Street and Glynn Avenue. He married Betsy Brown, my wife's sister. Bill later joined the 82nd Airborne Division and jumped in Holland, Normandy, and at Bastogne. He was one of the "Battered Bastards of

Bastogne" and earned a Purple Heart for being wounded and a Silver Star for bravery. He later went to Hollywood as a technical advisor when they were filming the movie *Battleground*.

Danny Minchew Herold

We moved to St. Simons in 1939 from Baxley, Georgia. My father had died and our home had burned. We needed a place to live. We had always spent a lot of time in the summer on the island and loved it. Mother was also impressed with the better school system and the cheap taxes in Glynn County. My mother bought Stanton Inn from Mr. Henry Cofer and successfully ran it for 15 or 20 years. During the war years, Stanton Inn was filled with mostly young couples who either worked at the shipyard or were connected with the military and enjoyed living in a homelike atmosphere.

I had my first airplane ride on December 7, 1941, at the airport on St. Simons. I don't remember the pilot's name, but he said it would probably be his last flight as a civilian as he was sure he would be in the Army the next day.

I graduated from Glynn Academy the following June. I went to work at once at the shipyard in the payroll department. I made 65 cents an hour and worked seven days a week with every other Sunday off. I later went to college for a year and then came back to work at the naval air station on St. Simons, where I stayed until the end of the war.

In spite of the country being at war, it was an interesting time for young girls my age. Between the soldiers at Fort Stewart and all the Navy men at Glynco and the naval air station on St. Simons, we enjoyed a very active social life. There was always a dance to attend, and we were always asked to wear evening gowns. We met many young men from all over the country. I eventually married a career naval officer, so my life was always entwined with the military.

I, of course remember the blackouts, the patrols on the beach, and all the barbed wire. Our cars were stopped and searched at the toll booth, and Mother always kept a sack of apples in the trunk so the soldiers could help themselves. I remember standing on the beach and seeing gunfire at sea and the torpedoed ships being brought in and anchored just off the pier. I was crabbing at the pier a few days later and a body floated up beside my crab basket. I screamed my head off and the soldiers came off the beach and retrieved the body.

A Liberty ship went out for its trial run in late December, got fogged in, and had to stay out over Christmas. There were several crashes of planes from the NAS and the loss of good friends. I recall that we had German prisoners of war at NAS, St. Simons for a number of months. They worked in the mess hall and looked so young to me even though they were about my age. They were well treated but always looked scared to death.

There was the rationing and difficulty of getting tires and gasoline for your cars, and a lot of food was in short supply. That was when I started drinking black coffee because there was never enough cream or sugar to go around. The whole area was very crowded. War housing was built to help house the people, and everyone who had a room to rent did so. You had to stand in line for everything, but overall everyone was very patient because people were doing their part and many lasting friendships were formed.

I remember the excitement of VE Day at the base and everyone running up and down the halls hugging and kissing and the parties we had that night to celebrate. That was followed in a few months by VJ Day and the end of the war and what we hoped would be a return to normal living.

Main Street at the Pier
St. Simons Island, Georgia
Courtesy of Coastal Georgia Historical Society

Evelyn Wallace Heinold
Evelyn Heinold's mother came from Norway to St. Simons in 1900. Evelyn married Fred Heinold, who was stationed on the island in the Coast Guard.

I was single and still living at home in 1941. I was working at Ward's Drug Store at the pier on St. Simons and shall always remember being at work when the news came over the radio that Pearl Harbor had been attacked. It seemed there was an absolute silence in the store. It was just unbelievable! Of course, we all know what happened after that in this area. The shipyard brought many people here to work and live in Brunswick and St. Simons. Most of all, many military bases were established in our area. The U.S. Coast Guard had already come here. It was opened in the mid to late 1930s. The main station was at East Beach and the boathouse was on the Frederica River. The U.S. Navy had a station at the airport on St. Simons, and the blimp base opened in Brunswick. Much building began taking place to accommodate the influx of people.

Blackouts, price control, and rationing became a way of life. We used ration books and tokens. Gas and many food items were rationed. Mama sold our car so our means of transportation was calling a taxi. I had a bicycle that I rode to work. On my way to work one morning I noticed a lot of activity out on the pier. It was unusual at that hour of the morning so I went by there and was told that ships had been torpedoed off our coast during the night. Rescue boats were coming in at the pier. An event like that sure brought the war a lot closer to all of us. That happened in 1942. On the weekends there would be a lot of people coming to the island as some of the military from Camp Stewart, now known as Fort Stewart, would be here.

It was in 1942 that I met Fred. He was stationed with the Coast Guard. We became engaged in December of 1943 and were married in July of 1945. My brother, Edwin Wallace, was in the U.S. Army Air Force and went through training at several places in the States. He was sent to England and lost his life in an accident at an air field in Hertfordshire, England, on January 10, 1945. He is buried in Cambridge, England. Toward the end of the war my sister, Thelma, and I were working at McLendon's Grocery Store.

Evelyn and Fred Heinold
Courtesy of Evelyn Heinold

Marian Tiller Young

My introduction to World War II came long before Pearl Harbor. The minister of the First Presbyterian Church, Mr. T. L. Harnsburger, was the son of Chinese missionaries and was married to a daughter of the first missionaries to China. He had a daughter, Agnes (my age), and three handsome sons. He spoke strongly of the aggressive Japanese who had run them out of China and felt the U. S. would soon be involved with fighting them. Another classmate, Mona Douglas, and her younger brother, Tommy, were British refugees. They had been sent to live with an aunt on Sea Island during Britain's air battle with the Germans. So early in my high school days, I was aware of the large conflicts starting to invade our peaceful life.

The E. R. Shermans of First National Bank lived in the 1000 block of Union Street. His father, a very elderly gentleman, had been knocked down and robbed in front of his house on Richmond Street. Mr. Sherman had awakened one night to find a strange man standing at the foot of his bed. The man left. Mr. Sherman said that he was drunk and confused. After that our doors were locked and people had to be more careful. The shipyard had been started!

I worked in the summer of 1943 for the Naval Radar Training School at the King and Prince Hotel, the summer of 1944 for the shipyard, and for the Navy again in 1945 at the St. Simons Naval Air Station. My father was too old for the draft, and they would not offer him a commission (he had a wife and three children). He was comptroller for the Sea Island Company but commuted every day from Brunswick. My mother and I would have moved to St. Simons, but my sister and brother objected to such a move and I guess Dad really didn't want to move either.

I had two uncles serving in the European theater. One was with the Texas 36th Infantry Division and served during the invasion of North Africa and Italy and the invasion of southern France until 1944, when he was captured by the Germans. The other uncle served in the Battle of the Bulge. Both were infantry sergeants.

I was young and enjoying dating. There was no personal family loss of life or injury, but I was well aware of who went off to war and did not return. The Whittle boy was killed on D-Day; we lost Jim Andrews; and T. L. Harnsburger, Jr., was killed in an airplane crash while an instructor of naval aviators in California; and a young man named Edwin Ludwig, who lived with the Condoles, joined the Marines and was killed at Iwo Jima. These are the deaths I vividly recall.

USO

The USO had a house in Brunswick. Mr. and Mrs. Albert Shelander turned the home over to the USO, and they moved to the island. Another small building off Glynn Avenue (Highway 17) was also a USO.

I was a member of a group of girls (16 years and older) who were selected by the Glynn County Defense Recreation Board. The county was divided into six districts, which provided chaperones for the girls. The chaperones were Mrs. W. W. Parker, Mrs. H. J. Friedman, Mrs. Harry Vickers, Mrs. W. L. Harwell, Mrs. Ralph Kammerer, Mrs. Ed Diemer, and Mrs. Hubert Lang.

Dances were held at Camp Stewart (now Fort Stewart) at Hinesville. We rode up and back in Army trucks. I found the buses going to the King and Prince Hotel to USO-sponsored dances with U. S. Naval officers much nicer and more glamorous. The house on Union Street was used by enlisted sailors from St. Simons and Glynco. The small building across from the Hercules was used a lot. Vivian Krauss held ballroom dancing classes, and several Brunswick girls married soldiers they met there, including my friend Anne Harwell North.

COLLEGE AND RETURNING VETERANS

My first year at college was manless! There were Navy and Marine V-12 units, but they were closely regulated and didn't have much chance to date coeds. We had German prisoners of war pulling ivy off our dormitories on the women's campus at Duke University. They were quickly removed when dormitory housemothers found their girls practicing German with the tanned, handsome prisoners of war.

Then in 1945 the men returned, and it was so obvious the difference between young high school graduates and the returning veterans enrolled under the G.I. Bill. I know . . . I met and married one in 1947. My husband was in the Ninth Air Force and was a gunner on a small attach bomber (A-20 Haroc). He flew 65 missions over France and Germany.

Leslie Hansen Strickland

I graduated from Glynn Academy in June of 1941 and, like all 17-year-olds, could hardly wait to get away from home. I went to Birmingham, Alabama, where I had an older sister. I lived with her and attended the University of Alabama. In December of 1941 along came Pearl Harbor. Everyone seemed to have to move to get involved during that time. Either you were joining up to fight or you just felt what you were doing didn't apply to the war effort. I was among that group. In 1942, I returned to Brunswick. Masses of people were moving in to either work at the blimp base or the shipyard.

Mayor Hunter Hopkins headed up the Housing Authority. I went to work in an office controlling rentals for the hundreds and hundreds of low, flat-roofed four-unit apartments that were thrown up to house all the new residents. Mr. Edwin Fendig was my boss at the housing authority. He was one of the many permanent residents who temporarily changed their occupations during the war years. I still see some of those units standing when I return to Brunswick. Some are well kept and don't look too bad.

The shortage of housing in Brunswick with the vast influx of people caused the government to ask residents who had excess room in their homes to take in roomers. Since my parents had a spare bedroom, a young Navy lieutenant and his bride moved in with them and remained there for the duration of the war. This young couple became another set of children to my parents, and the friendship lasted until my parents' death. My mother flew to Oregon, which was their home, several times after the war to visit and get to know their children.

My father, George Hansen, who was in the construction business, had a very difficult time of it. He was too old to change occupations. Materials were in short supply to civilians. Gas was rationed so he couldn't operate his trucks. The situation pretty much put him out of business. He did survive. However, it was kind of odd to see this little, rotund figure riding around on a bicycle. My brother, Warren, who was a chemical engineer and had worked at Hercules as a co-op while attending Georgia Tech, was deferred because of his employment. He didn't work at the Brunswick Hercules but at Blacksburg, Virginia. My sister and brother-in-law, Vera and Paul Wicker, moved away when Paul joined the Navy and have lived in Texas since the late 1940s.

While I was in Brunswick that year and a half to two years, I did attend a few of the USO dances. I was a bit shy and never felt comfortable. A boyfriend from my Birmingham days was stationed at Fort Stewart, and that was my love life while I was in Brunswick. I stayed in Brunswick until the end of 1943, when I moved to Atlanta to be with my sister, Vera, who was pregnant and whose husband was among the missing.

I'll have to say that, as a young person, I certainly met a large variety of people who moved into our hometown during the war. It prepared me for a life I could face in the world when I left that little town again. I did leave. My husband was in the Navy and made a career of it.

Kay McKeever

The reason I was in Brunswick during the war years was that I was sent there by my school, the Presbyterian School of Christian Education, to assist in conducting vacation Bible schools in the various war housing projects. I served under the leadership of the Methodist minister. At the end of the summer I decided to remain in Brunswick. I lived with a family who had moved there. Both my father and brother worked at the shipyard. I worked during the winter and through the spring of 1944-1945 at the Mark Carr apartments nursery for children whose mothers worked at the shipyard. I cared for the two- and three-year-olds. We were aware of the Glynco air base. I recall a little neighbor boy telling us, "When you hear a sound like that and look up, that *bees* a blimp." And so it was!

Sometime during the early spring a representative of the USO came to our church to ask some of the young women to serve as junior hostesses. I was one of the ones selected and was assigned an evening to be on duty. I was shy, but the senior hostess advised us, "As a hostess, it is your duty to welcome these servicemen and help them have a pleasant visit here." So I tried to be as friendly and gracious as she was. I must have succeeded because it was there that I met the man who later became my husband! He was stationed at the Navy radar training station on St. Simons.

Another memory I have of that year was the flood waters several inches high on the downtown streets of Brunswick. I recall looking from the windows of the city library (which occupied the second floor of a building) and seeing people sloshing about in the water.

When the war in Europe ended, people who had come from other places to work in Brunswick began moving away. My family moved back to North Carolina in April and I was with them. I did not know that I would live in Georgia for two different periods of time in the future.

Ben E. James, Jr.

My family moved back to Brunswick in the fall of 1938. My father, a salesman, worked for the Coastal Chevrolet Company. The economy in Brunswick was still reeling from the Great Depression. When civilian automobile manufacture stopped, the only job my father could get was that of night clerk and bookkeeper for the old Oglethorpe Hotel on Newcastle Street. It was during this time that the U. S. was attacked and drawn into the war.

My first taste of the seriousness of this conflict was when some ships were torpedoed off St. Simons Island. For some reason, the news had gotten out around town and my family drove over to the island. We were standing on the old St. Simons pier with other townspeople as the lifeboats with the survivors were towed past. I remember people crying and then cheering the survivors as they went past the pier. Many of the survivors were put up at the Oglethorpe Hotel. My father helped them call home to their families to tell them they were safe. My father also told us about the officers who survived calling the families of the seamen who were not so fortunate. All the local funeral homes were full of the seamen who had been killed.

Soon war industry came to town. First, war housing was built to accommodate the workers that would build the shipyard and the blimp base. My father started working for Daniel Construction, which was building the shipyard and war housing. Later, J. A. Jones Company took over the shipyard which built Liberty ships. The Brunswick Marine Company, which had in the past catered to shrimp boats, work boats, and cargo vessels, started building yard oilers. Brunswick, which normally had a population of around 17,000, swelled in size overnight. Many people commuted daily from as far away as Valdosta. I remember pulpwood trucks being converted with enclosed wooden bus-type bodies to haul workers from the inland towns. We referred to the workers as "pea-pickers."

There were all types of shortages. Meat, some canned goods, butter, coffee, sugar, shoes, tires, and gasoline were all rationed. Since tires were almost impossible to get and gasoline was strictly rationed, it took a lot of coaxing to get my father to let me use the family car on Saturday night. At that time, the bridges to St. Simons Island were all made from wood. The wood pilings were topped with a framework of wood decking and wood siderails. They were narrow and dangerous. As a result of tire and gas shortages and the danger of the bridges, I was forbidden to use the car to go to the island. When my father would let me use the car, he would first measure the gasoline and write down the odometer mileage. As soon as I would leave our house on the Old Jesup Highway, I would stop at a convenient spot and disconnect the speedometer. Later, in town, I would use black-market gas stamps (which were freely traded among the teenagers) to put some extra gas in the tank. I would then head directly to the island since that's where the action was. The only requirement to buy a beer at the old King and Prince Drive-In was that you had enough money to pay for it. My father never caught me!

I started, as many of my friends did, working at the shipyard. From late May until early September, we worked at various jobs. I started a few weeks before my sixteenth birthday on my first job in the mold loft as an apprentice lofts man (patternmaker). The following year, I worked as marine electrician apprentice in the fitting-out basin. After the hull was launched, we would install the equipment in the radio room. I got to go on some trial runs of the Liberty ships. My family was concerned about my safety because of the submarine activity. However, I can't recall of any incident where a newly built ship was in danger. Some of this was because the war in Europe was winding down, but the main reason was because of the blimps patrolling the coast.

I went into the Navy when I was 17 years old. I was thrilled to finally get into the action, and it was not until I had my own sons that I understood why when I was leaving for boot camp I saw my father cry.

Jack Jarriel

Darien, Georgia, just across the creek from Glynn County, was my home. My father worked for Scott Construction Company and was building several bridges across the rivers between Darien and Brunswick as a part of the war effort to improve transportation. My first cousin married a blimp pilot from Glynco, and I visited them often during the war. He was on patrol along the coast from Brunswick to Savannah looking for German submarines.

Do you remember that the top of auto headlights was required to be painted black so as to minimize the chances of being spotted by enemy aircraft? My job was to paint the tops of the lights for our car and truck. I couldn't find any black paint, so I cut strips of black friction tape and stuck them on. This lasted through the war with only a few minor repairs.

Scrap metal was selling for two cents a pound. I scoured Darien looking for anything made of metal to sell. Just one five-pound chunk (which wasn't much) would pay the nine cents cost of a movie and give me one cent change for two Tootsie Roll pops. I remember that the government asked people to turn in their used toothpaste tubes to help the war effort.

Remember that sugar was rationed and we got only a very small amount? Well, we owned a farm in Tattnall County, Georgia, and, as a result of being farmers, got an additional ration of 25 pounds of sugar for canning purposes. Do you remember taking your dimes to the post office to buy savings stamps to put in the little stamp books? When you filled one up, you could turn it in for a $25 savings bond. I think that I bought two bonds that were the result of my big scrap-metal business.

Don't know whether or not anyone noticed but it was during the war that the cornbread served in the school cafeterias changed from being made with white corn to yellow corn. The white corn was used to feed the troops while the yellow corn, formerly used for livestock feed, was used to feed the wartime civilians. Most of the butter went to the troops and margarine was invented. It was initially white and people objected to it. Then they came out with the little package of yellow coloring to knead into the margarine. The next thing was to sell it with the coloring in, and it has remained that way even today as I peck away on my keyboard.

Eugene Palmer
Eugene Palmer's parents owned Palmer's 5 & 10 Store at the pier on St. Simons Island.

I was only seven years old when the Japanese attacked Pearl Harbor, and it frightened me to death. I had no idea where Pearl Harbor was and felt that "they" (whoever "they" were) were going to come and attack St. Simons. I remember hearing about the Bataan Death March, and my recollection is that someone who lived up on East Beach had a relative who was caught in that and it distressed me terribly. I don't really remember any deprivation, but I have a vague recollection of yearning for something like, perhaps, chocolate candy that I couldn't have because of the war. I also remember hearing the song "The White Cliffs of Dover" and longing for the "peace ever after" that song promised.

My father, Gene Palmer, Sr., who at that time owned and operated Palmer's 5 & 10 on St. Simons, went to work at the shipyard as a shipfitter. He worked shift work and on the off shift would go to his store and try to manage the business. One of my father's brothers came and lived in our guest room for a time while he also worked at the shipyard.

My father also joined the Coast Guard Auxiliary. He and others, like Captain Leo Arnold and George Hay Stevens, who were our immediate neighbors, went out on private yachts at night to patrol for German submarines. I don't think I knew it at the time, but I learned later that the only thing they had in the way of a weapon was a submachine gun.

A nightclub was built on St. Simons at the corner of Arnold Road and Ocean Boulevard right in our backyard. I recall seeing the military men going into that nightclub in droves and finding empty beer and whiskey bottles just outside our back fence. I remember hearing the music, which must have been from a jukebox, while I was trying to sleep. That building was built over a fairly low spot. Rather than filling it all in, they simply built brick piers on which to set the floor joists and filled in around the edges. This made a rather cavernous crawl space underneath that building.

Fresh food was not too plentiful, so my father planted a victory garden in a vacant lot. We also had some chickens in a pen in our backyard that provided us with eggs and an occasional chicken dinner. I remember that neither my mother nor the black lady who was working for us had the nerve to kill the chickens. When it came time for us to have chicken, it was my job to cut off the chicken's head with a hatchet.

The combination of chicken feed and the proximity of that crawl space under the night club attracted rats. I can remember my father shooting rats with a small .22 rifle. I can also remember some of those rats getting into our attic crawl space, and one of them even chewed a hole in the ceiling.

Somehow my father managed to buy a new reel-type mower. My little brother, John, who was about four or five years old, decided that he was going to "fix" the mower. He removed and lost several screws that were used to adjust the clearance between the reel and the blade. Because of the war, spare screws were not available. We were never able to use that lawn mower.

I remember walking on the beach and seeing oil-soaked life preservers and other debris that had washed up on the beach as a result of a German submarine having sunk our ships just offshore. I never did find a survivor or a dead body, but I was always afraid I might. I once went with my father and George Hay Stevens on a boat out to a merchant ship that had been raised after having been torpedoed just off the coast. The ship was anchored in the St. Simons Sound between the pier and Jekyll Island. The hole where the torpedo struck the ship looked large enough to drive an automobile through. There were also what appeared to be wooden patches on the hull up near the bow of the ship, and I was told that those were holes where the submarine had surfaced and shelled the ship. I don't really know whether it was this particular ship or whether it was another one, but I remember hearing some of the men talk about a ship having been sunk in St. Andrews Sound, just off Cumberland, and that some of the sailors who survived were attacked by sharks and barracudas.*

Army maneuvers were held in the sand dunes on the beach. At that time there were large sand dunes just south of the King and Prince Hotel. They came and dug gun emplacements that my friends and I had fun playing in after they had left. The house that we lived in was almost exactly in line with one of the runways at the St. Simons airport, which was taken over by the Navy and used to train pilots. Those Navy planes took off right over our house. They made a terrific noise to which we finally became accustomed. An aunt, uncle, and cousins visited us during this time, and the first time they heard one of those planes come over the house, they thought it was about to crash.

Camp Marion
East Beach,
St. Simons Island, Georgia
Courtesy of Ida Atkinson Cecil

The substantial increase in population in Glynn County, caused mostly by the influx of new shipyard workers, seriously taxed the school system. I went to school in Brunswick through the third grade, but the year I was in the fourth grade, all St. Simons grammar school children had to attend school at a day camp on East Beach called Camp Marion. It was not large enough to accommodate all of us, so we had to attend school in split sessions while they were building a new grammar school on St. Simons. The new grammar school was completed in time for me to start the fifth grade there in the fall of 1944.

The street that is now called Ocean View Drive was known as Railroad Street. This was the street where the horse-drawn trolley traveled between the pier and the old hotel that was on the street near its intersection with Arnold Road. [This was before the causeway was built, so guests arrived by boat.] When I was a boy, Railroad Street dead-ended into Arnold Road. I remember what I thought were some old railroad tracks (now I know that they were probably the old trolley tracks) stacked in the dunes at the foot of Railroad Street just across Arnold Road. Those railroad tracks went in one of the first scrap-iron drives.

There was a nice lady, Mrs. Schnitcher, who lived on St. Simons and ran a yarn and gift shop out of her home. She was a German emigrant and spoke with an accent. I don't have any idea how long she had lived in this country and I am sure she was completely loyal, but everyone was a little bit paranoid in those days. There was some concern that this lady might be a German spy. Of course, she wasn't, but the thought certainly added some intrigue. The Lewis family, who had immigrated here from England and had sons involved in the war, destroyed everything that they owned that had "made in Germany" or "made in Japan" stamped on it.

* Possibly the *Esparta*, which was sunk in that vicinity.

Virginia Dean Foster

I'll always remember our peaceful island prior to World War II. The influx of summer folk disrupted the locals, consisting of approximately 600 families. What a relief when they finally went home! Fishing on the pier, rambling the beach, such heaven!

I was in charge of the playground on St. Simons and left to work for Southern Bell in its little office across from the (old) Casino. Back then we had "long" lines and were constantly interrupted by someone picking up the phone to tell us, "There is no one home, operator." This could be very frustrating on a busy switchboard.

I was on the switchboard on the beautiful Sunday, December 7, when Pearl Harbor was bombed. Usually a very quiet day, this Sunday the board lit up all over. The customers were asking,

"Is it true, operator, about Pearl Harbor?" As we weren't permitted radios in the switchboard room, I called the supervisor. She verified it had happened and came flying to help with the many calls. So many people wanted to call family or friends that we had to restrict many calls for only the essential ones. Then the Navy came in, taking over the St. Simons airport. I applied for a position with the Navy and was given the job as chief operator.

Virginia Kent and I were asked by Captain Alfred Brockington to go out deep-sea fishing about 35 miles out. Since we had never done this before, we were glad to be included in a party. By the time the anchor dropped, most of us were seasick. The rest were catching fish as fast as they could bring them in. Suddenly the boat gave a lurch. It was a very calm sea, but Captain Alfred told us that we'd go about five miles closer to shore to try fishing there. Well, I found out later we were about where the tankers had been blown up. He later indicated to my brother-in-law that the surge could only have been from a submarine watching us.

You probably heard about our German lady spy! She suddenly appeared on the island asking the various ladies for cakes, pies, and cookies for the military. She also asked around for pictures of the bases and the sea coast for her personal collection. I had a very uneasy feeling about her and told my sister, Lucille Kent, that I did not believe the lady was what she said she was. She disappeared and I later asked one of the men civilians on the island what happened. She was what I feared and had been sent away under protective custody until after the war.

My sister, Lucille, took many pictures of the tankers at the pier, not realizing cameras were being confiscated by the military. She used a place in South Carolina to have them developed and did not know the developers in Glynn County had to turn in developed pictures.

Mrs. Charles (Eunice) Daniel

We were living in Atlanta when Pearl Harbor was bombed. After that everyone wanted to get into something that would help with the war effort. My husband, Charlie, was working in real estate. He wrote Mr. Alfred Jones at Sea Island because he had previously done some work for him. Mr. Jones gave the letter to someone at the J. A. Jones Construction Company.

My sister, Nancy, had moved in with my mother, Mrs. Collier, in her house on St. Simons, which is near the Coast Guard Station at East Beach. Nancy had graduated from the University of Georgia in journalism and worked with Weetie Tift, who started *The Star* newspaper.

Charlie went to St. Simons in May 1942. He took our two dogs with him and stayed in the back room of Mother's house. Our son, Chip, who was 14 years old and our daughter, Susan, who was 11 years old, and I stayed in Atlanta until school was out. I was pregnant but had a miscarriage, so it wasn't until July that we moved to St. Simons. We came on the day train and moved to a house on Wood Avenue, just around the corner from Mother's. We thought it was too much for my mother to have four people come into her house, especially when two of them were very lively children.

When we moved here, it was not long after the two tankers had been torpedoed, and oil was still on the beach. Being so close to the ocean, we had to observe blackouts every night. Riding the school bus to Brunswick to school was a new experience for the kids and me. I had to get up at 5 a.m. to get them off to school. When Susan was in the fifth grade, she went to school in the two-story house on East Beach. Mrs. Ledbetter was her teacher. In December of that year, Mother died suddenly of a heart attack. She was only 60 years old. We moved into the house with Nancy so that she wouldn't have to live alone.

Meantime, *The Star* had gone out of existence, and Nancy went to work as a teletypist with the Civil Air Patrol. The CAP was moved across the airport road when the Navy took over McKinnon Airport. However, they still used the runways. The little private planes went out everyday with bombs attached underneath. The CAP was phased out when the blimp base came in. At the shipyard Charlie worked in the railroad department. He worked at night because he couldn't stand being out in that sun all day. The only thing that made him look like a railroad man was the red bandanna that he had tied around his neck. He was in charge of directing the trains that came in at night to the shipyard. One car would have to go to the restaurant with what we called embalming fluid. It was the milk that came in cars from Wisconsin. Another car would contain paint and would be shunted off to the right area, etc.

At the end of the war, my sister married one of the CAP men and moved to Philadelphia. We still had our house in Atlanta and were planning to move back, but Chip said that he didn't want to go back and Susan said she didn't want to either. My husband said, "What the heck am I going to do now that the shipyard is closed?" Nelson Niall, who was also from Atlanta and was a good friend of my husband's (they both had been born in the Kirkwood area of Atlanta), suggested that he start a small construction business. So Charlie got a pickup truck and a couple of men to work for him. He loved it! Nelson got him started with a lot of people. Charles always wanted to do things with his hands. He was good at it and so we stayed on St. Simons.

Virginia Stribling Blackshear

My family—consisting of Mama (Clara Stribling), two brothers, W. L. (Tee) and Guerry Boone, and myself—moved from Macon to St. Simons in 1938. Everyone of us loved living there from the very beginning. It was a great place to grow up.

The first time I was aware of any war was the Sunday morning Pearl Harbor was bombed. U-boats began to appear off our coasts. Once I saw survivors being towed in by the Coast Guard. At night, there was a total blackout . . . no candles or lights without heavy curtains. There was also a mounted patrol that guarded the beaches all day. My friend Dudley Traywick and I were walking down Bruce Drive on East Beach when someone came to take her home. Her father, a colonel stationed in the Philippines, had been taken prisoner. He survived but was forever scarred.

Mama and her friend Nora Cooper were plane spotters. They took their stations on top of the King and Prince Hotel two or three nights a week from 11 p.m. until dawn. They rode their bicycles to and from because of the gas shortage and the blackout.

Fresh produce began to rise in price, as did gasoline and car repairs. Rationing began with meat, sugar, and coffee. Mama became more concerned, having the responsibility of three young children, so regretfully we moved back to Macon to live with our grandparents until the war was over. We returned to the island in June of '46. What a happy day for us!.

From 1938 to 1943, Tee, Guerry Boone, and I rode the school bus to school in Brunswick. We waited on the corner of Bruce Drive by the Coast Guard Station to be picked up around 7:15 a.m., rain or shine, light or dark! The bus picked up all the children from first grade to high school seniors. It was wonderful!

Carolyn Butler
Mrs. Butler was 90 years old when she wrote this information. She taught at the St. Simons Elementary School from the time it began in 1943 until she retired.

My way of life completely changed when I moved to St. Simons. I had always lived on a street in Alachua, Florida, where four generations knew everyone. When I came to St. Simons to teach school, there was rush, rush, rush. At night drawn drapes . . . controlled lighting.

Mrs. Carolyn Butler's 3rd Grade Class
1944 - the year that St. Simon's Elementary School opened

Everything changed from my life in Florida. There was only a small Community Church on the south end of the island, which I doubt would seat one hundred people. However, from this little Community Church has come the Methodist, Baptist, and Presbyterian churches.

I witnessed the building of the St. Simons Elementary School from the clearing of a scrub oak field to when it was finished in 1944. There were six teachers, the cafeteria was not finished, all the tile was not down on the floor, and horseflies darkened the windows. After school began, I saw a truck with benches along the side come loaded with German soldiers. They worked there until the school was completed.

Now they are building a new school at Frederica to accommodate the island growth. "Time and tide wait for no man."

Frances Postell Burns

My first relatives came to St. Simons with Oglethorpe. My maiden name was Postell. My mother's maiden name was Joyce Symons. My grandfather Symons was the bookkeeper at the Dodge sawmill on Gascoigne Bluff. They lived near where the Sea Island Yacht Club was located [on the Frederica River]. Mama and Daddy went to school at the mill. A guy who worked at the post office asked, "How long have you been here?" I said, "About two hundred years!"

My husband, Allen Burns, was reared at the Dodge Orphan Home at Frederica. He worked at the ice house at the pier and also drove the school bus. He was a very strict bus driver. Said he wasn't going to let anyone on his bus get hurt. Of course, he had to put one or two ruffians off. He wouldn't leave them on the side of the road, though. He would take them home and tell their parents why they couldn't ride the bus for several days.

During the war, we were living in the old school house at Frederica. It had big, old windows that went from the ceiling to the floor. We didn't change them because it would have cost too much. When the ships were torpedoed, those windows rattled like a child was shaking them. When one of the ships was salvaged and brought into the St. Simons Sound, Allen called me to come down to the pier and see the hole in it. It was big enough to put a car in, yet it was enough above the water line that they could bring it into port and get it fixed.

We had to have coupon books to get gasoline. I remember I had to take Mama to Waycross. The doctor was watching her to see if there would be a return of the cancer. It turned out it was all right, but they gave us a little extra gas to take her to the specialist there. Because of the overcrowded schools, Zoe Ann, our daughter, started her first year of school at Camp Marion, the first elementary school on St. Simons, and her second year at the new St. Simons Elementary School. My first cousin's son, Postell Shadman, was killed in Germany during the war.

Sarah Frances Gragg Owen

My family and I moved to Brunswick the summer of 1940 for my father to run a sawmill and planing mill. The U.S. Maritime Commission bought his plant and location in 1941 and built the shipyard. With the money from the sale, my father, A. Wayne Gragg, built and operated Bailey-Gragg Motor Company. This company serviced the automobiles for the shipyard workers and tried to keep old cars running so that the workers could go back and forth to their jobs.

There were no new cars to buy during the war years, and it was very important to keep the old cars in good condition. I worked at the motor company in the summers when I was home from college.

Reginald Wilson

Prior to the war, we were living in a small town called Townsend in McIntosh County, adjacent to Glynn County on the north. My dad worked at a large sawmill called Townsend Bandmill Company, which was owned by my uncle, A. Wayne Gragg [who later became mayor of Brunswick]. Most of the mill burned in the summer of 1940, so my uncle decided to rebuild his planing mill operation in Brunswick on the waterfront. We were left behind to finish cutting a large tract of timber. The plan was to saw and dry the lumber at Townsend, then ship it to Brunswick for planing and selling.

We were living at Townsend when the war started in 1941. There was a detachment of soldiers stationed at Townsend to take care of the aerial gunner and bombing ranges nearby. Bombers would come from Hunter Field near Savannah to practice and train before being sent overseas. We left Townsend in 1943 or 1944 and moved to Brunswick. My dad went to work at Glynco, or as it was called at the time, the blimp base, because the shipyard had taken over the site where the sawmill relocated.

I started Glynn Academy that year as a sophomore transferring from Darien High. This was a tremendous change for me. It seemed that half the world was in Glynn Academy. Since I was the new kid on the block, I was immediately called a "pea-picker," as was everyone who moved to that area during the war. I can't say I really enjoyed school that much. It was very crowded and, being a pea-picker, I was expected to move back to the farm after the war. One thing I've come to realize over the years since I graduated from Glynn Academy is that it was one of the best high schools in the state. I will never forget some of the teachers, especially Miss Macon, who taught me in spite of my lazy attitude toward learning. We received a solid, well-rounded secondary education.

We attended church at the First Baptist Church in Brunswick, and soon I made some friends and lived down the pea-picker name. I rode my bicycle to school and, in so doing, had to pass the Hercules plant, where a detachment of soldiers was stationed. I was in a hurry to finish school so I could join the service.

We lived in Brunswick about a year before moving to St. Simons. I remember the naval air station on the island. The planes impressed me, as did the crash boats, which looked like PT boats except they lacked the torpedo tubes. There was also a destroyer escort, the *Reuben James*, on patrol duty that went to sea each day and returned to anchor between St. Simons and Jekyll Islands at night. Some of the sailors came ashore at the pier on St. Simons.

Frankie Quarterman Obuchowski

My aunt was a member of the "hot-bedder" industry. She had three eight-hour shifts of sleepers and a lot of big pots for meals!

We were meticulous in observing all the rules for the blackout drills. I think we would've been humiliated had we let any bit of light be seen. Supposedly, the planes would drop five pounds of flour on your roof if they spotted the light.

There was a truck that came by several times a month to collect what we now call "recycling." We saved and smashed cans, tinfoil from cigarette packages, and anything made of real rubber. God forbid that you needed a tire. There were only retreads, and you patched and repatched the inner tubes. When the inner tubes were past help, if you were resourceful, you carefully cut rubber bands to substitute for the drawstrings in your underpants. My mother was especially good at this, and we never had to depend on drawstrings. We had a huge garden even before victory gardens were patriotic. We also had a cow and chickens. Due to the extended family situation, our household never lacked meat, coffee, or sugar. In fact, we were able to share ration coupons and items.

When I started school, there was a banking program which later switched to war saving stamps. When a book was full of stamps, it was exchanged for a war bond. They later became savings bonds, and we still buy them for the grandchildren.

I'm firmly convinced that if kids today had to depend on the Saturday newsreels to follow the news, there would be lots less violence. Let's face it, we didn't even get to listen to the war "live" on radio, much less watch it happening in living color on television. Maybe we were innocent and uninformed, but we were safe on the streets. We *were* fortunate to have the opportunity to watch the launching of the Liberty ships built at the shipyard from the water side . . . aboard a shrimp boat. My folks had a few friends who worked at the shipyard, and they always felt that the boats launched were theirs for having worked on them.

How about V-mail? There were several cousins in service, and my mother and I corresponded with them regularly. A few times we received letters that were severely censored. About the only things left were "Dear Frankie" and "Love" with a few lines that said nothing. They actually cut out the sensitive material with any reference to time and location or the person writing. My fifth-grade teacher had a brother in service and he was tickled to get letters from anyone, so several of us corresponded with him. I remember always standing for the national anthem in the movies or anywhere it was played. It was an automatic response.

In the sixth grade I got really lucky because it was my turn to do the bulletin board on VE Day. There certainly was no shortage of pictures and text in *The Brunswick News* for my board. As I recall, all the sirens in town were activated and all the neighbors ran into the streets and cried.

We moved to Brunswick in the summer of 1940, before my seventh birthday, and in just a few days I started the second grade at Sidney Lanier School. My father worked at the Coastal Chevrolet Company. We lived on Union Street, not too far from the school. Brunswick was a quiet little town, but it seemed quite large compared to the small town of Lumber City in Telfair County. It wasn't long before things changed, though.

When the war began and the shipyard opened, Brunswick became a crowded, busy place. My daddy went to work at the shipyard as a burner (similar to a welder) and, like everyone else, made more money than he had ever made.

Because of the rubber shortage, it became difficult to find underwear with elastic in it. Suddenly I had to wear panties with a drawstring waistband and no elastic in the legs. Besides the tie being uncomfortable, the legs became loose fitting after a few hours' wear, so I'd change to have them fit tighter. My mother complained that I changed underwear three or four times a day. That seems like a minor inconvenience, but at age eight and nine, it was a big problem to me.

Another thing that was difficult to buy was chocolate candy. My sister worked weekends at a grocery store and had the opportunity to buy some when the store got it in. So every now and then she brought some home. That was always a treat!

Since we had moved from Telfair County, we had a steady flow of friends staying with us for several days at a time while they worked at the shipyard and looked for housing. Mother and Daddy were always glad to help friends, but sometimes it did become difficult having extra people in our house so often. Mother had a good friend who ran a boardinghouse, and I remember her telling us how people who worked different shifts shared the same room and same bed.

"War apartments," as they were called, sprang up everywhere. Almost all of the south end of town where the shipyard was located was nothing but apartments. Some of the new friends I made at school lived in them. It was fun when I went to see them and got to see what the apartments looked like on the inside. Every day around 4 o'clock in the afternoon, when the day shift at the shipyard got off, there would be a steady stream of traffic down Albany and Union Streets. I would occasionally get caught while playing at a friend's house and have to wait for a long time to cross the street to go home.

I remember how careful we had to be with our ration stamps, especially for sugar, gas, and tires. My grandparents lived in Telfair County, and every time we had enough gas to go see them on the weekend, we'd drive the 113 miles. It was not unusual to have a flat tire on the way because of the shortage of tires and ours were not very good. I remember one trip when we had three flats on the way there. Daddy would put a cold patch on the inner tube, pump up the tire with a hand pump, and away we'd go. My sister and I always liked watching him repair the tires. It amazes me now to think of how we all took it in stride and thought the trip was just wonderful.

As a little girl, I was addicted to the movies or, as we called it then, the picture show. I think I saw every show that came to Brunswick. I knew all the stars and bought all the movie magazines. I still have my movie star books (composition books with all my favorite stars' pictures pasted in them). During the shipyard days, if you wanted to see a movie, you stood in a long line for hours. There were only two theaters, the Ritz and the Bijou, one at each end of Newcastle Street in the downtown section. It didn't matter what time the movie started, you just went in when they had a seat for you. The movie ran continuously so you watched until you got to the part where you came in and then left so someone else could have your seat. Besides previews and a cartoon, they almost always had a newsreel before the movie. I really didn't like the newsreels showing all the war news with fighting and bombing and didn't pay much attention to them. I wish now I had.

I remember when they christened one of the new ships. My sister's best friend got to christen it. That was pretty exciting. I had a cousin in the Army, and he wrote to us every now and then. I always thought he was a hero, and we were glad for him to come home.

Ione Quarterman Parsons

My dad needed a job. We lived on a farm in Florida and coming to Brunswick meant a very different lifestyle for my family and me. My grandmother lived in Brunswick, and we moved in with her until my father got a job. He was eventually hired at the pulp mill, where he stayed until retirement. My grandmother had a big house and big heart. Taking in boarders was her income and she had lots of them. They were single men looking for a place to stay and do shift work at the shipyard. The need was so great for a while that "hot bedding" was developed. This meant while one person was working, another was sleeping in the same bed. There were two large rooms with as many beds as would fit and always someone was sleeping in them. We were not allowed to play on that side of the house. The men were always very kind to us and gave us treats, saying we reminded them of their children back home.

In his spare time, my dad closed in the back porch and built a dining room so all the men could eat boardinghouse style. They contributed their food stamps so that rationed items could be bought. There was only one bathroom, therefore, a bath schedule was posted on the door at peak times of use.

We were able to rent an apartment in a few months. After the war we were able to buy a house and own a car. For me the greatest thing about the war being over was panties with elastic . . . panties that didn't fall off . . . no more drawstrings or tie-on's! My dad was able to put tires on his jacked-up car. We saw a TV in the window of a furniture store. There were no blackouts. I didn't mind going to school for just a half day, but new schools were built and it was back to a whole day.

During the war I bought some war (savings) bonds during the school drives . . . 10 cents a week. I cashed them in recently and bought a woodstove for my cabin in Hiawassee. I am very happy that we came to the Brunswick area to live. We made some great friends, and I met my wonderful husband, Seabert.

Bessie Mormon

We were living in Atlanta in the early 1920s. Jobs were hard to find. My dad, Ernest Henley, was working at a Hercules knot camp. Hercules had a knot camp (pine stumps) at a place called Rockingham, Georgia. It was a turpentine place. He went there alone. In the meantime, he wrote to the Hercules Plant in Brunswick asking for a job. There was a job in Brunswick for him so he went there in 1927. My mother, my sister, and myself moved from Butts County, Georgia, to Brunswick when I was four years old.

Back in that time Hercules wasn't what it is now. My dad filled barrels with rosin and turpentine. He worked for Hercules for 38 years. During that time, he was head of the union, and because women were in the workforce during the war, he was in charge of the women workers. Of course, we all went to school in Brunswick. I first started school at Risley. It was called Colored Memorial. Then they changed it to Risley.

On December 7, 1941, I was at home listening to the radio as usual when it was announced about the bombing of Pearl Harbor. Like everybody else I said, "Where in the world is Pearl Harbor?" I had never heard of Pearl Harbor! Everybody kept wondering, and, of course, I was the bookworm so everybody thought I should have known. Then we went to war with Germany—one right behind the other. Some men signed up for service. Most were drafted. I remember that one of my classmates joined the WACS. Her name was Angie Mack. Over the years she never came back to Brunswick to live. I heard that after the war she got married and moved somewhere in North Carolina.

I remember when the ships were torpedoed. Those torpedoes shook everything. At the time, we didn't know what it was until we turned the radio on the next morning and they were talking about it. But it just shook and rattled everything.

The USO for blacks met Friday and Saturday nights at the pavilion at Selden School or in respectable homes. Mr. and Mrs. Holmes on Cochran Avenue had a big home. They would rent a jukebox. A bus picked us up and took us to the dance. They were very strict. They locked the front and back doors so no one could leave the building. We danced, talked, and had a good time. They served refreshments of sandwiches, cookies, and drinks. After the dance, the boys boarded the bus and went back to camp and the girls were driven home.

All of us remember rationing. Mother had to have coupons and a birth certificate to get Carnation (canned) milk for the baby. I usually went for the milk at City Drug Store. I went so often the lady at the drug store got suspicious and questioned me. So the next time I went I took the coupons, the birth certificate, and the big, fat baby!

I spent the summer of 1945 in Cleveland, Ohio, with my sister, who worked for the National Key Company. The day the war ended was one day we couldn't forget! In Cleveland people were in the streets . . . some crying, some went to church and prayed, and others were blowing horns and turning over cars as well as streetcars or buses.

Herbert R. Gordy

I worked in the J. A. Jones shipyard during the summers of 1944 and 1945, building Liberty ships. During the months I was in school, I delivered *The Brunswick News* and Western Union telegrams and also worked as a mechanic's helper at Joe Owen's Coastal Chevrolet. But first, a little family background.

Before the Depression years set in, around the mid 1920s, my mother's family moved to Brunswick from Lyons, Georgia, and my grandfather became the caretaker for a large tract of Union Bag Paper property near the Sterling area. He also did a little farming. Around 1929, my dad lost his job with the railroad, and we were forced to live with my grandparents. Times were very hard, and my dad would take any work he could get. Finally, after Roosevelt and the New Deal came along, Dad went to work for the Hercules Powder Company in Brunswick. The year was 1933 and $13 a week was good money then. We moved to an old house on Cook Street, which was the street that ran right down to the entrance of the Hercules gate. It was near Glynn Avenue. The house was an old, single-story frame house with two chinaberry trees in the front yard. We lived at the same address until 1950.

During the years 1941-44, there was an Army camp on Glynn Avenue, just across from Tait's Auto Service. I remember as a teenager being awakened by the sound of soldiers doing close-order drill on the street in front of our house. They would be out about daylight and stay half the day. I would feel so sorry for these poor guys marching for hours in the heat. The encampment had from two to three thousand soldiers. They lived in temporary square-shaped buildings, with wood siding and floors with a canvas on top. I would guesstimate they were perhaps 25 feet on each side and that they were built to last no longer than five years. Perhaps six men slept in each tent, surely no more than 10. It is hard to even estimate how many tent buildings or barracks were there, but the lot in front of the Hercules was filled.

One afternoon a soldier from the base stopped at our house and asked my mother if she had a room she could spare and an extra bed. He had recently married and wanted to bring his new bride to Brunswick from some place up north. He had been all over the neighborhood looking for a room to rent, with no luck. My mother felt sorry for the young man and told him that we had a studio couch in the living room and that if the young couple could stand this arrangement, she would let them sleep there. They soon moved in but didn't stay long. He was transferred, and his young wife went back north.

One of the things that I most remember about the war years was that you had to stand in line everywhere you went . . . at the drugstore, grocery store, post office. If you had the courage to go to the Ritz or Bijou Theaters on Saturday or Sunday afternoon, you would have to stand in line for some time before you could get in. There was a bus service in those days, and often the buses would be crowded. Everywhere were people, occupying facilities that were built for half their number. Temporary housing was put up in vacant lots all over town to accommodate those transients working at the shipyard or other defense industries. As a kid delivering telegrams, I soon learned where all the housing units were and knew where every street was.

During the war, our family was a busy one. My dad was working long hours overtime at Hercules. My mom was working in the Hercules cafeteria, and I was working wherever I could when I wasn't in school. The first summer I worked at the shipyard I was a welder, and the second summer I was a sheet-metal worker. I certainly got some rare experiences and met some rare individuals during the shipyard days. There were many unsavory people as well as good folks working at all different jobs . . . welders, shipfitters, sheet-metal workers, etc. A man that I worked with drove from near Waycross every day to work in the shipyard. He lived on the edge of the Okefenokee swamp and made moonshine whiskey at home, which he sold to some of his friends at work. There were a lot of ladies working at different jobs, but mostly the jobs where physical strength was not required. As you probably guessed, a lot of the ladies were not the church-going type.

During the war, with gasoline rationing, Dad, Mother, and I had bicycles. On Sunday afternoon, we all set out to ride to St. Simons from Brunswick. We finally made it over there and back, but we were completely bushed. Later, I rode my bike over to Darien to visit a girlfriend, but it was a terrible ride back to Brunswick. It took weeks to get over that escapade.

Mary Frances Smith Ewing

I had no family members in the service. However, the war changed the pace of Brunswick. People moved in from all over to work at the shipyard. The pay was very good, so it helped the economy. During the war, there were dances in the ballroom at the Oglethorpe Hotel. The decor was Victorian. The dances were sponsored by the USO, and most guys from the blimp base came. The music was grand . . . such songs as "Smoke Gets in Your Eyes," "Don't Sit Under the Apple Tree," "Stardust," "Sentimental Journey." The dress was casual . . . only dresses (no slacks in those days). Sometimes the dances were formal.

The Oglethorpe Hotel
Brunswick, Georgia
Courtesy of Jack Lang

Clara Larsen Klimp

Pearl Harbor . . . We always went to vesper services at the Lutheran church. I sang in the choir, and during the service (we always passed our little notes around in choir) Virginia Nuss passed a written note that said, "The Japanese attacked Pearl Harbor today." *"Where's Pearl Harbor?"* I thought. I had no idea what they were talking about.

However, it wasn't long before Army truck convoys came down Highway 17 from Fort Stewart. They were filled with soldiers on leave. The parish house of our church on Gloucester Street had always been such a bare room. Now it was set up with furniture, a ping pong table, and a piano for the servicemen to use. Since the parish house was located in back of the church, we placed a sign in front of the church on Gloucester Street inviting the soldiers to come in. Usually the teenagers of our church manned the meeting place on Saturdays and the pastor would walk in and out. The servicemen came and played the piano or cards, wrote letters, and just had a good time.

The biggest entertainment for the girls as teenagers was the USO. Boy was it strict! I remember Mrs. Stevenson and Mrs. Ed Diemmer were chaperones. When we went to the Fort Stewart dances, we met at the Y on Union Street. We traveled in either Army trucks or buses and would usually have one or two chaperones sitting in the back with us and one in the front with the driver. When they brought us home, they brought us to our house. When they let us out, they stayed until they saw you go in and close the door.

They were also very strict with the girls at the USO functions in town. I think that was important at the time. The only way I had to get to the USO was if somebody took me. Mr. Farley of Farley's Shoe Store where I worked sometimes took me to the USO after work. I didn't get off until after 10 o'clock on Saturday night, and it really was too far to walk that time of night. The first thing I had to do after I got out of the car was report to the chaperone. They didn't let you get away with anything.

During the war, a USO was located across from the Army camp near the Hercules Powder Company. They had a dance every Saturday night. Most of the time they had a jukebox. Chester Anderson's Band might have played for some of the dances. Later on this USO closed and one opened in one of the old houses on Union Street. After the war, the USO by the Hercules became Benny Burks Nightclub.

At this little Army camp by the Hercules were guys from North Dakota, Iowa, and other areas of the U. S. that were settled by Norwegians. Many were Lutherans and came to my church. Often we would get a group of them together and go to Aunt Sophie's house. She and Uncle Fritz were born in Norway. Once some Norwegians were hitchhiking to Brunswick from Charleston, South Carolina, where their ship came in. Somebody had picked them up and found out they were Norwegian and couldn't speak English. They immediately turned them over to Aunt Sophie. I remember one Norwegian sailor was Tony. The only American song he knew was the "Strip Polka."

At this Army camp was one special guy who took care of Pauline (my cousin) and me. We had so much fun together. Uncle Fritz would allow him to drive his car. He was 27 years old and we were giving him a fit. He went overseas and was in Germany. He wrote both of us letters. They both were love letters. I wrote him back and said I really was disappointed because I thought he loved only me. The letter I opened said, "Dear Pauline." Then he wrote back and said how disappointed he was in me because . . . he was crazy as all get out! Haven't heard from him since the war. Aunt Sophie thought a lot of him.

As I said, I worked at Farley's Shoe Store, and during the war shoes were rationed. Some of the shoes not made out of leather didn't require a ration stamp, but if they had any leather at all they did. I have forgotten how many stamps a family or each person got. I do know a lot of mothers and fathers went practically barefoot in order to get the kids shoes because their feet would grow so fast. The store was only allotted so many shoes. When we did get a shipment in, it was bedlam.

I believe each person got two pairs of shoes a year—two stamps a year. I hate to think what would happen if we had something like that today. Back then there were people who were honest simply to be honest. Some of them would get a stamp, lay it in their book, and take it out. We were not allowed to accept a stamp unless it came out of the ration book. It was an interesting time. Mr. Farley had the safety shoe concession down at the shipyard, where he sold safety shoes to the workers, so he was usually gone. He opened his store on Newcastle Street in the afternoon for a short time. I worked afternoons and Saturdays.

In downtown Brunswick, the streets were full of people all the time. Even though there was no gas, traffic would be backed up. During the Christmas holidays, people trying to find a parking place proved to be quite an interesting time. I remember Pastor Heglar used to have devotions for the German prisoners at the blimp base because a lot of them were Lutherans. Margaret Blumquist, a WAVE who went to our church, was at Glynco. She married one of Hank's (my husband) friends. Hank came to the blimp base in June 1945 before the war was over in August.

My cousin Pauline and I were in Ft. Lauderdale when the war ended. We had decided to take a week's vacation and went to see our uncle Haakon. The night the war ended, Haakon had taken us out on his boat in the Gulf Stream. I got seasick. We could hear the bells ringing on shore as we started to come in. We found it was the end of the war, but Haakon wouldn't let us go downtown.

Eloise Meadows Hoffmeyer

I will never forget the shock when all of us who were Glynn Academy students at the time were called into the auditorium on Monday morning December 8th, 1941, and heard President Roosevelt's message declaring war—nor D-Day when the churches in Brunswick were opened and filled with people praying for peace and victory—nor

VE Day when again we filled the churches, thanking God for the end of the war in Europe and for victory there.

I worked in the local shipyard in the summer of 1943 in the personnel department and attended college later in the western part of the state. The trains I took were filled with servicemen—standing in the aisle.

I stayed at home the next two years. Thanks to Pauline Torkildsen, I was invited to the Luther League at St. James Lutheran Church. There in January 1946 I met Ralph Hoffmeyer, an ensign in the Navy at the radar training school on St. Simons Island. He was released from the Navy in the summer, and we were married on January 1, 1947. By then he was back in college on the G.I. Bill.

Doris Murdock Camp

I was born and raised in Brunswick. I have a sister, Audrey, and two brothers, Harry (Buddy) and Charles Robert (Tony). Harry and Audrey worked for the FBI during the war. Charles Robert worked for Southern Bell. Our father, F. Murdock, worked for Southern Bell and did a lot of work on Jekyll Island. There was a radar point located there.

We lived on Niles Avenue near the Hercules where an Army camp was set up. Near the camp was a USO to which we went. Mother was a chaperone, and they were very strict with us girls. We had to stay in the building. We went dancing at the USO almost every night and dressed in evening dresses. When we dated, the guy always had to meet the parents. All dates were double dates, and no alcohol was to be on the date's breath.

There was a guy named Jimmy Fitzgerald stationed at the Army camp. He loved to polka, and the girls would line up and wait for him to come up and give them a spin around the floor. After the war, many boys who had been stationed at the Army camp in Brunswick came back and visited my parents. We also went to Camp Stewart, and I along with other girls in full costume, students of Vivian Morgan, would entertain the soldiers by tap dancing.

I remember the day the tankers were torpedoed. David Gould, Doris Lane, and I went sailing and got outside the marker. It was rough, and we had taken down the sails and tried to start the motor, but water had gotten into the gas tank. David rowed us back to Brunswick.

Mrs. Lane, who owned the Monte Vista Lodge on Lanier Boulevard, housed some of the survivors from the tankers. I remember seeing them in the living room. They were speechless. When they were offered food, they couldn't eat because of the shock of the experience. The beaches were a mess from the debris. The holes in the ships were large enough to drive an Army truck through. Mr. Woods, who owned a plumbing company, went with some of his men to retrieve some of the bodies from the twisted metal in the tankers.

I worked at Glynco Naval Air Station as secretary to the commander in 1944-45. I married a Marine paratrooper stationed there who had been overseas and was waiting to be discharged. We dated for a year, married, and moved to Washington, D. C., where he worked at the Pentagon until he was discharged. We moved back to his hometown in Hickory, North Carolina.

Frances O'Brien Glover

Brunswick was our home. My father worked at the Brunswick Marine repairing boats and was quite busy. Some of my younger brothers sold newspapers at the shipyard at the change of shifts; it was quite profitable. My mother helped. She had to get them up early in the morning. She also put their money in a "safe place." A friend and I set up a lemonade stand and sold drinks, comic books, etc. and caught the shifts as they left the shipyard walking along Albany Street. My oldest brother, even though he was not old enough, kept trying to join the Navy. He did finally enlist . . . just a bit over 17.

The USO was located on Union Street at the old Perry Business School. My sister was very active in the USO, and I was very envious. The ones who were too young to attend were invited on Sunday nights for movies. I considered this glamorous and could hardly wait until I was old enough, but, thank God, the war did end. Even though I was not part of the USO, I later took part in the Servicemen's Club. Not quite as exciting, but fun.

Lucille Way Reu
Mrs. Reu's husband, A. H. Reu, was plant manager at the Hercules Powder Company.

I was very busy during the war with volunteer work, and there were a great many phases of this work. Besides being a mother with three children, the oldest being a teenager and the boys each being four years apart in age, I was engaged in rolling bandages one morning every week. We had to be very, very particular about them, not because the bandage on the person had to be so good but because the bandage had to be packed just perfect so it wouldn't take up too much room. We worked very hard and very steadily all through the time that the war had need of them.

Another thing I did was airplane observation. We phoned every plane sighting to the Jacksonville station. That was quite busy and important work. I did get gas, which I needed very much to go out to the country club for this. Actually, if you were in Brunswick and you wanted to go to the island it took all your gas for the week to make one trip over and back.

I went to the USO, which was a big house in town that was bought or rented by the government and fixed over into recreation rooms. It had a big kitchen. There were big rooms where they danced and had other activities, which made it a nice place for the servicemen to relax, read, or enjoy other forms of recreation. We helped mend their clothes, sew on buttons, wash anything that they couldn't do for themselves, and entertain them. We had a brigade of girls who were invited to come down and visit and come to the dances when they had them. We were to help them in any way we could.

Red Cross Volunteers rolling bandages
Courtesy of Sea Island Archives

Those three things I did all during the war. I also was grade mother at the school for each one of the three grades. I carried refreshments to the school anytime they wanted to have a party. I also worked at the Sunday school as superintendent of the Bible school. As a rule I taught the Bible class because I did know the Bible.

Metal was very scarce. Every round tin can we opened we were supposed to cut out the top and bottom so there would be a cylinder with open ends. Then we stepped on it to flatten it, which made it easier to pack.

One of the things the Hercules made was an ingredient that went into one of the gun powders. They earned an E Flag, a War Effort Flag, in recognition of their having produced a special amount for the war effort.

I had an adventure getting food canned for ourselves in the war effort. The county agent came to one of our meetings and urged all of us to do some cooking and canning so that we would be helping in the war effort. We also would have our own food. I agreed to spend a morning canning. I had bought the things we were going to can and got the materials together, but cooking is not my talent. I was very slow about everything. I never did get through before the county agent had to leave. The jars didn't seal very well so I had to use the food right away. I hadn't canned much so we just used it up. My effort at that didn't amount to a row of pins!

Anne Harwell North

My maiden name was Harwell and I am a third generation in Brunswick. My mother was a Torras. I graduated from Glynn Academy in 1943. Our home was on Gloucester Street. Both of my brothers were in the service. My mother and I lived alone and held together as most women did in those days. We had stars on flags in our windows for my brothers and were fortunate enough to have them come home safely.

The small Army contingent that patrolled Highway 17 in Brunswick was built next to the Hercules on the corner of Highway 17 and L Street. The first outfit to be stationed there was a National Guard unit from Massachusetts. Quite a few of those fellows married girls from Brunswick and still live here. People in our area treated them like they were sons, and when they were transferred, there were many tears. The next outfit was an MP group—all over six feet tall.

The USO was directly across L Street on the corner. My mother, Grace North, Mrs. Harry Vickers, Marian Harley, and many more ladies chaperoned dances at the USO and served once or twice a week for the boys stationed there. I met my husband at that USO, and we were married July 31, 1943. When Lou and I married, people chipped in with their gasoline rationing stamps so we could go to Jacksonville on our honeymoon

The same USO ladies were in charge of getting a Greyhound busload of girls to go to the Service Club on Friday nights at Camp

Stewart. We all wore long evening dresses and danced every dance from 8 to 11 p.m. As we got on the bus for the trip home, off came our shoes, feet black and blue. We always stopped at Midway to go in for a Coke. One night I heard a soldier tell another, "I told you these Georgia girls don't wear shoes!"

During the summer, many times we rode our bikes to St. Simons, spent the day, and rode home. The drug store on the island was the only place to get something to eat. Since we had ridden our bikes facing the sun both ways, you can imagine how scorched we were. Occasionally, we rode on a bus, but those old, rickety wooden bridges were frightening on a bus.

We had a hurricane in 1944. I worked at the shipyard, and they told everyone to go home. It wasn't long after I made it home that the salt water was past our front door on Gloucester Street. Windsor Park was a lake, and Reverend Hornsberger waded in the street, stopping people trying to go through to get to the island. Most of the people working at the shipyard had come from inland Georgia and knew nothing about what tides and wind could do.

Edwina Tyson

At the beginning of the war I was 30 years old. Toby and I were married in 1937, and our oldest child was born in 1939. When my oldest child was born, I couldn't do anything for that baby! That was my parents' baby! I couldn't go across the street with her by myself . . . Mother always followed. So when she was 10 months old, I told them they could have her and I went back to work. I worked for the Sea Island Company from 1936 until my parents got sick and I had to come home. My father died in 1942 and my mother in 1943. Our daughter was three years old when they died. I said I was glad they had her because that was the only grandbaby they knew.

I had started working for the Sea Island Company in 1936. My husband also worked there. It was Depression times and it was a good place to work. As I look at it now, I wonder how in the world we made it on the wages of 22 cents an hour. They laugh at me when I tell them that it was during the Depression when I learned how to save a nickel. We would save a whole month to get 25 cents to go to a football game. Those were rough times.

The Ballads had a cottage on Sea Island, and it seemed that nobody could work for them. It looked like they were hard to get along with. They would always be trying to get somebody to work for them, so Mr. Compton, the manager, told Toby, "You know you've got a job here at the hotel. I'm just gonna see if you can work for the Ballads." Toby went down there and worked two or three years . . . till after Mr. Ballad died.

I worked at the hotel but stayed with Toby at the Ballads. We just didn't go home very much. It was hard for us to get transportation to and from work on Sea Island. If we hitched a ride to Brunswick, when we got there we'd have to worry about a ride back to the island.

The Ballads' cottage was on 13th Street on Sea Island. The night they bombed those ships, I was scared to death. Everything in that home just shook.

During the war, Mom rented out two rooms to shipyard workers since we were not living there. She considered these roomers her children and fixed their meals and washed for them. I think after my brother and I had grown up she didn't have anyone to fuss over. That's also why she took possession of my daughter.

Toby was called up for the Army, but he had gotten sick and the doctor wouldn't let him go. When his name came up again, his age kept him from going. Toby went to work at the shipyard. He would go out when they launched those ships. I would be worried sick because it would be midnight or one o'clock in the morning before he came home and he had to be to work at seven o'clock the next morning. My husband earned the most money he'd ever earned at the shipyard. He would not have left Sea Island at that time, but I had to come home to take care of my mother, lifting her and all. After the war, he went back to Sea Island and worked continuously there for 37 years.

Sea Island wasn't a year-round resort. They kept a skeleton crew on during the summer, but I was lucky enough to get on to that, and on weekends they'd have what they'd call "excursions" and I'd get so mad because all the servicemen would come down over the weekend. They cut the rate for the soldiers. They'd come in on Friday and leave on Sunday, and you'd have to clean up behind them. I had 17 rooms to take care of, and they'd all leave at one time and I had to get them all ready. The day the U.S. won the war I forgot about it, and whenever a group registered at the hotel . . . boy, did they get royal treatment from me! I'd say, "Lord, please forgive me for fussing with them like I did." Some of the bell hops that worked in the hotel had to go into the service. I'll never forget that Sunday afternoon they came down singing "Off to War We Go." I said, "They don't know what they are going into."

We didn't suffer because of rationing. I think we got along fine. Some others didn't. I have 'em laughing now 'cause that's when I stopped making biscuits and bread. I didn't care anything about bread and my husband didn't either. I'd make six biscuits and throw away four. Crisco and lard were hard to get, and I got tired of spending my stamps for something that we weren't going to eat.

I think the war kinda helped Brunswick. I imagine it helped everyone else because after the shipyard opened, people did get a chance to work and be paid a decent enough salary to live on. I think the people in Brunswick have always gotten along . . . the whites and blacks have gotten along with each other. You find a few bad eggs in everything.

Lot of people say, "Oh, if they could go back to the 'good ol' days.'" Well, they were good, but I don't want to go back to them. I can remember when peace was declared for World War I because I got a whipping. Mother was combing my hair . . . the whistles sounded and we all ran toward Gloucester Street. She had stuck the comb in my hair, and somewhere along the line while running, I lost it. That was World War I. I can't remember exactly the ending of World War II . . .

only that I was a happy soul. I had a lot of friends that went into the service, and a lot of them didn't come back. The first black boy to die overseas was Alex Maddox. He was a twin. His was the first black body shipped back into Brunswick. His sister and I were best friends.

My husband's name was Clifton Tyson, but everyone called him Toby. I was talking with one of Judge Scarlett's grandson's the other day. He asked me if I knew Toby. I said I knew him very well and I told him who I was. He said, "Lord, Toby used to whip us over at the beach club with those wet towels. But you know what? He kept us all straight."

After my parents died, I went back to work. I worked on Sea Island until I was 70 years old. Now my children are trying to get me out of this house and to stay with them. I tell them, "The day may come when I have to go, but as long as I can take care of myself, I'm gonna stay home." I was 81 years old in September of 1995.

Josephine Wilson Ekblad

In 1941, I was living with Thora Wallace on St. Simons and working at the Princess Beauty Salon. On Sunday afternoon, December 7, 1941, Mrs. Wallace, her son, Edwin, and I went to the cemetery at Christ Church, Frederica, where her husband was buried. We came back by Ward's Drug Store at the village where her daughter, Evelyn, worked. Evelyn told us that war had been declared. She had just heard it on the radio. There were no television sets in those days. Mrs. Wallace's son, Edwin, was drafted in the Army and was stationed in England, where he was killed.

My father, Arthur Wilson, was a superintendent in the shipyard in Brunswick where they built Liberty ships. During the war, my brother, John, was in the Navy. I went to work at the King and Prince Hotel Beauty Shop. I remember fixing the hotel manager's wife's hair and nails and she told me her husband was very worried. This was just before Christmas. About a week later, we knew why he was worried. The Navy was taking over the King and Prince Hotel and everyone was out of a job. He kept this to himself during Christmas so he wouldn't spoil the holidays for anyone.

After the Navy took over the King and Prince Hotel, I went to work at the Cloister Hotel on Sea Island. Many big companies sent their presidents and other officers there to rest and recuperate. After the war, the Chase Manhattan Bank of New York sent a bank officer and his wife to the Cloister. I was fixing his wife's hair and, noticing how thin she was, asked her about it. She then explained that her husband had been assigned to the Chase Manhattan Bank in the Philippines in 1940. They were living there when the Japanese invaded. They were captured and were in the Bataan Death March. She said she had gained over 30 pounds since being freed. She must have been a walking skeleton when they were released from prison. With only a

THE SATURDAY EVENING POST
"They say she made her wedding gown out of his parachute."

From The Saturday Evening Post
(used by permission)
Courtesy of Josephine W. Ekblad

daily ration of rice, the prisoners had barely enough food to stay alive. She said many people died of starvation and tuberculosis. Conditions in the prison camp were so primitive and everyone did his or her part to keep it as clean as possible. Her husband's job in the prison camp was to empty and bury the buckets of human waste every morning. There were no bathrooms in the camps.

I met my future husband, Carl, during the war. He was in the Air Force. My wedding gown was made of a silk parachute, which my husband-to-be sent me from England. When a parachute didn't pass a safety test, some girls were lucky enough to receive one.

Iris Horton Colletta

My mother and grandmother did the "patriotic thing" and rented out two bedrooms, actually in two shifts during the war. I remember the loads of laundry and the cooking involved. Rooms were scarce as hen's teeth, and every family was expected to do whatever they could for the war effort. With the opening of the Glynco Naval Base in Brunswick, our family invited some of the servicemen over for Sunday dinners. I remember getting to know some "Yankees" that were actually very nice, but I also remember how they teased us because of the way we talked. However, I think they learned some things about Southerners and the way we lived, the kind of food we ate, and our culture in general that helped dispel some of the negative impressions that they held about the South.

My uncle, Burwell Liles, was on the *W. D. Anderson*, an Atlantic Refining Oil tanker. It was torpedoed in February 1942. He was the first Brunswick man to lose his life in World War II.

Pat Lewis Spaulding

September 18, 1944, Tom Spaulding of Brunswick, Georgia, and Pat Lewis of Brooklyn, New York, were married at the First Baptist Church in Brunswick. The Reverend John H. Haldeman performed the ceremony. This true love story begins in October of 1942 when Pat, who was then 16 years of age, moved to Brunswick with her mother and younger brother, Teddy. They moved so they could join their father, who was already at work building Liberty ships at the J. A. Jones Shipyard. Mr. Lewis, known as Ted to friends and co-workers, was one of several executives of the company who were originally part of the New York Naval Shipyard. Mr. Lewis was well-known and respected and was a very imposing figure at the shipyard, particularly to the many hard-working men and women on the swing shift, where he supervised the complete operation to the very best of his abilities.

In the time that Mr. Lewis was in Brunswick, prior to his family's arrival, he didn't have too much leisure time as the shipbuilding part of the wartime effort in Brunswick was in full swing, but he made a few friends. One of these friends was Mrs. Ed Sherman, who was one of Brunswick's outstanding citizens. Mrs. Sherman was responsible for taking Pat Lewis to Glynn Academy to meet with Sidney Boswell and

---

The Brunswick News, February 28, 1942

LOCAL MAN LOST ON TORPEDOED TANKER
Burwell Liles was on W. D. Anderson,
Sunk Off Coast of Florida

Burwell Liles, 24, son of Mrs. I. Liles, 2112 Wolf Street, native Brunswickian, is the first local man to pay the supreme sacrifice in the present war. While two or three local men have had narrow escapes in the sinking of vessels, young Liles is the first to lose his life.

He was a member of the crew of the Atlantic Refining Company tanker, W. D. Anderson, sunk off the Florida coast, announcement of which was made by the navy last night, and of a crew of 35, it is believed only one man survived.

Young Liles was third assistant engineer aboard the torpedoed tanker and he had been with the Atlantic Refining Company for a number of years. His family has long resided here and he was born in Brunswick, and had a large number of friends here.

Burwell is one of three sons of Mrs. Liles serving on tankers, one of which narrowly missed being on another tanker when it was torpedoed. Andrews Liles was chief engineer on the tanker E. H. Blum. The day before it sailed, he was transferred to another tanker. Two days later the Blum was torpedoed off the Virginia coast.

Another son, Harry, is first mate aboard the tanker W. E. Yeager.

Mrs. Liles was notified a few days ago that the tanker on which her son was assistant engineer had been torpedoed off the Florida coast. The next day she was advised that all except one member of the crew probably was lost. Full details of the tragedy were not announced until last night.

Besides his mother and the two brothers mentioned, Burwell is survived by his wife, Mrs. Leila Liles of Philadelphia; a sister, Mrs. I. H. Horton of this city and a fourth brother, John Liles of New Orleans.

thus get her enrolled and started in high school. Little did Pat know that on that day she would meet her mate for life.

Being a teenager in Brunswick during World War II, entering an entirely different school environment, making new friends but missing old friends, and coping with a whole new way of life was very discomforting, at first. It could have been disastrous if it weren't for Tom Spaulding. Right from the beginning, he made the transition easier and made Pat's move to Brunswick an outstanding memory. This "Yankee" learned to eat "Georgia Ice Cream" (grits), did not like boiled peanuts, learned how to squeeze an orange to suck out the juice (too messy for her), and found out that the funny looking things her mother raked out of the yard into neat little piles along the curb were edible.

While living on Newcastle Street South, Pat saw the change of shifts at the shipyard as hundreds of people passed their home every day. Many had no wheels, so they had to walk. They were rewarded for doing so by bending down to pick up pocketfuls of these funny things. Have you guessed what these goodies were? Of course, pecans!

Then there was the day Mama ordered groceries from Pfeiffer's Grocery on Newcastle Street. She had ordered peas and, upon delivery, thought that they had sent her "bad" peas for all of them had black spots on them. Pat learned to like black-eyed peas, but not Mama.

Although some things took time, for the most part Pat loved Brunswick, Glynn Academy, First Baptist Church, St. Simons, and Lanier Field; the war bond rallies; the sights of all the soldiers, sailors, and Marines coming to Brunswick every weekend; establishing friendships that exist to this day; and, artistically speaking, being part of the first drama department at Glynn Academy and one of the featured soloists with the Brunswick Symphony Orchestra, which was composed mostly of shipyard employees and directed by Mr. Christos Vironides.

Although the war in Europe and the Pacific raged on, young fellas did their part in answering the call and young girls, along with the rest of the community, carried on day to day doing what was expected. Each one coped with situations as they arose and tried to be there for each other. Yes, there were tears and frustrations, but we came through all the wiser for the experiences and richer for the lessons learned.

September 18, 1994, saw a renewal of wedding vows for Pat and Ted Spaulding, who were celebrating their 50th wedding anniversary with their daughter, Nancy, and grandson, Wesley, present. Loved ones and friends witnessed their happy event, which was made possible because of World War II and the Lewis family coming to Brunswick from Brooklyn as part of the war effort. One of the guests from out of town was 81 years old . . . Mrs. Lucille Jensen, whose husband, Al, was one of the New York Navy Yard executives making the move the Brunswick.

Brunswick during the war years, for all its busy-ness, people, and more people—a boom town, if you will—was still a small town with all the specialness that one finds in small towns. And 50 some years later, that is the way Pat likes to think of it.

"The Victory Corps was organized at school for girls. We had three companies and each company had a captain. Anne Harwell North was captain of one. After school we practiced marching. I don't know why or where we were going to march and I don't remember marching in any parade. Anyway, we were all left feet!"

Betty Ann Gaynor Lundberg

Betty Joyner McConnell

My only bright gain during the war was meeting and marrying David McConnell. He was from Reading, Pennsylvania, and was stationed at the St. Simons Naval Air Station. My father, a brother, and a brother-in-law worked at J. A. Jones shipyard in Brunswick. With 12 children and two parents in our home, supplies and everything else were always in a shortage state of affairs—even in peace time.

Sara Corbitt

I married my soldier in 1942. We had known each other for a year. After we were married, I went to live in Augusta, Georgia, until he was shipped overseas. Then I came home. When I returned home, my bedroom had been rented out to workers, so I had to sleep in the dining room. I prepared eight lunches each day for men who worked in the shipyard. Each man paid me a dollar a day and furnished the sandwich material. I worked at Nolan's Photography Studio for a dollar a day, seven days a week. Here with the lunches, I made eight dollars a day. I also balanced a business friend's books each week and was paid $15 for a two-hour job.

Counting stamps for meat and butter was always a problem, and sometimes we had stamps but no meat. My father raised fryers, so we made out better than others. The night that the Allies invaded Normandy, all the whistles, horns, and church bells sounded. I still get chill bumps remembering that night. During this time, I gave birth to our son without my husband being there. He didn't get to see him until he was two months old and then again at six months of age. After that, it was two years until we saw my husband again. He spent those two years in the South Pacific. I had an invalid mother and a baby, so I never had much time for Red Cross work.

My father worked at the shipyard as a carpenter. I remember the shipyard workers being called "pea-pickers," but I wonder what would have happened without them. There weren't enough local people to have done all the work that needed to be done.

Barbara Haag Fahey

In late summer of 1942 I left Jenkinstown, Pennsylvania, for Brunswick, Georgia, with my sister, Bette Carson, and her new baby. Bette's husband, Bill, was a chemical engineer with Hercules Powder Company in Brunswick. Bette was returning to Georgia after the birth of her baby and a bout with appendicitis. I accompanied her to help her regain her health and take care of the baby over the summer. I was 16 years old and had never been allowed to travel. The train ride from Pennsylvania to Georgia was difficult because there were very few seats with soldiers traveling. We sat up all night. Bette's husband met us in Thalmann, Georgia, and drove us to Brunswick. After breakfast at the Oglethorpe Hotel, we drove to 1406 Lee Street, where they had a small second-floor apartment in the home of Mrs. Susie Hotch. Susie and Captain Hotch, as he was called, along with their children, became our new family. Shortly after I arrived, Brunswick became the hub of Liberty ship construction. Everyone found work and the city came rapidly to life.

I enticed my widowed mother, Amanda, to leave our home in Pennsylvania and rent an adjacent apartment in the Hotch home. My mother volunteered to serve and altered clothing for all military in the area. One of the fondest memories I have of my year as a 17-year-old living in Brunswick in 1943-1944 concerns my mother. One of our neighbors on Lee Street had received word that her son was missing in action. It touched all our lives and filled us with sadness hard to describe. One day when Mother was altering an Army uniform—the trouser length to be exact—our neighbor received word that her son was alive and well. My mother was so happy and excited over this joyous news that she accidentally cut one leg of the uniform shorter than the other. She gladly reimbursed the gentleman for his trousers. It was well worth the price.

I attended Glynn Academy through the tenth, eleventh, and twelfth grades. As a young girl I went to many USO dances and helped to entertain the troops before they went overseas. In school we had a Victory Corps and did a lot of marching around the school property. Sugar, leather, and gasoline were rationed. We dutifully saved tin and became very aware of the war with U-boats off the Georgia coast. There wasn't a street not hit with the loss of a loved one, and we knew everything was changing. The war came home to me personally when Louise Hotch's husband of only three months was killed at a naval air station in a training accident.

In 1944 I met my future husband, John A. Fahey, who flew blimps at the Naval Air Station, Glynco. John was an ensign and a pilot who conducted long patrol flights in airships seeking U-boats and escort-duty flights with convoys in the shipping lanes off the coast. Blimps were a constant sight and sound over the city. My family, neighbors, and friends became very used to hearing the familiar engines roaring above the street where I lived. As an added attraction, John was noted for using a loud speaker and calling down from the blimp, "Get up, Barbara. It's time for school." I was never late!

On D-Day I was visiting a friend on St. Simons Island. The ringing of the church bells woke all of us, and we knew the Normandy invasion had begun.

After graduation in 1945, I briefly left Brunswick, returned to Pennsylvania, and married my husband, John, at Lakehurst, New Jersey. We then returned for his duty back in Brunswick and lived at 1406 Lee Street in the same apartment until August 1946, when he was transferred to a Navy program at Brown University in Providence, Rhode Island. We celebrated our 50th anniversary June 1995.

Lynn Gillican Sikes

I was 12 years old on December 7, 1941, a very formative and vulnerable age. The war in Europe had already been indelibly stamped in our young minds. I have vivid memories of being at the movies, and

when the RKO and CBS News came on, I recall the cacophony of boos that went up in the audience when the "goose stepping" Hitler was shown with his men wearing swastikas and yelling "Heil, Hitler." I shall never forget the feeling of hatred that we felt at the mention of the Third Reich and the Nazi Party. We used to gather nightly around the little Emerson radio and listen to accounts of the war as told by Gabriel Heater in his doleful tones. After the news, we gathered for prayer and scripture reading. Each of us children had to present a memorized Bible verse every evening . . . my brother, Charles, my sister, Jo Ann, my parents, grandmother, and me.

I remember ration books with stamps for gasoline, sugar, shoes, and coffee. There were T-stamps. for trucks and C- or S-stamps for cars. We couldn't get any good brands of candy; Hershey, Brach, and Whitmans, along with Beechnut Gum, went to war.

I remember that we were to dim lights, cover windows, and half-blacken headlights on cars. Everyone drove cars that looked like they had heavy-lidded eyes at halfmast.

The huge shipyard went up overnight. It employed people from all around, bringing in thousands of folks to Brunswick and St. Simons. Construction companies worked endlessly to build houses and lean-tos for the overflow of workers. Everything stayed open all night, which, with all the flashing neon signs, lent a carnival atmosphere to Brunswick. Barbecue and hamburger stands stayed open 24 hours a day, and when we had slumber parties, we would go in mass with our khaki raincoats on over our pjs. These sojourns, of course, were unknown to our parents, for they usually occurred around 2 or 3 a.m. Once in a while we would walk out to the Recreation Park and climb the fence to swim in the pool . . . such fun! Slumber was certainly a misnomer for that time frame. Union Street was as busy at night as it was during the day. Heavy traffic!

Sometime during the war, a Victory Corps was organized at our school and I was made corporal. I was so proud of my striped armband. I took my duties seriously as I directed my troops in marching with real Army commands: "to the rear, march," "to the right flank, march," "left oblique, march," "about face." These Victory Corps, scrap-metal heaps, victory gardens, and the rest were just symbolic of the government's effort to make us aware of the "war effort." Just as were the signs at the post office and all the "Uncle Sam Wants You" posters.

I can remember my mother and older sister lamenting that there were no more stockings. All the silk went into making parachutes for our paratroopers. For the scrap-metal heap, we saved anything that remotely resembled iron, and we were advised to save cans and newspapers. I diligently enforced this rule with my family. My grandmother even had to guard her dental bridge 'cause I spied some metal on it!

When two oil tankers were sunk off our shores, my mother was on the Red Cross Disaster Committee that served sandwiches, coffee, and doughnuts to the survivors. My sister and I helped make sandwiches and send them to St. Simons. Mother's account of those oil-drenched men remains deeply etched in my mind. I remember the rivers and beaches were awash with oil and ship remnants. Several people gave accounts of having seen parts of humans. I never saw anything but dead, oil-drenched birds, a glove, or a shoe. There were German submarines sighted off our shores, and it was suspected that they were being refueled at some point in our coastal waters, possibly Darien. I don't think this was ever proven. When I was at camp in North Carolina, we were taken by open truck to visit Clingman's Dome and various places of interest. Many times on our way up high in the mountains, we passed German prisoners of war. POW was written on the truck and on their shirts.

All of our churches nursed young soldiers' homesickness, as did we as families. I never knew who would be sitting by me at the dinner table. Mother and Dad had loving and generous hearts, and our home was always open to them. Mother worked at the USO and also gave many hours to the church and youth activities, which also included many young Navy and Army men.

Everyone's constant prayer and thoughts were with our young men in the service on land, sea, or in the air. There was never any assemblage anywhere that their lives were not lifted to our God for their safety and quick return. I only remember a few names of those who didn't make it back. That was J. C. Strother of St. Simons, John Whittle and Harris Steel of Brunswick . . . probably many others whom I've lost through time.

Mary Kay Miller Cannon

I was born in Brunswick, Georgia. My dad was an architect and engineer. During the war, he had an office job at the shipyard that was very demanding, so every weekend my parents went to Lazy Lodge, a camp we had in Camden County, to relax and get away from the telephone. I did not like to go with them because I was involved in all the weekend things that teenagers liked to do (especially Methodist Youth Fellowship, which was called Epworth League at that time). I spent the weekends with my grandparents. I worked with my aunt, Mary Miller, at the rationing board, filing mostly. I remember walking on dates or riding with several couples in one car to pool our gasoline. Gas rationing helped boost the Baby Boomers because more couples parked (not me, of course).

Several of my friends and I, in Windsor Park and Urbana, formed a club to plant victory gardens. We called ourselves the Victory Girls and had fun, but I don't remember ever harvesting any vegetables. I remember Mr. Potter Gould in that funny air-raid warden's hat and his telling us to take cover. We got under the dining table and thought the whole thing was very funny. As a member of the Pirates' Club, I remember raiding the ships when they came into Brunswick. We would capture the captain, lower the flag, and raise the Jolly Roger. I met a sailor on one of those raids named Johnny Johnson. He came back many times to visit me. My mother wouldn't let me go out with him (I was too young), but we had "at home" dates. I think she liked him more than I did. He brought her precious sugar, and she made him cakes. My brother Laurie was in the Navy and was aboard what they

Pack Up Your Troubles (Tune)

*Dig up the dollars that mean VICTORY
And smile, smile, smile!
It's a small price to pay for LIBERTY!
Smile boys! That's the style!
Just buy War Bonds every month,
Get interest all the while!
So! Dig up the dollars for Uncle Sam,
And SMILE, SMILE, SMILE!*

called UP boats. He got most of his college education in the Navy. The war was just about over when Burr, my other brother, went into the Navy.

One of my first dates was with a boy named Gene who had come to work at the shipyard during summer vacation. I don't remember if he was in high school or college, but he had a car. I met him at church. There was another boy named J.D. Corbett, Jr., and I think they were roommates. I dated both of them. I don't know what happened to Johnny Johnson or Gene, but J.D. went on to become a Methodist minister. I remember another guy named Elmer who was a Seabee stationed at the Coast Guard Station on St. Simons. He sang in the choir at First Methodist with us. Johnny Jones lived with us for a while before going into service, and we had a star in the window for him as well as my brothers. Johnny was in the tank division of the Army.

During the war, John Sharpe was our pastor. He took a group of us young people down to the shipyard to give out little Bibles to the workers when they changed shifts. (The workers from the farms were lovingly called "pea-pickers.")

As you can tell by what I have written I didn't take the war too seriously and did not experience too many hardships.

Patricia Sikes Jobe

In 1941, I attended Sidney Lanier Elementary School on Mansfield Street in Brunswick. I was in the fifth grade that memorable December. Each classroom was equipped with a two-way radio and I recall listening to FDR's declaration of war speech. However, what really made a lasting impression was that during the day while Miss Nell Whiddon was out of the room, a certain student (and I remember his name) placed a sign just above the middle of the blackboard in the front of the room that read TO HELL WITH THE JAPS. That was strong language for anyone, especially for a fifth-grade class.

Sometime during the period, I remember new and different people moving to our area because of the shipyard and the military bases. I was especially glad to have new students in our school and to even have some "Yankee" friends. The best part of this was that Sidney Lanier became quite crowded, but our entire area was becoming congested. I recall how difficult it was to try to cross Union Street on a bicycle to get to the city library or the Bijou Theater during a shift change at the shipyard. Also, a worn-out saying going around was, "You have to stand in line everywhere you go except to church."

With Camp Stewart Army Base near, the area was full of servicemen, especially on the weekend and at church services. It was the custom at our church, First Methodist, for member families to invite the servicemen into their homes to Sunday dinner as guests. That was fun, too. Some of the saddest times I ever remember were attending memorial services at our church for servicemen who had been killed. The blue star was replaced by the gold star on the red, white, and blue satin banner and then someone in the distance would play "Taps" on a trumpet. Another somber time was when the tankers were hit by torpedoes off our coast and my mother started gathering spare blankets and quilts for the survivors in response to a WMOG radio plea.

My dad was a neighborhood air-raid warden. When we had an air-raid drill, my mother and I would huddle in the hallway with all of the doors closed so the light wouldn't project from the radio until the all-clear siren would sound. Even our street lights were shaded with a piece of metal on the east side so as not to be visible from the coastline.

We were able to get by with all of the rationing for gasoline, sugar, tires, shoes, and probably some other things that I fail to remember. I became quite adept at removing both ends of a tin can and flattening for the war effort. At our school, Band Day became Stamp Day, when we began purchasing war stamps each week for obtaining a war bond. The movie star Veronica Lake came to town for a war bond parade and sat atop a convertible! Nice shiny cars always attracted a lot of attention because no one had a new car during those war years

I recall the USO located in the big brick house on Union Street. Some good programs were held there, and I attended and was impressed with a parade of Easter bonnets that began with hats at the turn of the century through 1943. In 1944, when I was a freshman at Glynn Academy, I belonged to a teenage club, Gamma Alpha Beta, which held its weekly meetings at the USO.

Colleen Moore Sellers

This is about the Glynn Academy class of 1945 from the viewpoint of a person who moved here during World War II so the parents could work in the shipyard. It might not be the same viewpoint as a person who had lived in Brunswick or St. Simons all of their lives, although quite a few of the events would be the same since we all shared a common goal, winning the war. This was in our minds at all times even though we lived our daily lives in a quite normal way.

The class of 1945 was unique. We spent our whole four years in high school, with the exception of the first three months, during a world war. We were not able to have a band, and our football program was very restricted. We had rationing of gasoline, meat, and shoes and the constant fear and worry for our big brothers, cousins, and uncles in the war.

Nevertheless, we had a "normal" life, which included classes, music, dancing, lots of basketball, volleyball, football, and baseball. We had our shares of joys, sorrows, fun, first love with its attendant heartbreak, just the same as all the classes before and since. We wore "sloppy Joe" sweaters, pleated skirts, dirty saddle oxford shoes, and penny loafers. We had no TV, but we had radios, record players, and movies. Everything that we heard on the radio or saw in the movies would be G rated now. The air was not polluted, or if it was we were unaware. Of course, the grownups (mostly the men) and some of the kids smoked, and no one had any idea of the ill effects until many years later.

In those days Glynn Academy had its junior-senior prom at the Sea Island Beach Club, where we went swimming, then danced to records (with our hair kind of stringy from swimming . . . no one had

Colleen Moore - 1944
Courtesy of Colleen Moore Sellers

Above left:
Bonnie Faye Moore - 1944
Gordon Oaks War Housing Project
Courtesy of Colleen Moore Sellers

Above right:
Willa Crawford,
Playground Director - 1944
Gordon Oaks War Housing Project
Courtesy of Colleen Moore Sellers

a hair dryer in those days). We did have one fantastic dance in the gym, though. Our student council hired Sammy Kaye's orchestra (this was a big-time swing band like Jimmy Dorsey and Glenn Miller), much to the disapproval of Miss Jane Macon, our dean of girls. She thought we should have given that money to the Red Cross.

Speaking of the Red Cross, we volunteered in our respective neighborhoods for the Red Cross, rolling bandages and knitting scarves for the servicemen. In my neighborhood, a brick housing project called Emanuel Homes, I was a volunteer at the recreation building, keeping the library and overseeing indoor games like checkers.

Glynn County had a very comprehensive plan to take care of the needs of the hundreds of families who moved here to work in the J. A. Jones Shipyard, where they built Liberty ships for the war effort. Each of the war-housing projects had a recreation building and playground with a paid supervisor to watch over the children playing baseball, basketball, and horseshoes and arranging tournaments with the other housing projects. The movies and restaurants were open 24 hours a day, and some people rented their extra rooms to people who did shift work and took turns sleeping. We had regular dances at the recreation buildings, square dancing one Saturday night, "round" dancing and jitterbugging the next Saturday night. The music was supplied by jukeboxes, record players, and local bands.

My father was supervisor of the power house at the shipyard on the afternoon shift, and my mother, who had never worked outside her home since her marriage, was a welder on the Liberty ships. Every day she would cook a big lunch for her and Daddy and leave enough for our supper. She also washed and ironed our clothes. There was no "wash and wear," and everything had to be ironed. She had always made all of our dresses but started buying sweaters and skirts and dresses for us during the war as she didn't have as much time to sew any more.

I was 15, Leland 13, Bonnie 11, and Charlotte 9 when we moved here in 1943. I was a junior at Glynn Academy, where I was made to feel very welcome by the friendly students and teachers. Leland and Bonnie were in the seventh grade at Prep High across the street, and Charlotte was in the fourth grade at Ballard Elementary, where they were going to school in shifts. When Greer Elementary School at Norwich and Fourth Streets was finished, Charlotte was transferred there.

I was the "head honcho" at home while Mother and Daddy were working, but luckily I never had any trouble with my siblings as we were used to minding our parents, cleaning up the kitchen, as well as the house, and doing our homework without being told. Most children at that time were the same way. I wanted to work part time at the local dime store, but my parents felt that I was needed at home, so I only worked during the Christmas holidays . . . one year at Grant's and one year at J. C. Penny's. Leland was in the Boy Scouts, which met at the recreation building near our apartment, and he, Bonnie, and Charlotte helped to run the Fun Club, which met at the same place. The teenagers belonged to the Emanuel Homes Pirates. Each club had meetings every week, played games, played the piano, sang, and danced a little. We spent many hours playing tennis, baseball, basketball, jump rope, and horseshoes at the recreation ground, which was virtually right in our yard! We had very good supervision there and very few problems with the children.

The city had a bus system, and we all rode the bus or walked to school. I tried riding my bike sometimes, but soon gave up because I almost always got a flat tire and you couldn't buy new tires because of the rubber shortage. No one had new cars during the war. Gas and tires were rationed, so you couldn't do much traveling or visiting. There was also a shortage of telephones, so we didn't get a phone until the war was over. So most everyone wrote letters prodigiously to their relatives and friends, including boys in service. I wrote to my uncle, Sam Lingo, in Texas, who was in the paratroopers and was wounded at New Guinea.

My girlfriend Nell Shy had a brother who was killed in the war, and I'll never forget visiting her family at that time. It was very sad, but everyone kept their chin up and kept going with the work they were doing. We had memorial services at school where we would honor the Glynn Academy students who were killed. We were all very patriotic, but we knew a few people who were draft dodgers and nobody had any respect for them.

My daddy was 36 years old when the war started in 1941, and they wouldn't take him because of his family and his war work. Later on they took him and some other people to Knoxville, Tennessee, to work on the atomic bomb. Of course, nobody knew about it because back then people could actually keep a secret.

I graduated in 1945 in a class of 117. Two of our boys were already in service . . . Grady Ricks and B. P. Harris. Eddie Glover had received his notice but was allowed to graduate before he went. The war ended in August 1945, and I was spending that night with my friend Dot Newman on the beach at St. Simons. I went to sleep, but Dot and her parents stayed up all night listening to the radio.

Ernest A. Drury

Schools in Glynn County during my attendance there offered a national current events newspaper in the middle grades. I received the top grade every year but was tied for the award in the eighth grade. We both received medals, ranking nationally. The point to be made is that though the newspaper was not applicable to high school, an earnest attempt was made by the Glynn Academy teachers and principal to keep the students aware of the growing national and international happenings. For example, we attended an assembly where a Chinese official discussed the Japanese occupation of China, visually demonstrating on a large map of China with his hand the portion, relatively small, that Japan had control of. Then a few days later we went to the docks for a tour of a Japanese merchant ship. We students were aware of the type of products in our stores (Kress, Grant's, and Woolworth); we could see what the United States was selling to Japan . . . scrap metal. (The scrap metal would be used in a military war against us.) We students could clearly see the dumping of cheap Japanese merchandise (if it said "Made in Japan," it was junk). We knew Japan was an island, with lots of people and few natural resources, that had to manufacture or value-add to what they imported and resell, otherwise they must take land from countries like China. The potential for two types of wars was evident . . . military or economic. An assembly at school was held after Japan's attack on Pearl Harbor to listen to Roosevelt's "Day of Infamy" speech.

Those residents catering to tourists were particularly hostile to blackouts. (For the few days I was on the west bank of the Rhine River, miles from Bonn, Germany; that lit-up "open city" helped us in many defensive and offensive ways.) It is easy to see the advantage the lights of Brunswick and the coast gave to the German submarines.

While there were shirkers, self-seekers, and profiteers among the people in the area, both the natives and those moving in were patriotic and well-behaved citizens.

While a student at Glynn Academy I worked at the local theaters (Ritz, Bijou, Casino, and Roxie) for $1 per week, less one cent for social security, as usher, pop-corn boy, ticket taker, and projectionist. Mrs. Alma W. King, who was in charge of the theaters, was a very nice person to work for. If she worked late, she would offer me a ride for the 10 blocks home. She personally gave me a dollar to supplement my 99-cent usher job, plus she bought fryers and eggs from me. (My hobby was raising 100 chickens each spring.)

Stage shows were popular, and Mrs. King saw that they did not offend good taste: Western star Tex Ritter was cautioned about too much drinking, and a dancer with a near-delivery pregnancy was ordered off the stage for the next show. Policemen walked the beat, were known as neighbors, and handled the crowds magnificently. Most movies were accepted well. I remember some newsreels showing the Panay gunboat bombing and sinking, the Japanese soldiers throwing Chinese babies in the air and bayoneting them as they fell.

I enlisted in the Army and was sent to N.C. State until I was 18 years old, then to an infantry division when the Army Specialized Training Program terminated. An Atlanta newspaper described me, on the front page, as the seventh Georgian to disembark at New York when our division was the first deployed from Europe to the Pacific. Thirty days at home showed me a change in the shipyard status; my return from the Pacific in 1946 showed me that the shipyard days were no more.

Dr. Robert (Bobby) J. Henderson

I was born in Brunswick in 1930 and therefore was a student during World War II in Brunswick.

One of my recollections has to do with the summer of 1944. The country was in the midst of a tremendous military build up. The military was everywhere, and everything was for the war effort. A cousin of mine, Sam Herrin, had been injured in the services and was discharged and returned to finished high school at Glynn Academy. The year he was finishing high school, Sam decided to continue his education at Emory University in Atlanta and had made appointments with the officials there to discuss being admitted. He asked me if I would like to go with him to Atlanta. At that time I was a freshman at Glynn Academy. In those days an opportunity to go to Atlanta was great news to anyone, so, yes, I wanted to go with Sam to Atlanta.

Sam and I set out on our journey. We left Brunswick on the old streamline train called The Georgia Cracker or just The Cracker. We arrived in Jesup about 11 o'clock at night. We had to change trains in Jesup for Atlanta. As we were standing in the depot at Jesup, we both realized we were tired and sleepy and thought we might spend the night in Jesup and continue on to Atlanta the next day. As we were discussing this, the train to Atlanta came in, stopped, took on its passengers, and started leaving. We stood there watching the train as it left the depot and at the last minute decided we'd go on to Atlanta that night. We had to run a bit to catch the train. It had completely left the station and was on its way. We ran, threw our suitcases up on the back of the last car, and got aboard. We just made it as the train gathered speed.

It was a warm, beautiful night. We stood on the observation portion of the rear car enjoying the fresh air and listening to the sound of the train on the tracks. We stayed out there talking and enjoying the ride for about one and a half hours. Finally, we decided we would go into the car and sit down. We didn't have Pullman accommodations, so we would sit in the day coach. We turned and attempted to open the door into the car. It wouldn't open. It was locked. We banged on the door and carried on something fierce for some time.

Finally, the door was opened by a big, burly, tough first sergeant. He wanted to know what in the world we were doing out on the back of this car. We told him we were going to Atlanta and wanted to come in and have a seat. He said, "Well, you can't do that. There's no way. Look inside the car."

We looked inside, and it was full of soldiers in the seats and aisles. There were duffle bags, rifles, and soldiers everywhere we looked. There was no way to pass through that car. The sergeant told us that not only was this car full of soldiers, but there were 22 cars ahead full of soldiers. He said, "You're on a troop train! There's just no way. You'll just have to stay here." He went in and gathered up some newspapers for us to sit on. We tried to make ourselves comfortable . . . sitting/lying on the iron platform on the back of that car.

We arrived in Atlanta the next morning. The train had a coal-burning engine, and during the night flicks of soot had settled all over us and our clothes. We were a pretty picture arriving in Atlanta. It's an experience we enjoyed in a way and one that I'll never forget.

Soda Jerk at Rich's Pharmacy

During my high school years, I worked at Rich's Pharmacy in Brunswick. Being wartime, Brunswick was extremely crowded. The people working at the shipyard seemed to have lots of money and were anxious to spend it. On this particular day, I was a soda jerk at the pharmacy, which at that time was located at the intersection of Newcastle and Gloucester Streets across from Bennett's Drug Store and Gordon's Department Store. This was a Saturday in the summertime and very hot. People came in and bought the things that we offered at the soda fountain. We found ourselves running out of ice cream, fruits, and drinks. Except we had one supply of a substance called "War Cola," which was a substitute for Coca-Cola. We were selling this for five cents a cup and then ran out of ice, but the people kept on buying. We worked all afternoon and evening selling just this syrup and water in paper cups to people who paid their money very cheerfully.

Virginia Kent Jackson

Our family lived on St. Simons Island, but I was not on the island very much during the war. In June of 1942, I went to New Orleans to live with my sister and attend college. I was back on the island for about six months during the summer and fall of '43.

One of my most vivid memories was of the tankers being sunk about a mile off shore. About 5 a.m., I awoke to a *putt-putt-putt* coming from the channel. We lived only about one block from the beach. The noise disturbed me and I started to get up but decided that it was probably a fishing boat going out or coming in. However, when I was on the school bus, someone said that a ship had been sunk. After a few days, the ship was floated and brought into the channel. There was a hole in it the size of a small house. J. C. Strother, Jr., went out to help retrieve some of the bodies of the crew. He said the stench was terrible, but he did make several trips out.

A company of soldiers was bivouacked in Brunswick. Their purpose was to patrol the beaches. Also, there were Marines stationed on the island who did guard duty on Jekyll. They used a landing barge to go back and forth to Jekyll for the changing of the guard, departing from the pier at St. Simons. Colonel Haas of the U. S. Marines lived on Sea Island while the Marines were stationed there. Thanksgiving 1943 he gave them a party that lasted all day and into the evening. I was fortunate enough to be invited, and it was truly a delightful day. The weather was mild so we played games on the beach, went swimming, and had a wonderful dinner and dancing at night. Doris Duke also entertained a group of soldiers at her estate on the island. This was an evening party with dinner and dancing and rowboat rides in the creek. A lot of fun.

On the weekends, there were always a lot of soldiers on St. Simons. For the most part, the local people welcomed them and invited them into their homes, especially to Sunday dinner. We rented rooms because we had a large house, and I recall that there was a soldier who came down frequently and stayed with us. His home was in Alabama and since transportation was slow, he would not have time to go home on a weekend pass. He became so fond of my father that he called him "Papa Kent." On one Fourth of July he did not call ahead to reserve a bed, not realizing what St. Simons was like on a holiday. He came in about midnight, and there were no beds left. He said he was going to stay at Papa Kent's if he had to sleep on the couch. And that is what he did!

Camp Stewart had dances a couple of nights a week. Girls and young ladies were invited from St. Simons, Brunswick, and other nearby towns. The camp sent buses, sometimes trucks, to bring them to the dance and return them. Sometimes, if properly chaperoned, a group of girls would drive to and from the dances. Mary Jane Everett's mother and Mrs. Carl Svendson were two of the chaperones who frequently took us.

When I graduated from high school in June '42, I went to college to study to become a doctor. However, after the first year with so many friends going into the service, I decided to leave college and go into nursing. I felt that I would be of more help that way. When I went to Baltimore, I joined the Cadet Nurse Corps. Everyone in my class was a member.

The Reverend Hugh E. Baumgartner

I was a student at Lenoir Rhyne College, Hickory, North Carolina, when World War II began. I had just walked into my dorm after attending church when the radio announcement was made.

My time in Brunswick was limited after that because the Lutheran Church asked me to become a "test case" for what would become accelerated study for the ministry. The intention was to provide, as quickly as possible, candidates for the denomination's military chaplain quota. This meant all college and seminary from September 1939 to January 1945, which was usually a seven-year program, was accelerated to just over five years. The result was that I was too young to meet the age requirement for officers when I graduated from the seminary. In February 1945, I became a Lutheran pastor in Atlanta and was named Lutheran Contact Pastor for Lawson General Hospital where military amputees were treated.

On the day the war ended, my date and I came out of a theater in downtown Atlanta to learn the news and found people curb to curb celebrating the end of the war.

Dr. Earl E. Walker

My family had moved to Brunswick from Hazlehurst, Georgia (where I was born in 1923). My father was salesman for Armour and Company until 1933, when he was forced to resign because of decreased sales commissions for salesmen. He started Walker's Grocery in the south end of Brunswick near the old hospital and the shipyard and was there for many years.

I lived in Brunswick from the age of a few weeks until I graduated from Glynn Academy in June 1941. The years during the war I was away from Brunswick entirely. I was fortunate to win a scholarship to Johns Hopkins in pre-medicine, but along came Pearl Harbor. I enlisted in the Navy in Baltimore and was allowed to shift to Georgia Tech for the second half of my freshman year. I went on to and graduated from Annapolis in 1945. The four years were crammed into three years, with eleven months of classes, two-week cruises on old battleships, and two weeks of vacation each of the three years. We cruised the Chesapeake Bay as German subs had the bay entrance bottled.

Ida Atkinson Cecil (second row, on right) with students after a day of picking cotton.
Claxton, Georgia - 1943
Courtesy of Ida Atkinson Cecil

Ida Atkinson Cecil

My parents were Dr. and Mrs. Frank Atkinson. My father, a dentist, died before the war started. We lived on Macon Avenue, near the old Brunswick Hospital. On the south end of Brunswick from Second Avenue on south was a beautiful grove of oak trees with Spanish moss. I remember my daddy taking me for a walk through the grove before the war and how beautiful it was. When the shipyard was built and the housing projects were constructed on the south end in that grove, the moss turned black because they used coal for heating. After the war, the trees recovered from the black char.

During the war, my mother was in a civil defense corps. Each person in the corps received some training for the task they were assigned. My mother drove a car, and one of her training procedures was to practice driving in the dark in the event there was a blackout when they were on patrol. The main area where they practiced was along the marsh in Windsor.

We knitted sweaters, but I doubt if anyone could wear them!

I was in school at Georgia State College for Women in Milledgeville during the war. I started in the fall of 1939. The education was the best you could buy with your money. My dad had left an education insurance policy for my sister and me each in the amount of $1,000. My four years at college cost $1,200. I remember rolling bandages with the other students at college. My sister, Sally, joined the WAVES.

After I graduated from college in 1943, a lot of the men had been drafted or had gone to work in war industries. In Claxton, which is in the heart of the agricultural section of Georgia, school children were called on to do certain farm jobs, such as picking cotton.* School

Volunteer Cotton Pickers
Claxton, Georgia - 1943
Courtesy of Ida Atkinson Cecil

was dismissed early for the kids as well as teachers to pick cotton. The kids were good pickers. I remember working one afternoon and earning 35 cents for the cotton I picked. There is a lot of skill to it that I had not realized. The ag teacher from the vocational department of the high school headed up the project. He organized us and secured a school bus to take us out to the farms. He had picked a lot of cotton and said that all you had to do was reach in, pull it out, and put it in your bag. It sounded so simple, but I found out it takes some skill.

In Claxton, we also had a vocational canning plant. Many of the farmers' wives brought in great baskets of food to be prepared for canning. Some produce required more preparation than others. We would put the prepared produce into cans, seal them, and sometimes stay until midnight processing them in the big steam pressure cookers. We had to wear white cotton stockings.

A lady in an apartment where I lived after college asked me if I would help organize a victory garden** for her. So we all bought overalls and embroidered on them. Mine had caterpillars. I still have the overalls. We grew a lot of vegetables.

* In 1943, 133,032 volunteers were placed on Georgia farms to help with farm operations: 37,817 men, 38,701 women, and 55,514 youth. 30,000 individuals volunteered their assistance to farmers independent of organized placement programs but as a result of the education program on farm labor.
Lamar Q. Ball Collection - Georgia State Archives - Agriculture - Box 2124-02.
** Victory Gardens: As part of the State Nutrition Program, in 1943 about 100,000 more gardens than normal were planted in the state, resulting in the production of highly nutritious food which otherwise would not have been produced. Emergency Farm Labor Program: The Agricultural Extension Service was designated by Congress as the agency by which the Emergency Farm Labor Program would be administered. It involved recruitment and placement of intra state labor to assist farmers in the attainment of production goals. The program was conducted as a cooperative activity and agents of Extension Services worked closely with all agencies, groups, and individuals in helping farmers to secure their labor requirements and the utilization of all machinery and materials to the best possible advantage.
Lamar Q. Ball Collection - Georgia State Archives - Agriculture - Box 2124-02.

Ada Edwards Sweat

The home economics teacher at Glynn Academy, Mary Will Warren, resigned just before the beginning of the school term of 1945 because her husband had returned home from service. I lived in Fort Valley, Georgia, and saw the ad in the *Macon Telegraph* for the position. I applied by telephone to Mr. Boswell, principal of Glynn Academy, and he hired me over the telephone. The Glynn County Board of Education treated me royally. Teachers were hard to get. I came to

Brunswick by rail on The Cracker and was met by Mrs. H. B. Smith, a math teacher at Prep High.

Even though the war was ending, Brunswick was still bulging. The Glynn County Board of Education had rented several two-story Victorian houses as teacherages to sublet to the teachers since housing was hard to find. Mrs. Smith was assigned the task of showing me the housing to determine where I wanted to stay. The first house she took me to was on G Street. Being 22 years old and wanting to be with teachers close to my age, I was disappointed when I found that no one was under 45 years of age. The house was old and beat up. Under the kitchen sink was a hole that if you looked through you could see the ground.

Next, she took me to the Hotch House on Reynolds Street, then the Whittle House facing the Jewish Synagogue in back of the Episcopal Church. This house was full.

At the Wisteria Inn, I found a house that had all young teachers in it, but it had only a tiny room on the top floor facing west. Finally, she took me to the Brailey Apartments on Gloucester Street, which had 12 apartments that were painted on the outside a very dark green. Four teachers lived in each apartment. Mary Will Warren had roomed with Gussie Goss at these apartments, and I decided to do the same.

The Board of Education knew that with so many people in town, the teachers could not go out for every meal, so they got the cooks at the Sidney Lanier Elementary School cafeteria to come in early in the morning and have breakfast for us and stay late in the afternoon and cook our supper. Of course, we ate lunch there with the students. I must say that the board of education went out of its way to take care of us during that period, especially Mr. Hood, superintendent, and Mr. Boswell. The first Sunday night after school started, the Methodist Church had a reception for the teachers. We were told by Mr. Hood that he was going to be at the church and he expected to see us there, too!

After the first year living at the Brailey Apartments, all the young teachers at the Wisteria Inn rented the White Cap Cottage on St. Simons Island, which was located near the St. Simons Elementary School. I moved in with them. Mary Frances Launius had a car and we rode with her. However, she was the music teacher and had to go early or stay after school for rehearsals from time to time. We would go out to Gloucester Street and people going to St. Simons would give us a ride. Sometimes in the morning, the school bus driver would honk the horn, and if we were still in the cottage, we would ride the bus. Other times in the mornings, if we waited in front of the house, the businessmen going to Brunswick would take us to school.

Dr. Carl Ward at Ward's Drug Store on St. Simons would cash our checks—there were no banks on St. Simons at that time—and was so good to us. The little Methodist Church on St. Simons had an oyster roast to raise money to furnish a kitchen. They could always count on the White Cap gals to furnish them with a tub of coleslaw. I lived at the White Cap Cottage from 1946 to 1949, and things were beginning to get normal again in Brunswick. The people on the island "adopted" the teachers and were so good to us and made us feel so welcome.

Ruth Pope Williams

About 1922, when my sisters and I were quite young, my mother and father moved from Hawkinsville in Pulaski County to Brunswick, Georgia. My father's brother had moved to Brunswick and encouraged my father to come. At first, my father and uncle worked at the old Glynn Ice and Coal Company on George Street selling coal and ice. They worked there for several years. Eventually my father opened a dry cleaning business called Pope's Pressing Club. For years it was located on the corner of Gloucester and Wolf Streets, the site of the present fire department.

I went to school at Colored Memorial. When I finished in 1935, an older teacher who was a friend of the family secured a tuition scholarship for me to attend Spelman College in Atlanta, an all-girl's school. My older sister was always interested in hair dressing and attended a cosmetology school in Atlanta.

I had majored in French, intending to teach it. Unfortunately they had stopped teaching French in the four years I was in college. I had done my practice teaching of French at Atlanta University Laboratory High School. However, I was given a job teaching on the elementary level instead of the secondary level. I started out teaching third grade for about two years. Then one of the teachers went into the service as a WAC, and I was given her fifth-grade class.

I had some private French classes on Saturday in a building called the Boilermaker's Building, which was right around the corner from where the old Risley School is now. I was teaching the regular curriculum during the week and French on Saturdays. The Boilermaker's Building had two floors and they held dances on the second floor.

The black families moving into Glynn County during the war impacted the schools and we did not have a hot lunch program. There was a lady who lived across the street from the school who prepared and brought sandwiches wrapped in wax paper to the school. I am pretty sure those sandwiches sold for about a nickel or a dime. I remember, I laugh about it now, she made a baked bean sandwich that the kids just went all out for.

Some fellows would go down to the Bluesteins' bakery and get a dime's worth of scrap cake in a big bag, bring it back, and give it to the students. There was a grocery store right across the street that sold cookies for a nickel or dime a box. If you had the money you could buy the Social Teas, Fig Newtons, or Lorna Doone cookies that sold for maybe 12 or 13 cents a box. If a young man gave a young lady a box of Lorna Doone cookies, you were really in because they were more expensive.

After the war I taught social studies in the high school. This included American history, world history, geography, government, and basic economics. Some of the credit my former students give me now is the fact that I helped broaden their world by introducing them to the happenings in Atlanta. Atlanta was a big city and Brunswick was more or less a rural area of Georgia. My satisfaction in my waning years is that I had something to do with what they managed to achieve.

We were really children of the Depression years growing up. Having been a child of the Depression, the thing that stands out in my mind about World War II was the prosperity that became typical of Brunswick. Money flowed fairly freely then. In fact you probably have met people who came here during the war and remained because they were very well pleased with the area.

Georgia McKendree
Georgia McKendree was manager of the St. Simons Island theater located in the Casino. Her husband, Marion, worked for the Sea Island Company.

It was like a big family at the Casino. There were rocking chairs all around the open-air dance floor. That's where my girls learned to dance. There were three different movies each week. We had two shows each evening, 7 p.m. and 9 p.m. The fare was 35 cents for adults and 10 cents for children. We had a candy girl and an usher. The young girls usually worked at the theater.

During the war both shows would be filled and there would still be a line outside. We had good movies. Honest, you could leave your children with me and you knew they would be safe. We never locked our doors. At that time there were no banks on St. Simons. At the end of each day, I would bring the receipts of the day home and take them to the bank the next day.

I remember so much about things that happened and so much that we had to do without. Bacon was a specialty for us. We were lucky to live next door to a lieutenant who shared some of his rationed items with us. Gas was rationed, and Marion's mother was in the hospital in Waycross. We did not have a gas stamp to buy gas. Marion had taken up a collection at church one Sunday and in it was a gas stamp. So we got to make the trip! Times were really bad about buying a car. We were caught with an old car. McDonald Harley had two cars and sold us his Plymouth coup for $900.

Milk was hard to get so we bought a cow. Marion put it in the woods near by. Marion got sick, and since I never learned to milk a cow as a girl, I had to sell her. We sold her to Mr. Fennell, who worked at the Sea Island Golf Course with Marion. He put her on his velvet bean patch. She ate those fresh beans and died. We gave Mr. Fennell his money back. We raised rabbits and chickens for our meat. We took a lot of the soldiers home to Sunday dinner. They were so glad to come.

Since most of the people were working at the shipyard, it was hard to get anyone to help with housework. A friend had three boys and no washing machine. She came and did her laundry at my house. We had an old-fashioned laundry room outside. In those days we all had to help each other.

My husband, Marion, held on to his job at the Sea Island Golf Club. He never missed a check in all the forty-six and one-half years there.

George Parmelee
George Parmelee's parents, Ellis and Dorothy Parmelee, owned the Bon Aire Cafe at the pier on St. Simons Island. George has retired from the Air Force and lives on St. Simons.

On St. Simons during World War II, it seemed like the whole island had come together to help with the war effort. Being a young man, and just being old enough to join the Boy Scouts a year after the war started, I remember many things that took place on St. Simons, especially the number of military people who were in and around all the islands.

I remember the incident of the Beechcraft airplane that crashed off the sandbar near the King and Prince Hotel. We were living just south of the King and Prince in an old beach house. The house was about 350 feet off the high water mark. I don't even believe there's a high water mark there now. It's all gone. Anyway, we were out in the backyard playing badminton one foggy day. It was so foggy, we could hardly see what we were doing. Percy Brandies, my brother Jack, and I were batting the birdie around a bit when we heard an aircraft sputtering. We heard this *kabut* and then a *bang*. The aircraft was trying to come in. It was on a radar training mission and had just missed the lighthouse. I don't know the full details. It got too low in altitude and crashed right there off the sandbar in front of the King and Prince Hotel. Brother Jack and I went running down the pathway to the beach. The fog was so heavy you could just feel it touching you. We walked out on the sandbar because it was dead low-tide. There was no wind. You could see the tip of an aircraft and hear somebody hollering for help. Brother Jack told me to run back and call the Coast Guard. I ran back up the pathway and got on the old phone and managed to get a hold of the Coast Guard. They knew the aircraft went down but didn't know where it was. I told them exactly where we were, and they could locate the aircraft very easily, but it was so foggy they couldn't get a rescue in there. The tide was out long enough where they could walk out and pretty well do what they could. We just sat back and watched. We were too young to be of any help. They finally got most of the crew off the aircraft. I think most of them died on impact. I'm not sure, but they did manage later to get a recovery vessel in there and bring the people back to the pier at St. Simons. I remember them taking the bodies off. News traveled fast back in those days and everybody just got out and helped.

Another crash was down from the Sea Island Golf Club. We were on the beach and heard this aircraft sputtering and carrying on. It went into the mud flat by the golf course, plowed up through the mud for quite a ways, came to a stop, and flipped over. We weren't too far away so we ran down to see what we could do. About that time, an amphibious-type Navy vessel was plowing through the mud trying to get to him. They managed to cut a hole in the bottom of the aircraft and get the pilot out. As he got out, he said, "Oh, Lord. I forgot my hat. I've gotta go back in there and get my hat." Thank goodness the pilot was not injured. I think he had to put on his oxygen mask to keep breathing since he was covered up with mud.

The little Grumann aircraft were flying in and around St. Simons all the time, also the P47 Thunderbolts. They would come in and practice dogfights with the Hell Cats or whatever they had in the area. I remember watching those dogfights.

I do remember another incident at the airport. One of those Grumann F4s or, F3s, I forget what they were, was coming in for a landing. I was towing Frank Bankston on the handle bars of my bicycle. We were riding down the airport road. I told Frank, "Boy, watch that perfect three-point landing." This little Grumann came in, landed real good, and all of a sudden the wheels folded up. The plane started skidding down the runway with sparks flying everywhere. The prop was warped. It tore up real bad. We were not too far away, and no fence was up there then. We ran over to see what was going on and to see if the pilot was all right. Boy, he came out of that cockpit, jumped out on that wing, dropped to the ground, grabbed his hat and threw it on the ground, and said, "Doggone, I forgot to lock my gear." Then he looked at us and said, "You boys didn't hear that did you?" We said, "No sir. We didn't hear that."

Of course the main thing was the blimps. The blimps were really doing a good job patrolling the coast because, boy, those guys could sit there and hover over an enemy submarine and drop depth charges right on top of it. You just kind of heard unofficially that they would get one now and then. Of course, we knew they were in the area because there were stories about one of the submarines and some of the debris that came ashore. Some of the bread wrappers were from a local bakery in Georgia somewhere. I don't know if it was Brunswick or Savannah. These people had infiltrated the beach at Sea Island, I understand, at night and came in some way or another and got supplies. This is just the way the war went.

The military had 50-caliber machine guns about every 500 to 1,000 yards set up all along the beach. They had search aircraft and, at the pier, a crash boat. We spent a lot of time down there talking to the Navy or Coast Guard personnel who operated the vessels.

I remember the two tankers being torpedoed off the coast. We shook that morning. I'll never forget that. The stuff that washed up on the beach was just terrible . . . whole hams, whole rolls of baloney. A few of the animals, especially the dogs, were going crazy to get all that stuff that was washing up on the beach. Anyway, meat was hard to come by in World War II and they were getting their share. The tankers were brought in and anchored in the St. Simons Sound. We rowed a boat out to them. You had to have a permit to get a motor during World War II, so we rowed out. You could load a boat up in the holes that were blown in the side of them ol' tankers. I remember them getting the bodies out and bringing them in down to the pier. This was another terrible thing, but this had to be done.

Boy Scouts

The Boy Scouts became very active in the war effort. We collected tinfoil, tin cans, and newspapers. The Scout House would be so full, we would have our meetings outside sometimes. They couldn't come and pick it up fast enough. Everybody just made an effort.

There were some boys who wanted to join the Boy Scouts but couldn't afford to buy a uniform. We would all get together, go around and clean yards, do this and that, and scrape up enough money to get them uniforms. The first Scout master was Bob Kent. Of course, we had a lot of advisors and a lot of help. We went with that program for years, and just about all the boys joined the Boy Scouts to help with the war effort.

I'll never forget the training we got in the Boy Scouts. I was learning international Morse code. This was later on when our Scout master was Borden Barry. He was a disabled Navy veteran who took over our troop. I made me a little spark gap transmitter at our house, which was not too far from the King and Prince Hotel. I was learning my Morse code by sending signals on this. I had set it all up with a little high voltage neon transformer and made it arc. That thing could be heard on my radio real good. This went on for several days. One day this knock came at the door. I went to the door. It was two guys from the Navy. I noticed they had this little gray panel truck with this loop antenna on top of it. They said, "We have traced this interference to this house. Can we come in and check it out?" I said, "Oh, yeah. Come and look at what I've got in here." I was proud of it. Actually, this spark gap transmitter was radiating all over the entire area and they were picking it up real good down at the King and Prince. I guess they thought I was trying to get a message to some German submarines or something. Anyway, I was told to take that thing down and get it out!

In January of '48 when I joined the Air Force, they naturally gave me the aptitude tests. I passed the Morse code test with flying colors, but I didn't put in for radio operator. I put in for several other things with radio operator as my third choice. I guess they needed radio operators and I ended up being one. I stayed a radio operator for 21 years in the Air Force.

I remember well that we wore our Scout uniforms quite a bit. Every morning we would run the American flag up the pole at the old Casino. I'd blow the bugle, brother Jack would play the snare drum, and everybody over there in the village would stop, come out, and pay their respects to the flag. In the evening, we would lower the flag. I'd play taps. It got to be a routine down there. I think Ralph Bufkin came in and helped. He could blow the bugle, too. Teddy Brandies also played the bugle. In fact, Teddy and I lived about half a mile apart. We didn't have too many telephones back then. His brother, Percy, and I would send Morse code out on the bugle. We would send little messages like "I'm coming over." It worked real good.

Western Union

I worked for the Western Union. The office was right next door to the old Bon Aire Café, my parents' restaurant, down at the pier. I'd check in there several times a day for telegrams. As we didn't have a lot of telephones on St. Simons back then, very few messages could be delivered by phone. So I'd get on my bicycle and deliver these telegrams. Of course, I was always told that if there was bad news not to hang around.

Working for the Western Union, I relied very much on the little bicycle I had. It had those big, ol' balloon tires. There was a reddish colored rubber on them tires. One hot August day my bicycle was parked out in front of the café next to the Western Union office. When I went to get it, both the tires had blown out. You couldn't get new tires. We managed to patch up those old tires. When I didn't ride, I had to walk to deliver the telegrams. Later on, when I got one of those Victory bicycles (they were finally making a few of them), I thought that was really something, but those ol' skinny tires . . . I mean most of the roads on St. Simons were either oyster shells or sand, so what good did that little ol' bitty tire do? I ended up pushing that thing more than anything. This was when they made the tires out of that synthetic rubber. You could slide on brakes about a half dozen times, but you'd better be careful on that pavement. You'd wear right on through that rubber.

I had this old dog named Prince. He was a cross between a German shepherd and an Irish setter. He was very faithful. He followed right behind me everywhere I went. We knew every artesian well on St. Simons Island because we'd stop and get a drink of water here and a drink of water there.

The Fast Pace, Shortages, and Such

The shipyard activity was on a 24-hour workday. I mean they kept that place going three shifts all the time. I remember serving a lot of people in that old café we had down there at the pier. Things just seemed to run so fast. There was never a dull moment on St. Simons back during World War II.

I remember the rationing too. By golly, we couldn't even get ketchup or black pepper. We had imitation ketchup. Can you believe that? Even at the café we had imitation ketchup and black pepper. I guess they must have used that to make black gun powder because black pepper was limited too. We did manage to have sugar because we got our rations for the café. We had it locked up in the back cupboard. Big ol' 100-pound sack of sugar. That was like having gold back then. My father watched the sugar. Once in a while I'd sneak out a cigar-box full of sugar.

Bananas! I don't know too many kids who don't love bananas, and, lo and behold, we couldn't get any fresh bananas during the war. That meant no more banana pudding in the café. Then they came out with this dehydrated form of bananas. That helped quite a bit.

The war didn't seem to hurt the shrimping. We called them prawns back then, they were so big. I can remember the old shrimp boats going out right at daybreak. Nobody was allowed on the water unless they had a permit after certain hours, but most of the shrimp boats would go out at daybreak and they'd be back in the early afternoon. I can still hear the old shrimp boats churning up the water, and I can still hear the old bell buoy clanking off the coast out there. Those sounds stayed with me even when I was in basic training in Texas.

During the wintertime after school I would come home, and, if there was a little time left in the day, I'd work with my Uncle Pete Simmons. We were wiring houses. My job was to bore holes with an old brace and bit into some of the old green wood they used in building those houses in Oglethorpe Park. The old 2x4s were full-sized 2x4s, so the houses were pretty well built. If you wired one, you knew how to wire all the rest of them. I knew where to bore all the holes. The wire

St. Simons Beach and Lighthouse
Courtesy of Ida Atkinson Cecil

they used was a rubber-covered Romex-type wire. Later, when they built the homes at King's Terrace and rubber was needed for the military cause, the wiring we used was insulated only on the hot wire.

AUTOMOBILES AND GASOLINE

Of course we didn't get around much in a car. Most of our activity was walking or riding a bicycle. Everybody on St. Simons knew everybody so if somebody was walking down the road, they knew by the way you were looking whether you needed a ride or not. Once in a while we got to ride in a car. They'd stop . . . give you a ride and ask no questions. They knew right where you lived. During World War II now, it got a little bit different because we had so many people and so many strange vehicles. We didn't know whose was whose. We were used to Old Doc Ward's Model A Ford down there at the drug store, and Old Doctor Backus, I think he had quite a sporty looking old car.

Gas rationing. Now that was something. I remember the day that they lifted the gas ration after World War II. We had a 1939 Dodge. Of course, we hauled so much seafood in the back of that thing, it ate the floor board out of the trunk. Anyway, World War II came to an end and Mother told me to take that car and fill it up. I mean we're going to *fill it up!* So I took off, went down to Fitzgerald's Grocery, where he had a little filling station. I told him, "Fill it up." He said, "Where's your stamps?" I said, "Haven't you heard on the radio? They lifted all the rations and nothing's rationed anymore. Mother told me to get that tank filled up." And he says, "Boy, I ain't gonna give you no gas. I ain't heard of no such thing." I told him, "You'd better turn the radio on and listen." We sat there for about 15 minutes until another broadcast came on before he would fill that tank up.

DAYS DOWN AT THE PIER

I spent a lot of time down at the pier as a young boy. I remember people driving on the beach and parking. The tide would be way out. They'd be out there sunning with their cars parked close to the shore. The next thing somebody's telling them, "You better go get your car. It's about to float away. The tide's coming in." He'd say, "What you mean the tide's coming in?" A lot of cars got damaged that way. One day I was down at the pier and this truck was trying to go under the pier to get to the ramp to get off the beach. He lacked about an inch or so of clearance. He couldn't go under the pier where he had more height because the tide was up so high. I told them to let some of the air of out his tires. "Let the air out?" he said. "Yeah," I said, "Let the air out and that'll lower your truck, and then you can go on up the ramp." Well, by golly, he did it and it worked.

My youngest brother, Tony, was nine years behind me. He came along in June 1940. By the time he was two years old, the war was going pretty good. I remember him toddling around in the café. Every once in a while a sailor or somebody would pick him up. Tony would look him right in the eye and say, "You'd better put me down!" I won't say what language he used. He didn't like strangers picking him up. Tony would count the pilings on the pier and know where there was enough water to stand up in if he jumped off the pier. He would count them and then crawl out on the edge of the pier and jump into the water. He could swim a little bit, dog paddle, I guess. But we all spent a lot of time swimming around that pier.

Of course, it wasn't anything unusual to see the St. Simons Sound with maybe a cruiser or several destroyers anchored out there. Those big ships were really something. Jekyll and Cumberland Islands were fortified by the military. You didn't go onto these islands. They were restricted areas. We stayed on St. Simons. We could find enough to do.

It was a way of life for us to ride down on the beach at night before the war in whatever we could get a ride in. Over the years Brother Sonny had several Model A's. It was just routine to ride down on the beach, go all the way down to East Beach and come back. We knew where all the soft sand was. Then the restriction of the war came along and you couldn't go on the beach at night.

HAPPENINGS AROUND THE CASINO MOVIE TIME

The big event was the theater at the Casino on St. Simons. They had movies on Tuesdays, Thursdays, and Saturdays. The biggest thing was to be able to get up 11 cents to go the movie. We caught up on all the world news through the short "March of Time." I'll never forget the day I became 12 years old. Mrs McKendree was the ticket taker—the ticket seller too—she handled the whole program. And I no sooner walked up there and tried to get in for 11 cents when she said, "George, you just turned 12 years old and you're going to have to pay the 35 cents." Boy, that liked to have really killed me to pay 35 cents to go to a movie. But I managed to get the money because we had different ways of picking up some pocket change back then. Mrs. McKendree knew everybody on St. Simons, their age, too, I guess. In the movie, I was pretty good with my spit balls. There was one guy in there I could hit all the way across that theater with a spit ball. If he knew I was in the theater, he'd try to get just as far away from me as he could.

SETTING UP PINS AND SHINING SHOES

During World War II, there were four bowling alleys at the old Casino and several alleys down at that building on the waterfront. We used to set up pins. I remember we had quite a few sailors and soldiers bowling. I think it cost them 15 cents a line to bowl. The shooting gallery down at the pier during the war was not allowed to be open. So we got together and set up a shoeshine stand in it. Percy Brandies, Guy Bunkley, Ed Riggs, and myself. We had two working the stand and the other guys walking around with the shoeshine boxes. We were shining them big ol' G.I. brogans. They really liked to get a shoeshine, and we didn't charge much.

Mary the Wanderer

Night activity was pretty well limited during World War II, we had such a blackout restriction. Because of the reduced amount of light from headlights, we were able to pull the old trick about "Mary the Wanderer." Boy, it was dark on St. Simons. We got some black silk fishing line, hung it over one telephone line on one side, drooped it down and flipped it over the other one, then pulled the line down in the middle of the street. We got one of Mother's old nightgowns and hooked that thing up with a few lead sinkers in the bottom. When a car came along, we dropped that nightgown down. We were way back up in the trees toward the Casino. We could see everything that was going on. We could pull that string and shake it just right and it would look just like somebody walking out there. Of course, you know, the lights weren't very good. Anyway, we pulled that stunt. This young couple came along in their car. We dropped "Mary" down. Their lights hit her, and we could see them slowing down. They weren't sure what was going on, so they stopped. We gave her a big yank and she disappeared. They pulled off to the side of the road. I saw somebody running over to the telephone office, which was just a few hundred feet from where they were. Before long, the county police were coming all the way from Brunswick because this was not under the military police. You could hear the siren coming all the way across the causeway, but we decided to continue our little prank. We dropped the nightgown back in the road and here come the police. They had their spotlight on. (I guess they could get away with that.) We dropped her down again. They saw her and almost turned sideways in the road when they hit their brakes. We pulled ol' Mary up straight over the top of that patrol car. They got their spotlight out and were looking everywhere, but they didn't think to look right straight up. So we let it be. Nobody talked much about it. It was over the weekend we pulled that stunt. The following Monday an article appeared in *The Brunswick News* about the mysterious appearance of "Mary the Wanderer" on Beachview Drive on St. Simons. We weren't about to say anything.

And Other Pranks

At night we would get up in the big oaks in the driveway going to the old Casino, which was the new Casino at the time. We couldn't get any rubber balloons so we carried buckets of water. We managed to get the buckets of water up in those trees. When somebody came by in a convertible, coming to the movie or whatever, we'd dump that bucket of water on them. People weren't allowed to shine their lights, so we could sit up there all night and they never could bother us.

There were lot of things that happened around the old Casino. I was a little bit smaller than the other guys, and one night they challenged me. I can't remember whether this was during the war time or not, but somebody had a little dead cat and said, "George, you can't crawl up in that return air vent and put that cat in there. You couldn't do that!" Now this was a challenge for me. So I took the dead cat. It had a string on it and I pulled it all the way down around the return air grill just around the corner where you couldn't look down there and see it. Oh, my heavens, in a few days I wished I'd never done it. That dead cat stunk so bad they had to close the theater for about two weeks. I mean they left the doors open. I don't think they ever found out where that cat was.

Gardens, Cantaloupes and Watermelons

I guess everybody had a victory garden. I remember Mr. Brandies, who lived in the caretaker's house across from the old Strachen house. He worked as a pipefitter in the shipyard. He had some of the best tomatoes on St. Simons. Percy, his son, and I would get a little salt in our hands and go out there and get a tomato now and then. He had several kinds of vegetables, but I remember the tomatoes quite well.

Later on brother Sonny had chickens in the backyard of our little house down off Demere Road. (The house is still there.) When he went off to the war effort, I took over that old chicken yard. I plowed and turned it up real good and planted some cantaloupes. Lo and behold, those things grew like I had never seen anything grow in all my life. They would run up on the side of the fence and then go down the other side heading out in the street. If you wanted to find a ripe one you had to take your shoes off, go in there with your bare feet, and work through them because there were so many.

Speaking of cantaloupes . . . we opened a sandwich shop down in back of the restaurant in the summertime. With the military around, the farmers would come to town with their produce. This one farmer came to town. He stopped at our sandwich shop and got a bite to eat and he asked me, "Sonny boy, would you mind keeping an eye on my cantaloupe truck out there? I'm going in there to watch the movie and cool off." That was the only place on St. Simons that had air conditioning. So I said, "Yes sir, I'd be very glad to." Well . . . I got to looking at those cantaloupes, and I thought those probably would serve good in the sandwich shop. So I took my apron, went out there, loaded about eight or ten, brought them in, and put them in a big old toilet tissue box in the back room. I made several trips. When the fellow came back a couple of hours later, he said, "Now I want you to go out there and get all the cantaloupes you want." I said, "Yes sir, I'd be glad to." I went out there and loaded that apron two or three more times.

It was an art to be able to snitch a watermelon, but it wasn't real hard because we didn't have that much light at night. The farmers would usually sleep in their truck. Not saying that we were bad or anything. We just wanted a few watermelons and couldn't afford them. One night we had this old delivery bicycle that we used at the café to deliver meals. It had a little front wheel with a big old basket over the wheel. Guy Bunkley and I sneaked up by this watermelon truck and loaded two or three watermelons in that big basket. We started off down the road. Guy was riding on the back fender and I said, "Boy, whatever you do, don't fall off." About that time, doggone if he didn't fall off. The front of that bicycle went tumbling and I rolled over those watermelons and never touched the ground. Of course, it didn't really hurt them. Kind of bruised them up a little bit. We ate them later on anyway.

Playing Hooky

In junior high during the warmer months, we would always have a hooky day in the spring. Somebody would holler "hooky day" on a Friday and just as many guys as could would play hooky. This one particular Friday, we rode the bus over to Brunswick and just didn't go to school. We went on down to the Bijou Theater and were standing around outside waiting for somebody to come out the exit door. When they came out the exit door, we would grab it and four or five of us would slip in the corridor behind the curtain, crawl up, and then just pop up in a seat somewhere to watch a movie. We could watch the movie two or three times, spending a good bit of the day in there. Then we went back to catch the school bus to come home. Brother Jack was along this day with Dan Cody and me. Dan and I had sneaked in, gotten up into a seat, and were watching the movie. Brother Jack got caught by the usher coming up under the curtain. They took him to the front office and said, "You won't be able to go to any movie for another month in this area." That was the St. Simons, the Ritz, and the Bijou theaters. In the meantime, Dan Cody and I were sitting there watching the movie for the second time. We started squeaking the seats. This got to be kind of obnoxious and we were drawing some attention. The usher came down, and she said, "If you boys don't stop that, we're going to have to give you your money back and let you go." Well my goodness, we hadn't even paid to go in the movie to begin with and then they were going to give us 35 cents. Anyway, we started squeaking the seats so they gave us our 35 cents and we got on out.

The Hurricane

In the fall of 1944 we were let out of school early one day because a hurricane was about to hit. Coming back over the causeway by bus, the wind was blowing a pretty good gale. My uncle, Carl Smith, was driving the school bus and, of course, he was a strict disciplinarian. Even though the wind was blowing 40 to 60 mph outside, you could hear a pin drop inside that bus. As we drove over the old wooden bridge at Frederica River, the bridge squeaked and cracked. That wind caught the bus full on the northeastern side, and we "belly bumped" [sideswiped] the railing on that bridge several times. When we got onto St. Simons' solid ground, everybody on the bus let out a big ol' hoop and holler and thanked the Lord. The hurricane of 1944 was a real wet one. I was reading the Air Force magazine back in 1964. It said, "Twenty years ago, the first seeding of an Atlantic hurricane was off the coast of Georgia." The Navy flew into it from Jacksonville and seeded that hurricane. They were experimenting with it and tried to rain it out. It rained it out all right! In two days we had 23 inches of rain. When we got up the next morning we didn't recognize St. Simons. It was just one big mess. Massive oaks blown over . . . pine trees. There weren't many pine trees left on the airport road all the way down to the St. Simons Sound. And boats . . . row boats were everywhere floating loose. In Brunswick, Lanier Boulevard had its share of washed-up boats, even a shrimp boat. Of course when the tide went down all the boats that had been washed up were left high and dry. The Navy, Army, and Marines pitched in and helped to clean up the debris.

VJ Day

On VJ Day we were coming from school in someone's car. There was this big old Marine on Highway 17 hitchhiking to the island. We stopped. He said, "Y'all going to St. Simons?" We indicated we were and he got in. When we got up to the toll house, ol' man Bunkley was on duty. Let me tell you what, if you didn't pay that 50 cents for the car and driver and 10 cents for each additional passenger, you didn't go across the causeway. Of course, many a time we rode over to St. Simons in the trunk so we wouldn't be counted or hid down on the floor board with a blanket over us. Anyway, this big Marine was sitting in the backseat that day. When we came up to the toll booth the big Marine said, "Don't pay the toll. Don't give him any money. This is VJ Day." Mr. Bunkley insisted and said, "You ain't going nowhere. You pay your toll." About that time that big Marine, he looked like he was about six two or six four, started getting out of the backseat of that car. When he looked down at Mr. Bunkley, he said, "Mister, I told you, sir. We're not going to pay any toll today. This is VJ Day and I'm going to celebrate." Mr. Bunkley said, "Oh, well, I guess it'll be all right this time."

Oh, My Heavens!

Brother Jack came up from the beach one day and as he walked in the house he said, "You ain't gonna believe what I saw down there." I said, "What do you mean?" He said, "There was this man's head down there washed up on the beach." I said, "My goodness, a head washed up on the beach!" And you know, this could have happened in World War II. But anyway, I really bit, hook, line, and sinker. He said, "Yeah, he left a note. It was stuck between his teeth." I said, "My goodness. What did the note say?" The note said, "I ain't got no-body." Oh my heavens!

Charles B. Daniel

My father was in real estate in Atlanta when World War II started. As one might imagine, the bottom fell out of the real estate business the minute we were at war and my father had to look for employment elsewhere. He left Atlanta for Brunswick in April 1942 and started work for the Daniel Construction Company, which had begun to build the shipyard. The rest of the family spent the summer in Atlanta since my mother was expecting a child. After she lost the baby in August we moved to St. Simons, arriving in time to start school. We (my parents, my sister, Susan, and I, plus two dogs) lived originally in a house named the Sea Shell on Wood Avenue, about 300 yards south of the Coast Guard station. My grandmother, Molly Collier, lived near us. My grandmother died in December 1942, and we moved to her house, which we still own. We lived there for the balance of the war.

My earliest war job was plane spotting with my grandmother and aunt on top of the King and Prince Hotel from 8 p.m. until midnight. We had a telephone connected to Savannah. If we heard an airplane we had to predict if it was a one- or two-engine plane and which direction it was heading. We had a code name for our spotting station.

SHIPYARDS

My father was involved with the Daniel Construction Company in the building of the shipyard. He worked in the railroad department, which moved carloads of incoming materials around from place to place within the shipyard confines. After the shipyard was taken over by the J. A. Jones Construction Company, he transferred to its railroad department. He worked there for the entire war—most of the time on the third shift.

I only worked one week at the shipyard in Brunswick. It was the first week of June 1944, and I was on the third shift. I thought I could play in the daytime, still have my nighttime dancing at the Casino, then work from midnight to 8 a.m., but I had forgotten about sleeping. After a week of that I figured it wasn't for me. While there I worked in the pipe shop, where large pieces of steam pipe were bent to fit the interior of the ship in the engine room. During that week we had an announcement about 3 a.m. that the D-Day invasion of Normandy had begun. I vividly recall how everyone was screaming and hollering. Then we had about five minutes of silence and prayer for the servicemen involved in the invasion.

In August 1994 I noticed an article in the Jacksonville paper about the last remaining serviceable Liberty ship that was making a port of call in Jacksonville, having just returned from the Normandy Invasion 50th celebration. My wife and I went down and went through the *Jeremiah O'Brien*. I went down into the engine room to look at some of the pipes that were identical to those we bent in the pipe shop during the war at the J. A. Jones shipyard.

It's noteworthy that you can still see the ways that those ships were built on during the war. The fitting-out basin, which was dredged at that time and used for fitting out four to six ships at a time after they had been launched, has silted in to the point where most of it is unusable now.

SABOTEURS

Between early 1942 and 1943 there was a big scare that we might have saboteurs put ashore from German submarines on St. Simons, Little St. Simons, Jekyll, and the other islands along the coast. They would come ashore in rubber boats, and we had to be on a constant lookout for them. I believe the Georgia State Guard patrolled the beaches at that time.

I don't know of any documented saboteurs put ashore, but I do recall a big hoopla at Ponte Vedra Beach in Florida where some came ashore there. It was exciting and scary to think we could have a saboteur knocking on our door some time. What should we do? Who should we report it to and what might happen? Actually, I don't think the danger was very great since it is so shallow so many miles offshore for St. Simons. I think they would have gone to a place where deep water is closer to the beach because a submarine requires quite a lot of water.

Use of the Inland Waterway

The inland waterway was used a great deal during the war. It provided a safe means for transporting large quantities of material up and down the East Coast. It was nothing to have 10 to 15 tugs and barges come through every day. At that time we had the old swing bridge at the Frederica River. There was a lot of delay getting back and forth to Brunswick.

Maneuvers

One of the most spectacular things that would occur during World War II was when the anti-aircraft contingence from Camp Stewart would come down with their trucks and 40MM aircraft guns, have a week-long camp out, and target practice on the beach. Normally they would come in around the Coast Guard station with 50 or 60 trucks, 20 or 30 guns, and maybe a couple hundred men. They would set up as if they were out in the field in combat and fire at a target that was towed by either a Coast Guard or Navy boat about a mile off shore. This was always exciting. We were allowed to go down, stand behind the guns, and watch them shoot at the target.

The Old Casino
St. Simons Island, Georgia

Casino

The old Casino was where the movie theater was located on the east end and the bowling alley was on the west end. In between was a large courtyard where most of us spent our time dancing or just, as they would say today, hanging out. I recall the lines to get into the movie going twice around the courtyard for a movie at 7 and 9 p.m. Mrs. McKendree was the manager of the theater and put up with absolutely no foolishness from anybody as far as talking or doing anything that would disturb the other people. She was not at all bashful about kicking you out of the movie if you didn't "do to suit." The bowling alley was run by Mrs. Edwards, Buddy and Skippy Edwards' mother. I was always envious because the Edwards boys got to set up the pins. For some reason, I always thought I would love to set pins in the bowling alley. The jukebox was outside the bowling alley, and that was the source of our music for dancing. We certainly had a good time jitterbugging in the courtyard at the old Casino.

I think one of the most traumatic things that happened on St. Simons was when somebody decided they could go the old Casino one better and build a new one that would be much more usable and better. It just never quite got there, but at least the new Casino had a swimming pool.

RECOLLECTIONS FROM HIGH SCHOOL

I went to Glynn Academy from September 1942 until graduation in 1945. Every child from St. Simons was bused to school in Brunswick. We had two busloads from St. Simons each day. Bus #8 was for the children from the south end of the island and Bus #6 was from the north end. We were still operating with the original wooden plank bridges that were built in 1924. It was a somewhat scary trip to go to Brunswick on those old bridges with a busload of kids.

I worked most of World War II summers at Dr. Backus' St. Simons Drug Store at the pier. It was located where a T-shirt shop and Coconut Willies is now. We worked 10-hour shifts seven days a week. There were some "perks" that went with working at the drug store. Since most things were rationed, we got first crack at the little bit of chewing gum, candy bars, and the one ham the drug store got each week for sandwiches. Edwin Fendig, Ray Cameron, and several other people worked there the same time I did. I think we did a good job and had a good time too.

It sounds as if what I did during the war was a lot of fun and not at all what you would expect war time to be. This all changed for me as I began my senior year at Glynn Academy in September of 1944. As soon as the class of June 1944 graduated, the boys went directly into service. The main hall of Glynn Academy had an honor roll that was started several years before. There were at least six or eight names from the graduating class of 1944 who had been killed in action between June and September. This made it quite clear to all of us how near we were to finishing our high school days and being called to take our place in the war effort. I, luckily, was young enough that I did not have to go into service in World War II, but I was called up for my pre-induction physical at the Fort McPherson Army Base in Atlanta during my first year at Georgia Tech. There were about 20 or 30 of us called up for the pre-induction physical and there were about thirty or forty thousand servicemen being processed out of the service. Although I passed my pre-induction physical, I was never called up.

William H. Backus
Dr. William H. Backus was a pharmacist on St. Simons Island and owned the St. Simons Drug Store.

My wife, Ruth, was in New York the day Pearl Harbor was bombed. You can imagine how anxious I was to get her home. Ruth and I, returning late from a party, heard cannon fire from the explosion of the tankers off Sea Island. The salvage workers who worked on these tankers were very nervous about going to work. The salvaged ships were anchored in the St. Simons Sound. I went out in an outboard to look and was able to run the boat through the torpedoed hole into the engine room.

Once when we briefly went offshore to check on the lights from the island and Brunswick, we were fired on our return. The Coast Guard had ordered no lights. The MPs were ordered to shoot at any boats with no lights.

For a few days I had no help at all in the store (St. Simons Drug Store) because everyone had gone to work at the shipyard. I had to fill prescriptions and make hamburgers.

Olaf H. Olsen, Jr.

MODEL AIRPLANES

During World War II schools all over the country made little models of airplanes in shop class for civil defense to study. They were six to eight inches long, painted black, and were exact silhouettes of what our planes and enemy planes looked like. As they passed inspection they were hung up at different angles for identification. I think I made one or two. Pete Kalcos made quite a few since he was good at it. We were given a certificate for building the model planes.

THE FIRST WEEK AFTER THE TORPEDOING OF THE TANKERS

The first week after the tanker ships were torpedoed off St. Simons, Daddy took the captain and some of the crew out to the site. Then he got me to go to Brunswick and pick them up every morning before daybreak. I would pick the men up at the motel at 4:30 a.m., take them to the boatyard Daddy had on Terry Creek in Brunswick, and take them out to the STS [St. Simons Light] Buoy. A boat would pick them up there and take them to the ships. The ships weren't too far from the STS Buoy and weren't fully sunk. The boat I drove was 32 to 34 feet long and made by the Balsa Boat Company. Every day the men would bring me a little present. They brought me the bell, a life ring, and other stuff from the ships. I did this for about a week.

Life Ring and Bell from the Baton Rouge
Courtesy of Olaf H. Olsen, Jr.

BEACH PATROLS ON LITTLE AND BIG CUMBERLAND ISLANDS

I remember going with Reginald Taylor to Little Cumberland. He was in charge of taking the soldiers to guard the beaches. Mr. Taylor wasn't too sure about landing on the beach. There was no dock. I had been over with the Sea Scouts, camped in the lighthouse, and gone turtle egg hunting there, so I went with him, ran the boat, and showed him the deep-water places. I didn't go to the north point of Little Cumberland but laid out on the backside or the inland side of the island. With the stern anchor out, it held the boat and kept it from coming around sideways. Then we pulled the boat, which had a shallow draft, toward shore. It was a calm day. We were overloaded because we had about 10 men and their equipment. The men waded ashore. I don't think there had been any men over before that time to patrol because when we went to set up camp at the lighthouse, nobody was around

Soldiers unloading supplies for Coastal Patrol
Little Cumberland Island, Georgia
Courtesy of Olaf H. Olsen, Jr.

and it was all grown up. Besides the lighthouse, there was a well and two old houses there at the time. The men camped in tents but made their headquarters in an old house.

That was the time when one of the men was peeling potatoes and the lieutenant pulled out his pistol and shot near where the man was sitting. He killed a rattlesnake close to the potato peeler! The soldiers were just a bunch of kids hauling their clothes, equipment, and supplies ashore, you know, not much older than I was. On the north end of Cumberland Island they had a camp just as you were going to the beach. They put down little pilings, had barracks. They cooked there and had a cooler. There was a radio station in the old beach house on the north end. The bigger unit at Duckhouse had a radio relay station. Duckhouse, which was towards the south end of the island, was back off the beach and had a little radio room with a sign over the door. A lot of the soldiers and later Coast Guardsmen on the south end of Cumberland lived in the barracks at Dungeness.

The refrigerated ship was torpedoed right off Stafford Shoals at Cumberland Island. I have sat on the Cumberland beach with the Army patrol and listened to the German submarines offshore charging their batteries. By the time I went into service, they had blimps patrolling and ships traveled in convoys.

Shipyard Days

When I went to work at the shipyard, Dot Rogers Raulerson, Bernice Rogers, and Mrs. Padgett worked for the comptroller, named Mr. Oliver. The office was a big room. When I went in the office that first day there weren't but about five or six people working. They hired me to be a messenger. They didn't have any telephones at that time. The next day we must have had 15 or 16 more people working. Before the week was out there were about 25, and there were about six or eight of us as runners. That building just kept filling up and filling up with people being hired. They were building a little timekeeper's office right inside the gate and it had an upstairs to it. I had to go out there to check in after I had been working a week or two. Before that time you didn't check in because there was no place to check in! I have never seen so many people move in from so many places in my life! I was making 48 or 49 cents an hour. When I quit I was making $1.20 an hour. I became a shipfitter and worked until I went into the Merchant Marine after I graduated in 1944.

The Brunswick News, February 24, 1942

Local Students Will Construct Plane Models

During the remainder of the school term, volunteer students of Glynn Academy will construct 150 models of airplanes for the National Defense Program, R. H. Hartley, vocational instructor, announced today. According to a statement made by Secretary Knox, over 500,000 models are needed for aircraft recognition and gunnery sighting practice. Students will learn the value of precision and the importance of speed; and at the same time provide organized participation of the youth of the nation in the national defense. One of the greatest public benefits to be derived will be the use of these models by civilian "spotters" in identifying enemy planes, an ever increasing menace to seacoast cities.

During the week, the work will be organized among the students. Various civic clubs and organizations will be called upon for assistance in the project. Plans and specifications are furnished by the Bureau of Aeronautics, but, all construction materials are furnished locally. The completed models will be carefully inspected before acceptance. For those students achieving outstanding work, certificates of award will be issued by the Bureau of Aeronautics of the Navy Department.

Catherine Wynne Gleason

In 1934 our family moved from Atlanta to St. Simons, where we lived at Wynne Gables Hotel until 1944. Our father was a construction engineer for the King and Prince Hotel. After the tankers were torpedoed the beaches had many seagulls that were unable to fly away because of the oil on their feathers. Glynn Academy students were encouraged to plant victory gardens, prepare bandages for the Red Cross, attend USO functions, and build model airplanes. The planes were used to train air-raid wardens to distinguish our planes from the hostile ones at a glance.

The school newspaper had articles to promote buying defense stamps. In the March 1942 issue, we were reminded "The more defense stamps we purchase, the bigger saps we'll make out of the Japs." In April 1944, the armed forces stationed in our area contributed to the success of a school bond auction. The Coast Guard gave Jeep rides to high bidders. The Army had mechanized reconnaissance vehicles on display.

Lillian Marie Lang Meyers

I remember vividly December 7, 1941, the day the Japanese bombed Pearl Harbor. My mother and I were playing golf at the Brunswick Country Club. When we returned to the club house, we heard the terrible news and rushed home to tell our father. The next day my brother, Hubert, tried to join the Navy. As he was a senior in high school, my father would not sign for him. He had to wait until he graduated. As a 15-year-old sophomore in high school, to me the war really was more of an inconvenience than a reality. We had sugar and meat rationing and the worst . . . gas rationing! Most of us were just getting our driver's license. There were the blackouts at the beach, so our parties were curtailed.

I had a part-time job on Saturdays at an auto hardware store which sold auto parts, tires, sporting goods, etc. I remember the pea-pickers, as we derogatorily named them, would come in the store with more money than they needed and buy just about anything. I recall selling a man a complete set of golf clubs even though he had never played golf and was not even interested.

My mother got a job in personnel at the shipyard. As we had a servant, that did not affect my life too much, and, as a teenager, I continued to do my thing. By this time my brother was in the Navy, and, on some level, I guess I worried but he was still Stateside. My father was very busy as he owned a lumber company and business was booming. There were USO dances and some of the girls my age attended, but I wasn't interested as I was going steady with someone.

And then the war began to be noticed. Some of the boys I knew had died. One was Harris Steele, a good friend of my brother Jack and someone I played tennis with and liked a lot. He was a Marine and died on Iwo Jima. My next-door neighbor was engaged to J. C. Strother and he died somewhere in Europe . . . Normandy, I think. Hubert was now on a minesweeper in the Pacific and they were getting sunk regularly.

I Want A Girl (Tune)

I want a bond -
Just like the bond
that's backed by U. S. A.
It is the bond,
and the only bond,
I save for each pay day!
Good old fighting bond,
with interest due;
In ten years from now
I'll need it too!
I'll buy a bond,
each month a bond,
To win for U. S. A.

I began my first year at the University of Georgia in September of 1944. There were few men on campus and we girls used to wonder about the ones who were there . . . like "what is wrong with them?" Then President Roosevelt died. He was such a connection for me to the war, and I felt very bereaved. Suddenly, the campus was filled with men—of all ages, shapes, and mental conditions. As a psychology major, I had my few that I comforted and spent hours talking to. But the war was over, my brother was safe, and there were men to date and good times were here again.

Some classmates married servicemen from the North or just married young. I have never forgotten those whom I knew who died. But I think most of all of their parents, who will always miss them and long for them.

Robert C. Highsmith

When the World War II started, I was delivering milk from 4:30 a.m. until school time. At 16 years of age I went to work in the shipyard on the 12:30 a.m. to 8 a.m. shift and stayed out of school. The next year I worked on the 4:30 p.m. to 12:30 a.m. shift and went to school in the mornings. I did not have time to keep up with my old friends. Also during this year J. A. Jones had me teaching a blueprint class in a bus garage on Newcastle Street. I worked seven days a week at the shipyard. Sometimes on Friday and Saturday nights I worked 12 hours. I got lucky. I was competing mostly with farmers who had little education. Otherwise a 16-year-old kid like me would not have been getting instructor's pay. I had security clearance to work on some jobs where they kept the blueprints locked in the office safe. With these jobs I had to keep the prints on my person and not let anyone else have access to them. On most of the jobs, the prints were in a shack that was lifted onboard ship by a crane. I graduated in 1945 and went straight into the Army. I was 18 years old when I joined and had just turned 21 when I came out. When I was discharged, I came in on a train from Norfolk, Virginia, one morning and went to work the same night at Brunswick Pulp and Paper. I started on the bottom job in the machine room, later transferred to the electric shop. Worked up to A+ electrician on shift, a position I held for many years. In 1970, I became a supervisor and stayed there until March 1, 1989, when I retired.

About the tankers: my dad worked on one of the salvage tugs, the *Resolute*, for Merritt, Chaplin and Scott. This was before I worked at the shipyard.

The salvage tug *Resolute* was assigned to the torpedoed tankers *Baton Rouge* and *Oklahoma* in April 1942.

Nan Fowler Bailey

Although I wasn't born in Brunswick, my family moved there when I was four months old, so I consider myself a native. There were five children in our family: Carl, Glynn Academy Class '37; Nina, '39; John, '42'; Nan, '46; and Mary, '51. Dad worked with the AB&C

Railroad, later consolidated with Atlantic Coastline. The depot was next to the Oglethorpe Hotel. (It still pains me to know that grand old place is gone.) Across Newcastle Street was the Edo Miller Funeral Home. Carl died in 1975. Nina, John, and Mary still live in Brunswick.

My earliest memory of the war and the changes that took place was with my brother, Carl. We were sitting on the front porch and he was looking at *The Brunswick News*, reading about the shipyard coming to town. When he sadly remarked that it would drastically change Brunswick, I didn't quite understand. But he was right! All of a sudden, or so it seemed, everything was crowded. Before the war, we felt perfectly safe. I remember Stella Denty and I would often walk downtown at night to get a Coke at Holody's Drug Store. Holody's then was right next to the Ritz Theater.

Naturally, the schools were overcrowded. I know some of the elementary grades had two shifts. In high school we had Liberty bond auctions . . . bidding on things like a half day off or a Jeep ride, compliments of the local Navy or Army facilities. We had no interscholastic competitions. Lots of new teachers came in. Coach "Red" Adams went into the Navy as a commissioned officer. He looked so handsome in his uniform! (Several years later in California, I ran into him at the Officers' Club and blurted out "Coach" Adams. We did a lot of reminiscing. Sadly, he died a few years later.)

After school I worked in a neighborhood grocery store and remember collecting customers' ration points along with the money. For example, a pound of bacon was something like 45 cents and 8 meat points. When my brothers came home on leave, they'd go downtown to the rationing board for an allotment during their stay. Mother's women's society at church voted not to serve refreshments at their meetings to save their sugar and butter. This move wasn't well received by all the ladies, but I won't mention names! Speaking of Mother, she volunteered at the Red Cross making bandages. I believe the local head of the Red Cross was Mrs. Judy Corbett Krauss, Boysie's mother.

The war brought many servicemen to Brunswick. At our church, and it was probably so at all other churches, any serviceman attending church on Sunday was guaranteed a dinner at home with a member of the congregation. In spite of rationing and shortages, Mother always had plenty of food for visiting servicemen and she was a wonderful cook. I was a little young to date servicemen or attend USO dances, but my sister Nina did.

During the war, my brother Carl was in the Water Transportation Corps of the Army and was skipper of a tugboat off Belgium. John was in the Army Air Corps and was in Washington State waiting to be shipped out when the war ended. Nina was employed at Brunswick Pulp and Paper from its very early years. Just recently we were talking about that and she remembered that the personnel file was a manila envelope! She remained there as secretary to the president until her retirement a few years ago.

Laverne Anderson Mills

Our family moved to Brunswick in 1943 from Glennville, Georgia. My brother worked at the shipyard prior to Army duty and my father worked at the gas plant near the shipyard. The one thing that stands out in my memory is the patriotism felt by everyone—from the oldest to the youngest—and the desire to do everything possible to contribute to the war effort. At no time since, and probably never again, will we see a nation and cities so united toward a common goal.

William J. Harp, Jr.

After I had finished my freshman year at Cordele High School, we moved to Brunswick. My father had taken a job as a police officer in Brunswick. The year was 1943 or 1944 and Brunswick was bustling with activity. The shipyard was in full swing. Men and women were working. Money was plentiful, but goods were scarce.

Brown's Barbecue was downtown. It was small and always busy. They had the best cheeseburgers I ever tasted. The Doughnut Shop was near Brown's Barbecue. It had a plaque with the words "Keep Your Eye on the Doughnut and Not on the Hole."

We lived in Gordon Oaks, a modest brick housing under stately live oak trees near the shipyard. The Mark Carr Recreational Center was nearby. It was vast, with a soda fountain, cafeteria, and trading post. I worked there after school until I went to work in the soda fountain at Andrews Drug Store.

Andrews Drug Store on Gloucester Street had marble counters, cherry wood cabinets for tobacco, white and black checkered ceramic tile floors, black-top tables, an elaborate ceiling, and black columns in the prescription area. The drug store was so busy that merchandise was sometimes left in boxes rather than put on shelves. Evening in Paris, Old Spice, and Cara Nome were popular in the cosmetic and fragrance area. On my way to work I would pass a beautiful mansion on Union Street. The street then, as now, was lined with beautiful Victorian homes and spacious yards. One day I saw a beautiful lady with white hair gardening in front of the most imposing home on the street. She was wearing gloves, and to me, she represented the highest form of genteel southern aristocracy. My parents had decided to leave Brunswick, but Mr. Andrews, the owner of the drug store, asked me to stay and move into his home. He could do more for me than my parents could afford. My parents, after much discussion, decided it would be in my best interests.

Then I met the beautiful lady on Union Street. She was Mrs. Andrews! [Mr. and Mrs. Andrews owned Andrews Drug Store in Brunswick. Their son, Jim, died during World War II.] I love them both dearly and will always be grateful for their kindness and love that knew no boundaries.

How to describe my years in Brunswick? Happy and fulfilling?

Antonio Barboza and Eugene Cutinke
Courtesy of Mary Teresa Martin

Mary T. Martin

Six to eight blocks of the south end of Brunswick was a small community of Portuguese families. These were immigrants from the old country who had settled along the waterfront. They were all fishermen and didn't have any cars. They had to live close to the waterfront so they could get down to their boats around two or three o'clock in the morning to go out for the day's catch. Hanover Park was the center of this Portuguese community. The Catholic church and St. Joseph's School were all within walking distance of our homes. Every evening as you walked along Newcastle Street you could see groups of men sitting on the benches in the parks that lined Newcastle Street all the way from Hanover Park to the Ritz Theater. They usually would be talking about how many shrimp they caught that day and where they had been fishing.

One day the awful news came over the radio of the attack on Pearl Harbor. President Franklin Delano Roosevelt's words announcing we were at war were terrible! That day changed everyone's lives. All the church bells in Brunswick began to ring and people began to fill the churches. Masses were said and special prayers were offered for those who had died at Pearl Harbor. Also, we prayed for a speedy end to this horrible war that was just beginning. At that time I was about 13 years old. I had no idea of what was really happening. Soon all of our young men and women began to enlist in the services.

First-generation Portuguese who lived in the south end of Brunswick enlisted. They were eager to defend the country that had given their parents a new start in life, that had given them a good education and a better chance to make a difference. Three of these young men were killed in action: Lewis Romera, Eugene Cutinke, and Manuel Manita. I remember the day Mrs. Manita received the telegram that her son had been killed in action. It was as if a knife had been plunged into her heart. Her cries could be heard all over the south end until she finally collapsed from exhaustion. Eugene Cutinke was my cousin. He was born in Fernandina, but at age one his mother took him back to Portugal. When he was 18 years old my uncle sent for him to come live with us and learn how to captain one of his shrimp boats. Little did we know that two years later he would be enlisting in the infantry and at age 21 would be killed by machine gun fire.

My mother and all the women in the community rolled bandages and knitted scarves for the veterans. She read letters for those men who did not know how to read and write. There were quite a few fishermen who didn't have any education at all. She did this as a favor to them and also interpreted for them if they needed to go to a doctor.

Also during that time, two or three of my uncle's shrimp boats were used by the government to patrol our coastline for our protection. I remember when the ships were torpedoed off St. Simons. At church that Sunday the priest asked the people to invite some of the survivors to their homes. Mother invited three young men to have dinner with us. As it turned out two of them were Portuguese descendants and spoke the language. For many years we corresponded with Tony Barboza who was in the Merchant Marine.

Hanover Park took on a whole new purpose. At that time we were living at 206 George Street. Across the street was a large lot that was overgrown with trees and shrubbery. When people came to Brunswick looking for work at the shipyard, they had to find a place to sleep the first few nights until they got a job and some type of housing. They would pull their cars into this wooded area and sleep in the cars. Every morning you could see people coming out of the woods with their towels, bars of soap, and toothbrushes, making their way to the fountain in the center of Hanover Park. Also, if you walked through the park in the dark you had to be very careful not to step on a sleeping shipyard worker who hadn't gotten a place to live yet.

The U.S. bond rallies were a lot of fun. I remember Veronica Lake came to Brunswick. Later Goren's car was on display. My Uncle Joe always made sure I had plenty of money to buy U.S. bonds so that I could have my picture taken with the celebrities. Big deal!

Tony Martin, my future husband's brother, became a radio man in the Navy and was assigned to the USS *Pennsylvania*, which was hit by a torpedo the day that the treaties were signed, but he was okay. Arthur Martin and I were engaged during my senior year in high school. When he graduated from Glynn Academy, he also joined the Navy. Actually, Arthur had already received his papers as to which ship he was assigned, but, thank God, the war ended before he even left the States.

When the war ended, again all the church bells rang. This time their sounds brought us joy! Our boys came home. Picking up their lives was not easy. Many had been wounded, such as Manuel Santos. Many would never recover from the experiences of that terrible war. Some went back to school. Some tried to get jobs, but there were not enough jobs to go around. Our government did help them with their education and helped to create new jobs. Many of us married soon after the war and started the so-called "baby boomers." I remember our first class reunion when five seemed to be the magic number and Mr. Boswell (principal of Glynn Academy) made a joke about it.

Brunswick grew quite a lot during the war days and changed very much. The islands were never quite the same either. Those days for us who grew up during that time were, in a way, good days because we were so young. I suppose we never really thought then as we do now that we have our own children. We can remember with pride those who died and hope we never have to send our sons and daughters to fight such a war again. Patriotism never ran quite so high as it did during those World War days, and I guess that pride really stays with us who lived through that time—for we know the true cost of freedom.

"God is good! How fortunate we are that we did not suffer as other countries did where the battlefields were!"

Eleanor Smith Gathright

Stars in the Windows

CHAPTER THIRTEEN

Our Men and Women in Service

In honor of our loved ones who fought for our country during World War II and in memory of those who gave their lives for our freedom.

Across the United States, families honored their loved ones fighting during World War II by hanging blue stars in their windows. If a loved one was lost, they replaced the blue star with a gold star.

STARS IN THE WINDOWS
From *The Brunswick Mariner*
Friday, June 16, 1944

Personal Experience
By J.M.

My star changed today.

Last night it was a deep dark blue, reminding me of the boyish eyes it represented. And as a constant reminder of what I had given, my little blue star valiantly and proudly heralded to all the world, like a beacon in the night, the purpose for which it stood. Last night my mind was filled with all the many plans I had for the boy my little blue star represented. His future, his happiness, his success was all that mattered to us as we planned all those small, yet important items that were to make his life an easier, fuller and more complete one.

We wanted him to forget all the bitter hell that he had been through in this great war, and we wanted to forget rationing and black markets and bond drives. There was so much to remember, so much to forget, and there was so much to be planned and dreamed of.

But today my star changed from a deep dark blue to a flaming gold.

My plans, my dreams crumbled as I read "deeply regret to inform you." The end of time had arrived for me, nothing mattered now, all was lost. Could nothing remove the agony that was in my heart? No, not until I thought of the many, many other little blue stars that said to the world "I represent a soldier" did my mind respond to the hidden urge to take up the battle where my boy left off.

My task is easier now, no work too hard. Each day my resolution to do more and more becomes more firmly imbedded as the conviction that I am doing my part holds me to a greater determination to see the battle through. "Yes, I'll buy more bonds today, gladly and proudly, too, I'll love and cherish my little gold star, but I want yours to remain ever blue."

"I remember the five stars hanging in the window of our house because my five older brothers were in the service, four Navy and one Air Force. They all returned safely!"

Hollis Cate

G. Vassa Cate

I was born and raised in Brunswick, as was my father. My grandfather was one of the pioneer doctors in Brunswick. He came from North Carolina before the turn of the century. I graduated from Glynn Academy in 1936 and attended college through 1940. I taught and coached one year. In 1942 I went into the Navy. I was not discharged until 1946. This means I was not in Brunswick except a day of two during the years 1941-45. I was in the Pacific during those years. I do remember hearing through correspondence with folks at home how Brunswick had tripled in population, with people sleeping in cars because of lack of rooms.

There were six boys in our family. Five served in World War II and one in Korea.

Frances Foster Cofer

William and I married a few months after we graduated from Glynn Academy in 1941. When the shipyard was built, William worked there as a sheet-metal welder. My mother, Mrs. R. C. Foster, worked there in a tool house where they dispensed and collected the tools each day. William helped construct the model Liberty ship which was displayed at the Chamber of Commerce. They have replaced it since the original rusted away.

William was drafted when our daughter was six months old in December of 1943. My baby girl, Martha Lee, and I stayed with my parents while William served in the Navy in the Pacific war area. His brother, Edwin, was captured by the Germans in the famous Battle of the Bulge. He was in a root cellar eating rotten vegetables when the U.S. troops came in and set them free. William was stationed on a destroyer tender. Ships came to them with huge holes in them and they would work around the clock repairing them to go back into battle.

I was most impressed with the fact that people, because of their desperate situations, began to feel the need to draw nearer to God than they ever had before. I prayed earnestly that William would be spared to return to us, if the Lord had a plan for his life after the war was over. I even asked the Lord that, if in his plan he would need for William's life to be taken while he was gone from us, He would give us the strength to relinquish him, knowing that God does all things well. William returned completely unscathed. After William came home, our son, Billy, was born.

A funny little note: It had been announced everywhere that when V Day came, we should meet at church for a time of praise and thanks to God for the end of the war. It didn't matter what hour the word came, we would all hurry to the church to celebrate! When the day came, I was so excited and quickly got Martha Lee and myself dressed, so we could joyfully tear off to the church. I plopped a little dress on little Lee, who was around two years old. We were all screeching and laughing and she couldn't get a word in edgewise! I discovered too late that she had no underwear on as I saw a trickle running down the church floor. She was admonished to sit very still and quietly until we could get home and remedy the situation!

Joe Harwell
by Anne Harwell North

In September 1908, Joseph L. Harwell was born in Brunswick, Georgia. In March 1943, his cargo ship was sunk in the north Atlantic. The years between were of a boy growing up in a small southern town with a large loving family.

After graduating from the Naval Academy, he went into the Merchant Marine, still in the Navy Reserve. It wasn't long before he was made captain with the Isthmian Steamship Line, making many trips to foreign countries around the world.

World War II changed the cargo of the Merchant Marine fleet to carrying supplies to England and eventually Murmansk. The German U-boats came in wolf packs for the supply ships, and it was in one of these convoys that Joe's ship was sunk. All of the men from Joe's ship were saved, and they were returned to Newfoundland. As Joe was taken aboard the Canadian Corvette from his lifeboat, he heard the roster of officers and recognized a name. He requested to speak to the commander and here was a shipmate from the Naval Academy who had joined the Canadian Navy on graduation. Joe made many more trips during and after the war.

Stella Morton Harned
Stella M. Harned's husband, Irving, was general manager of the Cloister Hotel on Sea Island in 1941.

My husband, Irv, and I were living in a small house on Sea Island when in the middle of the night he woke me and asked, "Did you hear that?" I said, "Yes, is it thunder?" "No, " he said, "it is shelling." How do men know these things?

It was the procedure of the U-boats when they torpedoed a ship to surface and shell the ship at the waterline. The crew of the ships were allowed to take to their lifeboats before the U-boat shelled them. [Note: These were merchant ships and were not rigged at that time, early 1942, with any type of gunnery.] When the news reached us that the tankers had been torpedoed and the survivors were being brought into the Sea Island Yacht Club and Coast Guard Station on the Frederica River, we went to meet them. It was a frightening thing to realize that a German U-boat was right here in the waters off St. Simons.

After this, Irv was commissioned a first lieutenant in the Army Air Corps. We proceeded to Miami Beach, where he graduated from Officers Training School. In Miami Beach we had blackout curtains and drove with dim lights. This was to keep the merchant ships off shore from being silhouetted, which made it easier for the U-boats to spot them. We did see ships burning offshore in the daytime.

Before the war, skeet shooting had been a popular pastime at Sea Island, and there were many tournaments. Irv had an AA national

Irving Harned
Courtesy of Mrs. John A. Russo

rating. For this reason, he was transferred to gunnery at Tampa and then Barksdale Field, Shreveport, Louisiana, where he taught skeet shooting and trained the gunners in the bomber. These bombers were good in combat, but hard to learn to fly. More than one went down. When it happened, they closed the field and took all the personnel out on a bivouac . . . a glorified picnic, with lots of barrels of beer. It dispelled the gloom.

We were at Barksdale Field long enough to have our first child and for Irv to graduate from the first class of gunners to get their wings in Laredo, Texas. That meant flight pay and was an honor as well. Irv was next sent to Norris Field in Charlotte, North Carolina, as a wing gunnery officer. We were in Charlotte for six weeks when he was requested by the Air Transport Command and was on his way to "the black hole" of Calcutta, India. It was a very unpleasant assignment and dangerous. Air Transport Command was an airlift mission over the Himalayas, the highest mountain range in the world. It was called "The Hump."* They were keeping China supplied to keep the Japanese busy and hopefully distract them from the South Pacific. He was there a year and then the war was over.

The servicemen were anxious to get home but were not discharged right away. General Turner, who headed the airlift, told Irv that if he went to Shanghai and reopened the Cathay Mansions, a hotel that the Japanese had occupied during the war, he would let him come home. That was "duck soup" for Irv since he was in the hotel business. He just hired back the people who had been employed there before the Japanese took over. And then he came home!

*The Hump was the first great airlift in history. During World War II, it was the supply lifeline from northeast India across the Himalayas to China. From December 1, 1942, through November 15, 1945, the total volume transported from India to China was 776,532 tons. This instituted air freight transportation. The Hump crews mainly supplied the B-29s which flew out of bases in China with 100 octane aviation fuel. Each flight's cargo consisted of approximately twenty-five 55-gallons drums.

Barbara Harrison Drye

My first memory of World War II was of my daddy listening to the radio and President Roosevelt's speech announcing we were at war. Pearl Harbor had been bombed. Every airplane that flew over after that frightened me as I thought they were going to bomb us.

My family had lived in the area for as far back as I know . . . at least as far back as my great-granddaddy. We lived on the Old Post Road, which was five miles past Thalmann.* It was very isolated, and our nearest neighbors, about three miles down the road, were my dad's three brothers and their families. It was a wonderful growing-up experience, and I wouldn't take anything for it. We didn't have indoor plumbing, running water, or electricity. My grandfather owned several thousand acres of land on the Post Road, and Daddy bought several hundred acres from him when I was four years old and we moved from Brunswick. It was about 20 miles away, which back then seemed to take an eternity to drive. One of my uncles moved from the Post Road to Thalmann and opened a small grocery store. I would spend the night with a girl cousin. When the troop trains would come through, my aunt would fill up boxes with chewing gum and candy for us to go out and sell to the soldiers. They would hang out the windows of the train to buy it.

One of my sisters went to work at the shipyard and married a man she met there. Another sister married a local boy that we all knew and loved. Johnny Howe was his name. He was stationed in Columbus, Georgia. After they married, my sister, Alma, got to live with him less than a year. She became pregnant, and about her eighth month she came home to have the baby. Johnny was able to come home for a short furlough. The nurse wasn't going to let him see the baby, but my dad was there and told the nurse that Johnny had to go back to the base and maybe wouldn't get to see her for a long time. It turned out that was the only time he saw his daughter. She was born in December 1943, and he was killed July 12, 1944. He is buried at Normandy at St. Laurient. My sister saw in the paper that some of the men who were there were going back for the 50th anniversary of D-Day. She called one of them and asked him to take pictures of Johnny's grave. He did and sent them to her. I also lost a cousin who was killed exactly one month later in the same area. He also is buried in France. He was the only boy in a family of three sisters. I remember it nearly killed them. His name was Gerald Harrison. My husband-to-be was stationed with another cousin in Savannah at Chatham Air Force Base. My older brother worked at Brunswick Pulp and Paper. My youngest brother joined the Navy and was on a ship for the last year of the war.

This is about all I can remember about the war days. I just remember it being a sad time in all our lives and how glad we were when it was over.

* Thalmann was the location of the train depot for the Seaboard and Coastline railroads. People who were coming from the south or north used this station. People visiting Sea Island boarded or departed the train at Thalmann. There was a depot, water tank, and coal bin for the steam engines located there.

Frances Sumner Herrin

I have always lived in the Brunswick area. During my early childhood, my family lived in a five-room house at Kinstle's Dairy Farm on Kinstle's Road, which is now Goodbread Road. I had two older sisters and a younger sister and brother. My father, Clifford, was a dairyman and worked for Mr. Kinstle until the dairy burned. Mr. Kinstle never rebuilt. Then Dad worked for Blackerby's and Cason's dairies. During the war he worked at the Brunswick Pulp Mill. After I married, he moved to Baldwin, Florida, where he worked at a dairy.

My mother's oldest brother, Perry L. McDonald, Sr., had fought overseas during World War I. He had a wife, two daughters, and a son, Perry, Jr., whom we all called "Junior." They lived in Syracuse, New York. We had very little contact with them. Uncle Perry left this family and as years passed left several other wives. My mother and grandmother were always forgiving toward him, after all, he suffered from shell shock in World War I. Uncle Perry's son, Junior, brings the fondest and saddest memories when I think of World War II.

Perry L. McDonald, Jr.
Courtesy of Frances Sumner Herrin

One day, shortly after World War II began, Junior appeared on our doorsteps. Already crowded, Mama took him in and soon he became a part of the family. It was sometime later that we found out Junior had left home without permission and did not intend to go back. I never knew the circumstances, just that Mama made him welcome and he became a member of the family and for me, the older brother I never had. I suppose he was in his late teens.

Junior enlisted or was drafted into the Army. He was a paratrooper. I was so proud of this especially and so proud that my first cousin, whom I had known and loved for such a short time, was serving our country. Junior was stationed at Fort Benning and came home several times on short leaves. Then, on what was his last visit, he informed us that he was to be shipped overseas to the war zone. With childlike acceptance, we hugged, kissed, and bid farewell.

It was not until my mother received that dreaded telegram, "Killed in Action," that she realized Junior had listed her as next of kin. I still remember lying across the bed where my grandmother sat as she heard the news that her eldest grandson had been killed in action. With proper arrangements and contact with Junior's real mother, his body was sent to Syracuse, New York, and laid to rest. Then and now, I wonder, was he "killed while jumping from a plane?"

Junior had sent my mother a picture of himself in his uniform framed in one of those patriotic frames. She kept it all these years, until last year, when she gave it to me. Junior also gave me the last baby doll I received as a young girl. She stands about 24 inches high. I never gave her a name, but I still have her and cherish her.

Curtis E. Burch

My parents moved to Brunswick in 1924 from Montgomery County, Georgia. My father became a member of the Brunswick City Police Force. He was a mounted patrolman, which in those days included everything from rounding up animals to patrolling the waterfront dives on Bay Street. A policeman carried a big stick, even though he might walk softly. My father continued to be a patrolman until 1931, when he was appointed assistant chief of the Brunswick city force. The city bought a 1932 Ford coupe with the new V8 engine specifically designed to chase moonshiners and bootleggers. He had this position with the City of Brunswick until he retired around 1948.

I remember during the war policemen also had to carry a big stick because there were a great many barrooms, saloons, and dance halls in the Brunswick area and quite a bit of fighting and drinking. Brunswick was a pretty wild town. In 1949 my father went to work with the Glynn County police force as assistant chief, and around 1950-51 he was appointed the chief of the Glynn County force. He held this position until he retired in 1969.

My mother was a homemaker for many years, then in the early '30s she worked at a dress shop in the 1500 block of Newcastle Street across from where Kress is now. In 1940 she took the U.S. government census, and in 1941 she went to work with the Greyhound Bus Company as a ticket agent at the old bus station on the corner of Grant and Gloucester Streets. It later moved to the corner of Gloucester and Carpenter Streets. After many years with Greyhound, she went to work in the State Court or Misdemeanor Court of Brunswick in the Glynn County Courthouse and stayed there until her retirement around 1971. My mother passed away in April of 1988 at the age of 83. My father died in August of 1993 at the age of 93.

I started school in the old Glynn Grammar School on Mansfield Street in September of 1931 and completed the fifth grade there. In that time Sidney Lanier Elementary School was built, and I went there to the sixth grade. The Glynn Grammar became the Prep High building with seventh and eighth grades. (I believe, besides Glynn Grammar there was Purvis Grammar School on Norwich Street in about the 2000 block. There was also N.A. Ballard Grammar School, which is still there out on the old Jesup Highway and Community Road, and there was also a grammar school in the Sterling area. I do not remember if that was for white children or black children; at that time, as of course you know, there was segregation.) I graduated from Glynn Academy in the class of '43.

In the summer of '42 I worked just a couple weeks at the J. A. Jones shipyard as a messenger boy. I left that job and went to the Shepherd and Griffin Construction Company on St. Simons Island and helped build the naval air station that was under construction at that time. I drove a big dump truck, hauling everything from gravel and sand to various construction materials from Brunswick across the causeway to the site of the naval air station. That summer I was a member of the St. Simons State Guard. The St. Simons Guard would accept young men 16 years old who were somewhat large for their age, whereas the Brunswick Guard would not. After my seventeenth birthday, which was in September 1943, I transferred to the Brunswick State Guard and participated in that unit until I left for the service in 1943.

Upon graduation from Glynn Academy in June 1943, several of my friends (some of them had quit school) had already enlisted in the armed services. My mother and father insisted that I finish high school. I journeyed to Savannah to try and join the Marine Corps. Two very close friends, Roy Rolg and Harry Steele, were in there. The Marine Corps turned me down because I was somewhat nearsighted. It was back to Brunswick, brokenhearted, to say the least, that I could not join.

I went to work at the J. A. Jones shipyard again. I started out firing a steam crane [shoveling coal in an old steam crane]. I got a promotion a few weeks later to firing a locomotive [shoveling coal on a steam locomotive]. I traveled back to Savannah and enlisted in the Navy and was accepted there. Eye standards were not quite as strict as the Marine Corps. I left Brunswick in July and was sworn in at Macon, Georgia. From there I went to Pensacola, Florida, and did several weeks of boot camp. After boot camp I was assigned to a fire and crash unit at Saufley Field in Pensacola.

In the latter part of October 1943, I came home to Brunswick on leave. My sweetheart, Imogene Phillips, and her mother had moved back to Montgomery, Alabama. After spending a few days with my family in Brunswick, I journeyed to Montgomery. Imogene and I were married on November 1, 1943. In December she moved to Pensacola to be with me, and, believe it or not, the first real snow I had ever seen fell in Pensacola, Florida, in December of '43. Three inches of snow. This was unheard of and unbelievable. They turned the schools out so the kids could play in it.

My Job in the Navy

At the naval air station, I was a crash and building fireman. The Navy always kept crash trucks on the flight line just a short ways from where the planes landed and took off. At that time we were training not only our pilots but also pilots from Britain, France, New Zealand, Canada, Australia, Norway, Holland, France, South Africa . . . forces that were not under Hitler's occupation or pilots who had escaped to the Allied side. We were training them along with our own in Pensacola.

We had some awful crashes and fires in those days. Very tragic. I've seen a lot of people burned to death, but we also rescued a lot of aviation cadets and pilots. Although I never went overseas, some of these memories still are with me today. During this time I met many of the foreign servicemen who were training in the Pensacola area. Sometimes when we were off duty, which wasn't very much, the aviation cadets from these other countries would come by the firehouse or the crash station. We always had a guitar or harmonica. We sat around and made music together to pass the time. Made quite a few friends in those days.

In January 1945 the Navy shipped me from Pensacola, Florida, to the Brooklyn Navy Yard in New York. I went through several weeks of school, learning how to be a ship fireman—in other words, to combat ship fires and aircraft carrier fires. Sometimes they would take us downtown and train us there with the New York City firemen. After finishing this school in the Brooklyn Navy Yard, I was a rated firefighter, a specialist F third-class petty officer, which I held until the end of the war.

I was discharged in March of 1946 and returned to the Brunswick area and went to work for the city fire department. I worked with them for about seven years. I finally wound up going to work at the naval air station in Glynco in '67. When they closed Glynco, I transferred to the air force base at Warner Robbins, Georgia. I finished up my time there in 1989 and retired. My wife and I celebrated our golden wedding anniversary in November of 1993 with a trip back to Montgomery where we were married—"the scene of the crime," my wife calls it—and also to Pensacola where I was stationed. We went to the aviation museum there. Seeing those old planes that I had worked with gave me cold chills. It was just like being there during the war.

In closing out, let me say that I volunteered to serve my country in World War II. I'm very proud of that fact. I served with honor and distinction, perfect conduct record, and while I didn't see combat I did as I was told. If the same thing came up, I'd do the same thing again. I'd volunteer to defend my country. I am grateful to the almighty God that I did not sustain any injuries or have to go into combat, but I would gladly have done so if that had been the case.

Laurence S. Miller, Jr.

I graduated from Glynn Academy in 1942 and went to work in the shipyard for a while before joining the Navy. Before I went into the Navy, my father and I put two boats, *Two Friends* and *Ranger*, in the Coast Guard Auxiliary, as a good many of the boat owners did. Our main job was to patrol the sounds at night to keep any boats from entering or leaving as there was a curfew on all boats. I was on patrol duty when the two oil tankers were raised and brought into St. Simons Sound. I ferried Navy officials from the pier out to the ships and got to go aboard them. The dead were still in the flooded compartments. The ships were shelled with heavy guns and the superstructure was all shot up.

My father was plant engineer at the big shipyard when it was first started and later went with the Brunswick Marine at the little shipyard as outfitting superintendent as there was no private practice for architects or engineers during the war. I worked in the fabrication shop at the shipyard and helped layout the first seven ships, and later when I was home on leave from the Navy, I had occasion to be on the platform when one of the ships was launched. Mrs. A. M. Harris, Sr., broke the bottle of champagne. On another leave I went on a shakedown cruise on one of the smaller ships that were built at the Brunswick Marine. My father was the pilot and took me along—a sailor's holiday!

I was a boatswain mate in the Navy, and while on anti-submarine patrol off North Carolina, my boat got credit for sinking one of the German subs. I was discharged in April 1946, got married, and went to Georgia Tech to further my education, then joined my father to practice architecture and engineering. The war was over, and Brunswick was beginning to return to normal.

Robert J. (Bobby) Roebuck

I was sitting on the porch across from the First Baptist Church on Mansfield Street when I heard the announcement of Japan's attack on Pearl Harbor. My first reaction was disbelief, then anger. I was 17 years old, a senior in high school, and, along with most of my classmates, eager to join one of the services. My choice was the Navy, having always had a desire for nautical life, flying, and clean sheets to sleep on.

After graduation, I applied for the Naval Aviation Cadet Program called the V-5 Program. After months of disappointment, I was finally accepted on December 12, 1942. In the interim, I went to work building the shipyard, working 12 hours a day, seven days a week, making, as a plumber, $127 a week. This was a fabulous amount of money for a youth who had never made over $20 a week. When I went into service my mother rented my room to two young men until my family moved to St. Simons Island. I suspect they moved to avoid the congestion and noise generated by the hoard of people walking through the streets of Brunswick.

At the outbreak of the war, the United States was in a devastating depression. People had very little money to squander and struggled to feed and clothe their families. The war changed that. We were immediately brought into the war front, with many making more money than they could spend. Many saved and invested, and we became a true middle-class society.

A significant benefit from this war was the education, leadership, and discipline many of us derived from military life. We were exposed to people, interests, and culture. Without it, we would never have known the strides in transportation and medicine, or experienced the comforts of air conditioning, appliances, or multiple bathrooms. Many of the returning veterans took advantage of the G.I. Bill, which paid for job training and college education. Education and integration were all eventful products of World War II. The necessity of getting along with others gave most of us a fraternal and patriotic outlook we will never forget.

My own life has been very rewarding, having been president of a labor organization; organized and taught at a vocational school for young adults; served as president of a mechanical contracting firm; been a Naval aviator and making captain in the Navy; served as a member of city, county, and state plumbers examining boards and held a # 3 master plumber's certificate. I have been blessed with friends and acquaintances, good health, and a comfortable retirement. Many of these I attribute to my early association with the Navy.

Eunice Minor

My father was a letter carrier and died in 1921, when I was about 10 years old. My mother did the best she could. There were five of us children . . . Walter, Ellen, Willie, Julie, and Eunice. I was the youngest of the five. Willie drowned in 1915, when he was 13 years old. Ellen and Walter were young adults and had left home. There was a number of years between them and Julia and me. It looks like they had us in pairs. Since Julia and I were the younger children, we stayed with Mother. Julia married and had four children. I never married.

I was teaching in the public schools in Brunswick when the war started. At that time you could teach after having completed two years of college. I had gone to Spelman College in Atlanta for two years. During the summer of 1942, I took my mother to Milwaukee, Wisconsin, to visit my older brother and sister who lived there. While I was visiting, I read a Negro newspaper called *The Chicago Defender*. In it was this article about the WACS and I recognized the names of some persons whom I knew well that were officers in the WACS. They entered as second lieutenants. I liked what I read. I wanted to join, but because I had only had two years of college, I couldn't go in as a second lieutenant.

Before I left Milwaukee, my brother had said to me, "Oh, you can't take dictation. You shouldn't join." He had already broken up a marriage that I had wanted to make, so I wouldn't listen to him this time. I replied, "It's according to who's dictating." So when I returned to Brunswick, I joined the WACS. After I had taken the oath for induction into the WACS, I had to go whenever they called me. They called me before the school year was over, and I was first sent to Des Moines, Iowa, where I had my basic training. I guess my basic training

WAC Eunice Minor
Courtesy of Eunice Minor

was about three months. Then I was sent to Fort Lenardwood, Missouri. At Fort Lenardwood, I was assigned as a librarian's helper. That was the work that I did as long as I stayed there.

My mother was alive at that time, but after I left home—I don't know if it was because she worried about me too much—her health wasn't too good. It was then that I had to be released from the Army. It took about two or three months, you know the government works so slowly, but I was released in November of 1944. I was discharged at Fort Bragg, North Carolina, and came on back to Brunswick to be with my mother. I was able to substitute in the public schools for the remainder of the term. The following fall, which was 1945, I was rehired in the public school system in Brunswick and taught the 1945-46 term.

The G.I. Bill was a wonderful opportunity to complete my education, so in the fall of 1946 I entered Cheyney University in Pennsylvania to get my undergraduate degree. My older sister Ellen had always wanted to go to Cheyney but did not have the opportunity. She was my idol and I had grown up with that dream in my mind. When I got a chance to go, I went. I was able to complete that work in two years. In the spring of 1948 I received my BS degree from Cheyney. I wanted to leave the teaching profession and change fields and go into social work. That fall, I went to the University of Pittsburgh. I did well until winter came. The weather where those three rivers met was so severe, I couldn't stand it. So I came back home and taught in Camden County for the remainder of that school year.

During the summers I worked on my graduate degree at the University of Wisconsin and completed that in the summer of 1957. My mother had passed on then. I awarded myself the gift of a trip to Los Angeles for having received my graduate degree. I remained in the Glynn County public school system until the spring of 1973 when I retired.

When I joined the WACS, I had been out on my own for some eight to ten years, and to have another woman giving me orders didn't set so well with me. I didn't like the discipline in the WACS, but you know what, I wouldn't take a million dollars for having gone. I was able to serve my country, but I also profited because I wouldn't have been able to complete my education and better myself.

My mother and I lived here in this house. I'm right where my mother left me. I gave up everything for my mother.

Louise Holley Herrin

My mother and I moved to Brunswick in 1935 after the death of my father. Just before the war my mother worked at the beautiful Oglethorpe Hotel. My mother remarried in 1941, and I, at the tender age of 16, married in 1942. We were left alone after my dad joined the SeaBees and my husband the Navy. We moved in together in the Glynn Villa apartments. My aunt, whose husband was in the Navy, and my grandmother, who was a widow, got an apartment together just across the backyard from us so we could keep each other company. My other uncle, who was about 18 years old, went in the Army paratroopers. My brother went in the Coast Guard later in the war. During the war,

Mother worked at the pulp mill and I at the shipyard. When I started there, not too many women worked as a burner in the fab shop. After my first child arrived, we would go to the USO Servicemen's Wives luncheons and give each other moral support, which was truly needed in those times.

Our family was truly blessed. We had no casualties. My husband stayed in the Navy for 23 years. If he had stayed in Brunswick he would have spent the rest of his life here at the Hercules plant. But being in the Navy, we got to travel to Guam, Cuba, and many places in the states where he was stationed. Our three children got to see a lot of the world.

Ruth Croft Kent

My memories of World War II start in September 1940. My mother, Grace T. Croft, my brother, Carl L. Croft, and I went to the train station on September 16, 1940, and watched my father, Carl E. Croft, and his National Guard friends leave. The Brunswick Riflemen, Company E, Second Battalion, 121st Infantry and the Oglethorpe Guards, Headquarters Company, Second Battalion, 121st infantry were being mustered into federal service for duty due to war in Europe. When I would tell my friends my father had gone to Fort Jackson, South Carolina, to train because of the European war, they did not believe me. The United States was not at war!

My father was known as "Warhorse." He spent 1941, 1942, and early 1943 training recruits how to fight in combat and how to use a rifle. His first group of trainees and his co-workers in 1941 nicknamed him "Warhorse" and it stuck. In fact, he was called that until his death in late 1975.

Carl Evan Croft - 1942
"Warhorse"
Courtesy of Ruth Croft Kent

Besides missing my father, one of the hardest things was the lack of money. There were no allotments for Army families until 1943. My mother had to go to work. She was able to get a job at the W. T. Grant Company. This was quite a change for my brother and me. My father had been in charge of the mosquito control for the Glynn County Board of Health and always supported the family.

On December 7, 1941, my family heard the news about Japan bombing Pearl Harbor. We were having lunch with my father's sister and other members of the Croft family. The announcement came on the radio and the women started crying. It was quite emotional since we knew Brunswick's Company E and Headquarters Company would be part of the action. World War II restricted our activities. My brother and I went to school at Sidney Lanier Elementary and later Prep High, then straight home. There were so many people coming to Brunswick my mother was scared to let us go anywhere except to church (First Methodist) and some school activities. Our quiet town had been invaded due to the shipyard and the building of the Naval Air Station, Glynco.

Some of the Oglethorpe Guards and the Brunswick Riflemen became part of the 8th Infantry Division, First Army and were sent to

Ireland in December 1943 to train for the invasion of France. On D-Day, June 6, 1944, the 8th Infantry Division entered France at Utah Beach and helped secure the beachhead in the greatest invasion in history. Many of our local men who left in 1940 were injured or killed.

I'll never forget the day we received the telegram from the War Department. My father had been wounded in action on July 8, 1944, at La Du Rue, France. A German soldier shot him in the chest as he came over a hedgerow. According to my father, the biggest problem after the beachhead was the hedgerow country of Normandy. The American Army had only come a short way in 32 days due to the hedgerows. My dad was returned to Utah Beach, then taken to a naval hospital at South Hampton, England. After a week, he was sent inland to the 136th station hospital for three months.

Upon release, my father was placed with the 387th Military Police Company and returned to Cherbourg, France. At first he shared a tent with John Woods, hangman for the European theater of operations, who was involved with hanging American G.I.s who committed serious crimes. My father stated that Master Sergeant John Woods was one of the strangest men he had ever been associated with. Woods went on to gain notoriety as the hangman at Nuremberg.

Unable to cope with this assignment, my father was made provost marshal at Grand de Camp, France, a small fishing village. In June 1945, after the war ended in Germany, he returned to the United States under the point system. On July 2, 1945, he was released from active duty. On July 3, 1945, my mother, brother, and I returned to the same train station he had left from to meet the train. This time it was a happy event as my father had come home. It had been nearly five years since we all had been together as a family.

One can see that the war period was centered around my father. However, I did develop the habit of reading since our activities were limited. I'll never forget reading *Gone With the Wind* in 1942. Over 1000 pages was quite a feat for a young girl.

Being a Brunswick native, I did not get to know many of the people who came during the war until after 1945 when I was attending Glynn Academy. In 1950, I met my future husband, Harold F. Kent, who came in 1943 from Thomaston, Georgia. His father was employed as an outside machinist with the J. A. Jones Construction Company. He was involved in putting in equipment on the deckhouse of the Liberty ships. So one can say the war caused our paths to cross. We were married in 1951.

My brother, Carl, also met his future wife, Ann S. Moore, in a roundabout way due to the war. Her father was an officer at the NAS Glynco in 1943 and 1944. In 1951, the family returned with a group of girls for a vacation on St. Simons. Our next-door neighbor knew Mr. Moore during the war and arranged for Carl and some of his classmates to visit the girls. Ann and Carl were married in 1956 after he graduated from the U. S. Military Academy at West Point.

Gladys Cothran Long

My family moved to Glynn County about 1925. My older brother, Wyman Cothran, worked at the Hercules Powder Company during the mid '30s. Wyman and my other brothers, George and Otto, worked at the shipyard. I even worked for a few months at the shipyard in one of the offices.

In 1936, I had met one of the CCC boys and dated him from time to time until he left the CCC Camp on Blythe Island and returned to his home. He was born in Atlanta, but his family had moved to Smithville, Georgia, where he grew up. We corresponded and he came back for my high school graduation. On December 7, 1939, he joined the Navy. After training, he was sent to the West Coast and then to Hawaii. He was at Pearl Harbor when it was bombed on December 7, 1941. He was in the South Pacific area for two years and seven months before he got leave to come home. We were married March 20, 1944. He was sent back to the West Coast, where I joined him at Puget Sound, Washington. He waited about five months for a new ship to be finished. His ship, the USS *Cumberland Sound*, went on a shakedown cruise and then back to the Pacific theater of war. My husband was one of about 10 who were at Pearl Harbor and Tokyo Bay.

His enlistment was up in December 1945, and he got home just in time for Christmas. He hadn't been home for Christmas in seven years. A few weeks later, we went to Jacksonville to visit one of my brothers and his wife. They had never met my husband. We got stuck here in Jacksonville and have been here ever since. We have three sons and one grandson.

Mona Louise Traywick

My father, Jesse Thomas Traywick, Jr., a career Army man, was transferred to the Philippines in November of 1940. Our family—which included my mother, my sister, Dudley (age 12), my brother, Jesse (age 5), and me (Louise, age 10)—accompanied him. When we arrived, they were already evacuating the United States Navy dependents from the Far East, but the Army dependents were still coming into the Philippines. However, we didn't stay in the Philippines very long. We were there from November 1940 until May 1941.

My Grandfather Dudley had built several houses on St. Simons. There was still one house that my Grandmother Dudley owned that was located on East Beach. When the rumor started that we were to be evacuated, my mother wrote Grandmother and told her that she wanted to buy the house. At that time, my grandmother lived in Richland, Georgia. My Grandfather Dudley had died.

We traveled by ship from the Philippines to San Francisco. Most of the passengers were women and children. The only military men they sent home were those who were sick or elderly and not far from retirement. When we docked, there was my mother, us three children, and all our trunks and suitcases waiting to be cleared through customs. Our last name beginning with T put us way down on the list, and it took a long time to get cleared. We were on that dock for half a day.

Kids being kids, we couldn't stay still. We kept running off and on the ship. We played spy-type games. That only shows that there was a lot of talk going around that reached our ears or else we would not have thought up those games.

We arrived in Montgomery, Alabama, and stayed with my Traywick grandparents a couple of weeks. Since we had left our car in Manila, Mother bought one, and we drove to my grandmother Dudley's house in Richland. She went with us to St. Simons. We were halfway down East Beach when Mother said, "You know, I think we've passed the house." The blocks on East Beach are not very long and we had missed our street. We turned around and retraced our steps. The hedge around the yard was extremely high and had almost hidden the house. That was my first memory of the island.

We moved into that little house on the corner of Bruce Drive and Sixth Street. We had three bedrooms and one bath for five of us. Grandmother Dudley was living with us. My mother finally bought a sign and put it on the bathroom door that said OCCUPIED on one side and UNOCCUPIED on the other. At that time, there were still sand dunes on the left-hand side of Bruce Drive at The Point on East Beach. That is where we played.

Army troops from Camp Stewart put on maneuvers on East Beach, bivouacking in the sand dunes all along the beach. They had large artillery pointing out to sea. I remember seeing the torpedoed tankers brought into the harbor with huge holes in the sides and the trash from the tankers that washed up on the beach. We had a victory garden and chickens.

My sister and I attended school in Brunswick. She was in the eighth grade and I was in the sixth. That was the year that the sixth grade went up the back fire escape to the two back classrooms at Prep High School. Therefore, we both were in the same building.

We knew before we went to school that day that the Philippines had fallen. As I went into the classroom, my classmates were saying how sorry they were. Of course, at that time we didn't know if Dad was a prisoner or had been killed. I started crying. I got up and went down the fire escape to the girl's room and met my sister coming in from the inside of the building. She was having the same problem.

When General Douglas MacArthur left the Philippines for Australia, he took his staff with him and left General Jonathan Wainwright with his staff. My dad was on Wainwright's staff. When General Wainwright signed the surrender of the American armies in the Philippines to the Japanese, *Life* magazine published a picture of the signing with the caption giving the names of Wainwright and his staff. My dad was in the picture, but they had misnamed him "Diller." That should have been in a May '42 issue of *Life*.

Dad became a prisoner of the Japanese. He was first in a prison camp on Formosa and later was moved to Manchuria. On the way to the Manchurian prison camp they pulled into a port, possibly in Korea. American fighter planes flew overhead where the prisoners were crammed down in the hold of the ship. Dad said that the prisoners would stand on shoulders to look out the porthole and give a blow-by-blow account of what was happening. The planes were headed straight for the ship and the prisoners thought that if that was the way to go, that was the best way. They noticed that the Japanese sailors were going ashore. They don't know if one of the prisoners signaled out the porthole or what, but the planes turned and headed for the town and leveled it. No American gunfire or bombs touched the ships. The Japanese that survived returned to the ship and headed out of port.

While a prisoner Dad was able to send a radiogram to Mother in which he asked her to send him a fruitcake. Mother knew he must be starving to ask for fruitcake because he did not like it. However, he had two reasons for requesting fruitcake: it wouldn't spoil and its food value was high. Mother found one and sent it to him. When Mother could send a package to Dad, you'd be amazed at what came out from behind the counter in the grocery store. She couldn't get it for herself, but they came up with the scarce goods for that care package for Dad.

Concerning the food that was sent by the Red Cross, each prisoner got the same items. Dad had a partner, and when one opened a can of food, they shared it. This way the food didn't spoil and lasted longer. Dad told us that occasionally a prisoner would crack up and run through the yard yelling, "The war's over, the war's over!" They would look at him and he'd have a blank stare in his eyes. So someone would take him to the doctor.

One day someone ran through the prison yard yelling, "The war's over! The war's over!" Someone said, "Oh, there goes another one." But someone else said, "No, Look at him. He's got tears running down his face." Someone said, "Wait a minute," and went up to him. The guy said, "There's this great big, huge sergeant from South Carolina that's got the Japanese commander by the collar and pushed up against the wall giving him orders!" They all took off in the direction where the commander was. Sure enough, he was right! Americans had parachuted in.

The prisoners were going to be released in the best and most orderly way. As evacuation of the prison camp was set up, the order was given that no one could ask for or get a prisoner out of camp ahead of someone else. They were being evacuated according to their health. Since all could not be moved at the same time, the most critical came out first. Even though my father had lost a lot of weight and was not in good health, he volunteered to stay and execute the evacuation list and see that it was done orderly.

The Brunswick News: April 10, 1942

U.S. FORCES STILL HOLD CORREGIDOR

Corregidor, a tiny island fortress, proudly flaunted the Stars and Stripes before besieging Japanese armies . . . . But on Bloody Bataan peninsula, just five miles from Corregidor, it was apparent that Japanese hordes had crushed the last American-Filipino resistance . . . . General Wainwright declared that our flag still flies on the beleaguered island fortress of Corregidor.

> *The Brunswick News:* May 7, 1942
>
> ### WIFE OF OFFICER ON CORREGIDOR AWAITING NEWS
>
> Mrs. Jesse Traywick, Jr., wife of Lieut. Col. Traywick, who is reported to be among the Americans on Corregidor who are now captives of the Japanese, said that the last message she received from her husband was Easter Sunday.
>
> Mrs. Traywick, the former Mona Dudley who was born in Brunswick and spent most of her life in Atlanta, is now residing on St. Simons Island with her three children. She spent six months in the Philippines with her husband, who has been stationed there for more than a year, but she returned to the States in June, when all Americans were ordered to evacuate. There were more than 800 women and children aboard the vessel on which Mrs. Traywick returned.
>
> Lieut. Col. Traywick is a West Point graduate and therefore has seen many years of military service. He is from Alabama and resided in that state a number of years ago. He was promoted to Lieut. Col. in January.
>
> While she is naturally worried over the plight of her husband, Mrs. Traywick hopes he is safe in Corregidor. She realizes that it will now be practically impossible for her to hear from the officer, who is on the staff of General Jonathan W. Wainwright, who yesterday surrendered.
>
> Mrs. Traywick and her children will continue to reside in a cottage they have leased on East Beach and she is hoping that some encouraging message will be received from her husband in the near future.

We lived on St. Simons Island at East Beach for the duration of the war and a while after my dad came home. During the war we received a few letters from Dad. Mrs. Mary Everett, the St. Simons post mistress, would go to the post office on Sundays and if there was anything from my dad, she would call Mother. Mother would get in the car right away and head for the village.

Ralph Hoffmeyer

I arrived at St. Simons at the very end of November 1945, assigned to the Navy Radar Training School. The war was over, so there were no wartime restrictions in force. Most of the training was in classrooms at the airport. We lived at the King and Prince Hotel and were ferried to school at the airport by "cattle trucks." They were slat-sided semis with seats all around the sides and in the middle.

The main dining room at the King and Prince was set up as a simulated Combat Information Center (CIC). One drill was to go up in the tower at the K&P and control one airplane visually in an attack on the "enemy" plane. It was a great three months. I enjoyed the hospitality of the Olsens and the same kind of hospitality with Sophie Torkildsen, Pauline Torkildsen, and her friends. One of those friends was Eloise Meadows, who later became my wife. Luther League and worship at St. James Lutheran Church were the high point of the week.

Marion Waltower

    I was born in Lakeland, Florida, and was brought to Brunswick to live with my step-grandmother when I was one year and three months old. When the war started, I was in high school. For three years, I worked as a lifeguard during the summer months at the Selden Recreational Park. I also welded for six months at the shipyard.

    In April 1946, I joined the U. S. Army and was sent to the Allied Occupied Philippines. I was stationed at Manila with the Army Engineers.

    During that time, there were many Japanese who lived as guerrillas in the jungle and did not believe or didn't know that the war was over. I was wounded by a sniper on December 23, 1946. I was sent to an Army hospital where I stayed until July 1947, when I was discharged from the Army. I was then sent to a veterans hospital in Virginia where I stayed until 1948. I was in the Army a total of 14 months and came back to Brunswick as a 100 percent service-connected disabled veteran confined to a wheelchair. When I left the hospital, I made up my mind to accept my disability and I did.

World War II Memorial Monument
On the lawn of the
Glynn County Courthouse
Brunswick, Georgia

Honor The Dead By
Helping The Living

Dedicated To

The Men Of Glynn County
Who Gave Their Lives
For Their Country During World War II

Adams, George
Anderson, Woodrow W.
Barker, Perry, H.
Barr, Perry Daniel
Blount, Rupert
Braddock, Joseph, Jr.
Braddy, Willie P.

Breland, Clarence E.
Brown, Edward Lamar
Browne, Charles
Chesser, James W.
Collins, William O.
Criscoe, James R.
Crosby, John

Cutinke, Eugene
Dart, John Patrick
Davis, Jack Charles
Devine, Samuel A., Jr.
Dollar, Robert S.
Dorsey, Leroy
Drayton, John Henry

Driskell, Raymond W.
Dyal, William E.
Dykes, Robert Edward
Eschmann, John W.
Evans, Robert L.
Falton, Jack
Farmer, James
Floyd, Clarence R.
Freeman, Horace T.
Freeman, Nathaniel
Frese, Albert G., Jr.
Girtman, Warren L.
Greene, DeWitt T.
Hall, James B.
Hall, Marcus
Hardeman, Robert N. III
Harnesberger, Thomas L., Jr.
Harrell, Luther
Harris, William Thomas
Hill, Clarence E.
Hodge, Marcus
Holmes, Ollard E.
Holton, Edgar I.
Howe, Johnnie
Humphries, Lonnin V.
Johnson, Donald F.
Jones, Lawton M.
Kennedy, Fred A., Jr.
Kersey, Thomas Wesley
Kizer, Dewey J.
Knight, Dan
Knight, Robert Lee, Jr.
Knight, Willis
Krauss, William
Lackey, John P., Jr.
Lane, Martin E.
Lewis, Robert S.
Lewis, W. P.
Liles, Burwell Ernest
Lloyd, Thomas W.
Ludwig, Paul
MacKay, A. D., Jr.
McElroy, John C.
McMillan, Raymond, Jr.
Manita, Manuel John

Mattox, Joseph L.
Melton, Cortez W.
Milton, Johnnie James
North, Hugh Dorsey
Pennington, L. C.
Petalos, John G.
Popwell, Lloyd G.
Reese, Luther Curtis
Rogers, James T.
Romeira, Lewis J.
Rouse, John H.
Ryals, Daial A.
Sapp, Grover Durrel
Shadman, James Postell
Shadman, Leroy
Shelfer, Bruce J.
Smith, Leroy
Smith, R. V.
Smith, Woodrow Wilson
Steele, Harris W.
Strayer, Robert W.
Strother, John C., Jr.
Sumner, Edgar J.
Tarte, John W.
Tindell, Robert J.
Tippins, B. Akins
Tormer, James
Trammell, Robert H., Jr.
Tucker, Edward B.
Wallace, Edwin B.
Weathers, Edward L.
Westberry, William Robert
Whaley, Wallace C., Jr.
Whitfield, Bill
Whittle, John T., Jr.
Williams, Joe B.
Williams, Joseph P.
Williams, T. A.
Williams, T. Harris
Wood, Simon, Jr.
Woods, Luther
Woodward, Norris N.
Younger, James
Zabawa, Harold R.

EPILOGUE

The price of freedom is immeasurable!

We won the war, but at a tremendous cost. Our soldiers fought, were wounded, and died in battle. Those who stayed at home worked long hours wielding their weapons of rivets, welding rods, and plows. All contributed to the Allied victory.

When World War II was over, war plants closed, soldiers came home, and Americans got on with the business of living. Leaving the Depression and World War II behind, Glynn County slowly adjusted to peacetime, prospering from the changes brought about by the war.

In other parts of the world, where fighting occurred, visible scars were left on cities and towns, on fields and farmlands, and on the people who lived there. America's battle scars were carried in our soldiers returning home and in the families whose loved ones were sacrificed. But traces of World War II are still visible in Glynn County for those who know where to look. The shipyard's six ways where the Liberty Ships were built and launched are still there, though deteriorating. The fitting-out basin can be seen, even mostly filled with silt.

Other reminders have assumed new looks and identities. Glynco now houses the Police Academy (FLETC). The St. Simons Naval Air Station has reverted back to an airport and is the home of Sea Pak and other businesses. The King and Prince Hotel has been refurbished into a luxurious complex. Island summer cottages are now year-round residences, and war apartments have been remodeled into homes.

Newcastle Street in downtown Brunswick has had a face lift. Old renovated buildings are wedged between new ones. The Ritz Theater and Kress Five and Ten Cents store still stand, tangible reminders of the war era. Missing from the landscape is the majestic Oglethorpe Hotel, demolished a decade after the war's end.

Union Street, the main route to the shipyard, no longer bustles with the host of shipyard workers going to and from work. It has returned to a peacetime pace with new families moving into the Victorian homes.

Today, Glynn County draws people to its beautiful shore and attractive way of life, some for a short time, others as permanent residents. Most know little, if any, of the perils that beset the area during World War II or of the efforts and sacrifices of its residents to support the military and protect the coast. World War II was a very brief period in history, but its impact was profound. The generations directly involved in this global conflict, whether on the war fronts or at home, know that life was never the same after it. The legacies of the time and, most important, of the people are with us today.

Thora O. Kimsey

Appendix A

Contributors

Alexander, Betty Brown	Alexandria, Virginia	171
Allen, Calvin F., Jr.	Gainesville, Georgia	9
Atkinson, Elder Robert L., Sr.	St. Simons Island, Georgia	85
Avera, Doree	St. Simons Island, Georgia	51
Backus, W. H.	St. Simons Island, Georgia	44, 251
Baker, Samuel Winn	Griffin, Georgia	37
Bailey, Nan F.	Brunswick, Georgia	255
Baumgartner, Hugh E., Jr.	Newberry, South Carolina	233
Bell, Raja Potts	Jefferson, Georgia	166
Blackshear, Virginia Stribling	St. Simons Island, Georgia	202
Bluestein, Marvin	St. Simons Island, Georgia	159
Brown, Benny F.	Hurst, Texas	129
Brown, Hoyt, Jr.	Birmingham, Alabama	13
Brown, Susan	Brunswick, Georgia	116
Brown, William H.	Brunswick, Georgia	47, 91
Bufkin, Ralph	St. Simons Island, Georgia	136
Burch, Curtis	Lucas, Kentucky	2, 6, 267
Burns, Frances Postell	St. Simons Island, Georgia	66, 204
Butler, Carolyn	St. Simons Island, Georgia	203
Cameron, Ray	St. Simons Island, Georgia	41
Camp, Doris Murdock	Hickory, North Carolina	214
Campbell, Joyce McGill	Augusta, Georgia	142
Candler, C. H., III	Sea Island, Georgia	57
Cannon, Mary K. Miller	Macon, Georgia	225
Capers, Rudolph	St. Marys, Georgia	74
Carpenter, Elizabeth(Betty) Brown	Columbia, South Carolina	179
Cason, Julian	Brunswick, Georgia	148
Cason, O.J.	St. Simons Island, Georgia	112
Cate G. Vassa	Calhoun, Georgia	263
Cate, Hollis	Statesboro, Georgia	20, 149, 263
Cecil, Ida Atkinson	Griffin, Georgia	234
Childs, Mary Lee	Thomasville, Georgia	114
Cloud, C. A., Jr.	St. Simons Island, Georgia	140
Cloud, Franklin M.	Lithia Springs, Georgia	138
Cofer, Frances Foster	Brunswick, Georgia	263
Colletta, Iris Horton	St. Simons Island, Georgia	220
Conyers, Jack	St. Simons Island, Georgia	185
Corbitt, Sara W.	Brunswick, Georgia	19, 222
Daniel, Charles B., Jr.	St. Simons Island, Georgia	39, 44, 46, 58, 62, 72, 248
Daniel, Eunice C	St. Simons Island, Georgia	201
Daniel, Ruth	Brunswick, Georgia	132
Daniels, Viola Carswell	Brunswick, Georgia	141
Davis, Eugene T.	Brunswick, Georgia	133
Dorris, Ralph O.	Shalimar, Florida	42, 164
Drury, Ernest	Waverly, Georgia	230
Drye, Barbara Harrison	Charlotte, North Carolina	265
Dukehart, Catherine Warren	Atlanta, Georgia	58
Eggen, Helen Ann	Winter Haven, Florida	66
Eggen, Orvin	Michigan and Florida	65
Ekblad, Josephine Wilson	Jacksonville, Florida	219
Estes, Woodie	St. Simons Island, Georgia	29, 184
Ewing, Mary Frances Smith	Buchanan, Georgia	211

Name	Location	Page
Fahey, Barbara Ann Haag	Virginia Beach, Virginia	222
Fahey, John A.	Virginia Beach, Virginia	75
Farrell, Mary Kramer	Staten Island, New York	105
Fendig, Albert, Jr.	St. Simons Island, Georgia	20
Fiveash, Dorothy Deaver	Kinston, North Carolina	164
Flanders, Dyson	Darien, Georgia	116
Floyd, Agnes M.	Brunswick, Georgia	160
Foster, Virginia Dean	Lawrenceville, Georgia	66, 200
Franks, Don and Helen	San Angelo, Texas	75
Frith, Edward (Pete)	Atlanta, Georgia	89
Gale, Neal	Brunswick, Georgia	130
Gathright, Eleanor Smith	St. Simons Island, Georgia	145, 147
Gignilliat, Thomas	Kinchlow, Michigan	28, 187
Gleason, Catherine Wynne	Fairfax, Virginia	29, 254
Glover, Frances O'Brien	St. Simons Island, Georgia	215
Gordy, Herbert R.	Morehead City, North Carolina	210
Gould, Clara Marie	Brunswick, Georgia	179
Gowen, Charles	Atlanta, Georgia	40, 89, 174
Gragg, John	Brunswick, Georgia	67
Hardegen, Reinhard	Bremen, Germany	23
Harned, Stella Morton	Sea Island, Georgia	29, 264
Harp, William J., Jr.	Jacksonville, Georgia	257
Hart, Beverly Wood	Brunswick, Georgia	178
Harwell, Joe	Savannah, Georgia	264
Heinold, Fred C.	St. Simons Island, Georgia	59
Heinold, Evelyn Wallace	St. Simons Island, Georgia	192
Henderson, Robert (Bobby) J.	St. Simons Island, Georgia	231
Herold, Danny Minchew	St. Simons Island, Georgia	191
Herrin, Frances Sumner	Brunswick, Georgia	266
Herrin, Louise Holley	Brunswick, Georgia	272
Highsmith, Robert C	Brunswick, Georgia	5, 255
Hoffmeyer, Mrs. Ralph (Eloise)	Brunswick, Georgia	213
Hoffmeyer, Ralph	Brunswick, Georgia	278
Holmes, Knollis	McDonough, Georgia	2, 4
Holt, William L.	Savannah, Georgia	165
Howe, Lee	St. Simons Island, Georgia	65
Jackson, Virginia Kent	Fairburn, Georgia	28, 232
James, Ben E., Jr.	Atlanta, Georgia	196
Jarriel, Jack	Aiken, South Carolina	197
Jobe, Patricia Sikes	Emory, Texas	29, 226
Johnston, Elizabeth Reu	Conyers, Georgia	117, 168
Kent, Ruth Croft	Brunswick, Georgia	72, 75, 273
Kicklighter, Mildred Jenkins	Brunswick, Georgia	157
Kimsey, Thora Olsen	Monroe, Georgia	150, 180
Kinard, Sonja Olsen	Atlanta, Georgia	23, 150, 183
Klimp, Clara Larsen	St. Simons Island, Georgia	212
Lang, Jack	Atlanta, Georgia	23
Lang, Marie Way	Brunswick, Georgia	29, 135
Lawrence, Clarice Ray	Blairsville, Georgia	207
Lemmond, Vivian Overstreet	Brunswick, Georgia	180
Long, Gladys Cothran	Jacksonville, Florida	19, 275
Lowry, Gene	Lawrenceville, Georgia	A - 46
Lundberg, Betty Ann Gaynor	Fresno, California	166, 222
Manning, Arthur L.	Brunswick, Georgia	115
Manor, Frances Bankston	Roswell, Georgia	185
Martin, Mary T.	Brunswick, Georgia	258
Martin, Norma Jean Strickland	Petersburg, Illinois	103

Name	Location	Pages
McConnell, Betty Joyner	Brunswick, Georgia	222
McKeever, Kay	Statesboro, Georgia	195
McKendree, Georgia	St. Simons Island, Georgia	238
McMichael, Ann Wynne	Aiken, South Carolina	39
Melnyk, Mary S.	Brunswick, Georgia	35
Melvin, Alice	Brunswick, Georgia	162
Meschke, Karl	Brunswick, Georgia	13, 95, 145
Meyers, Lillian Marie Lang	Bethel Park, Pennsylvania	20, 254
Miller, Laurence S., Jr.	St. Simons Island, Georgia	270
Miller, Mary	St. Simons Island, Georgia	161
Miller, Sonny (James)	Brunswick, Georgia	19, 148
Mills, Laverne Anderson	Elberton, Georgia	257
Minor, Eunice	Brunswick, Georgia	271
Mitchell, Marjorie Few	St. Simons Island, Georgia	159
Moore, Betty Lou	Brunswick, Georgia	113
Moore, Mary Ann Whilden	Brunswick, Georgia	156
Moore, Willie	Brunswick, Georgia	100
Morman, Bessie	Brunswick, Georgia	209
Morris, John B.	Atlanta, Georgia	30, 146
North, Anne Harwell	Brunswick, Georgia	216
Novak, Patricia Brown	Clearville, Pennsylvania	172
Obuchowski, Frankie Quarterman	Parkridge, Illinois	206
Olsen, Olaf Helmer, Jr.	St. Simons Island, Georgia	16, 252
Owen, Sarah Frances Gragg	Brunswick, Georgia	204
Palmer, Gene	St. Simons Island, Georgia	198
Parmelee, George	St. Simons Island, Georgia	6, 239
Parsons, Ione Quarterman	Hiawasee, Georgia	208
Patterson, Paul	St. Simons Island, Georgia	177
Pearce, Thorwald A.	Warner Robins, Georgia	173
Pool, W. H., Jr.	Atlanta, Georgia	67
Prentice, Mr. and Mrs. James A., Sr.	St. Simons Island, Georgia	171
Ragland, Charles E.	Brunswick, Georgia	96
Ramsaur, Gloria Smith	St. Simons Island, Georgia	29, 158
Reu, Lucille Way	Conyers, Georgia	215
Reu, Michael C.	Camden, South Carolina	129
Richardson, Lucille	Acworth, Georgia	111
Rickenbaker, Scarlett Blanton	Atlanta, Georgia	178
Roberts, London C., Sr.	Brunswick, Georgia	155
Roebuck, Robert J.	Brunswick, Georgia	270
Rooks, Carl M.	Brunswick, Georgia	118
Rouse, Madeline Thomas	Brunswick, Georgia	44
Schopfer, Frank	Brunswick, Georgia	130
Seckinger, Malcolm	Brunswick, Georgia	6, 127
Sellers, Colleen Moore	Brunswick, Georgia	227
Shane, Ruby Johnson	Altamonte Springs, Florida	99
Shepherd, Clyde	Atlanta, Georgia	72
Sikes, Lynn Gillican	Hinesville, Georgia	30, 223
Smith, Carl	Brunswick, Georgia	174
Smitherman, Frances Stewart	St. Marys, Georgia	154
Spaulding, Bill	Dunwoody, Georgia	148
Spaulding, Pat Lewis	Port St. Lucie, Florida	220
Steinmann, Phyllis	Scottsdale, Arizona	81, B-2
Strickland, Leslie Hansen	Delray Beach, Florida	194
Sullivan, Wallace	Brunswick, Georgia	35
Sweat, Ada Edwards	Brunswick, Georgia	235
Torkildsen, F. H., Jr.	Brunswick, Georgia	84, 90
Traywick, Mona Louise	New Braunfels, Texas	275

Tyson, Edwina	Brunswick, Georgia	217
Vice, Burton	Wichita, Kansas	52
Walker, Dr. Earl E.	Newark, Delaware	234
Walker, Jacqueline Baumgartner	Atlanta, Georgia	157
Walker, T. R.	Jay Bird Springs, Georgia	63
Waltower, Marion	Brunswick, Georgia	279
Ward, Mary Curry	Marietta, Georgia	30
Waters, Richard	Greensboro, Georgia	33
Wilder, Marjorie, K.	Kennesaw, Georgia	105
Wilkes, W. L.	Townsend, Georgia	189
Williams, Ruth Pope	Brunswick, Georgia	237
Wilson, Elizabeth	Brunswick, Georgia	142
Wilson, Reginald	Macon, Georgia	205
Young, Marian Tiller	Jacksonville, Florida	193
Zell, Carley	Sea Island, Georgia	119

Notes from Chapter Two: Activities in Glynn County

Headlines and excerpts of articles from The Brunswick News documenting the subtle and not so subtle preparations that were taking place in Brunswick before December 7, 1941.

August 30, 1939:	EUROPEAN SITUATION DISCUSSED BY GIBBS "...Congressman (Gibbs) doubts seriously if nations will go to war at present...during a joint meeting of the Kiwanis, Rotary and Young Men's Club."
October 10, 1939:	RESERVE OFFICERS OF GROUP SCHOOL TO MEET THURSDAY "...subject: Military Background of the present European situation." (National Guard officers and civilians were invited to meeting.)
October 19, 1939:	DRILLS BY NATIONAL GUARD SOON TO BE DOUBLED... "Adjutant generals in the 4th Corps area will meet here November 1 to plan double duty drills and field training for National Guardsmen...Lt. General Stanley O. Embeck yesterday ordered the guards to begin drilling twice a week and to prepare for seven days of field training before January 31..The War Department announced on October 10th the speed up in the guard drills."
October 20, 1939:	COURSES OF STUDY BEING PLANNED FOR LOCAL GUARDSMEN... "after a conference with Major L. D. Tharp, regular army instructors for the 2nd Battalion, 121st Infantry, The Oglethorpe Guard non-commissioned officers club immediately began formulating plans for an intense course of study that will prepare them for the increase in work and responsibility which is anticipated...every effort must be made to push the efficiency of the National Guard to the topmost peak because the fact that the Guard is about twice the size of the regular army, its importance as a unit of national defense is most significant."
October 21, 1939:	**CANDIDATES FOR NAVAL AVIATION TO BE EXAMINED**
November 4, 1939:	AVIATION CLUB TO BE ORGANIZED AT MEETING TONIGHT "...sponsors (for the aviation club) announce that a new government-approved plane has been purchased and lessons will be given in both actual flying and in ground work"
February 2, 1940:	LOCAL FLYING CLASS HAS FIRST SESSION "...a number of students have enrolled for instruction in aviation...women are eligible."
February 6, 1940:	INCREASE IN NAVAL STORE "Harrisburg (Mississippi) and Brunswick Hercules Plants have found it necessary to increase the rate of production to fill orders..."
February 7, 1940:	**MORE STUDENTS JOIN FLYING CLASS**
February 9, 1940:	**LOCAL FLYING CLASS NEEDS MORE MEMBERS**
February 13, 1940:	**LOCAL FLYING CLASS FILLED**
February 24, 1940:	NEW MARKET FOR NAVAL STORES CREATED BY WAR
April 9, 1940:	OSLO AND COPENHAGEN CAPTURED BY GERMANY
	LATEST WAR TURN TO AFFECT PULP PLANT "...a shortage in pulp paper (due to the occupation of the Scandinavian countries)...but there is the possibility of greater expansion of the domestic market."
April 13, 1940:	FORMER ARMY MEN CAN NOT ENLIST IN THE REGULAR RESERVE

May 5, 1940:	NATIONAL GUARD TO HAVE THREE WEEK CAMP "...imperative national defense needs has moved General George C. Marshall, Army Chief of Staff, to appeal to the business men of the nation to allow their employees who are members of the National Guard to serve in training three weeks this summer."
June 1, 1940:	"Congressman Givis (says) 'no developments to cause panic in U.S.'"
June 3, 1940:	HOME DEFENSE IN ALL COUNTIES IN STATE IS PLANNED "...(Governor Rivers announced)...they (the counties) will be charged with defense of highways, manufacturing plants, hydroelectric plants, railroads, gasoline and telephone lines and similar public services."
June 6, 1940:	MOVEMENT STARTED FOR HOME GUARD HERE "...to prevent invasion."
June 10, 1940:	MUSSOLINI DECLARES WAR AGAINST ALLIES AS GERMANS REJOICE. GEORGIA COMPLETES STATE DEFENSE PLAN "...plans have been completed for immediate organization of a state defense corps upon declaration of war or similar national emergency."
June 12, 1940:	NAZIS ARE 12 MILES FROM PARIS PLANS FOR ANOTHER AVIATION SCHOOL (on St. Simons) 150 ALIENS HAVE BEEN REGISTERED AT LOCAL OFFICE GEORGIA MILITIA NOW PREPARING FOR MANEUVERS
June 18, 1940:	LOCAL RED CROSS TO MAKE SUPPLIES FOR WAR VICTIMS
June 20, 1940:	ST SIMONS AND SEA ISLAND ORGANIZE TO HELP THE AMERICAN RED CROSS
June 26, 1940:	SUPER ROADS WANTED FOR USE BY TROOPS
July 1, 1940:	BRUNSWICK CONSUMERS BEGAN TODAY PAYING TAXES FOR THE NATIONS FIVE-YEAR FIVE MILLION DOLLAR REARMAMENT FUND
July 6, 1940:	LOCAL CITIZENS NEEDED FOR STATE DEFENSE CORPS "...Ryburn S. Clay, State Defense Corps Manager for Georgia notified key men in every county in the state to call local meetings...the plan is to organize the volunteer service of loyal citizens who are over 35 years of age, of excellent character, in good health, and commonly recognized as being loyal and patriotic, so that, should the necessity arise, we will be prepared to assist in the preservation of peace and order; protect vital installations and public works; and keep the activities of aliens in the state under close observance.
July 8, 1940:	A NEW ARMORY APPROVED TO BE BUILT IN BRUNSWICK
July 9, 1940:	EPISCOPAL HOME (DODGE HOME FOR BOYS) PROBABLE HOME FOR WAR YOUTHS NEW PLANE AT MALCOLM MCKINNON AIRPORT "...N. Hassell (has secured) a Taylorcraft 55 for training students."
July 10, 1940:	PUBLIC BARRED FROM POWER PLANTS
July 11, 1940:	NATIONAL GUARD UNITS ENCAMPMENT...AUGUST IN MISSISSIPPI
July 13, 1940:	PLANS TO ORGANIZE DEFENSE CORPS HERE "...urged to take action at once...James Gould, J. M. Exley and Paul Killian (key men to organize)... Major Exley named Commander of Area."

July 29, 1940:	REPORTED (NATIONAL GUARD) TROOPS TO BE CALLED UP SEPTEMBER 15TH
August 1, 1940:	THIS COUNTY MAY SUPPLY 68 MEN ON FIRST ARMY CAL
August 14, 1940:	LOCAL TELEPHONE OFFICE CLOSED TO ALL VISITORS
August 16, 1940:	JACKSONVILLE NAVAL AIR STATION NEEDS USE OF AIRPORTS WITHIN 100 MILES
August 21, 1940:	SITE FOR PROPOSED ARMY (CAMP) IS REVEALED "…(the) city is negotiating for land on the Coastal Highway near the Hercules Plant."
August 28, 1940:	YOUTH OVER 18 MAY BE CALLED INTO SERVICE "…youth over 18 years of age and members of the National Guard may be called into service."
September 13, 1940:	MORE MEN NEEDED IN THE LOCAL TWO MILITARY UNITS (Rifleman and Oglethorpe Units)
September 14, 1940:	CADETS WANTED IN AIR SERVICE PRESIDENT SIGNS DRAFT BILL "…sets October 15 for registering"
September 23, 1940:	LOCAL TROOPS TO LEAVE FOR CAMPS JACKSON AND SUMTER FOR A YEAR'S TRAINING
September 24, 1940:	LOCAL DEFENSE UNIT ORGANIZED
October 10, 1940:	BRUNSWICK AIRPORT MAY BE DEVELOPED
September 28, 1941:	"…an aviation school is wanted on St. Simons at the Malcolm McKinnon Field with the definite purpose of at once starting a movement to create a great interest in the facilities of this airport, which is second to few in the state. The War Department is awarding contract almost daily to various flying services throughout the South where facilities are available to supplement the regular cadet training in the Army Air Corps. There has developed a bottleneck in facilities for training students eligible for cadet training and while the Army Air Corps is creating facilities as rapidly as possible, it requires at least six weeks to twelve weeks before an eligible student is called to start training. The War Department is therefore looking around for suitable facilities for giving students their primary training under civilian instructors and it is learned that such contracts have been awarded to the Carr Arco Tech, Inc.; the Graham Aviation Co., at Americus; the Chicago School of Aeronautics at Albany; the Georgia Air Service at Milledgeville and Bennettsville, S. C.; and another at Douglas. …Local persons interested claim that McKinnon Field is the only accredited airport in Georgia that could provide an auxiliary, naval or seaplane component to its already well developed landing field…McKinnon Field has recognized airline connections, a weather reporting bureau, hangar and servicing facilities, and the local group believes that by forming a representative body to sponsor a school here, one could be secured. It was pointed out…that if a well functioning organization is formed, it will receive the support of the city and county authorities in seeking a War Department contract, provided the group can attract private interest to supply flying equipment for training purposes to the modern airport that had already been provided. Lieut. N. I. (Buddy) Hassell, who is in charge of the airport, is now endeavoring to contact all of these interested persons…"
October 1, 1941:	OFFICIALS TALK OF ADVANTAGES OF NAVY…Point out that it does not require men of high school education……..Secretary of Navy Knox says: "Navy enlistees do not

have to be high school graduates. Any ambitious and patriotic young fellow who wants to serve his country has that opportunity now by joining the United States Navy or Naval Reserve. Of course, he must be of average intelligence, good character, and be able to pass certain physical and mental examinations. Now, more than ever before, the navy needs men of that type."

October 2, 1941: **GEN'L JARMAN HERE ON INSPECTION TRIP** "....Looks over various recreational centers here and on island. .... Major General Sanderford Jarman, who a few weeks ago assumed command of Camp Stewart at Hinesville, today had an opportunity of visiting places that hundreds of troops at the camp have enjoyed themselves during the summer, when he made an inspection trip here of recreational facilities.
It seems that the area around Camp Stewart and from Hinesville down the coast has a good many "dives and joints" and the General is planning to clean the area of such places.
...General Jarman described the area between Camp Stewart and Hinesville as becoming a "no man's land" and declared that shops of improper type will become a menace both to the soldiers quartered at the camp and the citizens of the community."

October 3, 1941: **AVIATION GROUP TO ORGANIZE AT MEETING TONIGHT** [This article relates that interested persons will meet to make the McKinnon Field a training center. This is a follow-up of the September 28th announcement that the War Department is seeking facilities to train cadets.]

October 3, 1941: **MEN 17-50 WANTED IN U.S. NAVAL RESERVE**...They will be help on duty only for duration of emergency "...all men now enlisting in the Naval Reserve will be retained on active duty throughout the period of this national emergency, but they will be released to inactive duty as soon after the emergency as their services can be spared, regardless of the length of time remaining in their enlistment" *Note: enlistment in the Naval Reserves was for four years.*

October 7, 1941: **WAR DEPARTMENT ASKS FOR CADETS**...1000 men wanted for non-pilot training as aerial navigators.

October 9, 1941: **2 DEFENSE UNITS IN THIS COUNTY MAKING PROGRESS** "Fine progress is being made by the two local state defense units, one in Brunswick and the other composed of St. Simons and Sea Island residents....Members of the island unit assembled last night for their first drill period. Carl H. Smith, in command of the unit, commended the company for the interest and splendid spirit displayed..... The local unit (Brunswick) under command of Capt. J. C. Kaufman, meets regularly each Wednesday night at the armory, Bay and Gloucester streets... The company hopes to soon receive rifles, which will be used in the weekly practice drills. However, it is not known when the unit will be supplied with uniforms."

October 9, 1941: **LOCAL TRAINEES LEAVE TODAY FOR FORT MCPHERSON** "Fifteen Glynn County trainees...left today by rail for Fort McPherson, Atlanta, where they will be inducted into military service. Later all of the men will be assigned to various branches of the services and will go to training camps in many sections. Those leaving today were the following: Ledley Silas Harden, John Anthony Murphy, John Doris Smith, Jesse Lloyd Fitzgerald, Jr., William Wright Parker, Willie Nution Griffin, Millard Paul Lightfoot, Grover Latimer Davis, Walter Elliott Morgan, Alva Gene Lindsay, Jack Paul Adams, Jr., William Fletcher Downs, David William Job, Leonard Harold Brown, and Robert Earl Strickland...

October 30, 1941: **INCREASE IN SCOUTS URGED BY EXECUTIVE**...Appeal is made to all leaders to add to present membership. "Citing President Roosevelt's statement,'The Nation is confident that the Boy Scouts stand ready to contribute to the national welfare in these critical hours.' Dr. James West, Chief Scout Executive, appealed today in a letter to 350,695 volunteer adult leaders of the movement to 'make a determined effort to make Scouting and Cubbing available to more boys as a patriotic service."

Notes from Chapter Three: The Torpedoed Tankers

The Brunswick News: July 1942

Local Member of State Guard is Commended

A Georgia State Guardsman whose courage and initiative were instrumental in rescuing a large number of survivors from two torpedoed ships has received a special letter of commendation from Rear Admiral William Glassford, commandant of the Sixth Naval District and the Charleston Navy Yard, it was announced by the Public Relations Office of the district in Charleston today, which said:

"The State Guard member, Olaf Helmer Olsen, was on transportation duty on a boat operating off the Georgia Coast, when word was received that the ships had been torpedoed.

He immediately picked up a civilian volunteer to act as his crew, filled his gas tanks, and headed out to sea to go to the aid of the survivors. On the way, he overtook another boat carrying Dr. Jack Avera, whom he took aboard to administer first aid to the survivors."

Other details of the rescue were not disclosed since they would give vital information to the enemy.

Admirals Glassford's letter of commendation praised Olsen for 'a high degree of initiative, foresight and courage,' and for action 'without regard to your own personal safety..'

ESSO BATON ROUGE

DECLASSIFIED
Office of Naval Intelligence
NAVY DEPARTMENT
Intelligence Report
ENEMY ATTACKS ON MERCHANT SHIPS

From: DIO, 6ND   At: Charleston, S. C.   Date: April 14, 1942
Subject: Sinking by torpedo
Name of Ship: **Esso Baton Rouge** Flag: American (U.S.)   Type: Steam tanker
                                                                                                                                              Twin Bulkhead
Gross Tonnage: 7989.35   Whether Armed: Not armed
Date of Attack: April 8, 1942
Position of Attack: 13 miles 23 degrees from Brunswick Lightbuoy
Whether Sunk, Damaged, Captured, or Escaped: Sunk.
Resting on bottom. All superstructure, half deck sticking out of water.

PARTICULARS OF SHIP AND VOYAGE

Questions   Answers

1. (a) Port of departure: Baytown, Texas
   (b) Date of Sailing: April 3, 1942 - 1300 C.W.T.
   (c) Destination: New York
   (d) Route Instructions: Inshore routing — 2 miles off buoys

2. Name of Owners: Standard Oil Co. of New Jersey
   1. Cargo:
   (a) Full or in ballast (type of ballast)   Fully loaded
   (b) Distribution and amount of liquids: 90,000 bbls. - 70,000 barrels lubricating
                                                oil in #3,4,5,6 and 7 center and wing
                                                tanks. 20,000 bbls. Esso Heat in #. 1,2,
                                                and 8 wing tanks. # 1 tanks empty.

3. Full Christian Name, Surname and   James Simeon Poche, American Citizen,
   Nationality of Master: born United States.

CONDITIONS OF ATTACK

4. (a) Ship's position, date, and time   10 miles N.N.E. Brunswick Buoy.
   when enemy was sighted: 0123 C.W.T.. April 8, 1942

     1. Date(local) and time(specify   April 8, 1942, 0123 C.W.T.
        whether GCT, Zone, War Time)
     2. Depth of water: 40 feet.
   (b) When attack commenced: 13 miles 23 degrees from Brunswick Buoy.
   (c) What warning given?   None
   (d) Ship's position, date and time
     1. When ship sank, or
     2. When chase was abandoned: Same as given under (b)
   (e) Ship's position, date and
       time ship was abandoned: Same as given under (b)

5. (a) What was the cause of   Torpedo-one-starboard bunker between
       ship sinking?:   bunker and engine room.
     1. Estimated type, weight,
        diameter of projectile,
        bomb, torpedo or mine: Unknown yet considered large.
   (b) Was she seen to sink?   Yes
     1. Manner of sinking?
       (a) Capsized
       (b) Even keel
       (c) Plunged (bow or stern first)   Sunk by stern

(d) Listed (to port or starboard, degree of list)	10 degree list to starboard.
(e) How long afloat after being hit?	Less than 5 minutes

6. Course and speed of ships when enemy was first sighted or when attack commenced: Course 22 degrees (true), speed, 12.8 knots when enemy first sighted

    1. Course and speed after damage   —
    2. Drafts, forward and after, before and after damage (approximate):   Draft before damage 28 feet forward, 30 ft. aft. After damage 17 feet forward, 40 ft. aft.

7. (a) Was ship zigzagging? If so   Yes
   (b) Nature of zigzag   Zigzagged to left 25 degrees
   (c) How long had ship been zigzagging previous to the attack?   25 minutes

8. State of weather and sea, direction and force of wind; visibility   Slight sea, good weather, half moon just rising, wind S. E. force 3.
   (1) Moonlight   Half moon just rising.

9. (a) Was ship attacked with torpedo by submerged submarine.   Not known
     (1) When torpedo was fired were any people still on board? If so, how many? If so was -   Yes - 38

   (b) Periscope of submarine   Not seen

   (c) Track of torpedo seen before vessel was struck? If so, at what distance from own ship and what avoiding action was taken?   Not seen

   (d) Did submarine subsequently come to the surface? If so, when?   Yes, 10 or 15 minutes afterwards between boat and shore.

10. (a) Was ship attacked with gunfire? If so,   No.

   (b) Was enemy seen prior to attack If so,   No.

   (c) Was any, and if so what, warning or order given by enemy?   None.

11. (a) How many look-outs were on watch?   Two

   (b) Where were they stationed?   One on each wing of bridge.

12. Speed and course of aircraft, raider, or submarine relative to ship when first sighted, or when attack commenced?   Not seen

13. (a) What colors, if any, was ship flying at time of attack?   None

   (b) When were they hoisted?   ....

14. (a) If attack took place at night, what lights, if any, was ship showing?   None

    (b) If navigation lights were burning were they dimmed?   None

15. How was ship maneuvered after sighting enemy?   zigzagged

16. (a) Were any other vessels in sight?   Yes, a tanker bound south.

    (b) If so, what were their positions and movements and names, if known?   S.S.E. just before attack, three or four minutes.

    (c) Did any signal pass between them and the ship or enemy?   No.

17. (a) Was ship equipped with radio and did she use it? What signals?   Yes - no signals sent

    (b) If so, was any reply received, and from whom?   No

    (c) How long before attack did ship last use her radio? And on what wave length.   Feb. 24, 1942. 600 meters

    (d) Did enemy order silence or jam radio transmission?   No

18. (a) What course was submarine, raiders, or aircraft steering when last seen, or if submarine, did she dive?   25 degrees on surface 3 or 4 knots speed

    (b) Time enemy ship was last seen?   0315 E.W.T.

CONFIDENTIAL DOCUMENTS

19. (a) Were there Navy or British codes on board?   Yes

    (b) Which ones?   Port Directory, Baytown, has inventory

    (c) What became of them?   Left on ship. Returned and secured later.

20. (a) Were there any other confidential papers or mails on board?   Yes

    (b) If so, what became of them?   Left on ship. Returned and secured them.

    (c) What did the confidential papers consist of?   British and American instructions to merchant ships.

(NOTE: If codes or papers came to enemy hands, Opnav to be advised immediately by dispatch.)

OFFENSIVE ACTS OF ENEMY

Gunfire

21. At what time and range did enemy open fire?   None
    (1) Relative bearing of enemy ship?   Unknown

22. Number of rounds fired by enemy: None
    (a) Before ship was abandoned
    (b) After ship was abandoned
    (c) Approximate rate of fire

23. Number of times ship was hit: None
    (a) Before ship was abandoned
    (b) After ship was abandoned

    Torpedo or Aircraft Bombing

24. Distance and bearing of submarine or   Not known. Not over 200 feet
    aircraft when torpedoes or bombs fired: according to the Captain.

    (1) Whether horizontal or dive
        release of bomb from aircraft;
        attitude of release, angle of
        dive if dive release?   ———

25. Was there any way on the ship at time torpedo
    or bomb was fired?   12.8 knots

26. (a) Number of torpedoes or bombs fired: One fired.
    (b) Number which hit   One hit.
    (c) Number which missed   No misses.

27. If hit: -
    (a) Position of damage and depth below   Starboard side between bunkers
        water (for torpedoes)   and engine room, 20 feet below
                                                               water.

        (1) Any outstanding circumstances or
            peculiarities of the explosion,
            (fumes, after-burning on surface, etc.)   Fumes - cordite

        (2) Single or multiple explosion with
            estimated time intervals.   Single explosion

    (b) Description of damage   Vessel sunk
        (1) Dimension of hole or indentation
            in ship's hull with general
            description   Not known

        (2) Extent of flooding. What large   Immediate flooding of engine
            compartments known to have   room and crew's quarters.
            flooded. Immediate or slow flooding.

        (3) Fires started by direct incendiary effect
            or subsequently as a result of
            dispersal of fuel oil, gasoline, etc.   None

    If missed:

    (c) Whether torpedo or bomb passed ahead,
        astern, under or short, and by how much.   ———

    (d) Any other reason to account for missing   ———

    (e) If torpedo or bomb failed to explode and if
        torpedo observed to be floating after
        attack failed   ———

A-14

Boarding

28. Was ship boarded by enemy and how?
Was not boarded.

29. Was Master interrogated by enemy officers? What questions were asked? Which officer(s) asked questions and what knowledge of the English language had he?
No

Explosive Charges

30. If ship was sunk by explosive charges:
    (a) How many were used?
    (b) Where were they placed?
None

DEFENSIVE ACTS OF SHIPS

Gunfire

31. What guns were carried
None

   (1) Was there an armed guard on board?
   No

Additional information desired in case a magnetic acoustic or other influence weapon is suspected:
None suspected.

1. Were engines running at a steady speed:
2. Propeller RPM's for each propeller.
3. Number of blade on each propeller and any known defects.
4. Degaussing equipment: current in coils
5. Were paravanes or bow protection gear in use?
6. If not acting singly, give position information.

32. At what time and range did ship open fire? —

33. Was ship showing her proper colors when she opened fire? —

34. (a) Number of rounds fired by ship? —
    (b) Approximate rate of fire? —

35. Number of times enemy was hit by gunfire —

Smoke

36. Was ship supplied with smoke apparatus?
None

   If so:
   (a) What pattern?
   (b) How was it used and with what effect?

37. (a) Were there any casualties?
    (b) What were they?
    (c) How caused?
Three
2nd Engineer, oiler, fireman.
Two killed by explosion, one jumped overboard, not seen again.

38. (a) What was the number and nationality of passengers and crew?
    (b) How did they behave?
38 crew members. 37 Americans
1 Spaniard, Joe VENTOSA
Very good.

39. (a) What became of the passengers & crew after abandoning ship?	35 rescued. Two were killed in fireroom. One jumped overboard, a naturalized German, Carl HOLLGER. Had on rubber suit.
(b) Were any taken prisoner?	Don't know.

PARTICULARS ON ENEMY CRAFT

40. (a) Number, if submarine or aircraft	Did not see number.
(b) Where was number seen and how distinguished?	—
41. With the help of a sketch or silhouette drawing give a general description of the enemy ship and especially of any peculiarities noticed. A drawing of the submarine or raider, however rough, should be attached and the following points of descriptive detail noted as examples:	Silhouette enclosed[1].
(a) Whether large or small	Medium
(b) Color and whether any streaks or stripes	Not seen
(c) Shape of conning tower	Can shaped according to some. Short and elongated according to others
(d) Shape, rake and position of stack	———
(e) Any irregularities or bulges on hull or superstructure	None
(f) Gun position(s)	Between conning tower and bow
(g) Whether any net cutter?	No.
(h) Shape of bow; of stern	Cruiser spoon; not known
(i) Relative height and position of masts	None
42. Guns, number, position, and nature?	One, probably 4 or 5 inch, between conning tower and bow.
43. Number of masts and king posts?	None
44. Radio aerials and gear, description of?	None
45. (a) What color was enemy vessel painted?	Not known
(b) Did paint look old or new?	Black
(c) Did ship bear any marks of damage?	No
46. Estimated speed	Not known
47. Estimated tonnage (gross)	1800, more probably 750.
48. Steam or motor ship?	Diesel
49. Officers of enemy vessel. Names and personal descriptions?	Probably German, spoke broken English

REPORT OF INTERVIEWING OFFICER

50. General remarks by interviewing officer.	See attached details.

ALBERT FENDIG   (signed)
Lieut. (jg) USNR

---

[1] Silhouette not included in materials received by authors from Maritime commission.

DETAILS OF ATTACK AND SUBSEQUENT SINKING OF
S/S Esso Baton Rouge

13 MILES 23 DEGREES FROM BRUNSWICK BUOY   0123 C.W.T.   April 8, 1942

    This report is based on interviews with the 35 survivors of the tanker *Esso Baton Rouge*, these interviews being participated in by Lieutenant D. C. Trexler, USNR; Lieutenant(jg) Albert Fendig, USNR; Ensign C. Allen, USNR; and by personal inspection of the wreck by Lieutenant (jg) Albert Fendig, USNR. These interviews took place in the Coast Guard Station on St. Simons Island, Georgia, on April 8, 1942. The bulk of the information is furnished by Captain James Simeon Poche, George W. Bill, First Officer; Ralph W. Durdle, Second Officer; Neo H. Robinson and James W. Robbins, both of whom were lookouts.

    The *Esso Baton Rouge* was a steam tanker owned by the Standard Oil Company of New Jersey. This vessel departed from Baytown, Texas, 1300 C.W.T., April 3, 1942, destined for New York. She was under the command of Captain James Simeon Poche, who is a Lieutenant Commander in the USNR, attached to the 3ND. The cargo consisted of 70,000 barrels lubricating oil and 20,000 gallons heating oil. The cruising speed of the vessel was 12.8 knots. The *Esso Baton Rouge* was zigzagging and blacked out at the time of the attack. The vessel was torpedoed about two miles west of a line between the Brunswick seabuoy and the Sapelo seabuoy, and about four miles west of the route prescribed by the Port Director in Baytown, Texas.

    This ship sailed from Baytown with a complement of 38 men, and 35 survivors were brought to the St. Simons Coast Guard Station. The Second Assistant Engineer James E. Layne; a fireman, William H. Scheich, were killed in the engine room, and Carl G. Hollger, Oiler, jumped overboard in a rubber suit and has not been seen since.

    At the time of the torpedoing, the seas were moderate, visibility was good, and a half moon was just rising.

    Captain Poche was on the bridge at the time of the torpedo attack. He reports that the tanker *Oklahoma* passed his ship approximately one hour before the *Esso Baton Rouge* was torpedoed. He states that approximately ten minutes before the *Esso Baton Rouge* was torpedoed, a small craft which looked like a patrol boat passed to the stern of the *Esso Baton Rouge* going S.S.W. Captain Poche reports that this vessel looked so much like a patrol boat that he remarked to the third mate, "She's all right. She must be one of our patrol boats." The Captain describes this vessel as being approximately 75 feet in length, with a beam of 25 feet, two houses, and one gun forward.

    James W. Robbins, who was a lookout on the port wing of the bridge, stated this vessel came within 150 feet of the port quarter of the *Esson Baton Rouge*. He estimated the length of this so called patrol boat to be 50 feet. He stated that its color was dark gray, with one house amidships, with a speed of five or six knots.

    The Third Officer, Ole Gjerstad, agrees with the Captain's description.

    Almost immediately after this patrol vessel passed, Captain Poche advised that he sighted three lights two points off the starboard bow. These lights were flashing intermittently, apparently low in the water, about 200 feet apart, and traveling south at a very low rate of speed.

    Neo H. Robinson, who was a lookout on the starboard wing of the bridge, reported that he saw three lights an equal distance apart. He stated that in all his experiences, he had never seen such lights; that they were flashing and giving off considerable illumination, but did not illuminate the type vessels they were coming from.

    Ralph W. Durdle, Second Officer, stated that he saw these lights away in the distance, and they apparently were surrounded by a haze.

    While the Captain, the Second Officer and the Lookout are of the opinion that these lights were three separate submarines, attentions should be called to the fact that the lights were noted in the general direction where the torpedoed tanker *Oklahoma* was sunk, and could have probably been life rings thrown from that tanker or flashlights in the lifeboats.

    Captain Poche continues, that while these lights were flashing, a small tanker, which Captain Poche estimated to be 5,000 gross tons, stood by to the southward, between the *Esson Baton Route* and the flashing lights. Captain Poche noted that this tanker was high out of the water and, therefore, apparently light.

    Ralph W. Durdle and James W. Robbins, also noted this tanker and estimated it to be about one half mile to the east of the *Esson Baton Rouge*, therefore approximately one and one half miles west of the *Oklahoma*. It should be noted in this connection that none of the crew members of the tanker *Oklahoma* saw this tanker. Within about five minutes after this tanker had passed to the southward, the torpedo stuck the *Esso Baton Rouge* on the starboard side of the vessel between the bunker and the engine room. The *Esso Baton Rouge* sank immediately by the stern, listing to the starboard approximately 10 degrees.

James W. Robbins, the lookout, describes the explosion as being a ball of flame followed by smoke emitting the acrid odor of TNT. In this description, the majority of the crew members who were awake, concur. Twenty minutes after the attack a submarine put in its appearance and could easily be seen in the light of the half moon.

All the survivors got into the lifeboats with the exception of Carl B. Hollger, whom the Captain states was German born and naturalized in this country. This man utterly refused to get into the lifeboat despite the Captain's commands and entreaties, and jumped overboard in his rubber life suit. Although the lifeboats looked for him carefully, he has not been seen since. The men in the lifeboats stated they could plainly hear a voice on the submarine say "come over here and we will save you" in broken English. No men were visible on the submarine, but apparently this voice was coming from the conning tower of the submarine. Captain Poche stated that a man attired in a rubber life suit should float for at least ten days, and it seems quite possible that this man was picked up and taken prisoner by the submarine.

Most of the survivors agree that the submarine was approximately 250 feet long; that the conning tower was just aft of amidships; that there was one gun between the conning tower and the bow. No net cutter or other guns were visible. Some of the men claim that the conning tower was can shaped, but Captain Poche and First Officer George W. Bill, who have served on submarines with the American Navy, stated the conning tower was low (not higher than six feet above the deck) and elongated.

Captain Poche drew a sketch of the submarine, in which the First Officer concurs, which is made a part of this report and attached as Enclosure B.[2]

First Officer George W. Bill stated that this submarine resembled the American "S" boats in type and size. He estimated that the submarine was a little longer than the "S" boats and looked very similar to them.

Electrician John J. Boyle, Jr., stated that the vessel heeled over when hit and righted itself slowly, settling by the stern.

Michael H. Reilly, Radio Operator, advised that he did not attempt to send any radio message because apparently the radio outfit was knocked out of commission by the explosion.

Captain Poche had a number of suggestions and comments to make. He stated that since we are shy of patrol boats, why not have a boom of vessels every 120 miles, and run only in daytime. These booms with vessels would be protected by patrol vessels and would be in lieu of putting into harbor.

The Captain stated that he thought all fishing vessels should be kept off the seas at night. He states that an armed tanker should start blasting away at any sort of light they see at night.

The Captain advised that he saw very few patrol planes and had been challenged only three times by them. Captain Poche stated that the lamps on these planes are so dim that you can't see them. Two of the planes challenged the *Esso Baton Rouge* on the morning of April 7th. The Captain thinks the planes should fly in a straight line so that they could be identified by the ship. He stated that when they dart and twist around the ship, you could not identify them..

Captain Poche stated that when he was near Cape Canaveral, a plane dropped a smoke bomb and forced him to move out further. The Captain explained that none of his instructions explained the meaning of smoke bombs.

The Captain complained about the patrol boats which requested him, not only to divulge the name of his vessel, but the port of departure and the port of destination. In the Captain's opinion, by divulging such information, the safety of his ship is compromised.

Captain Poche left his confidential codes and other documents aboard the *Esso Baton Rouge* when he abandoned ship, but returned on the Navy boat *Irene* (author's note: actually it was the private yacht, Lourine), at the suggestion of the interviewing officer, and removed the bulk of the confidential codes and papers. Those were locked in the Captain's safe and are, in interviewing officer's opinion, not compromised.

At this time, the tanker *Esso Baton Rouge* was personally inspected by the interviewing officer. The catwalk between the bridge and the stern was awash, but the poop deck was above water. The stern of the tanker was apparently resting on the bottom, and the vessel was listing to the port at an angle of approximately 8 or 10 degrees, and apparently there is a possibility of salvaging same.

Pictures were taken of the tanker and are included as a part of this report and attached as Enclosure C.

One of the survivors picked up a piece of metal which he thought to be a part of the torpedo. This piece of metal is forwarded with this report for examination as Enclosure to ONI.

BOARDING REPORT
DISTRICT INTELLIGENCE OFFICE — SIXTH NAVAL DISTRICT, Charleston, S. C.

Boarded at:	St. Simons Sound, Ga.	Date:	April 23, 1942
Name of Ship:	S. E. "Esso Baton Rouge"	Nationality:	American (U.S.)
Captain's Name:	James Simeon Poche	Home Port:	Wilmington, Del.
Mate's Name:	George W. Bill	Sailed From:	Baytown, Texas
Cargo:	Lubricating and heating oil	Next Port:	Indefinite

The steam tanker *"Esso Baton Rouge"* sailed from Baytown, Texas, April 3, 1942, at 1300 C.W.T., bound for New York. Subject Vessel was under the command of Captain James Simeon Poche, and had a complement of 38 men including the Captain. On April 8, at a point 13 miles 23 degrees from the Brunswick Lightbuoy, the vessel went down by the stern in 40 feet of water. The forward half of the deck and the superstructure was never under water. 35 of the members of the crew made the life boats and were picked up and brought into Brunswick, Georgia. Another crew member jumped overboard and was not seen again. The two remaining members of the crew were killed by the explosion of the torpedo.

Subject ship was salvaged by the Merritt Chapman Company and brought into St. Simons Sound late on the afternoon of April 21, 1942. This was accomplished by pumping out about half of her cargo of heavy heating oil in order that she would refloat. Subject vessel was boarded by reporting officer in company with Chief Boatswain, C. T. Christiansen, U.S.C.G., Captain of the Port, Savannah and Georgia District, at her anchorage just off St. Simons Pier.

A number of photographs were taken and these included shots made of the torpedo hole and shorts made showing the damage in the engine room.

Actual inspection of damage to the ship showed that the torpedo struck the vessel on the port side at the engine room, some 10 to 15 feet below the water line. The explosion of the torpedo left the engine in shambles. All machinery visible above the water now in the engine room is destroyed. The force of the explosion apparently directed upward as the deck above the engine room was ruptured and the bulkheads torn loose from their foundations. The hole in the ship's side and hull, from all appearances, is more than 30 feet in diameter. However, only approximately the upper one third of this hole is above the water and visible. There were no shells fired at the ship.

Mr. Johan Larsson, Chief Engineer of subject ships, was aboard assisting in salvage operations. Mr. Larsson was interviewed in regard to when, where and how subject ship could be repaired. Mr. Larsson had no definite information concerning this. He stated, however, that he understood subject ship would in all probability remain at her present anchorage for at least three or four weeks while arrangements for drydock facilities and towing power are completed. He also advised that subject vessel would probably be able to proceed in tow of a tug at a speed of about 5 knots. The general opinion was, however, that the vessel would be taken to Norfolk, although this was not official.

The bodies of James E. Layne, Second Assistant Engineer and William J. Scheich, fireman, who apparently were killed by the explosion, were found in the engine room and removed from the ship when she was finally anchored in St. Simons Sound.

Mr. Charles R. Monahan, Standard Oil representative, stated in regard to the only other member of the crew missing, that the body of Carl F. Hollger, an oiler, who was seen to jump overboard at the time of the torpedoing, had been washed ashore somewhere on the Florida coast. Mr. Monahan stated that he did not know how true this was, the exact location or when it occurred. He advised that his information was hearsay and that he had heard it from some of the employees of the oil company.

When the reporting officer boarded subject vessel, the salvage crew was at work, and only one watchman was encountered. There were no patrol craft of any kind operating near this ship and another torpedoed vessel, the *S. S. Oklahoma*, which likewise has been salvaged and brought into St. Simons Sound. As a result, there was a constant stream of curious sightseers in the Sound around the ships. Nearly all these sightseers had cameras and were snapping pictures of both this vessel and the tanker *Oklahoma*. Also aboard the *Baton Rouge* was a crew of workmen engaged in cleaning up the ship, which was covered with the heavy heating oil pumped from the cargo tanks when she was refloated. The clean-up crew was composed of 15 and 16 year old boys and several Negroes. There was absolutely no fire protection and the following incident illustrated the effectiveness of the watchman about the *Baton Rouge*. On April 23, an expensive kit of tools was purchased and delivered aboard the ship. That night these tools were stolen from the ship. The watchman on duty on this night was fired and another engaged.

In view of these conditions concerning the security of this vessel and the *Oklahoma*, which is laying about a mile away, the reporting officer assisted the Captain of the Port in forming a patrol around both vessels in order to keep all boats away from the vessels and to cut out the taking of pictures. This patrol was set up with the cooperation of the Coast Guard Auxiliary and the Coast Guard Reserve, which has recently been formed under the director of Lt. (jg) H. Hallett. Lt. Hallett called out three vessels of the Coast Guard Auxiliary and furnished small arms and two men to assist in the work. Other men were furnished from the St. Simons Coast Guard Station and the Captain of the Port's complement in Savannah. The Captain of the Port also ordered the vessel supplied with fire protection and consequently a tug with fire fighting equipment joined the patrol. Armed Coast Guardsmen are not stationed on each of these vessels.

AFFIDAVIT OF CAPTAIN JAMES S. POCHE
OF THE SS Esso Baton Rouge
TORPEDOED APRIL 8, 1942

I, James S. Poche, first being duly sworn, solemnly depose and declare:

I am an American Citizen, 48 years of age, and my home address is 829 Basler Drive, Baton Rough, Louisiana; I have been going to sea since 1911 and have been in the employ of Standard Oil Company of New Jersey since 1919, and hold a Master's License since 1922.

Since 1940 and until she was torpedoed on April 8, 1942, I was in command of the American Flag Tanker *SS Esso Baton Rouge* of 4,738 net registered tones; 7,989 gross tons and 12,950 deadweight tons; 442 feet long - 64 foot beam or thereabouts, owned by Standard Oil Company of New Jersey.

After the casualty occurred, I remained in Brunswick, GA to assist in salvage operations and subsequently brought the vessel to Baltimore, MD. On my recent return to New York, I was shown and carefully read the joint sworn statement of Chief Officer George Bill and Second Officer Ralph W. Durdle, describing the circumstances of the attack, and all of which is substantially correct.

The only amendments I have to make to the said statement, are that, as reported therein, I went into the Chart Room about 2:48 a.m., April 8th to determine our proximity to the southbound track. We figured out our position was Latitude 31 degrees, 12' North. Longitude 81 degrees, 4' west at 2:50 a.m., that is, at the very time we were struck by the torpedo. From inside the Chart Room the shock felt as if the vessel had collided with some object and caused me to go up to the bridge again where Second Mate Durdle informed me we had been torpedoed.

Mr. Durdle thought that the torpedo had struck on the starboard side but the Port Lookout, A. B. Robbins, believed the ship had been torpedoed on the port side; which later proved to be correct.

The ship settled rapidly by the stern until the weather deck between the pump room and the after house was awash and she apparently rested by the stern on the bottom in approximately 7 fathoms of water.

The ship's radio was put out of order by the explosion and the Radio Operator, Mr. Reilly, was not able to send out any message.

Our lifeboats were not fitted with any portable radio sets nor outboard motors. They were supplied with ample provisions and water. The ship had also been supplied with life-saving rubber suits for the crew but only a few of these suits were used owing to circumstances and to some difficulty experienced with the 'zipper.'

Further, that after landing at 4:00 p.m. April 8th in the vicinity of Brunswick, GA. and reporting to the U.S. Naval Authorities, a U. S. Coast Guard Vessel about 6:00 p.m., took me back to the vessel with First Mate George Bill, Second Mate Durdle and Chief Engineer Larsson; after inspecting the general condition of the ship, I got hold of the secret codes and documents which I later delivered to the Naval Authorities, as well as the ship's papers which I replaced aboard ship after her salvage.

Later we returned to the St. Simons Coast Guard Station and were interrogated by the U. S. Naval Authorities, after which we obtained lodgings for the night.

April 9th: About 9:00 a.m. I contacted my owners by telephone, advising them of the casualty and the possibility of salvaging the vessel. My owners informed me they would send Merritt-Chapman & Scott Corporation Salvers to undertake operations as soon as possible and that Mr. G. L. Bennett, owners' Port Engineer, would join me at Brunswick, GA where I was to remain to assist in the salvage.

About 11:00 a.m., Lieutenant Fendig, USNR, myself, my Chief Officer George Bill and Chief Engineer Larsson, went out to the *Esso Baton Rouge* in a Cruiser Yacht(named *Lourine II*) owned by Mr. Charles Howard Candler, commanded by Mr. Olaf H. Olsen, an employee of the yacht owner.

When we arrived alongside the *Esso Baton Rouge* we found a U.S. Navy Tug, with a 1 inch wire cable from the port bow attempting to tow the vessel to port, but the Commanding Officer of the tug advised us he would have to abandon operations since he could not move the *Esso Baton Rouge*, the weather at the time was good; sea moderate, with light breeze.

Our party boarded the *Esso Baton Rouge* and we observed she had taken an 18 degree list to port; little movement, if any, in the vessel was noticed.

At this time we also observed a British Patrol Boat patrolling the area and that one of the *Esso Baton Rouge's* lifeboats which we had left aboard, was being towed away from our vessel's side by a power boat in the direction of the British Patrol boat. An inspection of my vessel showed many articles and ship's equipment missing, among which were the water cooler, ship's radio receivers, all fans and clocks amidships; the linen locker had been broken into and all the personal belongings of the men who lived amidships had been taken away. I do not believe these things could have been taken by fishermen or other boats because I was notified the previous day, April 8th, by the authorities that the area would be patrolled.

Later we went ashore in Mr. Candler's yacht, *Lourine II*, and in the evening, April 9th, my owners' port representative, Mr. W. B. Kimball, arrived from Jacksonville, FL. to assist me in securing transportation for the ship's crew, all of whom, with the exception of myself and Chief Engineer Larsson, were dispatched to New York the same evening, April 9th.

April 11th: Mr. Bennett arrived about noon April 11th, and we discussed the prospects of salvaging the *Esso Baton Rouge*; we spent the day discussing salvage operations and in contacting owners of various local small craft to assist.

April 12th: About 7:00 a.m. we went out to the *Esso Baton Rouge* aboard a small boat known as the *Captain Fred*, which we had hired, and inspected the general condition of the *Esso Baton Rouge* without going aboard. We returned ashore about noon to await the arrival of the Merritt Salvage tug; the weather was unchanged, sea moderate; southeast wind; force 4, and later contacted the Coast Guard Station at St. Simons Island whether anything had been heard from the Salvage tug.

April 13th: About 11:00 a.m. April 13th, we received word from the Coast Guard Station that a salvage tug was approaching the St. Simons Sound; we secured the service of Mr. Candler's yacht the *Lourine II* and proceeded to meet the approaching tug which was the *Resolute*, with Captain Dexter in charge. After contacting him, he advised us that he would first have to proceed to the City of Brunswick, GA., to replenish his fuel and water supplies and take on two additional air compressors which he had ordered.

April 14th: Mr. Bennett, myself and Chief Engineer Larsson, left Brunswick, GA. at 5:00 a.m. aboard the *Resolute*, fully equipped with a complete salvage crew, and arrived at the *Esso Baton Rouge* about 8:00 a.m. The sea was slight to moderate, with a Southeast swell and Wind Force 3.

The *Resolute* came alongside the bow of the *Esso Baton Rouge* and I jumped aboard with several men; we lifted two air compressors on to the deck and managed to connect one of these compressors to the smothering line. Then we plugged the air vents on tanks 3,4, and 5 across and started to blow air into No. 3 port wing tank, forcing about 300 bbls. of Dewax Necton 60 contained in this tank, through the ship's pipe lines into No. 1 starboard wing tank which was empty; this was done with a view of shifting the weight and to straighten the ship which was listing to port.

Once the ship was brought on even keel as a result of these operations we shifted the air pressure into No. 5 center tank that contained about 7700 bbls. of aviation lube oil, forcing this oil into No. 1 side tank that was empty, as well as in No. 1 center tank which contained about 4300 bbls. of Esso heating-medium, but as the tanks reach the same ullage we were unable to blow any more oil into No.1 tanks due to the excess air pressure required to force it in; naturally this operation resulted in the contamination of the cargo in No. 1 center tank.

As it had become late, we decided to return to the St. Simons Sound for the night in accordance with the U.S. Naval instructions.

April 15: We returned to the *Esso Baton Rouge* at daybreak April 15th; the weather was not as good as the previous day; the sea having become moderate with southeast wind, force 4, causing the sea to break across and over the after weather deck of the *Esso Baton Rouge*. These conditions prevented us from blowing any oil during the morning but we worked on general rigging of the air compressors, smothering lines and air vents.

In the afternoon we managed to blow out into the sea through overboard discharge lines about 1,500 bbls. of 'Panhandle' aviation oil from No. 5 center tank; this required about three-quarters of an hour until we had to suspend operations on account of the late time. The ship had not yet moved as a result of these operations but she had obviously become more alive to the sea.

April 16th: We resumed operations early on April 16th and were able to blow overboard about 4,000 bbls. of aviation oil contained in No. 5 port wing and center tanks and all the Necton 60 contained in No. 5 starboard tank. There operations lasted all day and were successfully pursued on **April 17th**, and as the ship had raised sufficiently to enable us to reach the valves from No. 6 tank, we started shifting pressure therein and blew out to sea about 3,000 bbls. of aviation oil from No. 6 center tank.

April 17th: We then attempted to balance the *Esso Baton Rouge* closer into shore by putting the *Resolute* on a hawser from her starboard bow but she did not move any noticeable distance; however, by this time she had become so alive that the port anchor was let go with 60 fathoms of chain. Two more compressors were placed aboard in view of additional air required to blow the cargo as the levels in the tanks became lower.

April 18th: We then pumped about 600 tons of sea water into the forepeak tank by means of the fire hoses from the tug *Resolute*. We also kept blowing about 1,000 bbls aviation oil from No. 6 center tank into the sea. This lasted until dark.

April 19th: When we returned the next morning, we found the ship had swung 180 degrees and was now heading West-Southwest; weather was moderating. We installed a portable gasoline discharge pump into the pump room skylight and began pumping oil that had flowed 17 feet deep in the pump room. However, after working this pump several hours, we found that the level did not go down, which indicated that the pump room was open to the sea; another pump was placed on the poop which was free of water by this time, and a suction hose was put in the afterpeak, which was discharged overboard.

About 3:00 p.m. Captain Davis of Merritt-Chapman & Scott Corporation arrived aboard and after deliberation it was decided to continue operations, which were shaping well. We then blew overboard continuously until dark; the Necton 78 contained in No. 6 port wing and the Necton 60 contained in No. 5 starboard wing tanks; the Butterworth plate from No 6 port wing which had become loose was righted by the diver just prior to retiring for the night.

April 20th: We finished blowing out into the sea the Necton 78 from No. 6 port and starboard wing tanks and the aviation oil and Necton 60 from No. 5 wing tanks which took us all morning of April 20th. About noon the vessel was definitely afloat.

We than started to blow overboard the Necton 78 and Esso heat-medium, contained in No. 7 wing tanks. The vessel was then high enough to take Butterworth plate from No. 7 tank and to try to suck the Cantas 180 oil out of No. 7 center tank, but we found this oil was too heavy to lift. By the time No. 7 wing tank was empty we attempted to blow the Esso heat-medium, contained in No. 8 center, together with the Cantas oil contained in No. 7 center tank in order to make No. 7 run more freely. This permitted us to blow out into the sea about 1700 bbls. from No. 7 center and about 2,000 bbls from No. 8 center, but also resulted in the contamination of the cargo remaining in these tanks. That night we anchored this ship.

April 21st: On our way to the *Esso Baton Rouge* on April 21st, we sounded the dredged channel of St. Simons Sound to determine the draft which the *Esso Baton Rouge* could carry. On our arrival at the ship, we proceeded to finish blowing out No. 8 center tank and at the same time we filled the foredeep tank with sea water by means of the *Resolute's* pumps. These operations finally resulted in securing the draft desired, which was bout 26' 9" even keel. About 3:00 p.m., the Merrit tug, *Willett,* which was assisting in the salvage of the *SS Oklahoma* nearby, took the *Esso Baton Rouge's* bow hawser and proceed to tow her into port. The *Resolute* took her stern line to steer the *Esso Baton Rouge* and at 10:00 p.m. the ship was safely anchored in 13 fathoms of water with 60 fathoms of chain, in the St. Simons Sound north of the St. Simons Pleasure Pier. We estimated that we jettisoned about 33,000 bbls. of various grades of oil and that about 33,000 bbls. of cargo remaining in the ship were contaminated as a result of the various operations undertaken to save the ship.

Signed: James S. Poche
Master - *SS Esso Baton Rouge*

Information on the Sinking of the Tankers off St. Simons
Declassified - Navy Department
Office of the Chief of Naval Operations
Washington, D. C.

Memorandum

Subject: Summary of Statements by Survivors, *SS Baton Rouge,* American Tanker, Standard Oil Company.

1. The 7989 gross ton *SS Baton Rouge* was torpedoed without warning at 0123 C.W.T. on April 8, 1942 about 13 miles, 23 degrees, from Brunswick Lightbuoy. The vessel sank in 40 feet less than five minutes later.

2. The vessel was en route from Baytown, Texas, to New York on an inshore routing, 2 miles off buoys, with a cargo of 70,000 bbls. of lubricating oil and 20,000 gallons of heating oil. The lubricating oil was in tanks 3 to 7, both center and wing; while the heating oil was in 1, 2 and 8 wing tanks. No. 1 and 8 tanks were empty. The ship was on course 22 true, speed 12.8 knots, zigzagging, completely blacked out, radio not used, draft 28 feet forward, 30 aft. Two lookouts were on watch, one on each wing of the bridge. The weather was good, sea slight, wind SE force 3, half moon rising.

3. The torpedo struck the starboard side between bunkers and engine room, 20 feet below the water line. A cloud of smoke and flame followed the explosion. The engine room and crew's quarters were immediately flooded. The vessel sank by the stern with a 10 degree list to starboard, the stern resting on the bottom, and the bow draft was reduced to 17 feet. The radio was put out of commission by the explosion. The confidential codes were left aboard, but later recovered. The vessel was not armed.

4. Two of the crew were killed by the explosion. A third, a naturalized German refused to leave in a lifeboat but jumped overboard in a rubber suit and was not seen again, although it is possible he may have been picked up by the submarine. The crew heard a voice from the submarine say in broken English, "Come over here and we will save you." This may have been addressed to the naturalized German crew member.

5. The submarine surfaced about 20 minutes after the attack and could be clearly seen in the moonlight. It was believed by the Master that the submarine was no more than 200 yards distant when the attack occurred. It was described as about 250 feet long. The conning tower was aft of a midships and can-shaped according to some survivors, while others including the Master, state it was low (not higher than six feet) and elongated. The bow was high. One gun, probably 4 or 5 inch, was seen forward. No net cutter was visible. It resembled the American "S" boat.

6. The tanker, *Oklahoma,* passed the *Esso Baton Rouge* northbound about an hour prior to the attack. About ten minutes prior to the attack a small craft about 50 to 75 feet long, a beam of 25 feet, two houses and one gun forward passed astern at a speed of five to six knots. It was believed to be a patrol craft. Almost immediately after this craft passed three lights were sighted 2 points off shore the starboard bow, flashing intermittently, low in the water, about 200 feet apart and traveling slowly southward. They may have been on submarines or possibly lifeboats from the *Oklahoma* which was torpedoed in that location. A small tanker passed the *Esso Baton Rouge* to starboard at this time headed SSE. Three to four minutes later, the *Esso Baton Rouge* was torpedoed.

7. The Master of the *Esso Baton Rouge* suggests:

    1. A boom of vessels every 120 miles protected by patrol vessels where ships could stop at night instead of going into harbors. Vessels only to run in daytime.
    2. That all fishing vessels be kept off the seas at night, and armed vessels should fire at any light that they see at night.
    3. Patrol planes should fly in a straight line to facilitate identification by the ship. Patrol planes request not only the ship's name, but the ports of departure and destination which might compensate the ship's safety.

Crew List of "SS *Esso Baton Rouge*"

35 survivors   3 Casualties*

Poche, James Simeon	Master
Bill, George	1st Officer
Durdle, Ralph W.	2nd Officer
Guerstad, Ole	3rd Officer
Larsson, Johan	Chief Engineer
Cooper, Joseph M.	1st Ass't. Engineer
*Layne, James E.	2nd Ass't. Engineer (killed by explosion)
Montague, William H.	3rd Ass't. Engineer
Reilly, Michael J.	Radio Operator
Boyle, John J., Jr.	Electrican
Pinto, John	Steward
Ventoso, Jose A.	Chief Cook, Spanish, 1st papers
Haig, Alex	
Ekke, Michael	Pumpman
Landry, Claude T	
Fisher, Paul	
Gallego, Eugenio M.	
Dowling, James T.	AB Seaman
Aiken, John F.	AB Seaman
Robinson, Neo. H.	Lookout
Cabrepa, Dionisio, E.	
Robbins, James W.	Lookout
Grofik, John D.	
Trubisz, Frank H.	O. S.
Johnson, Aphonse	Oiler
*Hollger, Carl B.	Oiler (jumped overboard after explosion and not seen since)
Barboza, Antonio	
Young, Joseph A.	Storekeeper
Garcia, Jose	
Robertson, William F.	Fireman
*Scheich, William J.	Fireman (killed in explosion in engine room)
Torres, Franciso O.	Wiper
Wernick, Abraham	Wiper
Cozart, Edgar R.	Second Cook
Seegers, William M.	Salon Man
Koch, Kenneth M.	Petty Officer Messman
Lisofsky, Gregory	
Vizian, Arthur J.	Utility

Ships of the Esso Fleet in World War II
pp.178-183; c. 1946
Standard Oil Company (New Jersey)

"The *Esso Baton Rouge* was towed to St. Simons Sound by the salvage tug *Willet*, assisted by the *Resolute*, on April 21. Mr. Bennett, who then returned to New York, stated in his report:

'During the salvage work Captain Poche and Chief Engineer Larsson were of material assistance to the salvage tug officers and to the ultimate success of the operations.'

Sails Again

After temporary repairs were made, the *Esso Baton Rouge,* in tow, left Brunswick on May 14 for Baltimore, where she arrived May 22. There, at the yard of the Maryland Drydock Company permanent repairs were completed November 29, 1942, and the vessel sailed on November 30 for Houston, Texas. She was again commanded by Captain Poche. Her engine room was now in charge of Chief Engineer Earl Williams.

As previously stated, the cargo of 78,557 barrels of Navy fuel oil which she then loaded at Houston was discharged at Norfolk and on her next voyage she took on, at Beaumont, Texas, her last cargo, 66,592 barrels of Beaumont crude. Proceeding via New York, she discharged this crude at Swansea, Wales.

The *Baton Rouge* sailed in convoy from New York on January 22, 1943, arriving at Swansea on February 8. This convoy was attacked by enemy submarines continuously for more than a week. Several ships were sunk and others damaged. The North Atlantic weather was severely cold; aboard the tanker the men on deck watches kept warm by wearing their rubber lifesaving suits.

On February 13, the *Esso Baton Rouge*, with 43 merchant officers and men and Navy gun crew of 25, left Swansea in company with 7 other vessels in ballast. With these ships, she awaited instructions at Milford Haven and then proceeded to a rendezvous where about 32 tankers and freighters gathered to make up a convoy for the Atlantic crossing.

The convoy sailed on the morning of February 16, bound for Curacao, each ship taking position as directed by the commodore, a British rear admiral aboard the tanker *Athelregent*. In the escort were four American Destroyers (the *Madison, Lansdale, Hilary P. Jones* and *Charles F. Hughes)* and six British naval vessels-corvettes and destroyers.

The *Esso Baton Rouge* was armed with a 3-inch gun on the foc'sle head, a 5-inch after, four 20mm anti-aircraft guns on the after boat deck, and four more AAs on the bridge.

As stated by Chief Mate Martin Wiberg in his report, to which additions were made by Captain Poche:

'From the time of leaving Swansea, the weather was fine and clear; occasionally we had moderate light swells, but on the whole the weather was fine at all times.

Beginning February 21, the convoy was attacked by enemy submarines. During the succeeding days and nights depth charges were dropped frequently by the escorting vessels and especially by the destroyers running ahead of the convoy. At night, the corvettes and destroyers close by the convoy used a considerable number of depth charges, indicating the constant presence of submarines.'

On February 24, 1943, the Berlin communiqué asserted that 'A group of submarines attacked a strongly protected enemy convoy in the Atlantic. After hard fighting they sank 17 vessels, totaling 104,000 tons, and torpedoed three other steamers.'

Depth Bombs

To continue Wiberg's report:

About 7 p.m., February 23, while I was standing the 4 to 8 watch, the British corvette *Totland*, then about two miles to starboard of the *Esso Baton Rouge*, turned on her searchlight and began dropping depth charges. Later, when aboard the *Totland*, I learned she had sighted an enemy submarine on the surface close by. The U-boat immediately started a crash dive, which was the occasion for the searchlight and depth charges. It was believed that the sub could not have escaped and was sunk.

As reported by Captain Poche:

About 7:20 p.m., February 23, the *Esso Baton Rouge*, in No. 4-3 position in the convoy, was in latitude 31degrees 15' North, Longitude 27 degrees 22' West, or approximately 600 miles south southwest of the Azores.

Other Ships Hit

"The convoy," Wiberg said, "was proceeding at a speed of about 9 knots. Suddenly, the Netherlands flag tanker, *Morina*, in No. 4-1 position and the second vessel ahead of the *Esso Baton Rouge*, was torpedoed on the starboard side, but did not sink and was able to proceed with the convoy.

"At that time I was in charge of the bridge. Captain Poche was atop the wheelhouse directing a change of course then being made. Harry L. Clark, A.B., was wheelsman; Charles L. Haynie, A.B., and Charles D. McMurchy, A.B., were lookouts on the bridge. First Assistant Engineer Joseph M. Cooper was in charge of the engine room and on watch with him were Oiler David H. Owen and Fireman-Water-tender Howard C. Landiss.

"Within one to two minutes after the *Morina* was hit, a Norwegian flag tanker, directly ahead of the *Esso Baton Rouge* in the same column, began firing her stern gun to starboard. Almost simultaneously, torpedoes struck two British tankers in No. 1 - 1 and No. 2 - 1 positions - The *Empire Norseman* and the *British Fortitude*. The *Empire Norseman* was the first hit by a torpedo on the port side, followed by two on the starboard side; she subsequently rolled over and disappeared. The *British Fortitude*, torpedoed on the starboard side, was able to continue with the convoy.

Then the "Baton Rouge"

"Immediately after the two British tankers were struck, the *Esso Baton Rouge* was torpedoed on the starboard side after, in way of the bunker fuel tank. A sheet of flame rose high in the air from the burning fuel oil Flying debris was scattered all about. All the vessel's lights were out."

As reported by Chief Engineer Earl Williams: "The force of the explosion carried away the bulk heads between the bunker tanks and the engine room, which began to fill with burning oil. Various parts of the ship and superstructure were torn into fragments of jagged steel and blown a distance of fifty to sixty feet."

"The *Esso Baton Rouge*," said the chief mate, "settled by the stern, indicating that the engine room bulkheads had been blown out and the engine and fire rooms flooded.

Preparedness

"At the time the *Morina* was hit, the general alarm was sounded on the *Baton Rouge*, so that when she was torpedoed most of the crew were taking their stations near the lifeboats.

"No. 3 lifeboat was completely destroyed by the explosion. No. 4 boat was launched in charge of Chief Engineer Williams and was boarded by 22 men in all. As chief officer, I launched No. 1 lifeboat with a total of 27 men. Captain Poche, Second Mate William Hamilton, and Third Mate Roy V. Denton, with 12 of the crew, were in No. 2 boat. Captain Poche was the last man to leave the ship."

Three men were missing: First Assistant Engineer Joseph M. Cooper, Fireman-Water tender Howard C. Landiss, and a member of the Navy gun crew, Seaman 1st Class Gilbert C. Esham.

Four men were seriously injured: Boatswain Karl P. Martinsen, Oiler David H. Owen, Storekeeper John L. Chapelle, and a Navy gunner, Seaman 1st Class Joseph E. Jeanette.

Returning to the chief mate's report:

"Several rafts were launched while the vessel still had considerable headway and they were some distance away when she was abandoned, therefore being of little use. One raft, however, launched by Second Cook Charles A. Wilcox, proved to be important.

"Wilcox, who jumped overboard, was able to reach this life raft and he subsequently rescued Oiler David H. Owen, who had received severe burns. Wilcox and Owen were taken from the raft by Captain Poche in No. 2 boat."

As reported by Oiler Owen:

"At the time of the explosion, the first assistant engineer was at the ahead throttle and I was at the reverse throttle nearby. The engine room was enveloped in flames, followed by darkness. I floated in the water as it filled the engine room space and rose to the upper level. Then I got out to the after deck and put on two life preservers before I entered the water. I swam for about 15 minutes until I reached the life raft."

Boatswain Karl P. Martinsen reported:

"When the vessel was torpedoed I was standing on the starboard side of the poop deck behind the blackout screen. My hands, face, and scalp were burned by flashes of flaming oil. I was able, however, to go amidships and get into No. 2 lifeboat."

Storekeeper John L. Chappelle said: "I was standing on the after boat deck when the ship was hit. Fortunately, I was near No. 3 boat. I was covered with burning oil, which was extinguished when members of the crew rolled me on deck several times in their efforts to put out the flames in my clothing. I was then assisted into the lifeboat."

Several of the injured members of the crew were assisted into the port lifeboat by Galleyman Russell O. Wirtz, who had previously pushed two injured men overboard as the ship settled and supported them in the water until he and they were picked up by No. 2 boat.

"When last seen," Wiberg said, "the bow of the *Esso Baton Rouge* was upright at a 90 degree angle and she was slowly going down stern first. All the lifeboats were excellently stocked and provisioned, with about 80 gallons of water in each boat. No. 3 starboard boat (which had been destroyed by the explosion), and also No. 2 port lifeboat, had motors and portable radio sets.

"Instantly following the attack, our escort vessels went into action and dropped a great many depth charges. While the convoy proceeded with the escorts, the lifeboats remained near where the *Esso Baton Rouge* was torpedoed.

"At about 8:15 p.m., the corvette HMS *Totland*, which had rescued the survivors of the *Empire Norseman*, was observed close by. The men in No. 2 lifeboat shot a flare. The *Totland*, leaving the scene until the flare burned out, returned and picked up, in succession, the survivors in boats Nos. 4, 1, and 2.

The lifeboats, with the plugs removed, were then set adrift and the *Totland* proceeded, rejoining the convoy on the morning of February 24." (The *Totland* was originally the U. S. Coast Guard cutter *Cayuga*; constructed in 1920, she was one of the first turbo-electric vessels built in the United States.)

Martinsen, Owen, and Chappelle, suffering from second and third degree burns, were given skillful treatment aboard the *Totland* by Galleyman Wirtz, who in his earlier years studied medicine and had a good practical knowledge of first aid. Wirtz volunteered to assist in caring for the burned and injured men on the *Esso Baton Rouge* and the *Empire Norseman* and his services were promptly accepted by the corvette's commanding officer. The Esso galleyman's prolonged and tireless work, day and night for eleven days, which saved a number of lives, is described in his citation for distinguished service.

"About 11 a.m., February 26, owing to crowded conditions aboard the *Totland*, the merchant crew of the *Esso Baton Rouge*, except the most seriously injured, and some men from the *Empire Norseman* were transferred to the Netherlands flag freighter *Maskere*. At noon, March 4, the *Totland* bore off from the convoy and arrived that day at Antique, British West Indies.

"Martinsen, Chappelle, and the injured U. S. navy gunner, Jeanette, who had been left aboard the *Totland* in charge of Wirtz, were landed at Antigua and taken to the U. S. Navy Hospital. Owen, who had been transferred to the *Maskere*, was taken to a hospital in Port-of-Spain, Trinidad, when the Netherlands vessel arrived there on the morning of March 6 and landed 37 men from the *Esso Baton Rouge*. All personnel were given Red Cross emergency rescue kits."

As reported by Captain Poche: "The unlicensed men were given accommodations at the U. S. Army Camp, known as 'Torpedo Junction', at Port-of Spain, and the officers were taken to the Allied Merchant Marine Navies Officers' Club. At both places, everything possible was done for the comfort of all hands."

Of the survivors of the *Esso Baton Rouge*, 36 returned to the United States on the *SS George Washington*, operated by the Alcoa Steamship Company, which sailed from Trinidad March 7 and arrived at Baltimore March 13. At Baltimore they were met by an agent of the Company who furnished them with money and clothing and arranged for their transportation by rail. They arrived in New York on the morning of March 14.

Captain Poche and Chief Engineer Williams returned by Pan American Airways, leaving Port-of-Spain March 9 for Miami and arriving in New York March 11.

S.S. OKLAHOMA

(Note: see "The Torpedoed Tankers" in Chapter Four, for the summary of statements by survivors of *Oklahoma*)

Excerpts from declassified report entitled:

Details of Attack and Subsequent Sinking of S/S *Oklahoma*
Thirteen Miles North of Brunswick Buoy
April 8, 1942

(Information furnished as the result of interviews with the nineteen survivors and an inspection of the wreck of the steam tanker, "Oklahoma." Lt. D. C. Trexler, USNR, Ensign C. Allen, USNR, participated in the interviews. These interviews took place in the Coast Guard Station at St. Simons Island, GA. on April 8, 1942. Much of the information was furnished by Captain Theron P. Davenport, First Mate K. Reiersen, Second Mate Weston C. Small, radio operator Keith G. Martin, and Elize Hayes, AB seaman. All survivors were interviewed and others are quoted where their opinion or observations differ from those of the five above.)

The *Oklahoma* was a steam tanker owned by the Texas Company. She was practically new with a rated speed of 16 knots and a potential speed of 20 knots. This vessel departed from Port Arthur, Texas at 1600 on April 4, 1942, bound for Providence R.I. The ship sailed from Port Arthur with a complement of thirty-eight men. Eighteen were apparently trapped either in their quarters or in the engine room. One man died in a lifeboat from wounds received from flying metal fragments. Captain Davenport had his confidential codes and other documents with him intact.

At the time of the attack, the vessel was about two miles inside a line drawn from the Brunswick sea buoy to the Sapelo whistle buoy, in water of approximately forty feet in depth. The ship was not and had not been zigzagging. Captain Davenport explained this by saying that during the daytime, he was running so close to shore that he did not think it was necessary, nor did he think it was necessary after darkness set in.

Although the vessel was in comparatively shallow water, the lookouts and the Second Mate advised that they neither sighted a submarine or a torpedo prior to the explosion. According to most of the survivors, the torpedo struck in the engine room, about ten feet below the waterline. The ship remained afloat forty-five minutes sinking stern first until the stern rested on the bottom.. The men were of the impression that the ship had collided with another vessel and the radio operator sent out an SOS with an emergency set stating that the ship had been in a collision. The ship did not catch fire from the torpedo. Three life boats were launched. After the life boats had left the ship Captain Davenport heard screams from aft and his lifeboat returned to the ship. He, the radio operator Martin, Third Mate MacPhee and Bos'n Maahs boarded the ship to investigate. They found the 2nd engineer, W. Howell too badly injured to help himself or even scream. They lowered a rope, drew him up to the deck and then lowered him to the lifeboat. The screams were coming from a man trapped in the quarters below. The Captain stated that they could not reach him because they were barred by water. Evidently the doomed man's compartment had for a short time remained unflooded. The Captain ordered the radio operator to send other distress signals. The signals were sent "SOS - Torpedoed" and the position given.

Fifteen minutes after the Captain had left the ship the second time, the submarine appeared (surfaced). The submarine commenced firing. According to Quartermaster Stogaitis, the first shell fell short of the ship and emanated a reddish white glare, which illuminated the entire ship and everything surrounding the ship for a distance of approximately two hundred feet. The second shell went over the ship and exploded about 300 yards beyond. The third shell hit amidships on the starboard side, just below the houser. The fourth and fifth shells went over the ship exploding on impact with the water. The sixth shell went through the wheel house at a three point angle. The seventh shell missed. The eighth shell hit just forward of amidships, flaring up into a burst of flame and black smoke which quickly died out. The ninth and tenth shells went over the bow and exploded. The eleventh and twelfth shells hit the forepeak, flashed and exploded. The Quartermaster said he could see every shell as it left the gun and could follow it through the air until it reached its destination. The shells appeared to be incendiary.

While the submarine was shelling the vessel, it slowly approached the tanker. The submarine circled the vessel and proceeded on a course to the east, leisurely and on the surface. The survivors could clearly hear the "chut chut" of the diesels.

Most of the survivors heard the voices of the submarine's gun crew. Many of them could distinguish nothing, although the majority state that it sounded like German to them. The Quartermaster overheard the word "aspetto" which he states means "wait" in Italian. Two men stated that the order to "fire" was given in English. None of the other survivors agreed to this statement.

The 2nd Asst. Engineer Howell, died when the submarine started shelling the vessel. Dr. J. B. Avera, Brunswick, GA, examined this man and stated that a piece of metal had traveled through his head and another through his back.

The 1st Asst. Engineer Beckendorf, stated that if the *Oklahoma* had been armed with a three inch gun, "we could have shot hell out of that sub". He also added that "if we had a gun in our lifeboat, say a one pounder, we might have sunk the sub when it came up, if we had a crew especially picked for that position."

Quartermaster Strogatitis stated that he thought it necessary to call the interviewing officer's attention to Able Bodied Seaman Hayes. Stogaitis pointed out that Hayes was aboard the *Australia* when that ship was torpedoed. Stogaitis stated Hayes was lookout on both the *Australia* and the *Oklahoma* at the time each was torpedoed. Stogaitis states that the *Australia* was torpedoed at 1:05 p.m. and that the *Oklahoma* was torpedoed at 1:05 a.m. He places significance on the time element. In addition, Stogaitis states that when the *Australia* left Port Arthur, Hayes remarked to one of the employees of the "Rosemont Hotel" in Port Arthur, "I will bring you back a souvenir of Bayonne," the destination of the *Australia* according to Stogaitis. He stated that before Hayes sailed on the *Oklahoma* he remarked to the same employee, "I will bring you back a souvenir from Providence," the destination of the *Oklahoma*.

Hayes, according to his own statement, was lookout on the starboard side of the bridge of the *Oklahoma* at the time she was torpedoed. He stated that about three minutes before the torpedo struck the vessel he heard something that sounded like shellfire from a long distance away, but that he did not report this fact to the 2nd mate. He stated that he did not see the submarine or the torpedo, and added that the moon was not out and visibility was poor. (According to all survivors, the visibility was excellent for a dark night.) He advised that he was on the *Australia* and was starboard lookout at the time it was torpedoed. He denied stating that in either the case of the *Australia* or the *Oklahoma* he remarked to an employee of the "Rosemont Hotel" that he would bring back a souvenir. Hayes is not a prepossessing person but one who seems sure of himself. His appearance is decidedly Teutonic. A.N.N.I. -119 report is being made on this matter and will be forwarded under separate cover.

Crew of the SS Oklahoma

20 Survivors 16 Casualties* Buried in Palmetto, Cemetery in Brunswick, Georgia+

Theron O. Davenport	Captain
Malcolm A. MacPhee	Third Mate, U. S.; Wife; Brooklyn, N. Y.
Keith G. Martin	Radio Operator; 31; U.S.; Mother; Amarillo, Texas
Henry Maahs	Bos'n; 34; U.S.; Aungt; Port Arthur, Texas
James L. Stogaitis	Quartermaster; 35; U.S.; Wife; Philadelphia, Pennsylvania
Elzie Heyes	AB Seaman; 36; Mother; Morse, Louisiana
Anton H. Osttorp	Steward; 50; U.S.; Port Arthur, Texas
Sigvald K. Reiersen	Chief Mate; 42; U.S.; Friend, Mr. Patterson; Port Arthur, Texas
John Mowry	First Cook; 24; U.S.; Mother; Woonsocket, Rhode Island
Sverre Sorensen	Quartermaster; 23; Norway (1st papers); Sister; Brooklyn, New York
Weston C. Small	Second Mate; 26; U. S.; Wife; Port Arthur, Texas
Charles H. Phenna	Chief Engineer; 41; U. S.; Wife; Philadelphia, Pennsylvania
William D. Beckendorf	1st Engineer; 41; U.S.; Mother; New Orleans, Louisiana
William C. Max	3rd Engineer; 22; Philadelphia, Pennsylvania
James A. Pellow	Oiler; 26; U. S.; Father; Houtzdale, Louisiana
Joseph D. DeBlanc	Oiler; 22; U.S.; Mother; Port Arthur, Texas
J. B. Anderson	OS; 33; Wife; Mizem, Mississippi
Allen G. Fontenot	OS: 21; Father; Ville Platte, Louisiana
Gustave Cauthiere	1st Pumpman; 30; U. S.; Friend, R. W. Mouchette; Port Arthur, Texas
Robert M. McGregor	Wiper; 19; U.S.; Father; Patterson, New York
John Price*	Oiler; 25; U. S.; Mother; Savannah, Georgia
Arlis D. Edgar*	OS; 19; U.S. ; Mother; Hemphill, Texas
Herman V. Barker*	AB Seaman; 36; U. S.; Brother; Port Arthur, Texas
Frank J. Kroy*	AB Seaman; 43; U.S.; Wife; Port Arthur, Texas
Charles Rivette*+	OS; 20; U.S.; Father: Port Arthur, Texas
Charlie P. Sistrunk*	OS; 18; U. S.; Father; Mitchell, Louisiana
Joseph F. Boyd*	OS; 24; U.S.; Mother; Woonsocket, Rhode Island
Arthur J. Genter*+	Oiler; 41; U.S.; Sister; Evansville, Indiana
Stanley J. Majba*	Fireman; 21; U. S.: Father; Cambridge Spring, Pennsylvania
Lastie Hance*	Fireman; 38; U.S.; Father; Oberlin, Louisiana
James E. Mott*	Fireman; 26; U.S.; Father; Glenmore, Louisiana
Alfredo Cormona*+	Wiper; 46; Puerto Rico; Friend, Ms. Torress; Tampa, Florida
Joseph W. Geary*+	2nd Cook; 36; U.S.; Father; Providence, Rhode Island
Matthias J. Chorman*	Messman; 20; U.S.; Mother; Fort Wadsworth, S.I.N.Y.
James Riley*	Messman; 31; U.S. Friend; New York, New York
William L. Howell*	2nd Engineer; 33; U.S.; Wife; Port Arthur, Texas; (died in lifeboat from wounds received from flying metal..body recovered)
Osswald Ryder*+	Messman; 21; U.S.; Father; Ville Platte, Louisiana
Richard Dooley*	Utility; 22; U.S.; Father; Colorado Springs, Colorado

The Brunswick News: April 14, 1942

People Thanked for Aid Given Many Survivors

Mayor J. Hunter Hopkins today received a letter from W. B. Kimball, agent, marine department, Standard Oil Company of New Jersey, with headquarters in Jacksonville, extending through him on behalf of the officers and members of the crew of a merchant ship who were brought here after being torpedoed in the Atlantic, thanks for the very fine treatment accorded the survivors while they were here. The letter said:

"On behalf of the officers and men in the contingent of those crew members who were rescued from one of the ill fated American vessels owned and operated by the Standard Oil Company of New Jersey that met with disaster off your shore, I wish to express the highest commendation for the extreme kindness rendered by the citizens of your city.

Each one of the rescued has expressed gratitude at the attention which was given their every want by the citizens of Brunswick. In particular I would like to especially thank Mrs. C. W. Lane, who operates the Monte Vista Lodge, who, in her desire to be of help, offered rooms and meals for those distressed seamen. Such a display by your citizens is the spirit that has made this country the greatest on each, and it is that same spirit that will keep us there.

It makes me proud to pass on to you the thanks of these men, who are representative of American merchantmen generally and who themselves are deserving for their own gallantry."

Words of praise have been showered from other quarters on the people of this city for their kindness and courtesies to the survivors of two vessels who were landed here last week. Not only did the captains of the two vessels personally urge that The News thank the people for them, but practically every survivor made the same request.

S. S. ESPARTA
(The *SS Esparta* was sunk off the coast of Cumberland Island on April 9, 1942)

Memorandum

Subject: Summary of Statements of Survivors, *SS Esparta*, American Steam Freighter, United Fruit Company.

1. The 3,365 gross ton *SS Esparta*, was torpedoed without warning at 0115 EWT on April 9, 1942 twelve miles S.E. of the buoy at St. Simons' Sound (30.46 N-81.11 W. midnight position). Several hours after the attack, the stern of the ship was resting on the bottom with a 35 degree starboard list. The bow and the top of the bridge remained above water. *(note: This was off Stafford Shoals off Cumberland Island)*

2. The *Esparta* was en route from Puerto Cortez, Honduras, to New York with a cargo of bananas, coffee and miscellaneous goods. She was on course 12 true, 14.5 knots not zigzagging, completely blacked out, radio not used. Three lookouts were on watch, the Chief Officer and 2nd Officer on the bridge and an A.B. on the bow. The weather was clear, sea slight, visibility poor due to extreme darkness.

3. The ship was struck on the starboard side of the # 4 hatch after of amidships, depth unknown. Nos. 3 and 4 hatch covers were blown off, the port beam badly damaged, the starboard side damaged, and a small fire was started at the point of impact. The force of the explosion released 1,200 pounds of ammonia gas used in the ship's refrigerating system and the fumes forced several men to jump overboard. The ship listed 10 degrees to the starboard and began to sink rapidly by the stern. Distress signals were sent and acknowledged. The codes were thrown overboard in a weighted bag. The Esparta was not armed.

4. Nos. 1 and 3 starboard lifeboats and the forward life raft were used to abandon ship which occurred within ten minutes of the time of attack. The Master and radio operator jumped overboard later and were picked up by the life raft and later transferred to a lifeboat. Thirty-nine of the crew of forty were rescued 7 hours later by the Navy Crash Boat, *U.S.S. Tyrer*. One member became panic stricken and drowned.

5. The submarine was seen only indistinctly. It appeared about 15 minutes after the attack about one-eighth to one-quarter of a mile north northeast of the ship. It was described as large, from 150 to 300 feet long with conning tower 8 to 15 feet tall. Several members of the crew saw a dim blinking light on the submarine at the top of the conning tower. It disappeared at about 0130 EWT. While en route to pick up survivors, the *U.S.S. Tyrer* reported seeing a submarine close to shore in 25 feet of water. The craft when challenged did not answer but proceeded northward at a speed exceeding 20 knots. It was described as about 300 feet long with very little superstructure. The Inshore Patrol Boat YP-31 reported locating a submarine by sound in the vicinity of the *Esparta* several hours after the attack. Two depth charges were dropped but failed to explode since the water was less than 50 feet deep, the minimum depth at which the charged could be set. Planes were in the vicinity, but could not be attracted since the YP-31 could not communicate by radio or signal to them.

It was suggested that separate lanes for north and south bound shipping be established since there was a greater fear of collisions than of being torpedoed. It was also suggested that life preservers be placed at strategic points on deck where they can quickly be obtained.

Additional Information on U-boats

The German submarine base used for the launching of patrols to the United States was located in France on the Bay of Biscay.

Middlebrook, Martin. *Convoy*. New York. William Morrow and Company, Inc. c. 1976
Permission to use the following text given by author, Martin Middlebrook, Boston, Lincolnshire, England.

p. 12 : "One basic aspect of the battle for merchant shipping should be stressed. Britain's island position meant that all of her oil, most of her raw materials and much of her food had to be imported. The Germans were never strong enough at sea to impose a complete blockade, and so the campaign between the U-boats and the merchant ships of Britain, and eventually the ships of a growing number of Allies, was essentially a campaign of attrition of shipping tonnage. When a German U-boat captain torpedoed and sank an Allied merchant ship, he had not only destroyed that ship, the cargo it carried and probably some of its crew—the British Empire and America had more than enough men, war material and civilian supplies to crush Germany. What the U-boat captain had achieved was to deny the Allies the opportunity of transporting many more cargoes to the vital war theaters in that vessel on later voyages. The Germans called it 'The Tonnage War'. If more ships could be sunk than the Allied shipyards could replace with new construction, the German would inevitably achieve a tightening stranglehold on Britain's supplies.

If this had happened in that period before Pearl Harbor when Britain stood alone in Europe, Britain would have fallen however great the courage of her people. If the U-boats had strangled Britain in 1942 or 1943, there would have been no base for the Anglo-America invasion of Europe in 1944. In either instance the history of our times would have been immeasurably altered.

p.13-14: It would be appropriate to examine here the manner in which the Germans observed International Law on submarine warfare. Germany had signed the 1935 London Submarine Agreement in which all parties undertook to observe the rule of the Hague Convention. These rules laid down that a submarine must first stop its intended victim, then order its crew to take to the boats and, after sinking the ship, ensure that the lifeboats had the capacity for the entire crew. The rules would also apply to defensively-armed merchant ships, but not to ships in convoy.

In September 1939 Hitler ordered that these rules should be observed, hoping that Britain and France would not be unduly antagonized and might come to terms after Poland's defeat. But it is almost certain that the German Navy had made up its mind to be rid of these restrictions as soon as possible. The use by the merchant ship of its radio while the U-boat was giving the required warning would endanger the U-boat, and the responsibility for taking surplus survivors on board the U-boat would be a reduction in its ability to continue operations. When the *Athenia* was torpedoed and sunk the first day of the war, no warning was given and 110 of her civilian passengers and eighteen crew members were drowned. Oberleutnant Lemp afterwards claimed that he had identified *Athenia* as an armed merchant cruiser; no action against him was taken by his superiors, but the sinking had brought Germany much unfavorable publicity in neutral countries. On the day following *Athenia's* sinking, signals were sent to U-boats ordering that the agreed rules must be observed and, by Hitler's personal order, no more passenger ships were to be sunk even if in convoy.

This was a good start, within three months the German Navy had persuaded Hitler to drop all restrictions on attacks against all vessels identified as hostile; neutral countries were also warned that their ships would be attacked without warning in all areas around Britain....

Hitler's eventual approval of the admirals' policy marked the end of the short period during which agreements on submarine warfare had been honored and some degree of mercy had been shown to the merchant sailors. For the next five-and-a-half years there would be no such protection for them.

It should be recorded, however, that there were to be instances of U-boat captains helping survivors..

"Admiral Donitz never ordered us to shoot survivors. We had a clear order, which we always complied with as far as conditions allowed, to help survivors but they must not be brought on board. We ourselves certainly met English survivors in the North Atlantic and gave them food and cans of water. We even sent a signal giving their position. There was always the chance that our own boat would be sunk one day." (Funkgefreiter Werner Hess, U.530)

p. 16 : Admiral Donitz, commander of the German submarine arm, had discovered while commanding a First World War U-boat in the Mediterranean that a U-boat on the surface at night was almost invisible and, being able to use its air-breathing diesel engines, could travel fast. He had found little difficulty in getting through a convoy's screen of escorts and sometimes right into the convoy itself, calmly aiming and firing his torpedoes at the merchant ships all around and then making his escape at speed on the surface or by submerging.

...Donitz had always intended that the night attack on the surface should be the ultimate U-boat tactic.

p. 23: America's participation in the war would eventually bring immense reinforcement to the Allied cause and opened the way to final victory but, initially, the effect on the sea war was catastrophic. The Japanese attack on Pearl Harbor surprised the Germans, but they declared war on the United States a few days later without any apparent thought of the consequences. Donitz was quick to see the opportunity presented by the vast amount of unconvoyed shipping that sailed along the American Atlantic Coast and sent six of his new long-range boats to this area in January 1942. The U-boat captains were delighted. **The American coastal cities had no blackout; buoys and beacons were still lit; there appeared to be no effective anti-submarine patrols; ships were not sailing in convoy.** The second Happy Time had begun.

The next six months were to be disastrous ones. Although the American coast was 3,500 sea miles from the Biscay bases, the Germans were able to assemble and maintain there a force averaging eight U-boats, partly by the use of tanker U-boats. The way the American authorities reacted seems, in retrospect, to be almost criminal. Despite the fact that there had been an American Naval Mission at the Admiralty since August 1940 and that the members of the Mission had studied every development of Britain's U-boat war, the United States Navy seemed determined not to follow British methods. No attempt was made to form convoys, and the few available anti-submarine vessels were sent on the offensive sweeps that the British had found such a waste of time. It was not until April (1942) that the civilian authorities imposed a coastal blackout. Not a single U-boat was sunk for three months.

The British were not well pleased by the American failure to profit from the hard-earned British experience...

The U-boats men's Happy Time ran to the end of May 1942. There are no separate figures for sinkings off the American coast, but in these five months 362 Allied merchant ships were lost to U-boats and already the tonnage sunk exceeded the U-boat successes for the whole of 1941. The entire effort of the United States Navy off its own coast in these five months resulted in the sinking of just one U-boat, while a Coast Guard cutter had sunk a second...

In the end the United States Navy abandoned its sweeps, gathered together the available anti-submarine vessels, including some loaned by the British, and set up a convoy system. Immediately, the sinkings slackened off and more U-boats were sunk.

p 59: ...The Majority of the 1943 U-boat captains were men who had been junior naval officers on the outbreak of war and had served on all types of naval vessels from torpedo boats to battleships; many had been seconded to the Luftwaffe as observers in maritime reconnaissance squadrons. These men had then been drawn into the expanding U-boat arm in the heady days of 1940 and 1941, had sailed on at least two operational patrols as watch officers in other U-boats, and then attended a captain's course before taking over their own newly commissioned boat with a new crew. A few of the captains were older men who had been brought in from the merchant service or had been instructors at U-boat schools; these last were reckoned by their crews to be good men to serve under, as they had managed to amass a considerable submarine experience in safe waters. But most of the captains were in their twenties, were tremendously loyal to Hitler and to Donitz, felt greatly honoured to be in U-boats, and were delighted with the responsibility of command in a ship whose operations allowed so much scope for individual initiative. They wore with pride the white cap cover allowed only to captains of ships and thus giving them a status that could not be claimed by many officers far senior to them in rank. The U-Boat captains were the elite of the German Navy.

When you were on a big ship you were a nobody but when you were captain of a U-boat, if you had the confidence of your crew, you were almost a God. (Kapitanleutnant Kurt Neide, U.415)

p. 133-134: Many of the U-boats that had been on patrol for some time were in need of refueling. It was quite normal for a U-boat to operate well beyond its own fuel capacity; this was a great act of faith in the U-boat Headquarters staff officers who controlled the tanker U-boats or 'milch-cows' as they were known. There were two of these on station, U.119 which was a Type XB, really a minelayer but converted for tanker work and U.463, a Type XIV purpose-built tanker. These two had taken up position in the Air Gap just north of the normal convoy routes. Operational U-boats always added a small coded message to every signal to U-boat Headquarters indicating their fuel stocks in cubic metres. The condition of every boat was watched carefully and they were ordered to rendezvous with a tanker U-boat whenever fuel ran low. Both of the tanker U-boats were busy now in this interval between convoy operations. It was a great test of navigation and seamanship to find the tanker, float across fuel pipes supported by life jackets, take on fuel, provisions and essential stores and then get out of the way before the next U-boat was due.

Notes from Chapter Four: Civilian Volunteers

The Brunswick News. October 7, 1941

GOVERNOR ASKS CIVILIAN AID IN AIR ATTACK

Gov. Eugene Talmadge wants civilians to enlist in the state air raid warning service, saying that unless observation posts were established by October 30 army maneuvers scheduled in eastern and central Georgia might be canceled.

The Brunswick News. January 1, 1942

CITY NOW PREPARING FOR FIRST BLACKOUT
Every Effort Being Made to Notify All Residents About It

Tomorrow night at 9:30 o'clock whistles will blow and sirens will screech!

In short blasts the people will be given an air raid warning; a practice one, of course, and thereafter if another such warning is heard, it probably will be the real thing.
When the whistles blow and the sirens open up tomorrow night, it means that the city must immediately become dark....
...Here are the simplest rules which the people are urged to study:
- Immediately upon hearing the danger signal all lights should be extinguished.
- Automobile drivers who are on the streets in their cars should pull over to the curbing and put out the lights.
- Pedestrians should take cover in the nearest safe place.
- Occupants of all homes or business houses should turn out all lights or cover the windows with light-proof material.
- Streets should be kept clear for emergency traffic, which must travel without lights.
- Don't smoke in open or display any light whatsoever.

The Brunswick News. January 7, 1942

STATE AIR RAID WARDENS TO GET ORDERS MONDAY

The first general order for Georgia air raid wardens to assume their posts will be issued Monday, the State Defense Committee announced in Atlanta today.
The order will affect all counties in southwest Georgia and the eastern section of middle Georgia.
...The wardens will be ordered to man their posts and then report to the county headquarters for further orders..

The Brunswick News. February 19, 1942

AIR RAID SIRENS BEING INSTALLED

Eight air raid sirens, donated to the city by Franklin Horne of Sea Island, have arrived in the city and are now being installed at strategic points in the various sections of the city. As soon as they are all in position, they will be given a test.
Ten more of the sirens, donated to the county by Mr. Horne, will also be installed at various points in the county. All of them will be controlled by one switch in the city in order that they can be sounded simultaneously.

Notes from Chapter Five: The Georgia State Guard

The Georgia State Defense Corps, The Georgia State Guard

The Georgia State Defense Corps was established in 1940 by Governor Eugene Talmadge with Headquarters in Atlanta after it appeared that the Georgia National Guard elements of the 30th Infantry Division and other units would be Federalized. The initial strength authorized for the Corps was 6,000 officers and men, and a total of 2,955 officers and 3,000 men were mustered by September 19, 1940. The Defense Corps was originally organized into three major area divisions with twenty-five districts, and two additional districts were later added to the Corps. On December 10, 1941, Governor Talmadge issued a proclamation and ordered the entire State Defense Corps to active duty. In addition to guarding key railroad bridges, public utilities, and installation, **Corpsmen performed coast-watch duty from Tybee Light in the north to Cumberland Island in the south.** An interesting aspect of the State Defense Corps activation was that militia members were placed under the direct command of (then) Brigadier General Omar Bradley who was the Commanding General at Fort Benning, Georgia. Detailed secret plans were prepared dividing the state into two defense zones along interior lines from Okefenokee Swamp to Savannah, and the Corps was assigned the mission of "engaging enemy raiding parties and invading forces." **To the members of the Defense Corps who patrolled the beaches along the Georgia coast during the early months of 1942, the war seemed very close. Explosions could be heard far out at sea, and waves washed bodies, debris, and lifeboats up on the shore revealing evidence of ships blasted into bits by German torpedoes. Utilizing private yachts and other craft, the Defense Corps patrolled the Sea Islands along the Georgia coast while an Aviation Section of the Corps provided air support.** In addition to the districts which were organized along county lines, a total of 297 "Units" were activated throughout the states. Units were designated by their location and numbered from 1 to 197 in the order that they were formed such as Fargo Unit # 54, Waycross Unit # 72, Waycross Unit # 241, **Brunswick Unit # 262**, etc. Records were not available to indicate when the Defense Force was redesignated, but it is believed that this was accomplished early in 1942 as a document dated May 3rd of that year has a "Georgia State Guard" letterhead. Documentation regarding the shoulder patch worn by the Georgia Defense Corps could not be located, but the insignia was clearly visible on the left shoulder of a militiaman in a newspaper dated December 14, 1941.

The Georgia State Guard was established upon the redesignation of the Georgia Defense Corps with no change in Headquarters location. The Guard underwent a major reorganization in 1943 and replaced the district and numbered unit designations with battalions and lettered companies. For example, Carrollton Unit # 95 of District 16 (Columbus) became "P" company of the 3rd Battalion. A total of 20 battalions were inactivated, and the mustered strength of the Guard increased to over 11,000. At the time the State Guard was inactivated on April 21, 1947, the authorized strength was established at 9,700 officers and men. Except for training exercises, no record could be found of any State Guard activities...*Shoulder Sleeve Insignia of the U.S. Armed Forces, 1941-1945"*

In a letter dated August 6, 1940, Ryburn G. Clay, Commanding Officer of the State Defense Corps, appointed James D. Gould, Jr. as Unit Commander of Glynn County with the rank of Captain. J. M. Exley was Commander of the 23rd District which included Glynn County.

The following letter from James D. Gould, Jr. verifies the organization of the Glynn County unit with a roster of personnel.

August 6, 1940

Honorable J. D. Gould
Brunswick, Georgia

Dear Sir:

You have been appointed Unit Commander of Glynn County, State Defense Corps, with the rank of Captain. We deeply appreciate your acceptance of this appointment.

You will be advised within a few days of the date on which an organization meeting of your district will be held, at which time all appointees will be officially sworn in.

Please fill out and have notarized the enclosed enlistment record and return to this headquarters as soon as possible in order that our records may be complete.

In the meantime, if we may be of service to you in any way, do not hesitate to call on us.

Sincerely,

Ryburn G. Clay
Commanding Officer

RGC:mg
Encl:

ROSTER:

Ralph Henning Moureau
1413 Sycamore Ave., Brunswick, Ga.

Edward Hewes Messick
P.O. Box 16, St. Simons Island, Ga.

Villard Hopkins Royal
1017 Union St., Brunswick, Ga.

Jonathan McKay Armstrong
1201 Union St., Brunswick, Ga.

Robert Sommerkamp Browne
No. 2 Brunswick Manor, Brunswick, Ga.

Augustus Myddelton Harris
710 Carpenter St., Brunswick, Ga.

Jesse Norman Parham
801 Union St., Brunswick, Ga.

Carl Henry Smith
St. Simons Island, GA.

Robert Vort Tait
808 Dartmouth St. Brunswick, Ga.

Kennard Shields Trowbridge
1210 Pine Street, Brunswick, Ga.

John Christian Kaufman
1714 Norwich St., Brunswick, Ga.

Hoyt William Brown
1819 Niles Ave., Brunswick, Ga.

Isaac Means Aiken
802 London St., Brunswick, Ga.

Aubrey Raleigh Bates
c/o Western Union, Brunswick, Ga.

Edward Herbert Diemmer
Talmadge Ave., Brunswick, Ga.

Walter Simon Nathan
1804 Gloucester St., Brunswick, Ga.

Allen Thurman Ross
Darien Road, Brunswick, Ga.

John Carl Strother
P.O. Box 128, St. Simons Island, Ga.

Paul Nelson Thomas
803 Gordon St., Brunswick, Ga.

Norman Alexander Way
Sycamore Ave., Windsor Park, Brunswick, Ga.

A letter dated August 28, 1940, recommends the appointment of the following men as officers and non-commissioned officers:
   First Lieutenant: Ralph Moureau
   First Sergeant: John Christian Kaufman
   Sergeant: Edward Hewes Messick
   Corporal: Hoyt W. Brown and Villard Hopkins Royal

As the organization continued and members were added, the Medical Detachment consisted of:
   Dr. Millard Winchester, Dr. Paul Killian and Dr Willis.

A second Defense Unit was formed in August of 1941 on St. Simons Island and eventually Glynn County had four Units.

The Brunswick News, July 23, 1941

GENERAL HERE TO ARRANGE FOR CAMP

General E. F. Wood, stationed at Fort Benning, Columbus, is in the city making preliminary plans for an officers' training school for the Georgia State Guard on this district to be held on St. Simons early in August.

General Wood announced a few weeks ago that the training camp would be conducted for all officers of the local district, and he came here to confer with Major James. D. Gould, commander of the district. Full details regarding the camp will be announced shortly, it was stated.

An Article
by
Dr. Louie Devotie Newton*

Sapelo Island, Ga.   Aug. 8, 1942

Louie Newton was a journalist before he became a Baptist minister. He was an Army Reserve Chaplain during W.W.II and was appointed chief chaplain of the Georgia State Guard in 1942. He received a certificate of appreciation in 1943, signed by Gov. Ellis Arnall & M.E. Thompson.

Major, Georgia State Guard
Chief of Chaplains

Two hundred years ago, General James Oglethorpe successfully repelled the enemy along the Golden Isles of Georgia in notable battles at Bloody Marsh, Frederica and elsewhere. For the past week Brigadier General Eric Fisher Wood, U. S. Army, stationed at Fort Benning, and Instructor of the Georgia State Guard, directed quite successfully the First Command Post Exercise of the 27 districts of the Georgia State Guard, and the Field and Staff School which followed on Sapelo Island, one of the Golden Isles of Georgia's coastline.

Colonel Lindley W. Camp, Commanding Officer of the Georgia State Guard, **Lieut. Colonel O.C. Waters**, Chief of Staff, and a number of high ranking Army officers, declared this first Field and Staff school a highly satisfactory step in the program of final training for the men who are directing the more than 10,000 members of the State Guard.

The commanding officers of the 27 districts, with a few chosen officers from their respective commands, began their trek towards the coast last Sunday afternoon, August 2, sleeping on the ground at night, and cooking their meals with field equipment. During this CPX, they went through five situations of combat, converging upon Santo Domingo state park, between Brunswick and Darien, on schedule, on Tuesday afternoon, where they were received by General Wood and Colonel Camp.

They proceeded to Sapelo Island, transported by the Georgia State Guard fleet, commanded by **Captain C. Howard Candler, Jr.** and his staff of pilots, composed of **Captain Chas. H. King** and **Lieutenants Olaf Olsen, Frank Horne, Robert Ferst,** and **Newell Ward.**

Sapelo Island, now the estate of R .J. Reynolds, of Winston-Salem, and at present an officer in the Navy, has been placed at the disposal of the State Guard and the U. S. Government. The spacious buildings composing the residence, shop, garage, barns and hanger proved a perfect setting for the week of training for the 140 student officers and the school troops of some 60 officers and enlisted men. The Darien unit of the McIntosh county guardsmen had charge of the canteen, under the command of Captain W. H. Graham. A detail from the 725th M. P. Company, Fourth Corps Area troops, served as interior guard.

Captain Robert Stevens, commanding Company G of the 104th Infantry of the "Yankee Division", on duty at Brunswick, supplied the cooks and rations for the week, and every man present will join me in testifying that they really gave us a grand supply of food.

Brigadier General Wood is the easiest big man to interview I have ever encountered in my newspaper career, and I think I know the reason. The General is really sold on the Georgia State Guard. I had been with him more or less all day Thursday, observing with unspeakable admiration his ability to command the maneuvers through which he put us on the rifle and pistol ranges, the air patrols, and so forth.

Colonel Camp suggested to the General that he wanted to prepare a story for the press, and the General welcomed the suggestion. He told me how he had discovered the merit of the Georgia guardsmen from the moment he assumed the role of instructor and advisor. He declared the morale and efficiency of the Georgia State Guard to be par excellence.

"The Georgia State Guard is the finest set of Americans I have met in a long while," began General Wood, "And I go on to say that Georgia has the finest State Guard of any of the eight states in the Fourth Corps Area, and is probably rivaled in the nation only by Massachusetts, Washington and one or two others; and I doubt if either of these states excels Georgia in the efficiency and morale of its State Guard.

I cannot overstate my sense of appreciation for the work of Colonel Lindley W. Camp towards organizing and developing this wonderful outfit of men who mean more to your state and to the nation than the public perhaps realizes. I heartily congratulate Georgia upon its State Guard. This week of special training for these key officers is a further step in getting Georgia ready for any crisis that may await us."

With this shove-off, the General leaned forward across the table in the quarters building where we talked far into the night, and told me why this State Guard is so vitally important at this very moment, and why every other state needs a similar army of trained men to deal with what is ahead of us.

"When you were in that plane this afternoon with Captain Winover, what did you see?", said the General, his keen eyes fairly piercing my inner thoughts. "You saw the unspeakably beautiful island beneath you, with the many small lakes and keys that form a festoon-like coastline, and then you saw the expanse of open sea. I want you to think now about that open sea, and I want you to think about the stretch of coastline from Cape Hatteras to Palm Beach - one vast open door to attack of an enemy.

"More than that, I want you to think of our cities along this stretch of open coastline, not only the important cities immediately on the coast, such as Savannah, Jacksonville, Brunswick, Miami, Charleston, and so forth, everyone of them within reach of possible attacks from this open coastline - the possibility of which anyone must admit who will study his map and acquaint himself with the tactics of the present war."

The General went on to interpret what lies behind the Hitler technique. He told how Hitler, from the beginning of his mad determination to conquer the world, had adopted the precepts of Frederick the Great as his military Bible. The precepts of Frederick the Great are found in that code of rules and that military philosophy, composed and released in 1747, and known as "Instructions to My Generals."

What did Frederick say in these rules? I cannot fully state them within the limits of this necessarily abbreviated report of my interview with General Wood. But, in a word or two, those rules and that philosophy involved such salient points and principles as:

"Defensive operations are not practicable....I prefer the temerity of the offensive, even at the hazard of losing a battle....Strike at the enemy's rear, or surprise him in his base camp, or knife his communications with his home country by a surprise forced march....For the offensive I require a general to examine the enemy's frontier, and to wage a war of ruses and chicanery. Ruses of war are of great usefulness. Their object is to hide your veritable design from the enemy and thereby to catch him in the trap you have prepared for him....His self-confidence becomes your accomplice; false security lulls him, so that your coming may triumph.

"Above all, one must study the country against which he is going to act. The most detailed and exact maps must be obtained. The cities are visited, your own camp sites are chosen ahead of time, the roads are examined, the mayors and butchers and farmers are talked to....It is necessary to hide your secret intention with the most specious pretexts that you are able to invent.

"The best spies that one can have are members of the enemy's staff(Major Quisling), or even the servants of the enemy's general. Prince Eugene bribed the postmaster at Versailles, who thereafter opened the dispatches which went to the French army and sent him copies thereof....If greed for silver does not work, it is necessary to employ fear. In general it is necessary to pay spies well. A man who risks being hung in your service merits being paid well....To make your plans against a city without knowing how it is constructed within and without, is like ordering a tailor to make a suit without knowing if the man is tall or short, fat or thin, etc., etc."

General Wood leaned a bit nearer and said:

" It is manifest that Hitler has complied with Frederick's precepts, as far as they go. Hitler, the new prophet of German ruthlessness, has added a very important new element to the technique of Fifth Column work as compared with its older prophet Frederick. Frederick assigned his Fifth Column a mission that might also be called a sociological one. It operated without arms, by persuasion and bribery. It committed no overt acts either before or during the attack."

"Hitler immensely reinforced his Fifth Columns, and assigned them an additional mission - a tactical one. He thereby invented one of the important 'tactical surprises' of military history. Hitler's Fifth Columns assume combat duties. Not infrequently they have been reinforced by small detachments of parachute troopers, trained and heavily armed."

Their tactical actions include:

"Sabotage of commercial telephone communications. Assassination of leaders of Government and of the Army. Demolition of important bridges...Sniping at soldiers and at officers of the law. Dissemination of false alarms and of false orders, by Fifth Columnists disguised as policemen, soldiers, officers of the Army, Navy, etc. Sabotage of airplanes and Army motor vehicles. Demolition of ammunition and gasoline depots. Particular attention to industrial installations for the manufacture and distribution of war materials - to protect them if Hitler means to incorporate the country into his empire, to destroy them if his strategical mission is one of neutralizing the country's war efforts."

The General shifted quickly in his chair and asked me if I was following him - if I saw what he was coming to. I tried to reassure him, and he proceeded:

"So much for the technique, pro and con. What, if any, prospect is there of its becoming applicable in the general area in which we are operating - to that part of our country which lies along and behind the Atlantic seaboard from Cape Hatteras to Key West?

We must admit two things. First, that if Hitler continues to follow Frederick's precepts, his future points of attack, like all his past ones, will be selected from among the places (a) where damage to the cause of the Allied Nations may be attained, (b) where his spying has been completed, and (c) where his arrival is totally unexpected. Risk will not deter him. On the contrary they may invite his psychopathic 'institutions'. Norway, at the time it was attacked, fitted our three-point formula perfectly. The risk of attacking it did not deter Hitler.

We must admit, in the second place, that our Atlantic seaboard area appears to fit the above three-point prescription. In particular, the population of this area (in spite of specific warnings from President Roosevelt and his aides) leans towards an attitude of incredulity as to the possibility of German raids or attacks." General Wood then proceeded to outline, in overwhelming logic, the lines along which Hitler may attack the Atlantic coastline from Cape Hatteras to the tip of Florida. He described devastating havoc of Hitler's submarines along our coastline. And that statement brought to mind the ship we had watched Thursday afternoon, crawling along close to the shore of Sapelo Island.

He then described the surface war craft of Hitler - how his naval aircraft carriers may even now be lurking in the Atlantic, capable of transporting the airplane support for a naval or military task-force convoy. He told of a reserve of fast transports, capable of 20 knots an hour, of shallow draft, that might land hand-picked storm troopers with arms, including light tanks and artillery.

"We know," said General Wood, "that Hitler already has heavy bombardment planes that can carry a pay load of bombs for upwards of 4,000 miles. We suspect that he may have better planes designed or in production. Manifestly, he could bombard our Atlantic coast if he were willing to sacrifice his planes, and remember that Hitler has never hesitated to sacrifice either equipment or men. We see that illustrated in his present Russian campaign."

"At certain parts of this coast, say from Jacksonville to Parris Island, it is probably within his physical capabilities to attempt a coordinated simultaneous group of raids by sea-borne commando forces of all arms (by no means excluding carrier-borne pursuit aviation and paratroops), to include rapid penetrations of considerable depth into the interior behind the coast, with missions to demolish vital industrial and transportation installations. Integrated, of course, with concurrent support by teams of Fifth Columnists."

"We stick to the rule of not trying to guess at what the enemy has on his mind. We do not predict that Hitler will do any of the above things. We merely state that in our personal opinion, as a result of our personal estimate of the situation, Hitler CAN do one or more of the above things."

"If we plan on that basis, to include psychological preparations for the events, we cannot go far wrong."

The General then talked slowly and emphatically, measuring his words, and driving the meaning of them indelibly upon my memory, and I hope they will find such lodgement in the minds of my readers. Here are his words: "What obligations does this indicate for the Georgia State Guard, for the Civilian Defense forces and for the industrialists?"

"The Soldier of the Zone of the Interior needs to be prepared to hem in and destroy these highly mobile gangs that Hitler may land on our coast, by seizing with combat outposts a net of critical traffic bottlenecks, while combining with combat patrols the inside of the net. The most important, and potentially the most effective Soldier of the Zone of the Interior is the State Guardsman; because his units are, in effect, already deployed; and after assembling promptly at their home stations, are capable of moving out as outposts and patrols in their own vicinity with a minimum of time-lag."

"Second, the Civilian Defense man and woman must be prepared to conduct the passive defense, particularly against air bombardment. They must put out the fires, clear the streets of debris, help suppress the opportunist criminals, control the panic stricken citizen, dig out the maimed and bury the dead. They take the punching, with their hands tied against 'dishing it out'. They are the 'holding force' that is foredoomed to punishment, in order that all the planes and all the antiaircraft regiments and all the combat divisions may go the main attack in Australia or China or Northern Ireland or wherever our high command has decided that it shall be. For all we know, they may be fated to follow in the footsteps of the English civilians of London and of Coventry who said, 'We can take it'; and we must be organized to 'take it'. or WE LOSE THE WAR."

"And, third, the Industrialist must mobilize his own resources, by arming and rehearsing a part of his own workmen as Minute Men to defend his installations against sudden raids".

Thus ended the interview, and I knew I had listened to a man talk who knew what he was talking about. I realized as never before how important it is for those of us in the State Guard to be ready - how important it is for the Civilian Defense to be ready - how important it is for the Industrialist to be ready - how important it is for this country to be ready.

And, as I sit here, far into the night, writing this story, I can hear the drone of the patrol planes as they scour this coastline watching for submarines, for commandos, for anything that looks like the enemy; and I can also hear the roar of a thunder storm out at sea. The flashes of forked lightning seem to engrave yet more deeply in my mind what General Wood said to me tonight.

But I am more confident tonight than I have been for some weeks about the final outcome of this thing, and this renewed confidence stems from what I have seen and heard at Sapelo Island this week. Never have I seen a group of Georgians as deeply determined about anything in my life as these 200 men in this outfit. They represent about as fine a cross-section of Georgians as one could ever hope to assemble. Let me reinforce that rather strong statement by giving here the list of district commanders of the State Guard:

Major Frank Fling, Atlanta; Major A. L. Crowe, Marietta; Lieut. Colonel Wm.. P. Welchel, Gainesville; Major Paul H. Ponder, Madison; Major Scott Candler, Decatur; Major John M. Puerifoy, Griffin; Major Harry G. Thornton, Elberton; Major Cliff C. Kimsey, Cornelia; Major Clarence C. Hill, Dalton; Major Paul Hodges, Americus; Major J. H. Clark, Thomasville; Major Samuel A. Nunn, Perry; Major Marcus C. Balkcom, Macon; Major Levi Smith, Albany; Major H. B. Peas, Columbus; Major Hatton Lovejoy, LaGrange; Major Henry S. Wootten, Milledgeville; Major Thad J. Morris, Statesboro; Major John B. Spivey, Swainsboro; Major Lee S. Purdom, Blackshear; Major George Haines, Augusta; Major George A. Rice, Savannah; **Major James D. Gould, Jr., Brunswick;** Major M. A. Chapman, Dublin; Major G. C. McKenzie, Ashburn; Major J. L. Newbern, Valdosta; and Lieut. Colonel Mark A. Cooper, Rome.

When I look at these 27 district commanders and think of all the officers in their respective units, and all the men composing their ranks, I know we have 10,000 Georgians in the State Guard who will face the tasks at hand and ahead without fear or compromise.

And when I listen to men like General Wood and Colonel Camp and Lieutenant Colonel Waters, I know that we have a leadership that will take us through. And I must add here the names of the outstanding corps of Army officers who have served as instructors in this Field School. They have done a swell job. They are Lieut. Colonel Reginald H. Wood, Colonel Herbert E. Mann, Lieut. Colonel John H. Milan, Lieut. Colonel Herbert D. Mendenhall, Major Raymond C. Blatt and Major Ralph A. Glatt.

Major Thos. P. Goodwyn, Atlanta, leads the medical work, ably assisted by Captains H.D. Allen, Milledgeville; Thomas Harrold, Macon; N.J. Newsom, Sandersville; and Lieutenants J. D. Applewhite, Macon; B.L. Helton, Sandersville; and F.C. Wilson, Valdosta.

I could start from here and write another story about Sapelo Island - its surpassing beauty as represented in the majestic live oaks, the flowers, the lakes, the groves of satsuma, the fields of corn, the turkeys, the deer, the birds, the cattle, and the grand old house in which I sit and write tonight, the open sea and all. But before I got to all these things on Sapelo, including the glorious sunrises and sunsets, I would have to write about Frank Durant, Mr. Reynold's caretaker, and Louie Olsen, his assistant and the 200 natives, mostly Negroes. To hear the dialect of these Negroes, well, it is a story in itself.

But all this belongs to another day.

We are at war - a war that calls for sacrifice, and the beauties of Sapelo will be here, when we shall have won this war, and Freedom is reassured for the peoples of our Father's world.

Georgia State Archives - Lamar Q. Ball Collection - World War II

Atlanta Constitution, Sunday, August 30, 1942

GEORGIA STATE GUARD IS READY

by Lindley W. Camp, Colonel, Georgia State Guard, Commander.

"When war came to this nation in the midst of a peaceful Sunday afternoon, it found many parts of the country and many defense organizations unprepared.

There was one notable exception. Within two days, member of the State Defense Corps, now changed to Georgia State Guard, were in uniforms, armed, and on duty to what Army officials termed vital and sensitive points in Georgia.

Within a few days, they enlarged their sphere of duty, at the express request of high authorities, so that ensuing days saw units on duty literally from Rabun Gap to Tybee Light, guarding sensitive and vital points against acts of sabotage, such as had proved so hurtful in other countries in the opening days of hostilities.

Relieved Combat Forces

By these efforts, the State Guard was able directly to aid the nation by relieving combat forces of the U. S. Army for other duties. Today, not a single soldier of the U. S. Army is guarding a single sensitive and vital installation in Georgia.

When this first call for duty came, the officers and men of the Georgia State Guard, went in the service unquestioningly and without thought of their own interest, knowing only that their country had been attacked suddenly and savagely by a barbarous enemy and that their services were needed.

Today, the same spirit of patriotism is manifesting itself throughout the entire organization. The force consists of 11,054 officers and men divided into 27 districts under district commanders with 291 units in 159 counties in Georgia, without pay except when on active duty and performing guard duties in addition to regular duties of making a living.

These guardsmen have been training under direction and supervision of regular Army officers. Recently, a command post exercise was undertaken and successfully performed that extended from the Tennessee line to the vicinity of Brunswick where all the district majors and their staff officers were then taken to Sapelo Island for an intensive training program conducted by the Army. Immediately following this school, 200 line officers were detailed to Fort Benning, Ga., where they received the regular company commander course at this great infantry school.

High Praise from Regular Army

Today, the Georgia State Patrol is perhaps the best trained in fundamentals in the entire United States. Regular Army officers say it is an outstanding organization and capable of performing all of the missions assigned to it. They point with pride to its progress and accomplishments.

The members of the Georgia State Guard know that it is possible for our European enemy to attempt raids by air and land to include penetrations of considerable depth in the interior behind our Atlantic coast, with a mission to include demolition of American industrial, traffic and military installations.

If that emergency comes, the people of Georgia may have the satisfaction of knowing that a well-trained, efficient state guard will meet the situation with the same patriotism and with the same spirit that soldiers of America are facing the enemy wherever he may be."

Excerpts from:...

The Georgia State Guard
by Henry Taylor LTC, EN, GSDF

As a student at Atlanta's Boys High School and enrolled in Junior ROTC, the Army and everything associated with it was exciting to me. All magazines, newspapers, and radio news reports told of the war's progress and the country's home front activities in the support of the war effort.

My close friends and I felt that we could do our part by enlisting in the Georgia State Guard.

The newspaper often carried articles in support of the Georgia State Guard, so it was not difficult to locate the nearest unit which was "A" company, 4th Battalion, which was located on the school grounds between Boys High and Tech High. The Armory was an "L" shaped room with a secure storage area, office area, and assembly area.

After riding our bicycles to the Armory on Thursday night, we were sworn in (Parents' Permission Required)... the supply sergeant issued us our uniforms and equipment

The uniform consisted of a wool blouse, khaki shirt, wool overseas cap, wool pants, high top brown shoes, heavy wool jacket and insignia. They were surplus uniforms used by the CCC.

Individual recruit training was practically non-existent by the time we joined the Georgia State Guard. From Boy Scouts and the war movies we had seen, Martin and I were able to stand in line and stay out of the way of **Lt. C. O. Waters**, the platoon leader and Sgt. James Smith, the first sergeant.

Headquarters for the Georgia State Guard was located on Confederate Ave.

Although the Georgia State Guard was a volunteer organization, serving without pay, its worth was recognized by the Federal government as its members received a "B" gasoline ration book, so that the members would have sufficient gasoline to attend drills and mobilize when called.

Source: Georgia State Defense Force, *Best Defense*

"The Georgia State Guard As I Remember It."
by Gene Lowry, Civil Affairs Section, Headquarters, Georgia State Defense Force

Sometime during 1942, after a number of men from Lawrenceville, Ga. had joined or had been drafted to serve in one of the Armed Forces during World War II, Company C, 5th Battalion of The Georgia State Guard was formed. Those men who did not join one of the services or who had been deferred from the draft for various reasons were the ones who made up the Guard in Lawrenceville. The age group ranged from high school students to men in their 40's and 50's. A number of the guardsmen had served in World War I and provided some know-how to the new recruits.

The Lawrenceville Company was commanded by Lt. Tom McGee who was either in the reserves or who had some previous military training, plus some support officers from Decatur attended and assisted during drill night. The city of Lawrenceville and Gwinnett County were very supportive of the Guard, furnishing the softball field for drill, also paying for the lights during the nights the drill was held. We had mock air raids, constructed observation towers to watch for enemy aircraft and various other exercises that were overseen by The State Guard and Civil Defense authorities. I'm not aware of any classroom activities in conjunction with the Guard, however, there could have been some.

Our weapons consisted of 12 gage shotguns, single barrel with plastic stocks and plastic forearms, but I don't recall the make. Then we were issued new weapons, the old British Eddystone Enfield .30 cal. that must have weighed 15 pounds, also one Thompson .30 cal. sub-machine gun and one .45 cal. revolver. Included with this, we received two or three cases of ammo for each of the weapons.

Our uniforms were Army khaki's. After I became a member, we were issued "New Uniforms." These weren't really new uniforms, in fact, they were surplus uniforms of the old Civilian Conservation Corps, *The C.C.C.* The composition of our "New" uniforms was 100% wool pants, blouse, cap and overcoats. After you wore the pants for one drill there were no hairs left on your legs because the heavy wool pants just shaved them off. If your uniform became wet, the weight more than doubled and it was a chore just to walk around much less perform any type of close-order drill.

One year our company met with other companies of the battalion at Buford, Ga. for inspection. The inspecting officers arrived by train, conducted the inspection and then left by train. I guess to inspect other companies up the railroad line, Gainesville and Toccoa.

It was during my senior year in high school that we spent a week-end at some type of camp in Toccoa, Ga. Some branch of the Army had been training there and had moved out for assignment, so we were allowed to use the barracks and training area for our exercises. Transportation to and from Toccoa was provided by school buses from Lawrenceville.

During the summer of 1943, we spent a week at Ft. Benning in classroom activity, close-order drill, map reading, cross-country marches and, of course, the rifle range. That was my first experience (and at that time, I swore my last experience) with a military rifle. The rifle range Army cadre enjoyed seeing a bunch of high school students and old men trying to qualify with a 15 pound "cannon." Our instruction as to the proper way to fire a weapon was somewhat lacking, after you had fired the first clip there was no skin left on your shoulder. Needless to say, very few of us qualified.

In 1944 we received a new company commander, Lt. Robert Kelly from Lawrenceville, who had attended school where R.O.T.C. was taught and was qualified as a company commander. We continued to meet until the Japanese surrender in August of 1945. Then everyone just quit attending the meetings.

The war was over and we in The Georgia State Guard had done the job that was expected of us...

Source: Georgia State Defense Force, *Best Defense*

Notes from Chapter Six: Civil Air Patrol

Initial Staff of Coast Patrol Base # 6

Base Commander - Major Thomas A. Daniel, Jr.
Operations Officer - Capt. Francis A.(Sam) Baker
Personnel Officer and Assistant Operations Officer - Lt. J. W. Clayton
Intelligence Officer - Lt. L. Lex Benton
Assistant Intelligence Officer - Lt. H. McKee Nunnally
Administrative Officer - Lt. T. B. Sutton
Administrative Section Head - M. C. Patterson
Radio Operator - A. S. Bauman, H. M. Mitchell
Plotting Board Operator - E. S. Clayton, J. M. Louise
Engineering Officer - Capt. J. M. Cloud, Jr.
Assistant Engineering Officer - C. B. Guest, Jr.

The Brunswick News - March 5, 1942

STATE AIR UNITS WILL BE UNDER SINGLE COMMAND

The Civil Air Patrol in Georgia and the air force of the Georgia State Guard have been consolidated under a single command to eliminate duplication of duties and organization, Wing Commander Winship Nunnally announced Wednesday.

The move shifts into Civil Air Patrol ranks some 200 pilots, and brings the C.A.P. close to top strength, according to Commander Nunnally, who said that Lieut. Col. R. W. Ferguson, who headed the State Guard Air Arm, was made group commander for the coastal area.

Other group commanders are Major Lion Mason, Atlanta, who has charge of North Georgia, and Major William J. Graham, Americus, who has charge of South Georgia not including coastal areas.

Notes from Chapter Seven: Reserve, Auxiliary, Sea Scouts

The Brunswick News: July 27, 1942

THOUSAND SMALL YACHTS NEEDED IN PATROL WORK

Yachtsmen who own boats capable of cruising off shore can get into the battle against U-boats...

Secretary of the Navy Frank Knox said, "...Yachtsmen of America willingly have accepted wartime restrictions and regulations. Their patriotism has been magnificent. Their only complaint, up to now, has been that they have not been permitted to cooperate to the fullest extent. There is now no limit—the Navy needs them and wants them! These boats are needed right now—not only for harbor patrol duties but for actual offensive operations against enemy submarines."

The Brunswick News, June 9, 1943

THE YACHT BERNICE IS CALLED TO SERVICE

...Lieut. C. T. Christiansen, captain of the port of this district with headquarters in Savannah and Capt. H. B. Keller, U. S. Navy...announced the local vessel, *Bernice*, owned by Edwin Royall, had been acquired by the Coast Guard to be stationed in Brunswick's harbor for security purposes...the vessel will be fitted out at an undisclosed shipyard with several types of weapons and fire-fighting equipment...the boat will carry a double crew in addition to a skipper. The *Bernice*...has been in commission here for a number of years, and under command of Captain Royall has engaged in various work. The comfortable boat has frequently been chartered to take out pleasure parties on fishing and other trips. It is probably the largest boat in the harbor licensed to transport passengers.

Notes from Chapter Nine: St. Simons Naval Air Station

The Brunswick News: July 14, 1942

AIRPORT TAKEN OVER BY NAVY DEPARTMENT
ORDER OF U.S. COURT RECEIVED HERE AND OFFICIALLY TRANSFER OCCURRED AT 10 O'CLOCK TODAY

St. Simons Naval Air Station
(Handout for a tour of the St. Simons Naval Air Station)

THE TRUTH ABOUT ST. SIMONS....

Commissioned on December 22, 1942, the United States Naval Air Station, St. Simons Island, Ga. served originally as a training station for pilots of Navy fighter planes. With the transfer of this activity of the Naval Radar Training School - one of the most important military projects of the East coast - the station's mission was vitally changed and the activities tremendously expanded.

In the "top secret" classification until recent weeks, the mystery of radar had not yet been entirely revealed to the public. Many of the developments of radar warfare are still restricted from general circulation. You, our guests here today, will understand why we cannot invite you to tour the Radar School.

Other activities on this station are open for your inspection. Step in, look around, ask questions! We want you to see and understand what we have been doing these past two and one half years toward winning the war.

Your host today, Captain W. D. Thomas, USN, has been in command since the station was commissioned. Many of your know him personally and share our admiration for him. The executive officer, who reported aboard a month ago, is Commander A. M. Chamberlin, USNR.

As you entered the station, you passed the marine guard which is on duty 24 hours a day, in fair weather and foul, safe-guarding the men and property of this activity. They are the same Marines who fought at Guadalcanal, Iwo Jima, Okinawa, and other bloody stepping stones on the road to Tokyo.

On your left, inside the Main Gate, is the athletic field where departmental softball teams will play at 2 o'clock and at 4:30 on Thursday afternoon and at 2:30 on Monday afternoon.

Beyond the athletic field, on the left, is the dispensary where the Navy cares for its men and their dependents in the immaculate building which rates an "excellent" at every weekly inspection.

As you entered, your eyes probably turned first to the right where are on exhibit some of the types of planes which fought overwhelmingly victorious battles against the Japanese fighters. On display, (in order, as your enter) are the Amphibian J4F Widgeon; Primary Trainer N25, Yellow Peril; Advanced Trainer SNJ Texan; FM-2 Wildcat, Amphibian J2F Duck; Advanced Trainer SNB2 Navigator; and the SB2C-3 Helldiver.

Battle-experienced mechanics, men whose know-how keep the planes in operation and are in a large measure responsible for the station's low accident record, will be happy to explain the aircraft's distinquishing features and to answer your questions.

The planes face the guarded Administration Building where administrative officers and their staffs of enlisted men and civilian workers perform the vast amount of "paper work" necessary in the operation of a military establishment.

On your right, as you continue along the roadway, is the photographic laboratory where work the skilled technicians who keep an up-to-date pictorial record of the station's activities. Graphic aerial maps of the entire Brunswick area have been made by photographers at this station.

Beyond is the maintenance department where work the men who "keep 'em flying." Their unsung work of grease and grind and repair is appreciated by the men who take the planes aloft and whose safety depends upon the faithful performance of the men on the ground.

Also appreciated by the fliers are the officers and men in the tower (that's where you see the red flag flying) who are the nerve center of the station, maintaining contact at all time with the planes in the air. No plane takes off or lands until it gets the "okay" of the tower.

On the ground floor of this building is the aerology office where the "weather birds", on the basis of information collected here and at stations all over the nation, keep the fliers informed of what kind of flying conditions can be expected at varying altitudes.

In the adjoining building is the pilot's "ready room" where the fliers play pool, cards, or swap tall stories with their companions. In the same building is the link trainer where the aviators, under simulated flying conditions, get valuable flying experience without actually leaving the ground. In this building are packed and stored the parachutes, life rafts and other safety equipment.

Next on this little Cook's tour is the "line shack" where pilots get "the word" on which planes are in commission, and other valuable trade information. Further down - the last building in this line - is the armory where the guns and ammunition for safeguarding the station are stored.

The big building dwarfing the armory and turreted by the radar antenna is the Radar School where you are invited to witness the showing of a great double-feature, "The Fighting Lady" and "This Is It" at 4 o'clock.

Continuing down the main road we pass the supply building where everything from a cotter pin to a complete airplane engine may be obtained on requisition. The next two buildings you pass are barracks. Then you reach Ship's Service, the Navy man's general store where everything may be purchased from a pineapple sundae to a pair of lace trimmed unmentionables.

Ship's Service faces the Bachelor Officers' Quarters. The larger building at the rear of Ship's Service is the Recreation Hall where facilities are available for the physical fitness program. Daily gymnastic classes are conducted by officers and enlisted men of the department.

The recreation building is the play center for the enlisted man. There are facilities for playing pool or checkers, a library which includes both the current "best sellers" and classics and a place where a sailor can write a letter home.

That's all. We hope you have enjoyed your tour - that you will come back again sometime.

Notes from Chapter Ten: U.S. Naval Air Station, Glynco

The German U-boat menace made the protection of the Atlantic seaboard a "high priority" project in Washington, D. C., in 1942. Establishing airship operations along the coastal shipping lanes off the coast of South Carolina, Georgia and Florida.

In 1942, a site was selected approximately six miles north of Brunswick, Georgia, for the proposed Naval Air Station, Glynco. Construction began that year, was commissioned 1942. During the war years, Glynco served as an integral part of the anti-submarine network.

With the conclusion of World War II, Glynco was utilized as an airplane and aeronautical storage point. The two airship hangars are the largest wooden structures in the world.

From 1953 to 1955 construction projects included a new 8,000 foot jet airstrip, operations building, new barracks, new Bachelor Officers Quarters, a new Enlisted Mess, and a multi-million dollar Combat Information Center Training Building.

In 1953 Naval Auxiliary Air Station Glynco became a member of the Naval Air Training Command; the U. S. Naval CIC School, both elements of the Naval Air Training Command; and Airship Squadron TWO, a fleet unit. NAS Glynco has grown into a complex military unit which has become a very vital part in the defense of her country.

Notes from Chapter Eleven: Shipyards

Shipbuilding Beginning in 1941

The Brunswick News, October 2, 1941

Shelander Tells of Shipbuilding Plans
President Returns Today and Says Preliminary Work Progressing

The Brunswick News, October 9, 1941

Orders Are Placed By Local Ship Plant
Steel and other supplies soon to be received by Brunswick Marine

Steel and other material and equipment for the Brunswick Marine Corporation has been ordered, it was announced today, and other plans are progressing rapidly in preparation for beginning work on four steel tugs a contract for which was awarded the local company several days ago by the U. S. Shipping Board.

...The ship plant site, which adjoins the present machine and repair shops of the company, has been cleared, it was stated today, and work of running spur tracks, one between each of the launch ways.

The office of the company is being enlarged to accommodate engineers and draftsmen and considerable other work is in progress. The company hopes to lay the keel for the first tug within 60 days, it was stated, and if preliminary plans progress as well as they have during the past ten days, work may be started before that time.

...Due to the fact that it is not necessary to fill in the site, drive piles and complete other extensive work, much time will be saved in starting the actual construction work. The site is hard ground, and no ways will be required, except when the tugs are launched.

The Brunswick News. January 3, 1942

Keel Is Laid For First Steel Tug
It Is Also Announced That Practically All Steel For Four Vessels Has Arrived At Local Plant

.........The date for laying the first keel was tentatively fixed for December 15. The delay was occasioned by the delay of the steel mill in supplying the steel plates.........

United States Maritime Commission
INTER-OFFICE MEMORANDUM

March 23, 1942

To: United States Maritime Commission
     Via Commissioner Vickery

From: Acting Director, Construction Division

Subject: Brunswick Marine Construction Company - Plant and Facilities

For Construction of Approximately 30 EC2 Cargo Vessels

In order to augment the program of shipbuilding upon which the Maritime Commission is now embarked, it is necessary that additional shipyard facilities be provided. The Brunswick Marine Corporation proposed to build 30 EC2 cargo vessels for the commission, all of which will be delivered in 1943.

For the purpose of providing the necessary plant and facilities with which to execute this contract, the contractor requests an allotment of $6,721,000.

A site has been selected on which to construct a six-way shipyard, with complete facilities for fabrication, assembly, and erection of the ships. The site comprises approximately 345 acres, is located on the outskirts of the City of Brunswick, Glynn County, Georgia, at the conflux of Plantation Creek and Oglethorpe Bay, and which is generally described as Dennis Island. It has a water frontage of approximately 2,500 feet on Oglethorpe Bay and comprises two pieces of property, the easterly being owned by the Southern Railway Company and the westerly by the A.B. & C. Railway Company.

The A.B.& C. Railway Company's property comprises an existing ship basin approximately 300 feet in width with approximately 2,300 feet of docking space which is available and suitable for outfitting purposes. Also located on this property is an existing warehouse and several other existing buildings, some of which are currently used and which will be vacated and used in the shipbuilding operations. Located thereon, are also fire pumps and miscellaneous water lines and hydrants and one 100,000 gallon high water fire and water supply tank.

The property is generally level and has an average elevation of approximately 15 feet above mean low water.

The Contractor purposes to develop the upland section of this property only for shipyard purposes. The depth of this property is approximately three-quarters of a mile. It is served by the spur line from the A.B.& C. Railway Company, which now parallels the property and entails the minimum of new spur rail trackage therefrom. The plans submitted by the Contractor, indicate that an existing telephone line crosses the property and that it is partially crossed by a concrete roadway which will aid considerably in advertising the construction work of this project.

It is stated by the Contractor that the property of the Southern Railway Company, which comprises the major acreage involved, is available at a purchase price of $30,000, or an annual least rental of $1,800; and that the A.B. & C. Railway Company's property, which embraces several structures and the existing ship basin is now under option by others at a purchase price of $200,000, or an annual lease rental of $6,000. It is understood that the option is about to expire and will not be renewed by those presently occupying the property, and that a similar option will be advanced and made available to the Brunswick Marine Construction Company.

The existing electric service of this property, indicating a maximum capacity of 2,500 kilowatts, is available at an approximate distance of three-quarters of a mile from the property. It is estimated that the over-all requirements of this yard will be approximately 6,000 kilowatts. While it is considered feasible to bring in additional power to meet the overall requirements of this yard by extending the existing power lines from other localities, the Contractor has given consideration to the installation of a power plant at the site and proposes to generate the entire requirements of the yard with the proposed plant. For this purpose it is proposed to purchase and install available second-hand generating equipment which comprises one 3,000 KVA steam turbine generator, one 5,000 KVA steam turbine generator, one 1,500 KVA steam turbine generator, five 600 H.P. boilers in the existing boiler house on the property. The Contractor states that this equipment is under option and is immediately available at once. It is believed that under this arrangement, an adequate and satisfactory power supply will be made available, it being understood by the Contractor, and so stated, that this proposal contemplates installation of this equipment only in the event that satisfactory arrangements may not be consummated with the existing power company to supply the necessary overall power requirements.

A review of the Contractor's proposal indicates that the development of the project for the purpose is feasible and the cost thereof is not excessive. A summarized estimate of the cost as stated by the Contractor is as follows:

COST OF CONSTRUCTION AND EQUIPMENT

A	Yard Grading, Roadways, Fencing, etc.	$193,000.00
B	Railroads, Gentry & Whirley Tracks	565,000.00
C	Dredging & Filling	41,000.00
D	Six Shipways	342,000.00
E	Buildings (without equipment - See N)	944,900.00
F	Platens, Storage & Layout Areas	650,000.00
G	Water & Fire Protection & All Water Piping	127,000.00
H	Compressed Air System	73,400.00
I	Oxygen & Gas System	31,000.00
J	Electrical Installations (Power & Light Distribution)	295,000.00
K	Fitting-out Docks (Repairs & Extensions)	111,800.00
L	Cranes, Locomotives, Flat Cares, etc.	1,565,000.00
M	Light Transportation Equipment	105,000.00
N	Equipment in Buildings	649,000.00
O	Miscellaneous Portable Equipment	417,000.00
P	Electric Power Line, Plant & Equipment	291,000.00
		$ 6,401,100.00
	Contingencies 5%	321,000.00
		$ 6,721,000.00

This estimate is exclusive of any cost or carrying charges on land and existing improvements.

Recommendations: It is recommended that a facilities contract be entered into by the United States Maritime Commission and the Brunswick Marine Construction Corporation for the purpose of constructing a six way shipyard, located in Brunswick, Georgia, in the total amount of $6,721,000.

Carl W. Flesher, Acting
Director Construction Division

APPROVED BY:
H. L. Vickery, Commissioner
March 26, 1942

Excerpts from: Jones Construction Centennial: Looking Back, Moving Forward 1890 - 1990. Smith, Beth Laney. Kluever, Karen Trogdon. Laney-Smith, Inc. Charlotte, N. C. c. 1989.

Chapter 5 - "Ships for Victory"

"You learn by working. You select the right people and you work; you put all your heart and your mind in the project, and again you work; then you can do anything–army camps, ships, everything!"...Edwin Jones, Sr.

It was after nine o'clock at night in March 1942 when J.A. Jones was awakened by "Miss Rose" to take a phone call from Washington. It didn't put him in the best of moods. He had never liked his sleep interrupted, and at age seventy-three his habits were set.

The caller identified himself as an admiral with the Maritime Commission and explained that the United States Army and other branches of government had highly recommended J. A. Jones Construction Company.

"Would your company have an interest in building ships?" the admiral asked.

"Do you mean boats?" asked J. A.

"Well, you might call them *boats*. I'm referring to ocean-going vessels, Mr. Jones."

J. A. terminated that conversation quickly, "I'm sorry, but we're *building* contractors. Thank you anyway, sir, for thinking of us."

The following morning Edwin returned from a trip to the Panama Canal Zone. As they were ending a catch-up conference, J. A. said, "Oh, Edwin, some sailor called yesterday from up in Washington, and he wanted to know whether we would build some boats." J. A. didn't remember the name of the admiral, but Edwin got on the phone and ferreted it out...Vice Admiral Emory S. "Jerry" Land of the Maritime Commission.

When Admiral Land arrived in his Washington office the next morning, Edwin Jones was waiting for him. The disgruntled admiral had to call upon his military discipline to display courtesy. But after some few minutes, the modesty and sincerity of Edwin Jones melted away his gruffness, and Admiral Land explained that enemy submarines were sinking American cargo ships faster than they could be replaced. The United States was desperately in need of new ships, and the Maritime Commission was mounting a drive to have them built faster than ever in the country's history.

By the end of their meeting, the admiral decided to give Jones seven days to prepare a feasibility study on why they should be given a contract to build ships...a seemingly impossible task..

Construction Men in Action

By the time he reached his hotel, Edwin Jones was ready for the challenge of a completely new kind of construction. He got on the telephone and found the names of all U. S. shipyards and their locations. He contacted key people in his company and gave them data-gathering missions. Raymond [Jones] was asked to visit one shipyard, Emil Kratt another, Philo Caldwell a third, Hank Appen a fourth. Edwin told them the type of information he wanted and established a timetable. They all met in Charlotte two days before the deadline and complied their study, which included a recommendation that a shipyard be built in Panama City, Florida.

Their study addressed equipment and where they would find it: cranes, welding machines, air compressors...all the key machinery that the war had made scarce. Jones' men had contacted companies whose production had been interrupted by the war and made deals to buy idle, used equipment.

Their study also dealt with personnel...the strength represented in their project superintendents and seasoned engineers. After having built more than a dozen military cantonments, Jones had developed an expertise in recruiting labor...those stalwart men who would do the welding, pattern-making, burning, pipefitting.

The most impressive aspect of the study, however, was that it was submitted a day before the deadline. The Maritime Commission was convinced and signed a contract on April 4, 1942, calling for construction of the shipyard at Panama City and the building of **thirty-three** Liberty ships.

Wainwright Shipyard

The Panama City area that became Wainwright Shipyard began as swamp. Jones' assessment quickly established that there would be inadequate housing in Panama City for all the workers they would need to recruit, so housing became a first priority. As housing proceeded, so did construction of a shipbuilding plant with six "ways," fitting-out piers, machine shops, fabrication shops, roads, railroads, cafeterias, and all supporting utilities systems...

Becoming Shipwrights

Jones' men had a spectacular record of producing buildings and support facilities in military cantonments, so they unleashed this capability in another undeveloped setting. In the pathfinder days of their shipbuilding, they relied upon naval architects and engineers for guidance. They were also able to hire a few shipwrights experienced in the traditional ways of building ships.

The good news of their learning days was that they were building one type vessel. Liberty ships were cargo carriers of approximately 10,500 ton capacity. After some few months, they concluded that fabricating ships was little different from buildings and gained confidence in their own methods. C. H. "Doc" Graham, a career Jones man working at Wainwright, summed it up: "When you realize that a deck's nothing but a floor, and a bulkhead ain't nothing but a wall or partition, and you use steel instead of wood, there's nothing to it."

Indeed, the lessons learned in prefabrication of components for military camps were introduced into shipbuilding - and Jones was off to meet or beat the deadlines set by the Maritime Commission...

Training of Workers

...They [workers] were recruited from the surrounding small towns and farms. Before they became shipbuilders, they were clerks, filling station operators, plow hands, mill workers. They were taught their new skills at Wainwright in technical schools set up and conducted by the Jones company. The schools could never close because the draft was constantly depleting the cadre of trained men...

Brunswick Shipyard Contract

The Maritime Commission was watching closely how the Jones company coped with obstacles. When they launched their first ship in record time, and another was following in its wake, the Commission brought foward a new assignment. The shipyard at Brunswick, Georgia, also a six-way yard, was not being productive. In February 1943, Jones was asked to take over this yard... To superintend this operation the company chose Emil Kratt, that master of motivation. At the launching of the second ship at Wainwright, Emil Kratt was a fascinated spectator. He had never built ships before either, and he was absorbing all the details of this brisk operation.

Emil Kratt Shapes Up Brunswick

...Emil Kratt returned to Brunswick with a plan of action... Their problem was unlike that facing Jones men in Panama City. The Brunswick yard was built, and its former operators had ships under construction, using traditional crafting methods.

...As Emil or John [Pellett] walked through the operation, they observed that 10 percent of employees were not working, and it was always the same 10 percent. So they instructed supervisors to discharge 10 percent of their work force. This brought vehement protests and statements that an additional 10 percent of workers was needed, not fewer - but the order stood. When asked how they were to decide whom to fire, they were told, "Fire those you find not working." This policy was maintained until manpower was reduced by 30 percent - and each time a cut was made, total production improved. Seemingly heartless methods produced a lean and earnest work force, and Brunswick began to set production records.

List of Liberty Ships Built at Shipyard

No.	Name of Ship	Way No.	Yard Hull No.	M.C.E. Hull No.	Keel to Del. Days	Keel Laid	Launched	Dock Trial	Sea Trial	Delivery
1	JAMES M. WAYNE	1	105	1489	305	7/6/42	3/13/43	5/1/43	5/4/43	5/7/43
2	WILLIAM B. WOODS	2	106	1490	314	7/21/42	4/7/43	5/28/43	5/29/43	5/31/43
3	JOSEPH R. LAMAR	3	107	1491	320	8/1/42	4/29/43	6/12/43	6/15/43	6/17/43
4	THOMAS TODD	4	108	1492	320	8/14/42	5/19/43	6/28/43	6/30/43	6/30/43
5	ROBERT TRIMBLE	5	109	1493	325	8/29/42	6/21/43	7/16/43	7/19/43	7/20/43
6	JOHN CATRON	6	110	1494	331	9/3/42	7/11/43	7/19/43	7/30/43	7/31/43
7	JOHN MC KINLEY	1	111	1495	150	3/23/43	7/31/43	8/16/43	8/18/43	8/20/43
8	JOHN A. CAMPBELL	2	112	1496	140	4/13/43	8/14/43	8/28/43	8/30/43	8/31/43
9	JOHN M. MARLAN	3	113	1497	134	5/5/43	8/29/43	9/11/43	9/15/43	9/16/43
10	HOWELL E. JACKSON	4	114	1498	126	5/22/43	9/6/43	9/21/43	9/24/43	9/25/43
11	EDWARD D. WHITE	5	115	1499	100	6/22/43	9/20/43	9/29/43	9/30/43	9/30/43
12	HORACE H. LURTON	6	116	1500	99	7/12/43	10/7/43	10/16/43	10/17/43	10/19/43
13	HENRY W. GRADY	1	117	1501	91	7/31/43	10/22/43	10/28/43	10/30/43	10/30/43
14	JAMES A. WETMORE	2	118	1502	89	8/14/43	10/30/43	11/8/43	11/10/43	11/11/43
15	FREDERICK BATHOLDI	3	119	1503	83	8/29/43	11/9/43	11/17/43	11/19/43	11/20/43
16	JOHN B. GORDON	4	120	1504	81	9/6/43	11/16/43	11/22/43	11/24/43	11/26/43
17	EDWARD P. ALEXANDER	5	121	1505	70	9/21/43	11/23/43	11/28/43 11/30/43	11/30/43	11/30/43
18	ROBERT BATTEY	6	122	1506	63	10/8/43	11/30/43	12/7/43	12/9/43	12/10/43
19	SAMDEE	1	123	1507	55	10/23/43	12/9/43	12/15/43	12/17/43	12/17/43
20	JOE C. S. BLACKBURN	2	124	1508	58	10/30/43	12/15/43	12/21/43	12/24/43	12/27/43
21	JOHN B. LENNON	3	125	1509	51	11/10/43	12/22/43	12/29/43	12/31/43	12/31/43
22	GEORGE G. CRAWFORD	4	126	1510	58	11/16/43	1/1/44	1/10/44	1/12/44	1/13/44
23	DAVID B. JOHNSON	5	127	1511	62	11/23/43	1/13/44	1/21/44	1/24/44	1/24/44
24	HOWARD E. COFFIN	6	128	1512	62	11/30/43	1/21/44	1/28/44	1/31/44	1/31/44
25	R. NEY MC NEELY	1	129	1513	63	12/9/43	1/29/44	2/7/44	2/9/44	2/10/44
26	BENJAMIN H. HILL	2	130	1514	65	12/16/43	2/7/44	2/16/44	2/18/44	2/19/44
27	JOSEPH M. TERRELL	3	131	1515	65	12/23/43	2/14/44	2/23/44	2/25/44	2/26/44
28	ROBERT W. LIVINGSTON	4	132	1516	57	1/3/44	2/21/44	2/27/44	2/29/44	2/29/44
29	SAMALNESS	5	133	1517	56	1/15/44	2/29/44	3/8/44	3/10/44	3/11/44
30	ISAAC SHELBY	6	134	1518	56	1/22/44	3/6/44	3/15/44	3/17/44	3/18/33
31	SAMFAIRY	1	135	2350	57	1/31/44	3/16/44	3/25/44	3/27/44	3/28/44
32	SAMFOYLE	2	136	2351	52	2/8/44	3/23/44	3/29/44	3/31/44	4/31/44
33	SAMFINN	3	137	2352	59	2/14/44	3/31/44	4/10/44	4/12/44	4/13/44
34	SAMVIGNA	4	138	2353	58	2/22/44	4/8/44	4/17/44	4/19/44	4/20/44
35	SAMSELBU	5	139	2354	56	3/1/44	4/16/44	4/23/44	4/25/44	4/26/44
36	SAMLEYTE	6	140	2355	53	3/7/44	4/20/44	4/27/44	4/29/44	4/29/44
37	SAMAUSTRAL	1	141	2356	58	3/16/44	4/28/44	5/5/44	5/8/44	5/13/44
38	SAMINGOY	2	142	2357	50	3/24/44	4/30/44	5/11/44	5/13/44	5/13/44
39	SAMLORIAN	3	143	2358	55	4/1/44	5/14/44	5/20/44	5/23/44	5/26/44
40	SAMOLAND	4	144	2359	60	4/10/44	5/20/44	5/29/44	6/6/44	6/9/44
41	DONALD W. BAIN	5	145	2360	61	4/17/44	5/25/44	6/12/44	6/15/44	6/17/44

List of Liberty Ships Built at Shipyard

No.	Departure	Allocated To	Sponsor	Co-Sponsor	Destiny
1	5/8/43	WATERMAN STEAMSHIP CO.	Mrs. Edwin Lee Jones	Mrs. W. Franklin Brown Mrs. Edgar A. Wohlford Miss Burton Jacobs	Scrapped
2	6/1/43	A. H.. BULL & CO.	Mrs. Emil J. Kratt	Mrs. Frank Kylack Mrs. John D. Pellett	Torpedoed - Italy Sank
3	6/19/43	A.G.W.I. LINES, INC.	Mrs. Ellis Arnall		Scrapped
4	7/2/43	STANDARD FRUIT STEAMSHIP CO.	Mrs. G. N.. Mc Ilhenny		Reserve Fleet
5	7/22/43	A.G.W.I. LINES, INC.	Mrs. Thelma L. Groce	Mrs. Ina White	Scrapped
6	8/2/43	AMERICAN FOREIGN STEAMSHIP CO.	Mrs. John S. Gibson	Mrs. R. W. Griffin Mrs. T. M. Trash	Reserve Fleet
7	8/21/43	DICHMANN, WRIGHT & PUGH	Mrs. E. Mc Cranie	Mrs. Barbara Ray	Scrapped
8	9/2/43	MOORE MC CORMACK LINES, INC.	Mrs. Frank Dowd		Scrapped
9	9/17/43	MOORE MC CORMACK LINES, INC.	Mrs. Henry V. Mason		Scrapped
10	9/26/43	MARINE TRAMSPORT	Mrs. Robert Ramspeck	Mrs. John S. Leedy Mrs. Jarrell Dunson	Scrapped
11	10/3/43	A.H. BULL & CO.	Mrs. George Klosterman	Miss Dorothy Klosterman	Reserve Fleet
12	10./20/43	COSMOPOLITAN SHIPPING CO.	Mrs. W. J. Belk	Miss Sara Belk	Scrapped
13	11/2/43	WILMORE STEAMSHIP CO.	Mrs. Eugene Black	Mrs. Henry W. Grady, III	Reserve Fleet
14	11/13/43	WILLIAM J. ROUNDTREE CO., INC.	Mrs. W. M. Keniver	Mrs. P. F. Hyer	Scrapped
15	11/21/43	WEST INDIA STEAMSHIP CO.	Mrs. O.H. Hall	Mrs. Ruby Johnson	On Rocks - Scotland
16	11/27/43	T.J. STEVENSON & CO., INC.	Mrs. Charles Allen	Miss Annabel Allen Miss Carol Wolford	Scrapped
17	12/2/43	WILMORE STEAMSHIP CO.	Mrs. elston A. Lotz	Miss Helen Lotz Mrs. Norris Deaver, Jr.	Aground - Veracruz
18	12/12/43	COSMOPOLITAN SHIPPING CO.	Mrs. Edwin L. Jones, Jr.	Mrs. Edward K. Bryan	Aground - Mindannao
19	12/20/43	HIS MAJESTY'S SERVICE	Mrs. Katherine Geraghty	Miss Marjorie Ann Stuart	Scrapped
20	12/29/43	BLACK DIAMOND STEAMSHIP CO.	Mrs. Robert M. Hanes	Miss Ann Hanes	Floating dock-Portland
21	1/4/44	SMITH & JOHNSON	Mrs. F. R. Bustin	Mrs. C. L. Parks	Scrapped
22	1/15/44	AMERICAN RANGE LIBERTY S. S. CO.	Mrs. I. M. Aiken	Mrs. Walter Rylander	Scrapped
23	1/27/44	WILMORE STEAMSHIP CO.	Mrs. David B. Johnson	Mrs. W. R. Wallis Mrs. Roland	Scrapped
24	2/2/44	SOUTH ATLANTIC STEAMSHIP CO.	Mrs. Alfred W. Jones	Miss Monda Douglas Miss Dorothy Torras	Scrapped
25	2/11/44	SOUTH ATLANTIC STEAMSHIP CO.	Miss Lanelle Rimes	Miss Martha Ann Moore Miss Elaine Clark	Conversion - USN
26	2/20/44	A.L. BURBANK CO.	Mrs. J. D. Pellett	Mrs. Jackson W. Burnett	Reserve Fleet
27	2/27/44	R.A. NICOL & CO.	Mrs. Franklin W. Jones	Mrs. A.C. Mc Duffie Miss Doris Roberts	Scrapped
28	3/3/44	A.H. BULL CO	Mrs. Morton Funkhouser	Mrs. John W. Morris, Jr.	Scrapped
29	3/12/44	HIS MAJESTY'S SERVICE	Mrs. F. W. Prather	Mrs. Roger Stewart	Aground -Spain -Sank
30	3/20/44	SMITH B. JOHNSON CO.	Mrs. K. D. Nichols	Mrs. M. L. Darrieulat Mrs. Harry S. Traynor	Mine - Italy - Sank
31	3/30/44	HIS MAJESTY'S SERVICE	Mrs. Frank O. Sherrill	Miss Ruth Sherrill	Scrapped
32	4/4/44	HIS MAJESTY'S SERVICE	Mrs. Harry A. Debutts	Miss Van Meter Debutts Mrs. S. C. Cumming	Scrapped
33	4/15/44	HIS MAJESTY'S SERVICE	Miss Betty Dean	Miss Bessie Swails Miss Virginia Fowler Miss Janice Leavy	Scrapped
34	4/22/44	HIS MAJESTY'S SERVICE	Mrs. Alex s. Brown	Miss Jackie Rose Mrs. F. M. Bolding	Scrapped
35	4/29/44	HIS MAJESTY'S SERVICE	Mrs. W. A. Barnhardt	Miss Nancy Barnhardt	Mine - Belgium - Sank
36	5/3/44	HIS MAJESTY'S SERVICE	Mrs. Edwin Palmer Hoyt	Mrs. A. Burks Summers	Scrapped
37	5/14/44	HIS MAJESTY'S SERVICE	Mrs. J. B. Efird	Mrs. A. B. Walker	Scrapped
38	5/19/44	HIS MAJESTY'S SERVICE	Mrs. Parks M. King	Miss Mary Norton King	Reef - Veracruz
39	5/28/44	HIS MAJESTY'S SERVICE	Mrs. A. M. Harris	Mrs. G. H. Morrison	Scrapped
40	6/11/44	HIS MAJESTY'S SERVICE	Mrs. H. B. Jones	Mrs. Frank Caldwell	Aground - Ymuiden
41	6/19/44	THE NORTON LILLY MANAGEMENT	Mrs. J. Melville Broughton	Mrs. Clifton Beckwith Miss Adelaide Bain	Aground-Civitavechia

List of Liberty Ships Built at Shipyard

No.	Name of Ship	Way No.	Yard Hull No.	M.C.E. Hull No.	Keel to Del. Days	Keel Laid	Launched	Dock Trial	Sea Trial	Delivery
42	AUGUSTINE B. MC MANUS	6	146	2361	64	4/21/44	6/10/44	6/17/44	6/20/44	6/24/44
43	JAMES B. DUKE	1	147	2362	62	4/29/44	6/19/44	6/25/44	6/27/44	6/30/44
44	W.P. FEW	2	148	2363	63	5/1/44	6/22/44	6/28/44	6/30/44	7/3/44
45	ALEXANDER S. CLAY	3	149	2364	61	5/15/44	6/30/44	7/10/44	7/13/44	7/15/44
46	F. SOUTHALL FARRAR	4	150	2365	59	5/22/44	7/4/44	7/14/44	7/20/44	7/20/44
47	JAMES W. CANNON	5	151	2366	62	5/25/44	7/12/44	7/21/44	7/26/44	7/26/44
48	FRANK PARK	6	152	2367	51	6/10/44	7/21/44	7/28/44	7/31/44	7/31/44
49	EUGENE T. CHAMBERLAIN	1	153	2368	55	6/19/44	8/1/44	8/9/44	8/12/44	8/13/44
50	THOMAS B. KING	2	154	2369	57	6/23/44	8/7/44	8/16/44	8/18/44	8/19/44
51	R. WALTON MOORE	3	155	2370	56	7/1/44	8/14/44	8/23/44	8/25/44	8/26/44
52	NIELS POULSON	4	156	2371	61	7/6/44	8/18/44	8/26/44	8/29/44	9/5/44
53	ARTHUR J. TYRER	5	157	2372	49	7/13/44	8/22/44	8/30/44	8/31/44	8/31/44
54	CASSIUS HUDSON	6	158	2373	54	7/22/44	8/31/44	9/10/44	9/12/99	9/14/44
55	LUNSFORD RICHARDSON	1	159	2374	51	8/2/44	9/9/44	9/20/44	9/21/44	9/22/44
56	JOHAN PRINTZ	2	160	2375	53	8/7/44	9/18/44	9/24/44	9/21/44	9/29/44
57	CHARLES S. HAIGHT	3	161	2376	49	8/15/44	9/23/44	9/30/44	10/3/44	10/3/44
58	R. J. REYNOLDS	4	162	2377	54	8/19/44	9/30/44	10/9/44	10/11/44	10/12/44
59	DUNCAN L. CLINCH	5	163	2378	59	8/22/44	10/6/44	10/16/44	10/18/44	10/20/44
60	ABIGAIL GIBBONS	6	164	2379	54	9/1/44	10/12/44	10/22/44	10/24/44	10/25/44
61	CHARLES W. STILES	1	165	2380	52	9/9/44	10/18/44	10/29/44	10/30/44	10/31/44
62	MURRAY M. BLUM	2	166	2381	49	9/19/44	10/25/44	11/4/44	11/6/44	11/7/44
63	LAURA BRIDGMAN	3	167	2382	51	9/23/44	10/30/44	11/8/44	11/10/44	11/13/44
64	RICHARD RANDALL	4	168	2383	45	10/2/44	11/4/44	11/13/44	11/15/44	11/16/44
65	EDWARD R. SQUIBB	5	169	2384	46	10/6/44	11/9/44	11/18/44	11/20/44	11/21/44
66	JOHN H. HAMMOND	6	170	2385	45	10/13/44	11/15/44	11/23/44	11/25/44	11/27/44
67	ALBERT K. SMILEY	1	171	2386	41	10/20/44	11/21/44	11/28/44	11/30/44	11/30/44
68	IRA NELSON MORRIS	2	172	2387	43	10/26/44	11/25/44	12/5/44	12/7/44	12/8/44
69	GEORGE W. NORRIS	3	173	2388	42	10/31/44	12/2/44	12/9/44	12/11/44	12/12/44
70	ARTHUR M. HULBERT	4	174	2389	42	11/4/44	12/6/44	12/13/44	12/15/44	12/16/44
71	M. E. COMERFORD	5	175	2390	40	11/10/44	12/12/44	12/18/44	12/19/44	12/20/44
72	FELIX RIESENBERG	6	176	2391	40	11/16/44	12/14/44	12/22/44	12/23/44	12/26/44
73	ROBERT J. BANKS	1	177	2392	39	11/21/44	12/20/44	12/28/44	12/29/44	12/30/44
74	WILLIAM F. JERMAN	2	178	2393	34	11/27/44	12/23/44	12/30/44	12/31/44	12/31/44
75	WILLIAM COX	3	179	2394	37	12/4/44	12/30/44	1/6/45	1/9/45	1/19/45
76	GEORGE R. POOLE	4	180	2395	43	12/7/44	1/8/45	1/16/45	1/18/45	1/19/45
77	HAROLD O. WILSON	5	181	2396	43	12/12/44	1/12/45	1/20/45	1/23/45	1/24/45
78	JAMES BENNETT MOORE	6	182	2397	47	12/15/44	1/19/45	1/29/45	1/30/45	1/31/45
79	HALTON R. CAREY	1	183	2398	48	12/21/44	1/25/45	2/3/45	2/6/45	2/7/45
80	HAROLD DOSSETT	2	184	2399	51	12/26/44	1/30/45	2/10/45	2/13/45	2/15/45

List of Liberty Ships Built at Shipyard

No.	Departure	Allocated To	Sponsor	Co-Sponsor	Destiny
42	6/26/44	WM. J. ROUNDTREE CO., INC.	Mrs. William H. Harrison	Miss Nancy Meschke	Reserve Fleet
43	7/2/44	WESSEL DUVAL CO.	Mrs. Doris Duke Cromell		Reserve Fleet
44	7/6/44	ISBRANDTSEN STEAMSHIP CO., INC.	Mrs. J. Elmer Long	Mrs. Ralph Long	Scrapped
45	7/16/44	SOUTH ATLANTIC CTEAMSHIP CO.	Miss Zaida W. Clay	Mrs. Lucias D. Clay	Scrapped
46	7/22/44	UNIION SULPHUR CO.	Mrs. James A. Jones	Mrs. Frank Poole Miss Frances Gorrie	Scrapped
47	7/28/44	INTERNATIONAL FREIGHTING CORP.., INC.	Mrs. Charles A. Cannon	Mrs. Robert G. Hayes	Scrapped
48	8/3/44	U.S. NAVIGATION CO.	Mrs. Prince G. Finlayson	Miss Florence Finlayson	Scrapped
49	8/14/44	ISBRANDTSEN STEAMSHIP CO., INC.	Mrs. L. D. Cox	Mrs. James H. Garlington Mrs. Thomas W. Brooks	Hold for Vietnam
50	8/21/44	WESSEL DUVAL CO.	Mrs. F. D. Aiken	Mrs. H. B. Maxey Mrs. C. D. Parker	Reserve Fleet
51	8/27/44	PARRY NAVIGATION CO.	Mrs. Charles P. Howze	Mrs. Edmund Parry	Scrapped
52	9/6/44	DICHMAN WRIGHT & PUGH CO.	Mrs. W. H. Mc Whirter	Mrs. J. B. Caddell Mrs. A. D. Roach	Mine - Italy - Sank
53	9/4/44	GRACE LINES	Mrs. Hugh D. Ussery	Miss Nina Smith Miss Dorothy Ussery	Reserve Fleet
54	9/14/44	ALCOA STEAMSHIP CO., INC.	Miss Frances Hudson	Mrs. C. R. Hudson	Mine tow mine - Sank
55	9/23/44	WM. J. ROUNDTREE CO., INC.	Mrs. E. W. Stetson, Jr.	Miss Mollie Richardson	Scrapped
56	9/30/44	PARRY NAVIGATION CO.	Mrs. Glenn Fite	Miss Etheldra Kinard	Reserve Fleet
57	10/5/44	MARINE TRANSIT CO.	Mrs. James J. Harris	Mrs. Henry Clay Simpson	Aground - Burned - Mass.
58	10/13/44	BLACK DIAMOND S.S. CORP	Mrs. Richard J. Reynolds, Jr.	Mrs. J. T. Barnes	Scrapped
59	10/21/44	AMERICAN EXPORT CO.	Mrs. Harry B. Vickers	Mrs. William Healy	Mine-Havreroads-Sank
60	10/26/44	AMERICAN FOREIGN S.S. CO.	Mrs. W. Franklin Brown	Mrs. James Huntington, Jr. Mrs. George Moore	Reserve Fleet
61	11/1/44	SEAS SHIPPING CO., INC.	Mrs. P. Q. Murphy	Mrs. J. H. Green	Scrapped
62	11/9/44	MISSISSIPPI SHIPPING CO., INC.	Mrs. Sylvia Blum	Mrs. Walter Nathan Mrs. A. A. Nathan	Reserve Fleet
63	11/13/44	SEAS SHIPPING CO., INC.	Mrs. Clare Purcell	Miss Claire Purcell Mrs. Isaac Andrews	Scrapped
64	11/17/44	ISBRANDTSEN STEAMSHIP CO., INC.	Mrs. E. C. Marshall	Mrs. Norris Broyles Miss Benton Broyle (Jr. C. S.)	Scrapped
65	11/22/44	WEST INDIA STEAMPSHIP CO.	Mrs. Paul S. Jones	Mrs. Jack Hyland Miss Martha Jones (Jr. C.S.)	Reserve Fleet
66	11/27/44	WILLIAM J. ROUNDTREE CO., INC.	Mrs. R. Gregg Cherry	Mrs. O. H. Lineberger Miss Anne Lineberger	Mine - Elba - Sank
67	12/2/44	INTERNATIONAL FREIGHTING	Mrs. Harry H. Straus	Mrs. Elizabeth Candee Rabell	Scrapped
68	12/9/44	SEAS SHIPPING CO., INC.	Mrs. Ira Nelson Morris	Mrs. Virginia Jenckes	Scrapped
69	12/13/44	PRUDENTIAL STEAMSHIP CORP.	Miss Gretchen Rath	Mrs. George W. Norris	Aground- Japan - Sank
70	12/17/44	ALCOA STEAMSHIP CO., INC.	Mrs. W. Hunter Wynn	Miss Mary Daude Myrick Miss Jean Adams	Scrapped
71	12/20/44	MERCHANT & MINORS TRANS. CO.	Mrs. M. E. Comerford	Mrs. Mariel C. Friday	Scrapped
72	12/28/44	AMERICAN WEST AFRICAN LINE	Mrs. N. M. Campbell	Miss Addie Ruth Brown	Renamed - Nenana
73	1/2/45	NORTHASIP (Norwegian Gov't)	Mrs. George H. Buchanan	Mrs. Susan Hayward Miss Betty Buchanan	Scrapped
74	1/4/45	BLACK DIAMOND STEAMSHIP CORP.	Mrs. Charles W. Tillett	Mrs. Wm. I. Coddington Miss Sara A. Tillett	Scrapped
75	1/11/45	BLIDBERG ROTHCHILD CO., INC.	Aralee Cox	Julia Dowells Lillian Cox	Scrapped
76	1/20/45	STOCKJARD STEAMSHIP CO.	Mrs. Robert D. Strachan	Mrs. L. J. Turner Mrs. Gary Thompson	Scrapped
77	1/25/45	U.S. NAVIGATION CO.	Mrs. J. S. Bragdon	Lt. (J.G.) Dorothy Bragoon	Scrapped
78	2/2/45	A.L. B URBANK & CO. LIM.	Mrs. A. J. Peavey	Mrs. Leroy Mark	Reserve Fleet
79	2/8/45	AMERICAN LIBERTY S.S.	Mrs. A. W. Henson	Mrs. Frank C. Martin Miss Elizabeth Marie Henson Miss Martha Olsen (Jr. C. S.)	Scrapped
80	2/16/45	MORTON LILLY MANAGEMENT CORP.	Mrs. L. R. Groves	Miss Gwen Groves	Reserve Fleet

List of Liberty Ships Built at Shipyard

No.	Name of Ship	Way No.	Yard Hull No.	M.C.E. Hull No.	Keel to Del. Days	Keel Laid	Launched	Dock Trial	Sea Trial	Delivery
81	PATRICK S. MAHONY	3	185	2400	54	12/30/44	2/10/45	2/19/45	2/21/45	2/22/45
82	RICHARD A. VAN PELT	4	186	2401	50	1/9/45	2/17/45	2/26/45	2/28/45	2/28/45
83	CHARLES C. RANDLEMAN	5	187	2402	57	1/15/45	2/25/45	3/6/45	3/8/45	3/13/45
84	ROY JAMES COLE	6	188	2403	66	1/23/45	2/28/45	2/28/45	3/13/45	3/15/45
85	PATRICK B. WHALEN	1	189	2404	60	1/29/45	3/15/45	3/27/45/	3/30/05	3/30/45
86	LOCK KNOT	2	190	2474	119	2/5/45	3/23/45	5/28/45	5/29/45	6/4/45
87	RING SPLICE	3	191	2473	137	2/13/45	4/12/45	6/23/45	6/27/45	6/30/45
88	SINNET	4	192	2476	147	2/20/45	4/21/45	7/9/45	7/11/45	7/17/45
89	CROWN AND DIAMOND	5	193	2477	157	2/27/45	4/28/45	7/23/45	7/25/45	7/31/45
90	BELL RINGER	6	194	2478	162	3/2/45	5/8/45	8/3/45	8/8/45	8/11/45
91	RIGGER'S EYE	1	195	2479	160	3/20/45	5/22/45	8/17/45	8/24/45	8/27/45
92	SPAN SPLICE	2	196	2480	163	4/2/45	5/29/45	8/29/45	9/5/45	9/12/45
93	TRUE KNOT	3	197	2481	180	4/16/45	6/6/45	10/6/45	10/10/45	10/13/45
94	SHELL BAR	4	198	2482	151	4/30/45	6/19/45	9/14/45	9/18/45	9/28/45
95	MOORING HITCH	5	199	2483	169	5/7/45	6/28/45	10/16/45	10/19/45	10/23/45
96	TAG KNOT	6	200	2484	137	5/15/45	7/14/45	9/24/45	9/26/45	9/29/45
97	COASTAL MARINER	1	201	2726	158	5/26/45	8/11/45	10/26/45	10/29/45	10/31/45
98	COASTAL CAPTAIN	2	202	2727	166	5/31/45	8/17/45	11/5/45	11/9/45	11/13/45
99	COASTAL RANGER	3	203	2728		6/7/45	8/23/45	11/18/45	11/20/45	11/21/45
	COASTAL CHIEF	4	204	2729		6/20/45				
	COASTAL PIONEER	5								

List of Liberty Ships Built at Shipyard

No.	Departure	Allocated To	Sponsor	Co-Sponsor	Destiny
81	2/23/45	BLACK DIAMOND STEAMSHIP CORP.	Mrs. Christine Mahoney		Scrapped
82	3/3/45	ATLANTIC OVERSEAS CORP.(Belgian Gov't.)	Mrs. Duncan Morton	Mrs. Dorothy W. Latimer Miss Betsy Morton (Jr. C.S.)	Scrapped
83	3/14/45	AMERICAN FOREIGN S.S. CO	Mrs. Mary R. Baggett	Mrs. Vera Ferree	Reef-Phillipines-Sank
84	3/17/45	BLIDBERG ROTHCHILD CO., INC.	Mrs. Kenneth Cole		Renamed - Dolphin
85	3/31/45	ISBRANSTSEN CO.,INC.	Mrs. Leo W. Regan		Scrapped
86	6/6/45	AMERICAN EXPORT LINES, INC.	Mrs. J. F. McInnis	Hopefully	Brunswick Museum
87	6/30/45	AMERICAN EXPORT LINES, INC.	Mrs. Paul J. Kiker	Miss Ethel York Kiker Mrs. James I. Avett, Jr.	
88	7/18/45	U.S. LINES COMPANY	Mrs. Harry L. Dalton	Mrs. W. J. Carter	
89	8/2/45	LYKES BROTHERS S.S. CO. INC.	Mrs. W. R. Cuthbertson	Miss Marie Hagood	
90	8/11/45	WATERMAN STEAMSHIP CORP.	Mrs. Howard P. Powell	Mrs. S. A. Maxwell	
91	8/28/45	U.S. LINES COMPANY	Mrs. Preston B. Wilkes, Jr.	Mrs. A. S. Rachel, Jr. Miss Anne W. Wilkes	
92	9/12/45	LYKES BROTHERS S.S. CO. INC.	Mrs. R. S. Dickson	Mrs. R. A. Bigger	
93	10/14/45	MARINE TRANSPORT LINES, INC.	Mrs. H. C. Sherrill	Mrs. Charles Bunch Mrs. R. G. De Quevedo	
94	9/29/45	MOORE MC CORMACK LINES, INC.	Mrs. Paul N. Beall	Miss Virgina Beall	
95	10/24/45	STATES MARINE CORP	Miss Nanvy Beall	Miss Emily Russell	
96	10/2/45	AMERICAN EXPORT LINES, INC.	Mrs. G. G. Purcell	Mrs. W. L. Varnadore	
97	11/1/45	A.M. BULL & CO	Mrs. Frank M. Scarlett	Miss Mary Louise Scarlett	
98	11/14/45	NORTH ATLANTIC & GULF S.S. CO.	Mrs. C. C. Keiger	Mrs. Henry Bagley, Jr. Miss Jean Keiger	
99	11/23/45	NORTH ATLANTIC 7 GULF S.S. CO	Mrs. W. M. Roberts	Mrs. Robert Rankin Miss Patsy Boren	

Notes from Chapter Twelve: Stories from the Homefront

The Atlanta Journal, August 26, 1943

VENEREAL DISEASES CUTTING MANPOWER.
Dr. Winchester Tells How Brunswick Program is Improving Public Health.
By Rosalyn Bradshaw

Venereal disease is causing more loss in man-hours in Georgia industry today than all other diseases combined, Dr. Millard E. Winchester, nationally known authority on the treatment of syphilis and pioneer research worker in the use of atabrine and sulpha drugs, stated here Thursday.

The jovial, rosy-cheeked health commissioner of Glynn County has received international recognition for his major contributions to public health-success in stamping out malaria and work in the eradication of syphilis in Glynn County.

"A man with an acute case of syphilis who is employed operating a machine doing precision work is a liability to his company.," Dr. Winchester said. "The greatest health problem of the state at the present time is venereal disease."

With the co-operation of the United States Health Service and the Georgia and Glynn County boards of health, Dr. Winchester launched his campaign against syphilis among the residents of Georgia's piney woods in 1937.

Bad Blood Wagon

In a trailer equipped as a doctor's office and known to patients as the "bad blood wagon," he carries medical aid to the scattered inhabitants of the swamp lands of Glynn, McIntosh and Camden Counties. For many years ignorance and lack of medical facilities had left venereal disease uncurbed to take its toll. The "bad blood wagon" travels more than 500 miles weekly, conducting from three to six clinics every day.

Recent Selective Service examinations in Glynn County prove the effectiveness of his work. The number of syphilitics among the residents of the county was 50 to 60 percent lower than among non-residents who had migrated to Brunswick in the past 18 months.

Dr. Thomas Parran, surgeon general of the United States, has written Dr. Winchester: "Your county is going the finest piece of work in syphilis eradication that is being done in this country today."

"The population of Brunswick increased from 15,000 to 60,000 in the last year and a half," the health commissioner reported. "With the growth in population, I have noted a marked increase in the syphilis rate, but is has been confined to the new settlers."

Fortunately, the doctor says, syphilitics among the new residents have co-operated in taking treatment at the county clinic, probably because of the changed attitude of the public toward venereal disease. "We treat syphilis as a disease not a disgrace.

Pioneering In Health

Brunswick and Glynn County have pioneered in many health measures, Dr. Winchester says, and the success of their experiments has won the attention of the United States Public Health Service.

A Brunswick city ordinance now forces all employees of eating establishments to have periodical blood tests, and where it is found that facilities for sterilization of tableware are inadequate, the establishment must use paper cups and plates.

Glynn became the first section to make county-wide use of atabrine in malaria control, and he revealed: "The results of its experiment have proved, in my opinion, that atabrine is as effective as quinine. Not one case of malaria has been reported in Glynn County this year. Because of the shortage of quinine, atabrine is being used in the armed forces all over the world."

Appendix B

Letters written home by a
WAVE stationed at
Glynco Naval Air Base,
Brunswick, Georgia

May 17, 1944 - November 26, 1945

Phyllis Rhoades Steinmann

Phillis Rhoades served in the WAVES during World War II. After completing her training as an aerographer (meterologist) at Lakehurst, New Jersey, she was stationed at the blimp base at Glynco for the duration of the war. Her mother kept all the letters that she sent home even ones that she wrote to her brothers and father. The following are excerpts from those letters almost on a day to day account of what was happening. Unless otherwise indicated, all letters were addressed to her mother.

May 17, 1944
(from the Naval Air Station at Glynco outside Brunswick)

I guess you think I have forgotten you...well, I haven't. The Navy just doesn't believe in wasting time, so I was put to work immediately.

My train was late, as usual, getting into Brunswick. Mrs. C's granddaughter met me and took me out to the station on a bus. It is only a few miles. It was close to 11:00 a.m. when I finally started checking in. That and chow lasted until about 3 o'clock. Mrs. C's son came by then and took me into town. I bought one summer uniform as that was all they had. It really felt good after that wool suit. I stayed at their house for supper and finally got to bed about eleven that night. At seven o'clock Sunday morning I was rudely awakened and told that I had to report for work. I have to work every day for two weeks from seven to four. After that I will stand watches night or day and will have more time off.

My suitcase hadn't come in Saturday night, so it is still at the depot, I guess...My roommate is a radioman, but don't get excited...she is a WAVE, too, and a very nice one...by the way, when you send the cookies, please send about half dozen coat hangers.

May 24, 1944

...Monday I was given the day off, so I went to Jacksonville and bought another seersucker suit and a white dress uniform. They cost me $15.00 each. Since I only was paid $40 and other little items entered into the picture, I'm pretty flat until the next payday...the girls say the dress uniform looks better with long sleeve shirts, so if you have time to "rit"* the one I left a home, you might send it to me and I won't bother to buy another one.

*rit is the brand name for fabric dye.

June 2, 1944

...Have they quit making snap fasteners? I have tried to buy some in Brunswick and they don't seem to have any. We have shoulder pads in our dresses and they should be taken out every time they are washed. As I have to wash them often, it gets to be a bore tacking in shoulder pads every morning...Did I tell you about the bathing suit I bought? It is a dude. A two pieced affair with nothing in the middle. It is blue and white striped...I had my first evening watch from four p.m. to midnight. I was pretty sleepy when I finally came to the barracks, but I had to put sheets on the bunk before I could hit the sack. Did you ever try to make a bed in the dark?

June 10, 1944

Those cookies are really going to taste good when they get here!...I am going to the beach this afternoon if the weather clears. It is cloudy this morning and looks like it might rain. I really have it easy as far as work is concerned. I work three day watches, one evening watch and then I have two days off.

June 13, 1944

The box came yesterday and I was glad to get everything...especially the cookies. Ensign Andrews, my boss, said to tell you they were the best he had ever eaten and of course, everyone else who had some thought they were good, too. In other words, when you get around to it, some more would be appreciated.

I played badminton in the red dress yesterday and it felt good to have on a civilian dress. We have to do three hours' exercise every week and can't wear socks with our uniform so the dresses will come in handy. I don't like to wear shorts when there are so many men around.

June 23, 1944

...Thanks for the box. I was really glad to get the shoe socks and of course the snaps.

July 3, 1944

...It is nice and cool here today, because it has been raining since yesterday afternoon. We had only three days with rain in June and there were four days when the temperature was over 100 degrees. One day it was 102 degrees.

July 8, 1944
(to brother Donnie)

... Have I told you about the little black dog that lives in our barracks? It belongs to one of the girls, but everyone feeds it and plays with it. Its name is "Flicka." She is always carrying our shoes or whatever we leave on the floor and hiding them. She will sit up to beg for food or play dead. She can also dance on her hind legs when she wants to.

July 11, 1944

I do manage to go to the show once in a while. There have been a few good ones on the station lately. Last night I saw, "The Ghost of Centerville" with Margaret O'Brien and Robert Montgomery. It is a spooky picture but very good. The last one I saw was "Going My Way" with Bing Crosby. It was different than most of his pictures and very enjoyable. We go to the movies free on the station and it is a temptation to go too often even if the picture isn't good....we have more poor ones than the other kind. A USO Troup is here tonight, but I am working...We are eating emergency rations today and tomorrow while the boiler in the galley is being cleaned out...Last week was the first time since I have been here that I missed going to the beach on my day off.

July 28, 1944

...Seems like when I work nights, that I sleep days and evenings most of the time. We have a schedule of two mid watches (midnight to 7 a.m.); two day watches (7 a.m to 4 p.m.); and two evening watches (4 p.m. to midnight). Then we have two days off. You don't work long enough at the same time of day to get used to it.

August 2, 1944
... It started raining about an hour ago. I always hate to be on duty when the weather is bad because there is a lot of traffic through our little office. It seems that no one can tell if it is really raining without asking us about it. There will be pilots and other officers all over the place...I guess I told you that we didn't have any hot water for four days. My clothes really piled up...they finally turned the hot water back on...I am in no condition to take any cold showers this week. They didn't feel so bad last week because it was quite hot!...There were twelve new WAVES who came in last night. Two of them are a mother and daughter. The mother has been put in cleaning compartments and the daughter to driving a truck.

August 8, 1944
We have had quite a lot of excitement this last week. About 5 days ago, one of the planes crashed and killed two fellows in it. Then just last night one of the blimps caught fire in the hanger and burned to a crisp. Luckily no one was hurt.

August 14, 1944
I really feel G. I. now, because I have some dog tags to wear on my chain around my neck.

August 22, 1944
...We are going to have to get rid of "Flicka" because the captain doesn't like dogs. We will really miss her around the barracks. She was always jumping on our bunks and waking us up when we slept in the day time. The Captain didn't like that.

October 2, 1944
I guess you had better send my heavy pajamas soon...I didn't realize that it was going to get cool so quickly. Please send my blue jacket and my hand mirror, too.

October 16, 1944
My roommate has signed up to go to Alaska. That is all I hear from morning til night.

October 22. 1944
My roommate would like to know if the Fuller brush man still makes hair brushes like mine. She wants one, if he does...Thanks a lot for the persimmons. I had the only ripe one for breakfast. It tasted good.

October 23, 1944
...If you haven't sent the box yet and if there is a little room left, would you ask Aunt A. if I could borrow her tatting shuttle* and a bootie to use as a pattern. Don't get excited. I want to make a pair for Rosalie...We had quite a lot of weather the other day when the hurricane passed here. There were 8 1/2 inches of rain in 12 hours and the wind blew at 64 knots, which is almost 75 miles per hour. The worst of it lasted from early morning until about 3 o'clock in the afternoon. It didn't do a great deal of damage. Some trees were blown over and a metal top of a delivery truck was blown off, some shingles are missing and trash was washed up all over the highway between here and Brunswick.
*a small hand-held shuttle for making lace.

November 4, 1944

I've been wanting to write you all week, but I've been busy. Monday and Tuesday I slept after my mid watches. Wednesday I went to Jacksonville to do some shopping, and Thursday and Friday I worked. Thursday night I went to the movie,"Our Hearts Were Young and Gay," which was very good...Friday night I pressed my suit, shined my shoes, filed my nails and cleaned the compartment for the Captain's Inspection we had this morning.

I certainly do thank you for all the boxes you have sent me. The cake was wonderful. All the kids enjoyed it. There is just a little piece left and I am saving that for me. The pajamas were cute.....I enjoyed the nuts, too. I made some olive-pimento cheese sandwiches to eat tonight and put some of them (nuts) in them....Since I've started wearing my suits and shirts, I've really needed the coat hangers...Jenny said to tell you that she would really be glad to get the hair brush. She is worried, though, for fear it won't come before she goes overseas...

...P.S. I'll send the cake box home soon. All the girls said they hoped you'd take the hint. Me too!

November 12, 1944

Guess what? I am going to write you a whole letter and not ask you to send me a thing! Do you think you can stand the strain? ...I am going to see Howard.*

*Howard is her brother who was in Orlando, Florida

November 19, 1944

...My little trip to Orlando, Florida was a little harder on me than I expected. I got off work about 6:30 Monday morning and slept until 11 o'clock. I ate dinner and hitched-hiked a ride into Brunswick. It took me from 2:00 p.m. until midnight to get to Orlando on the bus. They hadn't received my letter, so no one met me...I left Wednesday morning about 8 o'clock and got back to the base around 5 o'clock that afternoon. I had to go to work at midnight...

November 24, 1944

...We had a very nice time Wednesday night. Some of the girls went in to the U.S.O. and cooked a Thanksgiving dinner, turkey and all. It was delicious. My roommate made the biscuits. It seemed like I was at home. There were 17 of us. I haven't been so very hungry since... One of the girls is going overseas. She is to be sent to Hawaii. I guess she will be the first group to go over. Everyone is excited about it.

December 16, 1944

I'm sorry I worried you by not writing sooner. I didn't expect you to be gone so long and I wrote a letter home, but I guess you know that by now. I'm not sick. I've just been pretty busy getting all the things ready for Christmas and with the big washings I've had, there wasn't much time to write. I have had a bad cold, but it is nearly gone now. I've been going to the dispensary to have my nose sprayed twice a day with an electric sprayer. They used some sulfa powder on my throat and gave me a short wave treatment for my sinus.

My roommate is leaving a week from today for Hawaii also. She has a few days at home and then she goes to California. It is almost impossible to live with her, she is so excited. Of course, we talk of nothing else. I've asked Lucy, the pigeon girl* to live with me.

* The Navy kept homing pigeons at the station, but for no practical purpose since the airships had radios. However, they trained them and would take them out in pairs in a blimp and release them within 100 miles of shore. When training at Lakehurst, N. J. they were used to send messages back to the base when using free balloons since there were no radios on board.

December 19, 1944
(to brother Donnie)
    You should have seen the big blimp that was here the other day. It is so big that a plane can be hooked on the back of it. It was supposed to make a very long trip and be up for 8 days, but something happened to the motors, so it landed here.

December 19, 1944
(to father)
    We have been having some very cold weather. It was 23 degrees one morning and was below freezing about five mornings in a row. Yesterday was very warm, but today it is cold again...They are sending out quite a few fellows and WAVES right after Christmas. I guess I'll be here, though, until they close the base. Some people think we might all be sent to the west coast, but I've not packed my bag yet.

December 29, 1944
    I just washed my hair and am sitting on the deck next to the radiator trying to get it dry enough so I can take it down and go to chow in a few hours...I had quite a Christmas myself. I had to work Christmas Eve from 7:30 a.m. until 4 p.m. One of the boys in the office took me into town for supper and then we went to Church. The service was nice. We only sang Christmas Carols and "White Christmas"! I've never heard anything like that in church before! We came back to the barracks, and since there was a party going on, my friend came in, too. He didn't stay long as we had to go to work at midnight. I took my gifts over and opened them right at 12 o'clock.

January 4, 1945
    ...Nothing much has happened around here lately. The London fog that was visiting us must have gone back to London. Yesterday was a beautiful day, but it clouded up and rained last night and is still gloomy today. I'm sure glad I don't have to forecast for a living. I've been doing it just for fun to see how bad I am and I'm pretty terrible.
    Donnie, (brother) do you know what a PBY* is? One flew in here the other day and I had to tell the pilot what the weather was between here and Lakehurst. It was a funny looking duck.
    Captain McAffee, the highest ranking officer in the WAVES is supposed to be aboard tomorrow and Saturday. We have personnel inspection Saturday, but I have to work and won't be there. Any other time I'd like to get out of it, but I would like to see her.
    We have to turn our liberty cards in when we don't rate liberty. The other day mine was missing. I had turned it in, but no one had seen it after that. The penalty for losing that little piece of red paper is 30 days restriction. Just when I was about ready to believe that I had lost it, they found it. I was really relieved.
    I shouldn't have said anything about the fog because since I wrote it, the fog has started to come back.
*A PBY Catalina is an amphibious airplane built during World War II.

January 11, 1945
    I don't think I have written since I received the little box. Thanks a lot for the tatting shuttle, and also the nuts. I guess Daddy picked out the nuts. They really are good. In fact, so good that I had a hard time saving any for me. There are a few left and I keep them locked up. Where did the toothbrush come from? I needed some new ones, so it came in handy.
    The lights went off about 2:45 this morning and we had to work by candlelight and flashlights for almost an hour. It was our busiest time, too. Seems like things are always happening when I'm around. The other day I got stuck in the jeep. That is the jeep got stuck in the wet sand and I was in the jeep.

January 15, 1945

I am sitting outside without even a jacket. It's so nice and sunny...I have Rosalie's booties almost done...They are to change the watch schedule so we are on duty 24 hours and then off 24 hours.

February 8, 1945

...While I think about it, I'll tell you about the doll. One of the fellows in the office has been trying to make an impression on me, so he took me out to the Cloister Hotel for dinner one evening. I guess it is the swankiest hotel in all of Georgia. The poor sailor didn't have must left of a $10.00 bill when we left. I had squab on toast and all the trimmings. It was very nice, but too fancy for me. Gov. Thomas Dewey of New York and his family were there for a couple of weeks after the election in November. There is a beach and private swimming pool that is operated by the hotel. That is where we went swimming. last summer. Anyway, we found the doll in the gift shop, so he bought it for me...We have another new schedule. I work eight hours every other day and three hours on the in between days...I finished the booties, but naturally I can't find any ribbon to go in them. I have some white (ribbon) that I used on Christmas packages, but it isn't very long.

February 11, 1945

...This is my weekend off and I'm really enjoying it. I'm going to a Church tomorrow that was started by Charles Wesley a couple of hundred years ago. It is on St. Simons Island about 15 miles from here.

I just finished my work on the logs for January. The hottest day we had was 73 degrees and the coldest was 30.5 degrees. It rained quite a few days but only little showers. One day it rained an inch and a quarter in 11 hours. That was about half of the total rain for the month.

Since this is Saturday night, my roommate and I are going to have a big time. We will go to chow and then to the movies. "Summer Storm" is on tonight. Then we will come back to the barracks and maybe drink a coke before we hit the sack. Doesn't that sound exciting?

There is a big plane flying round and round the field. It is quite unusual to see planes as we only have blimps here. There is a "heavier than air base" close by, though, so I guess he is just hunting for it.

February 14, 1945
(to brother Howard)

...I'm down at the pigeon loft with my roommate, Lucy. The pigeons are cooing and flapping. She has about 150. You should see them. Lucy will let them out and they will fly around for about a half hour and they will all come back.

February 16, 1945

I had a nice sun bath just a little while ago...under a pine tree, but the gnats are terrible!...There is going to be a picture about Lakehurst tonight. I don't know the name, but Wallace Beery is in it. I don't know if it will be any good or not, but it will be fun to see all those places up there in a movie...How is Rosalie? Time, I hope...I have some books to send home as soon as Lucy reads them. I'm reading one now by Ernie Pyle that is very good. As soon as I get my new luggage, I'm going to send my old brown suitcase home full of stuff. I bought some chocolate dots for making toll house cookies. Maybe someday you could make some, if you feel like it. Is there anything else you can't find. I'll get it, too. They have marshmallows sometimes. Would you like a box or two?...Do they have any hose in the stores in Shreveport? I haven't been able to buy any since before Christmas and I'm down to three pair that have more patches than the law allows. I've even started patching patches which is bad. If I can't find any in Jacksonville when I go next time, I'll just have to go bare legged and there ain't no two ways about it.

February 17, 1945
(to brother Donnie)
...Have you been to see Rosalie's little baby? What's its name? I'll bet it is cute...Has the movie, "This Man's Navy" been to Shreveport yet? Be sure to see it when it comes. It was taken at Lakehurst and shows all about blimps. The "K" ships are what we have here. The hangers are just like those there, too.

February 20, 1945
(to her father)
... I haven't heard any more about my income tax since the Revenue man from Brunswick came out to see me and sent me a form to fill out asking to wait until after the war to pay it. Did they send anything home?...I had a letter from Leslie today. He seems very encouraged about the war in Europe. I hope it is over soon. The letter only took 7 days to get here.

February 26, 1945
The package came today with the hose in it...They are pretty and if you could have seen my old ones, you would not be surprised that I was glad to see them.

February 28, 1945
(to brother Donnie)
There is the prettiest rainbow in the sky right now. It is very bright and I can see where it touches the ground on both ends. One of the blimps was flying right under the middle of it and the sun shining on it made it look like silver...Have I told you about the little black cat that decided to make his home in our office? He is so dumb that he won't chase mice and is afraid of bugs. He sleeps on the desk, on the book shelves, or in the mail basket. One day I opened the door to the cabinet to get something and out he jumped...He begs for food on his hind legs just like a dog. If anyone is eating, he will worry him to death until he gets some. Whenever we sit down to write or work he will jump up in our laps. We call him "Goony."

March 3, 1945
Your box of cookies came and just in time.
Don't get excited if you receive word that I've received the Purple Heart for being wounded in action. It happened this way. I was going out to the thermoscreen the other day. A beautiful sunshiny day it was, too. When all of a sudden, kerplunk, and I'm flat on my face. After I got up enough courage to survey the wreckage, I find one brand new pair of hose torn to pieces and about 2 square inches of skin gone from my knee. Later on a beautiful red, blue and green spot appeared on the other knee. Other than that, I was comparatively all right, so to speak. Three days have elapsed by now so I am able to bend my knee without it leaking. The girls teased me about having water on the knee as well as on the brain.
Goony, the cat, just jumped up on my skirt and left two dirty paw marks there.

March 8, 1945
(to father)
...Why don't you and mother come to Georgia to live? The climate is much nicer than at home...think you could be a shipyard worker? Although we have heard that the shipyards are almost closed in Brunswick. I guess this base will close as soon as the war in Europe is over...By the way, how is the war going on? I never read a paper and very seldom listen to the radio. I just know that some day I will receive my discharge papers and learn for the first time that the war has been over for 6 months.

March 22, 1945

Number One topic is: When I'm coming home. Of course, you surely realized when I told you that I could come home any time that I wanted to that I had to have the consent of the Captain. Even then things can come up so when I say that I had asked for a leave to start the evening of the 6th of May, that it might be the 6th of Juvember before I arrive. Anyway, I'm making big plans to be home then. I have sent the ration books on their merry way. But, don't think I'm sending them home for nothing. You must buy a can of pineapple with the necessary points so that when I arrive you can bake a pineapple upsidedown cake. With the rest you can buy whatever you desire...Someone knocked my watch on the cement deck while I was washing my hair last night and it didn't like it as it has refused to run ever since. The girls say that it isn't a good idea to take watches into Brunswick to be repaired so do you think I could send it home and have it fixed?

March 25, 1945

I'm working on my menus for when I come home. You had better feel like cooking, as I am forced to bring my tape worm with me.

March 30, 1945

We had booster shots the other day. I had two in my left arm. It has been so long since boot camp that I had forgotten how much they hurt. But, now I'm free for another year. I'll not need them by then...Since we have been put on Port and Starboard, we don't have liberty except after 4:30 p.m. That means we don't get to the beach except every other Sunday...The war news sounds very good these days, but then it has been for a long time and it is still going on. Wish it would hurry up and be over.

April 13, 1945

I hope you know the news by now that I am coming home next week.

April 30, 1945

Here it is 0330 and I'm working! What's more, I have mids all this week. They thought up a new and more fiendish watch list while I was gone. Now instead of working every other day, we work every day. The only redeeming feature is that we have liberty when not on duty.

The black cat should have never crossed my path on the way to the train (when I left home coming back to Glynco). It seemed like everything happened except my missing a train. We were only about 3 hours late arriving in New Orleans. I called Dorothy Jane and she met me at the Ferry and took me out to her base and showed me around. She took me to her apartment which is in the French Quarter on Royal Street. Since she had the afternoon off, she fixed lunch and later we went through a museum. The time went so quickly that I almost missed my train. I had just found a seat when the train pulled out. When we arrived in Montgomery(Alabama) at 0230 I was pretty tired. Some sailor talked me into trying to get a place to sleep at the Red Shield Boy's Club run by the Salvation Army. The man was quite shocked and annoyed, but he put me up in a room that he had reserved for men and their wives. He said it was a bit irregular, but he guessed it was all right. Anyway I got a couple hours of sleep with my knees not touching my chin. We were 10 minutes late getting into Waycross(Ga.), so I had 15 minutes to catch the bus. It was about 3 blocks away and I had to run because it had just begun to rain. It took 2 hours to come that 58 miles to Brunswick. Then I had to wait another hour for a bus out to the station. Anyway, I made it to the barracks 48 hours after I left Shreveport, lacking 10 minutes...I sure hated to come back and miss all that good sleeping and eating and just having fun. I hope they will let me come back soon.

May 8, 1945

They really gave me a rousing welcome when I came back...I told you about one of my roommates getting married and then wanting a divorce a few weeks later. When I came back from leave she was at home getting rid of a six weeks old pregnancy. She was supposed to have stayed in bed for a week, but her leave was up so within three days she was working again. She is the most fouled up piece of human I know. She seems to come from a nice family. I can't understand how anyone old enough to be in the WAVES could let themselves get into such a mess. I sure hope she doesn't have any trouble...I am having to work ten hours today because one of the fellows asked for an emergency leave to go home. A family whom he knew quite well was all burned to death last night.

May 10, 1945

...Since the war has been over in Europe everyone is looking for signs of this base closing. If anything is sent out or if supplies are slow in arriving, then it is a sure thing that we won't be here much longer.

May 14, 1945

...It is easy to tell that I have been here at Glynco too long. I'm for sure cracking up. Do you know that today is my first anniversary? I guess I'll have to go out and celebrate with a chicken dinner tonight.

May 16, 1945

I went to Jacksonville yesterday and tried to get some dresses. I bought a new hat and a skirt...At the bus station in Jacksonville(on the way back to Brunswick) I met two of the girls from the base. We stayed in Brunswick to eat and as a result missed the bus out to the base. Therefore we went by air! The man that picked us up was driving a very nice car and he decided to bring us all the way out to the base. Not only that, but when we got to the gate he said he would drive us in to the barracks. That is unheard of as it is very hard to get a pass to come in. Anyway he showed the Marine at the gate a card and sure enough he was let in. Then he told us he was Senator George from Georgia. I'd never heard of him before, but he is quite a character. Is there such a senator?...I met a lot of interesting characters yesterday...There was a WAVE from Arizona on the bus going out to the station carrying a pound of butter and was so afraid it would melt, it was so hot...the man who sat by me on the bus from Jax to Brunswick told me his life history and invited me out to see his wife sometime. They own some apartment on St. Simons Island. His wife reads cards as a hobby...when I finally arrived back at the base, I found out that a Marine who is stationed at St. Simons Island had been calling me all day. He followed me on the bus the night before when I was coming back from town. He wouldn't get off until I told him my name and phone number. He said that if I didn't make a date with him, he would tear Glynco apart until he found me. Do you think he had been drinking? Anyway, he left a message that he would continue to call until I stayed at home. Should I hire a bodyguard? Tune in tomorrow for the further adventures of "Rhoades and the Marine."

May 18, 1945

I took a balloon sounding this morning and followed it for 17 minutes. The wind was so strong that it was over 11 miles away and I couldn't see it anymore...The scuttlebutt about the base closing keeps on without end, but we are all still here and probably will be for a long time. In the imagination of some people, we have been shipped to the west coast, Charleston and St. Simons!

May 20, 1945

...I have been here for a whole year now and the highest off the ground that I have been is the second story of the WAVES barracks. So, yesterday when one of the officers who came to see about the weather asked if I would like to go up in a blimp, I said "yes." Naturally I thought it would be a joy ride and the weather was as perfect as it ever is. So, bright and early this morning I got up and went to chow because I had heard that one should not go up on an empty stomach. Then about nine o'clock we settled down in the blimp while it was still in the hanger and start floating out to the center of the mat where we were released like a toy balloon. From then on it was like being bounced on someone's knee. And I guess I am a little bit too old for that. My stomach is still going up and down and sideways and I have been down for five hours. It was an interesting trip non-the-less. We went over Brunswick and then out to sea. After some target practice we headed back to shore and by then we were off the coast just north of Jacksonville. By then I was pretty sick and the fellows were having a good laugh at my expense. They furnished me with a paper sack to use in case I decided to see if my breakfast would taste better the second time. However, I fooled them on that score and didn't use it. Finally the pilot found out how I felt about the whole thing and told me to come up and work the rudder for a while. It was fun and I felt better. He let me take it up the beach and we all waved at the people and they waved back. I'll bet there were even some who said that they wished they were up there with us. Silly people. Then we ate lunch. I was feeling better, so I ate some, too. In fact, I think that eating helped for a while. Then we went back out to sea and dropped a live bomb which exploded right under us. It caused the bag to go up and down several times. By the time we finally landed, I didn't care if I lived or died. I'm sure it was just as bad as being sea sick...that concludes today's chapter in the exciting life of "Rhoades, the Aerographer's Mate." Another chapter like today's and we will probably hear the last of her.

May 26, 1945

Well, I finally recovered from my blimp trip. I can't say as I'm the same, but at least I can walk a straight line and eat something besides Mexican Jumping Beans. All the fellows in the crew have been trying to get me to go up again tomorrow, but as far as they are concerned, I have the duty all day!...I went to the beach on Wednesday. It was a beautiful day until about a half hour before we were scheduled to return. Since we had come out in an open truck with a bunch of Marines we decided to wear our bathing suits so we wouldn't get our clothes all wet. Yes, a front was coming through with lightening and even some hail. Into the truck we piled...about 10 WAVES and 7 or 8 fellows. The truck was like the army used during maneuvers except there was no canvas on top. It was so cold that I decided to sit down on the floor just behind the cab of the truck. It looked like such a good idea that the next thing I knew, 9 girls and 8 fellows were sitting on top of me. You have heard the saying, "What's crackers without cheese, what's a hug without the squeeze?" Well, I got the squeeze without the hug. Oh, well I always did admire bowed legs...The next night there was a dance at the St. Simons Naval Air Base. It is about 15 miles from here. Since we were invited guests, they furnished transportation. It turned out to be what they call a "cattle-car." They use them to take the ship handlers out on the mat to land the blimps.

Anyway, we made it there without much trouble. We had a very nice time. They had cakes, coke and ice cream. One of the cooks from over there took a shine to me and wanted to have his picture taken with me. He posed with me cutting the cake that was on our table. He promised to send me one if they were good. He'll probably not remember my name, but if he does, I'll let you see it. It was nearly one o'clock in the morning by the time I got to sleep.

June 10, 1945

I guess you got my card, I sent from Silver Springs. One of the tower operators and I went on a 48 (48 hour leave). We both had had a "mid" the night before. I managed two hours sleep before we left, but she didn't have any. We got to Ocala by 3:30 p.m., but by the time we ate and found a place to stay and waited for a bus, it was 5:30 p.m. before we could lay our weary heads on a pillow. We were asleep by 6:30 p.m. and slept until 8 o'clock the next morning. The place we stayed was a Tourist Home, just about a quarter of a mile from Silver Springs. We walked down after we were dressed and ate breakfast. Then we went on the three tours they offered. The one in the glass bottom boat was the same one we took years ago…Then we went on a larger boat down the river about 5 miles. It was called the "Jungle Cruise." We saw monkeys and turtles, long-nosed gars, alligators and some funny birds. The guide also pointed out the place where some of the scenes from "Tarzan Finds A Son" were taken. He also showed us where they were planning to take some of the scenes of a new picture, "The Yearling." MGM is in Silver Springs now and they are shooting pictures about 2 miles from the River. Gregory Peck is the only star I knew that is going to be in it. We didn't see anyone or anything though. We also went down in the Photo Sub and could see the people swimming under the water and the fish would come right up to the window. It only lasted 15 minutes.

We still had some time before eating dinner, so we went to see Ross Allen's rattlesnakes. They had alligators, too. It was quite interesting, but not exactly what one would desire for an appetizer.

That afternoon we went swimming for about an hour and a half. We took the train back to Jacksonville and just missed a bus (to Brunswick) by 15 minutes. We had to wait 4 hours for the next one. It was 4 o'clock in the morning when we arrived at the base and we both had to go to work at 7 a.m.

If you have noticed more misspelled words in this letter than usual, blame it on Helen (Merrill). She was married about three months ago and day before yesterday got out of the Navy for the usual reason. And what does this all have to do with the way I spell words? It was her dictionary that I have been using for the last year…

Do you remember the dance I told you about where the fellow took my pictures cutting the cake? Well, the fellow who was supposed to get me a copy of it saw one of the girls in town the other day and said that he had the picture. We are going to have a dance here Thursday and he is going to try to come and bring it.

June 17, 1945

If this place gets any duller, they will probably bury us all while we aren't looking. There just isn't a thing going on…If something doesn't happen soon, we will all atrophy from such idleness. It is too bad they won't let us off when there ain't anything to do. But, no, we have to stay here just like we were helping to win the war.

June 27, 1945

I have gotten so brown that I have begun to have a few freckles…I haven't been to the beach for a few days. I surely would like to go today and cool off. It is always cool there when it isn't anywhere else…Are you getting more gasoline now? I saw something in the paper the other day about an increase in the amount of A (Gas Coupon) Book holders.

July 8, 1945

Do you remember the pictures of the girl in the "Bungee Bugle"* who had on my overseas cap? I sent the paper home a long time ago. Anyway, she was married Friday night. We were all invited to the wedding and reception. She is a good friend of all of the officers on the base. The Captain gave her away. She was married in a dress that belonged to the groom's grandmother. It was quite fancy and well-preserved for such age. The reception was given by a Doctor and his wife who live in town. I think everything was spiked except the cake. Naturally, I was quite thirsty before we left. I was afraid to even drink a glass of water someone found for me. However, it tasted like the straight stuff! At least I didn't feel any ill effects. But my roommate still can't find her shirt that she wore that night. She swears that she had it on when she came home...I told you about the dance I went to and the sailor asked me to cut the cake and took a picture of me. He said he would get me a copy. Well, I went to see if I could get a copy. I did.

* The Glynco Naval Air Base Newspaper

July 15, 1945

...Lucy is changing her rate to Yeoman, so I guess she will be here for a while yet. She has gotten rid of all the birds. They gave them away. She said that they were worth from 40-100 dollars apiece...We have had rain almost every day this month so far. Some days it wasn't at the station, but close enough to see. When it doesn't rain things are so damp that they feel like they have been rained on anyway.

July 21, 1945
(to brother Donnie)

There is a pretty sunset tonight. It is the first time in a week we have seen the sun. We have had so much rain that all my clothes feel damp and my wash cloth never dries out before I have to use it again. The envelopes all stick shut before I put the letters in. I don't have to lick them, just press down and they are sealed. It looks like we will never have more sunshine.

The PBY took off this afternoon while I was on duty. The pilot came in to see about the weather. They are funny looking planes!

July 21, 1945

...How is the toothpaste and Kleenex holding out? Can you buy either one yet?...Did Leslie tell you about the photographer who took the picture of me at the dance? We saw him and his wife and two children in town. Well, he called me up the other night and wanted me to go to the movie or supper with him. He couldn't understand why I refused him. Aren't men silly?

July 30, 1945

...Well, my chance to make 2nd class has been ruined again. We were all set to take our examinations next month and everyone could advance a step. What happened? They send in a Chief and no one can go up. Such is life in the Navy...The USO gave the WAVES a birthday party the other night. We are 3 years old now. It would have been fun except there were too many civilian girls and not enough men!

August 5, 1945

...Tell Carrie not to join the WAVES unless she can get a commission. It is too hard to make a rate now and seamen don't have a chance. It's fun, but gets to be an old story after a while...Guess what? I think I'll be leaving here soon. Maybe this month. They have at last decided what to do with the base. The new plans call for closing our office at night. There will be no need to keep so many people here and the lowest rates(that's me) will be sent out. Mr. Foster asked me when and where I wanted to go just like I'd have a choice. Naturally, I told him home, New Orleans, Corpus or Chicago. So, I'll probably be sent to Key West, San Diego or Seattle, Washington. Anyway, I haven't left yet, so keep sending my mail to Glynco.

August 7, 1945

It's for sure that I'm leaving, but I don't know when or where I'm going yet. I'll keep you posted.

August 11, 1945

I took my test for second class this morning. If I passed it, I'm sure it was an accident. I worked until midnight last night, so I slept through breakfast and only had a cup of tea before I went over...Anyway, I'll not make my rate here even if I did pass the test...Unless the end of the war changes things it is for sure that we will leave here soon. It is supposed to be before the 1st of next month...Isn't the war news wonderful! Looks like Leslie might be home to stay soon, Herbert and I, too. Won't that be swell? I can hardly wait.

August 16, 1945
(to her father)

...Well, the war is over but according to the point system it will be ten months before I can come home. I hope it won't be that long though. Nobody seems to know for sure what will happen to us yet. I guess we will not be sent out as was planned. If they change the base to a receiving station as some people say, then we'd have to stay. One never knows....how does it feel to be able to buy gasoline by the tank full instead of the gallon? I wish it had happened sooner. I would have insisted that you drive out here to see me on your vacation.

August 23, 1945

...I had a letter from the company asking me if I wanted my old job back. They also asked if I would take one like it or did I want something different. I guess I had better tell them that I'll take the old one back. I hope I don't have to work for them much longer. I can't make up my mind what to do, but I don't want to spend my life looking at a calculator five days a week.

August 30, 1945

...Well, I'm still here and I have no idea what will happen to me. Nothing has been said about our leaving or about getting out of the navy. I guess some day I'll just wake up and be a civilian..

September 1, 1945

...You asked if I had thought about going back to school. I've thought of everything from getting married to staying in the Navy. I guess what I'll do is go back to work for the company for a while and see what develops...The butterflies have been giving us a preview of autumn. There are some bright orange ones and yellow ones. When they flutter round they look just like falling leaves.

September 9, 1945

...You said something about my letters having a bored tone. I'm just that. When you have to get up in the middle of the night to do a lot of unnecessary work, you can't be enthusiastic. We haven't been needed for months now and they are just slow with the discharges. They will be slow in sending us some place that we are needed. Maybe when cool weather comes, I'll have a little more pep and energy. I'm not sick, so don't worry.

September 16, 1945

...I think it is wonderful about Leslie coming home...I think it is terrible the way Rosalie keeps imposing on you, making you look after Dickey. I'm just fooling. I'll bet you haven't had so much fun in years...I am glad that you can find a few things in the stores again. I'd planned to send some more toothpaste, but Ship's Service has been out for a long time...

You asked me to tell you about my trip to Orlando recently...I exchanged a mid watch for an evening so I would get off work at midnight before my days off instead of working until morning. I got up at 0515, dressed, and finished packing my overnight bag and walked to the gate. (about a mile). It was dark and foggy, so by the time I was half way to the gate, my hair was as frizzy as it could be.

It was still dark when I finally arrived at the highway and put my bag down so I could fight the mosquitoes with both hands. In a few minutes, some big vehicle with lights on it like the bus came down the road. I picked up my bag to be ready to get on as the bus driver doesn't like to wait. It turned out to be a fisherman with a load of shrimp. Anyway I rode all the way to Jacksonville with him. He bought my breakfast and was very nice to me. We were in Jacksonville by 0930 so I had time to catch a train that was supposed to leave at 1010. I was an hour late in leaving and two hours late in arriving. That made me just an hour earlier than I had planned on the bus. I took a taxi into the courthouse and found Uncle Al...You have probably heard about our hurricane. It began about 4 days ago and has been coming up this way getting more severe as it came along. Miami got the worst of it with winds over 100 mph. Orlando has already reported gusts to 72 mph. It is due here sometime tonight. By the time it gets here it will probably be well tamed down as the winds are decreasing all the time...We have been hearing some pretty bad stories about the blimp base out from Miami. It is the one where the one and only blimp we have comes from. The radio reported last night that the three hangers were all on fire, that several hundred planes and twenty-six blimps had been destroyed. They were reporting 75 mph winds when it happened.

September 21, 1945

...The hurricane didn't do any damage here. We had about six inches of rain in eighteen hours. That was the worst of it. The wind never got any higher than 39 knots or about 45 mph. I had the mid watch the night it passed so I had a good chance to observe it. When I went out at 0200 to measure the rain, one of the fellows drove me in the jeep within 20 feet of the rain gauge. The wind blew so hard that I was wet to the skin through my rain coat. The water was standing so deep that it came over the tops of my galoshes. I felt like I'd been dunked in a pool. I had the boy take me by the barracks to get some dry clothes and I changed in the head at the hanger. I didn't venture out again until 0530, By then the wind had died down to 20 knots and the rain was nearly stopped...Well, I guess you need to get new glasses. I wasn't going to tell you about making 2nd Class, but it has been a month now and you still haven't noticed it on the return address. I was quite surprised to get it. The station compliment was changed at the last minute, otherwise there wouldn't have been an opening. I haven't felt very happy about it, though, because one of the other girls who has been 3rd class two months longer than I thought she would make it. The reason she didn't was because my test grade was higher than hers. I haven't felt like sewing on my new stripes or anything. She is gradually getting over it, thank goodness.

September 30, 1945

Guess what I did the other day? I went up in a Cub. We circled the field and then landed again. We were only up 10 minutes, but it was plenty long for me...On the way back to the barracks from chow this morning, I picked all the different kinds of wild flowers I saw. There must have been 12 of them. I thought it would be nice to press them...The latest scuttlebutt, which may have some truth in it as it was in one of the Atlanta papers, is that this base will close by November 30th.

October 10, 1945

...Keep your eyes and ears open. If you hear on the radio or see in the paper that the points for WAVES discharge have been lowered to 25, you can mark on the calendar that I'll be home in a month or less. I'll go to Memphis for discharge.

W onderful
M arshes
O of
G lynn............local radio station named after a poem of same name. This is Glynn County! Glynco!

October 23, 1945
(or 38 more days)

I'm sitting on the porch of my penthouse overlooking the beautiful station of Glynco. Our office just moved up here about 4 days ago. It is on the 3rd floor of the Administration Building and very cozy. We make all our observations from the roof. It is nice and cool here and quite apart from everyone.

I have also moved my place of abode recently. There are only 29 girls left so we all had to move down stairs. It isn't as clean as the upstairs and is much more noisy.

Nothing better happened, so I have to stay longer than December 1st. Of course, there is always a possibility. They can hold you as long as 120 days as a military necessity which they might do if more men aren't sent in soon.

Navy Day 1945

34 more days to go. Ain't it wonderful?

We're having a bit of excitement around here as 2 of the girls are being married. One today and one next week. They have been in a dither for so long that it will be a relief to get them settled.

We are all dressed up for visitors today and not a soul has come. I'm not sorry because it is more peaceful just like this.

November 1, 1945
(or 29 more days)

I just got your letter tonight. Someone has been hiding my mail, so I don't see it for several days. I'll really be glad to get out of here...I think I'll go over to the dance for a while. There is supposed to be a good Marine band playing for it.

November 1, 1945

I'll really be glad to get away from these stinky girls here. One of the girls got herself into trouble and somehow it got out and an officer reported her to the Doctor. Now, of course, everyone knows it and they have been talking up a breeze since. It wouldn't be so bad but most of the girls doing the talking are just lucky that it hasn't happened to them. The fellow responsible for the whole thing was discharged today and I guess she will never hear from him again. My two virtuous roommates are breaking their arms writing all the girls who used to be here telling them the latest. It is all making me too sick. I have known it two weeks and haven't had to tell anyone yet.

November 5, 1945
(to father)

The other day I had to go to the Air Station on St. Simons about 15 miles from here to get some information for our office. The only transportation available was a Plymouth pick-up truck. It is on it's last wheels, if you know what I mean. It has more squeaks than a pigpen full of hogs and more rattles than a baby carriage for twins. It was fun being out on the highway behind the wheel even in that old trap. It made me wish that I had my car here. I made it over there and back all in the same day, but I haven't felt the same since...As far as I know now, I'll be home sometime soon after the 1st of December. I'll not know for sure until a day or two before I leave. I am going to start sending stuff home soon so don't be surprised.

November 9, 1945

Did you know that two years ago today I became a WAVE? For two years I have been wearing the Navy blue and gray. But in less than a month, I'll be right back in Shreveport and a civilian again. There is little doubt now that I will be held because there are three new AerM's scheduled to arrive at any moment. The sooner, the better for me because when they do get here, I'll be sure then that I can leave...My two roommates moved out the other day. It was so terrible that I kept moving the junk they put on the upper bunk over mine. It is an empty one and every time I was out for a while they piled it up with everything they could find. I guess they thought they would make me mad by leaving me alone, but they couldn't have pleased me more. I'm living alone for the first time since I left home. It really seems queer but I'm getting used to it fast.

November 19, 1945

...I should be leaving here two weeks from today. I'll really be glad to leave, too. It will be swell not to have to work at night any more.

November 23, 1945

I got your letter today asking about the sugar stamps, so I'll send the whole book. I heard today on the radio that after tonight nothing but sugar will be rationed.

November 25, 1945

As far as I know I'll leave next Monday, December 3rd. It will be about another week before I'm home because we have to be at Memphis for 3 days.

November 26, 1945
(last letter, to brother Donnie)

Just so you won't think that I never answered your last letter I'm sending you the evidence. I don't know where it has been since October 13th, but I don't guess it left Glynco. Someone found it yesterday and gave it to me....be seeing you soon.

BIBLIOGRAPHY

Books:

Ball, Lamar Q, *Georgia In World War II, A Study of the Military and the Civilian Effort.* Volume I. c. 1939

Bishop, Eleanor. *Prints in the Sand.* Pictorial Histories Publishing Co., Missoula, MT, 1989

Gannon, Michael. *Operation Drumbeat.* Harper Perennial, 1990

Hoyt, Edwin. *U-boats Offshore: When Hitler Struck America.* Scarborough House/Publishers. First Scarborough House Paperback Edition, 1990. *U-boats Offshore* was originally published in hardcover by Stein and Day/Publishers, 1978

Kuhn, Clifford M., Harlon, E. Joye and West, E. Bernard. *Living Atlanta: An Oral History of the City, 1914 - 1948.* The Atlanta Historical Society, Atlanta. The University of Georgia Press, Atlanta, 1990

Laney-Smith, Beth, and Kluever, Karen Trogdon. *Jones Construction Centennial: Looking Back-Moving Forward 1809 - 1990;* Laney-Smith, Inc. Charlotte, N.C., 1989

Middlebrook, Martin. *Convoy.* New York. William Morrow and Company, Inc. c. 1976

Ships of the Esso Fleet in World War II. Standard Oil Company (New Jersey). President, Eugene Holman. c. 1946

Smith, Richard W. *Shoulder Sleeve Insignia of the U. S. Armed Forces, 1941 -1945.* Ed. Roy A. Pelz. c. 1981

Thiel, Roger. *When Antiques Go to War...The 50th Anniversary of the Civil Air Patrol.* 1319 Naylor Court, N. W., Washington, D.C. 20001.

Thorne, Bliss K. *The Hump: The Great Himalayan Airlift of World War II.* J. B. Lippincott Company. Philadelphia and New York. c. 1965

Manuscripts:

Batten, Colonel H. CAP 62149. *Civil Air Patrol Historical Monograph # 17. History of Coastal Patrol Base # 6, Civil Air Patrol, World War II, St. Simons Island, Georgia.* National Historical Commission. Headquarters CAP, 1988

Georgia State Archives:

Lamar Q. Ball Collection

Periodicals:

The Brunswick News: Brunswick, Georgia

The Atlanta Constitution: Atlanta, Georgia

The Atlanta Journal: Atlanta, Georgia

Best Defense: "Georgia State Best Defense Force"; Georgia State Archives; Lamar Q. Ball Collection - World War II.

The Mariner: publication of the J. A. Jones Construction Company Brunswick Shipyard

United States Archives:

National Archives. Modern Military Records (NWCTM). Textural Archives Services Division

U. S. Department of Transportation. Maritime Administration